LANE KIRKLAND

CHAMPION OF
AMERICAN LABOR

Arch Puddington

WILEY

John Wiley & Sons, Inc.

Illustration credits: page 155 courtesy of Katherine Moore; pages 156 (bottom) and 157 (top) courtesy of the White House; page 160 (top) courtesy of the *Washington Post*; page 160 (bottom) courtesy of United Mine Workers of America; pages 156 (top), 157 (bottom), 158–159, and 161–162 courtesy of George Meany Memorial Archives.

Published by John Wiley & Sons, Inc., Hoboken, New Jersey
Published simultaneously in Canada

Design and composition by Navta Associates, Inc.

For general information about our other products and services, please contact our Customer Care Department within the United States at (800) 762-2974, outside the United States at (317) 572-3993 or fax (317) 572-4002.

Wiley also publishes its books in a variety of electronic formats. Some content that appears in print may not be available in electronic books. For more information about Wiley products, visit our web site at www.wiley.com.

Library of Congress Cataloging-in-Publication Data:

Puddington, Arch.
   Lane Kirkland : champion of American labor / Arch Puddington.
      p. cm.
   Includes bibliographical references and index.
   ISBN 0-471-41694-0 (cloth : alk. paper)
  1. Kirkland, Lane. 2. Labor leaders—United States—Biography. 3. Labor unions—United States—Officials and employees—Biography. 4. AFL-CIO—History—20th century. 5. Labor unions—United States—History—20th century. 6. Labor union democracy—United States. 7. Labor unions—United States—Political activity—History—20th century. 8. Labor movement—United States—History—20th century. I. Title.

  HD6509.K57K57 2005
  331.88'092—dc22

                                              2004008489

Printed in the United States of America

10 9 8 7 6 5 4 3 2 1

CONTENTS

Photographs follow page 154.

To Nick

ACKNOWLEDGMENTS

Several months after Lane Kirkland died in 1999, his widow, Irena, asked if I would be interested in writing Lane's biography. My response was immediate and enthusiastic. Years earlier, I had worked for several organizations on the periphery of the labor movement, including the A. Philip Randolph Institute, an organization founded by civil rights leader Bayard Rustin. I also served as executive director of the League for Industrial Democracy, a think tank that focused on issues of concern to organized labor. Aside from these experiences, I had a long-term intellectual interest in the role that American trade unionists had played in the Cold War struggle against Communism as well as in labor's role in the creation of the movement to promote freedom around the world. I was, in addition, an admirer of the men who made American labor into a powerful voice for working people and a unique force for global democracy. Finally, I was convinced that Kirkland's role as a labor leader and a democracy advocate had been insufficiently understood and appreciated.

First and foremost, I owe Irena Kirkland deep gratitude not only for asking me to undertake this book, but also for sharing her penetrating insights into her husband's career and character. Irena is a formidable woman in her own right, whose life story and achievements could easily be the subject of a fascinating biography.

Several of Lane's close colleagues from the AFL-CIO were particularly generous in discussing his stewardship as president and in providing an assessment of organized labor's history over the past half century. Most invaluable here are Tom Donahue, who served as secretary-treasurer during Kirkland's years as president and then, for too short a time, as president of the AFL-CIO after Kirkland's retirement, and Ken Young, Kirkland's executive assistant during most of his presidency. Other important sources of material on Kirkland's years in labor were Rex Hardesty, Jack Joyce, David St. John, Jim Baker, and Rachelle Horowitz. I am also indebted to Dick Wilson, who gave extensive interviews and provided me with important material concerning labor's work in Poland and other Communist countries during Kirkland's presidency.

Carl and Laurie Gershman were crucial sources of support and friendship during the research and writing. Carl Gershman, president of the

National Endowment for Democracy (NED), also provided important insights into Kirkland's contribution to the modern democracy movement.

Much thanks to Lane's brother, Rannie, for his recollections of their youth in South Carolina, for family histories and other material about the Kirkland family, and for a tour of historic Camden, where Lane spent his childhood. A number of Lane's other relatives were also generous in their assistance, including his brother, Tom; his sister, Katharine Kirkland Crockett; and his daughters, Luci Kirkland Schoenfeld and Rikki Kirkland Condon. I am also indebted to Lane's daughter Katherine Kirkland Moore for her invaluable assistance in providing photographs of the Kirkland family.

During the course of this project, I continued my affiliation with Freedom House, an organization that shares Kirkland's passion for democracy and where Kirkland served as a trustee. I owe a debt of appreciation to Jennifer Windsor, Freedom House's executive director, for her support and to Adrian Karatnycky, who had served as an aide to Kirkland on international affairs matters before he joined Freedom House. Adrian was an invaluable source of information and insight about labor's foreign policy, especially its project to assist Poland's Solidarity trade union. A number of Freedom House staff and interns provided important research and administrative assistance. They include Amy Phillips, Mark Rosenberg, Ben Isaac, Kate Abrey, Romolo Isaia, and Orysia Lutsevych.

In the course of my research, I had the good fortune to interview a number of Solidarity's key leaders from its early years and its period of underground existence. My special thanks to Irena Lasota and Eric Chenoweth for their insights on the Solidarity period. John Kubiniec, the director of Freedom House's Central European office, provided invaluable assistance in arranging the interviews that I conducted with Solidarity veterans during a trip to Poland in 2002. I am also grateful to Lukasz Michalski, who served as my interpreter in Poland.

I could not have written the chapter on Central America without the recollections of David Jessup, who was a key member of the AFL-CIO's team involved in Nicaragua and El Salvador during the 1980s. Dave also provided crucial assistance by giving me access to the voluminous files he maintained concerning labor's involvement in Central America.

Kerry Candaele provided important assistance in the archives of the Ronald Reagan presidential library in Simi Valley, California.

The staff of the George Meany Center for Labor Education went out of their way to assist me in research into Lane's personal files. Particular thanks go to Lynda DeLoach and Robert Reynolds. I am also grateful to Kathrine Stevens, my assistant, who helped me sift through documents at the Meany Center.

The project would not have been possible without the financial help of the Albert Shanker Institute. My thanks to Sandra Feldman, president of the American Federation of Teachers, and to Eugenia Kemble, director of the Shanker Institute, for their confidence in this project. I am equally indebted to Bob Georgine, who gave the project strong support during his term as president of the Union Labor Life Insurance Company. Others who helped this project financially include the ILGWU Twentieth Century Heritage Fund, the Atran Foundation, the Bayard Rustin Fund, and Steve Forbes.

Much thanks to Martha Kaufman Amitay, my agent, whose hard work and, especially, patience are much appreciated. I am similarly indebted to Hana Lane, my editor at John Wiley & Sons, for stylistic insights and for her faith in the project.

I could never have finished this book without the love and support of my wife, Margaret. Margaret's support was critical during several difficult periods. I say without exaggeration that I could not have completed the book without her.

Prologue

"ALL SINNERS BELONG IN THE CHURCH"

LANE KIRKLAND APPROACHED THE PODIUM AT THE SHERATON Washington Hotel. It was November 19, 1979, and he had just been elected by acclamation as president of the American Federation of Labor and Congress of Industrial Organizations (AFL-CIO), the largest and most influential instrument of trade unionism in the United States. He had begun his life's journey in modest circumstances in a small southern town and left college to go to sea and take part in World War II. Now he stood before the assembled convention delegates as the leader of organized labor in the United States and thus the most powerful trade unionist in the world, a position that many claimed, with only slight exaggeration, was more important than the presidency of the United States.

Kirkland's acceptance speech was brief, lasting less than ten minutes. It had all the earmarks of the Kirkland style: direct, intelligently crafted, featuring a vocabulary seldom encountered in the public statements of prominent Americans, and replete with tributes to labor's history and ideals.

He described the convention delegates as "the finest body of men and women in this or any other land." He expressed his deep respect for George Meany, the man he was succeeding, who for a quarter century had served, with rocklike solidity, as the undisputed leader of American trade unionism.

Then he brought the delegates to their feet when he observed that in taking on any challenge, "the proper course of action becomes simple, easy, and clear once you have answered that first necessary question: 'Which side are you on?'"

"As president of the AFL-CIO," he added, "I tell you now that I'm on *our* side, first, last, and always."

1

He had learned, he said, "that the proof of whether a decision on a course of action is right or wrong is not necessarily inherent in the issue, but depends upon whether you stand fast and see it through." Throughout his tenure, Kirkland would earn a reputation for being an uncompromising and tenacious leader of America's working people and an advocate for freedom for the world's oppressed.

Kirkland then spelled out his major objective: labor unity. By this, he meant bringing into the federation those unions—including two of the largest and most influential labor organizations, the United Auto Workers and the Teamsters—that at the time lay outside the federation's fold.

"I say now to those who stand outside that I have too high a regard for the caliber of their leadership to believe that they can really be governed by petty personal or pecuniary considerations or ancient and tedious grudges.

"All sinners belong in the church; all citizens owe fealty to their country; all workers belong in the unions of their trade or industry; and all true unions belong in the American Federation of Labor and Congress of Industrial Organizations."

Kirkland did achieve labor unity. Within a decade, all the sinners had come back to the true church, and a few that had never joined signed up as well—not only the two big industrial unions, but the Mineworkers and a number of smaller unions representing dockworkers, railwaymen, and writers. Labor was unified and thus better prepared to face the challenges of an increasingly hostile political and economic environment.

Kirkland achieved much more, although the American public never fully understood or appreciated his contributions. Within a year, a young electrician named Lech Walesa joined with other Polish workers to form the independent union Solidarnosc ("Solidarity," in English). Solidarity shook the foundations of Communist power as no freedom movement ever had. Kirkland emerged as Solidarity's most stalwart friend outside Poland. Abiding by his stricture that the test of leadership is to stand fast and see a cause through to the end, he established a broad network of support for the Polish union, prodded the international labor movement to embrace Solidarity as a cause, refused to compromise despite the entreaties of high American officials, and kept the heat on wavering policymakers in the West. His steadfastness was critical in those dark hours after the Communist authorities declared martial law, when Solidarity's leaders languished in prison or exile and Western diplomats urged a coming to terms with the regime. Kirkland was also among the very few who believed from the onset of the Polish crisis that Solidarity, a movement inspired by the struggle of ordinary workers, could be the crucial force that would lead to the collapse of the entire Communist edifice. Events were to vindicate that judgment.

It was a long journey from small towns in South Carolina to the corridors of power in Washington, D.C., and from there to a trade union congress in Gdansk, Poland, where, in the aftermath of Communism's fall, Kirkland was venerated as a hero of that country's freedom struggle. Lane Kirkland was a son of the Deep South. Although he did not come from poverty and could claim Confederate aristocracy in his lineage, he was familiar with mill towns, racial segregation, and grinding rural poverty. Ironically, his home state has the distinction of having the lowest percentage of unionized workers in the United States.

Although born in Camden, Kirkland spent most of his younger years in Newberry, a South Carolina mill town. His father's cotton brokerage business went bankrupt when the crop market collapsed—this actually took place before the great stock market crash—and his father spent years paying off his creditors, an example in ethical conduct that Lane would never forget. If blacks were the most impoverished of Newberry's citizens, poor whites were not far behind. Kirkland attended school with children who were one step away from complete destitution, whose families could lose everything if times were bad at the mill. Although it was not Kirkland's way to moralize about political issues, his experiences in the South led him to believe that something was fundamentally amiss when a wealthy society like the United States refused to adopt the measures required to alleviate human misery.

At the same time, the South of Kirkland's boyhood was a place where doors were never locked, car keys were left in the ignition, and children could wander about in an environment of security that is alien to today's America. A South where, despite the legal separation of the races, black and white children played together; a South where, despite its reputation as an American backwater, children had access to a first-rate education from dedicated teachers in the public schools.

Kirkland was also a child of the New Deal. The policies of assertive government initiated by the Roosevelt administration had a transforming effect on the rural South. The New Deal brought electricity to homes that had relied on kerosene lamps, produced cures for pellagra and other regional diseases, and gave the elderly a dignified alternative to the county poorhouse. For Kirkland, the lesson of the New Deal was that government intervention, intelligently applied, could bring a measure of justice to the poor and could level the playing field for ordinary people. Kirkland was convinced that what the New Deal had done for the South, a similarly generous government could do for other communities that suffered from poverty—blacks, for example. It was a conviction that instructed Kirkland's political philosophy until his dying day.

The New Deal was one shaping experience in Kirkland's life. The

other was the struggle against totalitarian evil, which Kirkland participated in during World War II and then, in a major way, during the Cold
War. He served in the Merchant Marine during World War II, where he
was in every theater of conflict. The experience left Kirkland with a
healthy appreciation of the dangers of combat and the conviction that
military intervention is not to be undertaken lightly. But it also convinced
him that free societies had an obligation to resist totalitarian evil and that
freedom's triumph depended on American leadership.

Throughout his long public career, Kirkland remained a New Dealer
and a Cold Warrior. He never abandoned his belief that the United States
possessed the strength and the wealth to expand freedom throughout the
world and promote the welfare of its own people. Kirkland believed that
the answer to most of the world's problems lay through an assertive
America, at home and abroad.

Cold War liberalism was the reigning idea behind the policies of the
Truman administration and, later, the administrations of John F. Kennedy
and Lyndon B. Johnson. But the proposition that the United States should
wage simultaneous wars against totalitarianism abroad and poverty at
home fell into disfavor and was undermined by a combination of developments: the Vietnam War, racial conflict, student protest, economic stagna-
tion, the energy crisis, and political polarization. Many liberals adopted a
position of reflexive opposition to a robust defense and the struggle against
Communism. Others retained their belief in the necessity of American
policies to curb Soviet influence but began to doubt the wisdom of the liberal domestic policies they had once championed. At the same time, a new
strain of conservatism gained influence in the Republican Party. Among its
principal goals was the wholesale weakening of labor's ability to represent
workers and its power to influence the national political agenda.

Only Kirkland, along with a handful of trade union leaders and others, retained the Cold War liberal faith. Kirkland was no prisoner to intellectual fashion. He never abandoned his principles, even when the ideas
or the causes to which he was attached were derided as passé or outmoded. His commitment to anti-Communism, certainly an unfashion-
able cause in the 1970s, was vindicated with the collapse of the Soviet
empire and the embrace of democracy by the people of Eastern Europe.

Kirkland faced a complex series of challenges when he succeeded
George Meany at labor's helm. Simply to take over the reins from Meany
was a daunting assignment. Meany was the guiding spirit behind the
merger that had created the AFL-CIO; he had been the federation's first
and only president. He enjoyed the respect of presidents, members of
Congress, and the elites of the corporate world. He had his critics, but no
one doubted his credentials as a leader.

Kirkland was well aware that he would face problems that had been spared Meany for most of his tenure. The era of Meany's leadership had been marked by strong economic growth, low rates of unemployment, and a political environment that was relatively favorable to labor's ambitions. In 1979, however, the American economy was stagnant, with inflation and unemployment on the rise. Looming on the not-too-distant horizon was a series of threats to the country's basic industries: an increasingly globalized economy that posed a challenge to the very concept of the well-compensated industrial worker and technological change that threatened to render entire crafts obsolete.

Nor was the political climate propitious. Labor prospered when Democrats occupied the White House, liberal ideas enjoyed popular support, and a bipartisan spirit ensured that the importance of a strong labor movement was appreciated by a critical mass of Republicans. It was Kirkland's lot to assume the leadership of American labor at a time of conservative ascendance. Bipartisanship was also under assault by extremes in both parties, and the Republican Party was coming under the domination of forces that regarded labor as an obstacle to a sweeping agenda of domestic change and not as a partner in the revival of the national economy.

As a trade union leader, Kirkland was able to combine his pragmatic approach to social problems with a strong idealistic streak. He fought for measures that would bring concrete benefits to ordinary working men and women. He left an imprint on practically every piece of significant social legislation from the 1950s onward, from Social Security to the laws that eliminated racial segregation, to Medicare and health and safety legislation.

One of Kirkland's proudest achievements was a plan for industrial revitalization that was killed off before it had a chance to succeed. This was the so-called National Accord that he negotiated with the Carter administration in 1979, a plan that represented what Kirkland hoped was the first step toward an agreement between business, labor, and government to join together in the rebuilding of the country's core industrial base. To have a chance at success, the National Accord required the full commitment of the administration. Carter, however, was preoccupied with a difficult reelection campaign and with developments in Iran, Afghanistan, and elsewhere. Prospects for the National Accord were nullified with the election of Ronald Reagan.

Had Kirkland served as the leader of American labor in another era, he might have left a significant legacy on labor-management relations and strengthened trade unionism's position in American society. Given his wide-ranging intellect and willingness to experiment with new ideas, Kirkland might well have taken the lead in the transformation of relations between labor and management from the traditional adversarial model to one based on tripartite cooperation. Instead, Kirkland was destined to spend much of his time fighting off one threat after another to labor's interests. Republican presidents occupied the White House during the first twelve years of his tenure, and while both Reagan and George Bush had a great deal of personal respect for Kirkland, they opposed practically every item on labor's domestic agenda. Unions also found themselves on the defensive in dealings with the corporate world, as the social contract that had governed relations between trade unions and business unraveled in an environment of intense global competitiveness. In many key industries, collective bargaining was dominated by management's demands for concessions from unionized workers. Then came deindustrialization, a euphemism for the closing of hundreds of factories that made automobiles, steel, machine tools, and other core products, with the resulting loss of millions of jobs and the decimation of some of America's largest and most fabled unions.

For different reasons, these were crisis years for liberalism as well. The belief in economic growth, equal opportunity, and an informed patriotism that had inspired Kirkland and others of his generation gave way to a corrosive combination of cultural radicalism, identity politics, and Cold War neutralism. If these new ways of thinking did not pervade liberalism, they were sufficiently widespread to transform liberalism from a universalist and optimistic creed to one marked by special pleading, confusion, and self-doubt. Kirkland, by contrast, never entertained second thoughts about his core beliefs and was thus not prepared to see the party of Roosevelt, Truman, and John F. Kennedy become the party of George McGovern and Bella Abzug. Under his leadership, organized labor—still, Kirkland believed, the "people's lobby"—was the only mass constituency within the Democratic Party coalition that was committed to mainstream American values, broad-based reform that transcended racial and gender lines, and a diplomatically engaged and militarily prepared America. One of his projects as president of the AFL-CIO was to encourage policies, values, and candidates who generally shared labor's commitment to broad reform. When he assumed office, labor was politically fractious and thus had little influence over the course of presidential politics. Within a few years, Kirkland had forged the disparate and often feuding unions of American labor into a unified and powerful political machine, powerful enough to secure the 1984 presidential nomination for a mainstream liberal, Walter Mondale.

Kirkland believed that trade unions were a key—indeed, the key—institution of a democratic society. Whatever the issue—health care, arms control, tax policy—Kirkland insisted that the voice of working Americans be heard through their representatives in the labor movement. From 1979 to 1995, that voice was most often Kirkland's. Seldom, perhaps never, has a major institution of American society had as its leading representative a man who could speak as fluently and on such a wide range of issues as the labor movement had during his tenure. He grasped the intricacies of trade policy, could discuss the pluses and minuses of exotic weapons systems, and could speak with authority about the financial stability of the Social Security system.

Kirkland also believed that labor's mission included the promotion of freedom around the world. Although he has been given credit for his contribution to the collapse of Communism in Poland and elsewhere, Kirkland was occasionally the object of criticism from those who opposed his anti-Communist principles or who simply felt he devoted too much time to international issues that were peripheral to trade unionism's concerns. Kirkland had little patience for his critics. He reminded those who charged that he was too involved with developments in the Communist world that free trade unions were among the first targets for obliteration by Marxist dictatorships. He also noted that it was the sons and daughters of the working class who risked their lives when American troops were committed to war. And it was the tax dollars of steelworkers and seamstresses that sustained America's costly military establishment. Given these realities, it was essential that labor's opinion be heard and taken seriously in the debate over America's role in the world.

Kirkland believed that the fight for freedom against the world's tyrannies and the struggle for expanded worker rights and civil liberties in the United States were essential components of one great cause. During his leadership years, labor led by example in the campaign for liberty. Kirkland had a broad interpretation of what constitutes freedom: elections, of course, but also the freedom of association that enables trade unions to establish themselves and exercise influence. He also included such basic rights as freedom of speech, belief, and thought, as well as the right to be free from abuse by the police or other instruments of state power. As president of the AFL-CIO, Kirkland presided over a vast project to promote democratic trade unionism throughout the world. American labor played a role in virtually every significant struggle for freedom that took place during the 1980s. The roster of countries where American labor's involvement contributed to the overthrow of some form of dictatorship and its replacement by democracy extends well beyond the countries of Eastern Europe. Andrei Sakharov and Lech Walesa visited Kirkland to express gratitude for American labor's stalwart commitment to the cause of freedom, but so did Nelson Mandela and the leaders of the opposition to the Pinochet regime in Chile.

Kirkland had a broad international vision. The Cold War having been won, he urged that the lessons learned in that struggle be drawn on to set in place the foundations of a new policy centered on the promotion of democracy as a basic element of international diplomacy. He was among the founding spirits behind the National Endowment for Democracy; his views on the obligation of America to the cause of freedom influenced leading figures in the political and journalistic world. Kirkland is as responsible as any single individual for the enhanced role that the promotion of democracy plays today in American diplomacy and foreign assistance programs.

In the later years of his presidency, Kirkland was increasingly preoccupied by the confluence of domestic and global trends that were eating away at labor's organizational strength. As far back as the 1970s, Kirkland understood that labor's problems could be resolved only by a strategy that addressed their origins in international economic and trade trends. His commitment to global freedom was in part motivated by a recognition that dictatorships would invariably suppress wages in an effort to draw investment, and jobs, from the democracies. It vexed Kirkland that while he understood the reasons for labor's problems, he was unable to devise a strategy to turn the tide and restore trade unionism to its former strength. Although the AFL-CIO's campaign to defeat the North America Free Trade Agreement (NAFTA) did not succeed, it did establish the precedent that trade accords could no longer be negotiated outside the bounds of vigorous public debate. The NAFTA struggle also advanced the principle that worker rights provisions should be incorporated in international economic agreements. And Kirkland set an example of informed criticism of the functioning of the global economy that stands in glaring contrast to the often mindless sloganeering that marks the commentary of the contemporary antiglobalization movement.

Kirkland was very much a man of Washington. He had an eclectic group of friends that included freedom advocates from abroad, labor leaders from the United States and Europe, notables from the world of art, and members of Congress. He was also part of the Washington elite. He served on innumerable commissions, such as the body appointed by President Reagan to recommend a solution to the crisis in funding Social Security. And he served on the boards of many important foundations and private institutions. Kirkland was also a member of several organizations, such as the Trilateral Commission and the Bilderberg Society, that have provided fuel to the wilder speculations of conspiracy theorists. Of his role in such organizations, Kirkland would quip, "I'm opposed to any conspiracy that I'm not a part of." In fact, Kirkland understood that the way to power and influence in Washington ran through these elite networks. Kirkland made use of his circle of friends and contacts to advance the interests of labor by settling strikes, passing laws, or resolving conflicts. At the same time, Kirkland had a skeptical attitude toward segments of the elite media and the intellectual classes and toward the business community generally. He was convinced that many intellectuals were disdainful of ordinary people's values and that businessmen would invariably place profits before human freedom. Where the expansion of free institutions was a concern, Kirkland looked to working Americans and their unions, rather than to professors, corporate executives, and members of Congress.

Although Kirkland's achievements and his significance as a leader were appreciated in Washington circles, they are not widely known in the American heartland. This is unfortunate, first, because Kirkland deserves broader recognition for his contributions to working Americans and global democracy, and second, because his views on freedom are altogether relevant to many of today's crucial debates. The lack of familiarity with Kirkland's career and ideas is due in part to the lack of esteem that labor suffers in the United States. The reasons for this peculiarly American attitude toward unions are numerous and complex, but the consequences are that the contributions of far-sighted labor leaders like Kirkland are insufficiently recognized by journalists, academics, and public officials. Another important part of the story, however, can be found in Kirkland's temperament. Kirkland seized every opportunity to remind Americans of the role labor played in generating prosperity, broadening democracy, and enhancing the quality of life for ordinary people—the "democratization of leisure," he called it. But Kirkland never claimed personal credit for these achievements. Self-effacing to a fault, he was generous in heaping praise on his fellow trade union leaders but scrupulously refused to claim any personal part in labor's successes, whether at home or on the international scene. He even disdained asking his public relations staff to promote his leadership role. Kirkland enjoyed the friendship and respect of a number of important press commentators. But while he would speak to them on behalf of an embattled union, he never asked them to write about his triumphs, even when he came under fire from a disgruntled faction within the labor movement.

Kirkland's acquaintances often remark on the complexities and the seeming contradictions of his life. He was a small-town southerner who rose to the pinnacle of success in a movement dominated by men from the big cities of the North. He took pride in his southern and Confederate roots but was a strong champion of racial equality and an advocate of aggressive government initiative to expand civil rights. He had the respect of the leaders of America's toughest unions, as well as of its most sophisticated intellectuals, journalists, and public officials. He was an ardent domestic liberal who remained a committed anti-Communist and a supporter of a vigorous American defense posture. He was unique among trade unionists in his ability to speak to journalists and academics on their level, yet he remained aloof and suspicious of intellectuals and the press. He had an intellectual's grasp of labor history, politics, and international affairs, yet was little understood and certainly unappreciated by most intellectuals.

Part of the answer lies in Kirkland's total commitment to two ideas: trade unionism and freedom. Everything he did in public life was meant to advance these two causes. Thus the story of his life is also the story of these two causes and how they fared in the second half of the twentieth century. On a personal level, it is the story of a man who was at the center of much of that history. The columnist George Will, who had a deep understanding of Kirkland's significance, put it this way: "Lane could have played a role as a public servant, perhaps as secretary of state or head of the CIA. But I'm glad he didn't. He was enormously important at the beginning of the last phase of the Cold War. His role was too important."

Kirkland was also a leading representative of that generation of American leaders that was shaped by World War II, the Cold War, and the struggle for racial equality in the United States. These were men who believed in the best kind of patriotic values, who were convinced that freedom is always preferable to its alternative, who believed that politics ends at the water's edge, and who could set partisanship aside for the good of the Republic.

When a group of Kirkland's trade union colleagues organized what amounted to a coup against his leadership in 1995, they contended that he was overly preoccupied with international affairs, that he paid too little attention to public relations, and that he failed to provide leadership toward the organization of workers outside the labor movement. After Kirkland's retirement, his successors implemented a regime of sweeping change in federation policy. But the new course has not led to labor's revival. The American labor movement today is smaller, less influential, and more narrowly focused than it was under Kirkland. Labor today is more marginal and less respected than at any time since the 1920s.

Lane Kirkland's life encompassed a remarkable period in our history. The Depression, World War II, the Cold War, and American prosperity, followed by the transformation to a postindustrial economy, the civil rights revolution, and the collapse of Communism—he lived through it all and left his imprint on some of the most important events of the time. He was among that generation of Cold War liberals whose quiet leadership and sober judgment helped the United States emerge strong and triumphant from the chaos of war, global change, and domestic upheaval. Although Kirkland never received the broad credit his unique contributions merited, in the great struggle for freedom that convulsed the world during the last half of the twentieth century, the contribution of this modest, unassuming leader of the working class was remarkable.

1

SOUTHERN ROOTS

AMONG LANE KIRKLAND'S ANCESTORS WERE POLITICIANS, JUDGES, planters, industrialists—men of distinction, and mostly of wealth. There were also adventurers, like the midshipman who sailed with the first American naval vessel to circumnavigate the globe, and eccentrics, like the great-grandmother who lived in mourning for sixty years in an upstairs bedroom of a decaying mansion. The male forebears were, for the most part (according to contemporary accounts), upright Christian gentlemen who adhered to an ethical standard in the conduct of business, behaved with courtesy toward women, and treated subordinates, including servants and slaves, with consideration.

Nor do any men who made their living at proletarian occupations figure in Kirkland's lineage. Had Kirkland's ancestors been around to witness his climb up the ranks of organized labor to eventual occupancy of the presidency of the AFL-CIO, they would no doubt have taken pride that a Kirkland had attained a position of such prominence and influence that he was consulted by presidents and treated with respect by world leaders. Whether they would have approved of labor's role in the economy is another question entirely.

That there were Kirklands in South Carolina in the early eighteenth century is confirmed by the state's first census, which was recorded during those years. Those bearing the Kirkland name had presumably emigrated around that time from Scotland and settled in the low country around Charleston. A distant relative served as a captain in the Revolutionary War; his son, Joseph, was a physician of obvious prominence who married Marianne Guerard, the widow of the state's governor, Benjamin Guerard. Joseph Kirkland lived in Charleston, where he died while tending to the sick during an outbreak of yellow fever in 1817.[1]

His son, William Lennox Kirkland, was born in 1797 and died in 1831. He left a son, also named William Lennox—Lane Kirkland's great-grandfather—who was born in 1828. The son owned a large rice plantation in the Charleston area and married Mary Miller Withers, the daughter of Judge T. J. Withers, a plantation owner from Camden, in the South Carolina midlands.[2]

The Kirkland and Withers families were prosperous members of the South Carolina planter aristocracy in prewar times. Both families owned slaves. A census taken in 1860 showed that William Kirkland had fifty-six slaves in twelve houses in Camden and a hundred slaves in the Colleton district. Judge Withers had twenty-three slaves in three houses in Camden. William Kirkland's wealth was placed at $30,000 in real estate and $75,000 in personal property. Judge Withers owned real estate valued at $7,000, and his personal property was placed at $100,000, a small fortune by the standards of the time.[3]

The father's wealth made for a privileged upbringing for Lane's great-grandmother. A fragmentary memoir left by Mary Withers tells of a girlhood of fancy balls, trips to New York, summers in Newport, and a grand tour of the European continent prior to her wedding.

Mary's education was not ignored. Judge Withers donated money for a class for Mary and eight other girls, who were taught a curriculum that included heavy doses of the classics and the memorization of the works of the great poets, Lord Byron being the girls' favorite. The teacher, Mrs. McCandless, though strict, seems to have recognized who was paying her salary, for while the other girls received unsatisfactory grades, Mary, whose performance, by her own account, was no better than the others', was given a rating of satisfactory.

At around age sixteen, Mary attended the St. Cecilia balls, a highlight of the Charleston social season, to which she was escorted by the governor and his wife and attended by her "faithful maid Selina." It was around this time that she met the young and wealthy William Lennox Kirkland. Kirkland was flattered that Mary had worn the camellias he had presented her, and a period of courtship ensued.[4]

Even as he wooed Mary, William was aware that he faced a tragic destiny—at least that is what a fortune-teller had predicted when he was just a boy. William would die in battle; so said the soothsayer to William's terrified mother, according to a story passed through the generations. Her belief in the fortune-teller's vision was such that when the war with Mexico broke out in 1848, she took William and a tutor and departed for Europe, where they all remained until she was convinced that conditions were safe back home. The three returned, the mother married the tutor, and William went on with his life. Because of the recent death of Mary's eighteen-year-old brother from injuries suffered in a riding accident, only six relatives attended William and Mary's wedding ceremony in 1859.

When the Civil War broke out, William Kirkland joined the Charleston Light Dragoons. He was badly wounded at the battle of

Hawe's Shop in 1864, near the war's end, and died in Richmond. The fortune-teller, it seems, had seen into the future. Kirkland's plantation was overrun during a Northern offensive that was notable for the role played by the slave rebel Harriet Tubman, who arrived with a convoy of five steamships to take the plantation's slaves away, after which some were drafted into the Northern army. In the end, war had brought doom to the young man and economic ruin to his family.[5]

Mary was spared the ignominy of witnessing the plantation's destruction by the combined forces of the Northern army and a brigade of freed slaves. On May 9, 1860, shortly before the war began, Mary had given birth to a son, Thomas Jefferson Kirkland, and William had moved Mary and her newborn back to Camden, where they remained for the war's duration. Judge Withers was there as well, as a delegate to the convention at which the Southern states voted to secede from the Union; he also served briefly as a senator in the Provisional Confederate Government.

Mary Kirkland withdrew into seclusion after her husband's death. For the rest of her life—she lived until 1924—she never left her home, an old mansion called Kamchatka, which was located on what were then the outskirts of Camden. According to a legend, Mary seldom emerged from her upper-story bedroom. As the years passed, the house fell into disrepair, and the grounds grew wild with weeds. (Kamchatka was eventually purchased and renovated, at considerable expense, by the family of the political writer William F. Buckley.) Mary stayed upstairs, consumed with memories of happier times.

Her son, Thomas Jefferson Kirkland, the grandfather of Lane, was a respected lawyer, politician, and civic leader in Camden. A reserved and dignified man, he served several terms in the state legislature, in both the assembly and the senate. He was at one time a partisan of the farmers' movement and its populist leader, Benjamin "Pitchfork Ben" Tillman, though he later broke with Tillman. Kirkland aspired to a judgeship, but when the opportunity arrived, certain conditions were attached to the appointment that clashed with his scruples, and he withdrew his name from consideration. T. J. Kirkland was part-owner of the local newspaper and was involved in a number of civic enterprises in Camden and Kershaw County. He was also something of an amateur historian and coauthored a two-volume history of Camden that was published in 1926.[6]

Although T. J. Kirkland was accomplished as a historian, a horticulturist, and a community leader, he demonstrated little aptitude for making money. Part-time service in the state legislature brought in little cash, and at the turn of the century the practice of law in a small southern town did not produce great wealth. Nor was his career as a banker especially successful; a savings and loan bank of which he was president failed at the

time of the Great Depression, bringing considerable reversal to the
family fortune. As for his long and plodding chronicle of Camden's
history, this brought in no money whatsoever—indeed, he and his coau-
thor, Robert Kennedy, had to borrow money in order to get the work
published.[7]

Money was an issue in the Kirkland family, because T. J. and his wife,
the former Fredericka Alexander, had nine children to feed, clothe, and
educate. Fredericka Alexander came from Manassas, Virginia, the site of
a major Civil War battle. Her father, Lawrence Sterling Alexander, was a
surgeon who served in Moseby's battalion in the Virginia cavalry. The
family had been well-off before the war but was financially ruined by
Reconstruction. Although Fredericka and her six sisters did not grow up
in dire poverty, they were familiar with the tensions and the disappoint-
ments that came with their father's declining fortunes. Fredericka was
deeply affected by the experience; in later years, she tried her mightiest to
instill in her children and grandchildren the importance of pursuing
careers that would guarantee financial security.[8]

Thomas, Fredericka, and their children lived in Cool Springs, a large
house of many Greek columns built a few miles outside the Camden town
line, and somewhat isolated. Because there were no white children for the
ever-expanding Kirkland clan to play with in the immediate vicinity,
often the Kirkland offspring played with black children who lived in
shanties on or near Cool Springs. William L. Kirkland, an uncle of Lane
Kirkland, wrote with fondness of days spent playing baseball with black
neighbor children. The girls, he reported, were allowed to play the field
but were prohibited from batting. On Sundays, the black children played
ball among themselves but made it a practice to select a white friend as
umpire; the umpire's decisions were never challenged. The black children
played without gloves or masks, and it was not uncommon for the catcher
to be knocked unconscious by a smash to the head from a foul ball.[9]

Among those who engaged in these interracial games was Randolph
Withers Kirkland, Lane Kirkland's father, who was born on May 5, 1897,
the third of the nine children.

On Lane's mother's side, his ancestors were, in their own way, as
notable as the Kirklands. But while all of Lane's relatives and ancestors
were equal, those from the North were a bit less equal—at least, in
Kirkland eyes—and it was the bad fortune of the Richardsons to have
come from Yankee stock.

Kirkland's great-great grandfather, Joseph Lane Richardson, was a
businessman and judge from Auburn, New York. His son, Charles
Richardson, was generally known as the Commodore, based on his having sailed on the historic 1835 voyage of the SS *Peacock*, the first American

naval vessel to circumnavigate the globe. By some accounts, this voyage played an important role in paving the way for diplomatic and trade relations between the United States and the Orient. Its major purpose was to exchange ratified treaty documents with several Asian principalities and to open negotiations with Japan. Richardson was a gifted writer; his letters home are the source of much of what is known about the *Peacock*'s famous voyage. The *Peacock* stopped in such exotic locales as Zanzibar (then ruled by the sultan of Muscat), Bombay, and Siam. In Zanzibar, Richardson reported the "heartrending" spectacle of children being sold after having been "imported" from East Africa. The *Peacock* was idled for several weeks after striking a coral reef off Muscat, during which time the crew was forced to keep a wary eye out for pirates who plied the seas of the region. Wrote Richardson, "The intention of the Arabs was not known, but we surmised that they would be glad to relieve us of our money, arms, and other valuables." The ship's officers stayed some days as the guests of Prince Momfanoy of Siam, whom the Americans mistook for a washerman because of his unpretentious attire. During his stay there, Richardson saw a dead boy floating down the river and was told "that it was a very common sight, it being the only way the poor, who are unable to purchase the wood to burn them, have of disposing of their dead." The *Peacock*'s diplomatic mission ended abruptly when its captain, Edmund Roberts, took ill and died en route to Japan. The ship thereupon reversed course and returned to the United States via the Cape of Good Hope.[10]

This was to be the Commodore's final voyage as a seaman. He divided the rest of his life between Auburn and San Francisco, working as a lawyer and trying, apparently without success, to make a fortune as an industrialist and as a mining investor during the California gold rush.

His son, Joseph Lane Richardson—Lane Kirkland's grandfather—was born in 1864. Given the Commodore's lack of success at business—an iron works he owned in Auburn failed—Joseph Richardson left home early on to embark on a career in the railroad business. He began near the bottom with the Pullman company, starting out as a conductor and then moving up to ticket agent. He worked his way quickly through the management ranks at Pullman, then left for a higher position with the Southern Railroad in Jacksonville, and finally, in 1896, accepted the post of commissioner of the Southern States' Passenger Association.[11]

Of Joseph Richardson and his wife, Mary Jacobs Jones Richardson, their son, Alan Richardson, wrote that "both were beneficiaries of a heritage and lineage of ladies and gentlemen of refinement and breeding" who displayed "graciousness and dignity coupled with a lively appreciation of the Christian religion as well as of the good tidings of this world." The Richardsons settled in Atlanta after Joseph accepted the position with the passengers' association. They lived a prosperous life in a large house just outside the city, with their children and half a dozen or so black servants, cooks, and mammies. Music played a central part of family life; the Richardsons were patrons of the opera and often hosted white-tie musicales, where local professional vocalists or musicians performed.

Mary Richardson was said to have been gifted with extrasensory perception. She once sat bolt upright in the middle of a conversation with friends and claimed that some misfortune had befallen her son, Alan. According to Alan's account, he in fact suffered a heatstroke while fighting a forest fire at precisely the moment his mother experienced her vision.[12]

Lane Kirkland's mother, Louise Beardsley Richardson, was born on May 6, 1897, the fourth of five children. She was working as a nurse in Charleston when she met Randolph Kirkland, who was attending college at the time. Soon after they met, he was given the "white feather"—white feathers were handed out by women to able-bodied young men who were not in uniform and had not enlisted for World War I, signifying a lack of patriotism. He thereupon joined the Charleston Light Dragoons and served in France in a reconnaissance unit, shuttling back and forth as a motorcycle courier. He and Louise were married on December 31, 1919, after his return from Europe.[13]

Randolph and Louise Kirkland settled in Camden, where Randolph's parents still lived. They produced five children: Joseph Lane Kirkland— he was named for his maternal grandfather—was the second, born on March 12, 1922. His brother Randolph Withers III was two years older; his two sisters, Mary (known as Mollie) and Katharine, were born in 1926 and 1928, and his brother Thomas Jefferson was born in 1933.[14]

By his own account, Lane Kirkland enjoyed a happy, albeit not prosperous, childhood. Randolph Kirkland made his living as a cotton buyer. A good cotton buyer like Randolph could provide a decent living for his family, but with little left over. In the late 1920s, Randolph tried to establish himself as a cotton broker, a profession with a more lucrative potential. His timing, unfortunately, could not have been worse; the bottom fell out of the cotton market, and his brokerage and warehouse business was ruined. Although it took years, Randolph made a point of paying off his creditors in full. For the rest of his working life, he made his living as a buyer for Kendall Mills, a corporation that operated textile mills throughout South Carolina, including several in Camden and Newberry, where the Kirklands moved in 1932, when Lane was about ten years old.[15]

Randolph Kirkland was blessed with the combination of qualities that were unique to a good cotton buyer: an eye for quality and an affable charm. Each textile mill required the particular type of cotton best suited for whatever it produced, whether gauze for medical dressings or terry cloth for bathrobes. Randolph traveled from one small town to the next throughout the South—his trips took him as far as Oklahoma—visiting warehouses, inspecting samples, and buttering up the warehouse managers. Randolph was adept at making friends among the warehouse managers; he knew which cut of meat or brand of liquor each preferred and regularly plied them with presents. In return, the managers directed him to the highest-quality fiber in their warehouses.

Young Lane accompanied his father on some of these trips, which took him to the more remote areas of the rural South, often reachable only by dirt roads that took a toll on the Model A Ford that the company provided. Much later, Kirkland wrote that buyers' abilities "resided in their eyes and fingertips, used to pull apart and judge the staple in cotton samples to determine whether a given lot would 'mill' at a particular plant making, say, gauze, or was more usable for another plant making sheets or towels. They lived on the edge of their nerves for misjudgment brought dire career consequences from remote impersonal Northern quarters."[16]

In a fragmentary memoir he wrote before his death, Lane Kirkland described his childhood as full of the kinds of adventures that might have provided the basis for episodes of the *Our Gang* comedies, which were popular among young moviegoers during the 1940s. During the summer, children were sent out of the house in the morning and were not expected to return until suppertime. They swam in ponds, played baseball, and sought out minor sorts of mischief. Even after moving to Newberry, Lane and his older brother, Randolph (or Rannie), spent summers in Camden with their grandmother, Fredericka (known as Miss Freddie), who thought it essential that the boys have the proper adult direction—the kind of direction, she was convinced, that their mother could not provide. For Lane and his brothers Randolph and Tom, life in small-town South Carolina was never boring.[17]

Both Lane and Rannie smoked what was known as rabbit tobacco, a weed that was crushed and smoked in a corncob pipe or as a cigarette. Adults tolerated the boys' habit on the grounds that rabbit tobacco didn't carry the potency of a Lucky Strike or a Chesterfield. In Lane's case, rabbit tobacco was the first step toward a life-long addiction to cigarettes.[18]

Of their various youthful escapades, the two older Kirkland boys had a special recollection of an incident that occurred in the mid-thirties in Newberry. There was a vaudeville hall in the town that ordinarily featured girlie shows; Lane recalled the marquee as advertising "12 Beautiful Girls! 12! Count 'em." On this occasion, the featured performer was an itinerant magician, who boasted of his ability to summon ghosts from the grave. The magician recruited Lane, Rannie, and other local boys as his stooges, with the promise of a free ticket to a Western movie, featuring such beloved heroes as Ken Maynard or Buck Jones, at the local opera house. Before the performance, the magician smeared the boys' faces with fluorescent grease and instructed them to seat themselves at scattered sites throughout the auditorium. After performing the usual routine of tricks, he came onstage with a tray of flash powder that, when set on fire, caused the boys' faces to glow in the dark. The boys were then to stand and face the audience, giving the impression of a collection of grimacing ghosts among them.

Lane recalled the unexpected reaction of the audience:

> As it happened, [the magician] reckoned without appreciation for the culture of the community. The county folks and mill hands present for the show, while truly believing in ghosts, did not take their immediate presence lightly or without active response to protect their children and womenfolk. Heavy work shoes came off and bludgeoned the supposedly disembodied spirits to their knees. Rannie and I, bruised and semi-stunned, crawled out amid the turmoil and fled homeward, shrieking and sobbing and unaware that our faces still glowed in the dark.
>
> As we reached the home path through the trees, we were observed by our family cook and child-tender, Mary Thomas, who promptly fainted dead away. Our parents being away visiting friends, we felt obliged to get Mary home, on the edge of town where most of the blacks lived. We managed to get her ample form into a wheelbarrow and, each taking a handle, pushed her down the unlit road, lined with the shanties among which she dwelled.
>
> Our ghastly chariot stirred panic, as the houses emptied and their occupants fled, trailing screams of fright and horror. Only then did the nature of our role in the drama dawn on us. We took to our heels, leaving Mary unescorted in the wheelbarrow, and ran home to scrub the glow from our faces.
>
> Having no rational account of our night's activities to offer in place of the awful truth, we admitted nothing and assumed an air of innocent bewilderment at the version of the event that circulated in town and ultimately passed into legend. Our parents, fortunately, wrote off Mary's incoherent account as superstitious fantasy and no penalties ensued.[19]

Lane and his friends often pestered a northerner named Ledley to give them supplies of the patent medicine "little liver pills" that he peddled for the cure of pellagra, rickets, and other diseases common to the region. But the boys wanted the pills for nonmedicinal purposes; they used them as ammunition for slingshots—"ballistically far superior to pebbles." Recalled Lane, "Instead of curing disease, the pills brought a further menace to birds, squirrels, street lights, and windows of the town." Slingshots were not the only weapons available to the youth of South Carolina. There were magnolia burr launchers, homemade musket pistols, air rifles, 22s, and of course, shotguns when a boy reached age sixteen. And there were other forms of excitement for young boys. As Lane wrote, years later:

> We dammed creeks to create swimming holes, and dug labyrinthine caves in their banks. We swam in ponds infested with water moccasins, exiting with super-human speed when we felt them brush against us.[20]

For contemporary Americans, the most striking, and enviable, feature of life in small-town South Carolina was the sense of total security that children enjoyed. Tom Kirkland, Lane's brother, who graduated from the U.S. Naval Academy, served with distinction as a naval pilot, and worked in Washington for the Defense Department, recalls his childhood in Newberry in near-idyllic terms:

> Many of the boys from Newberry did well; there was something about the town that gave us a good foundation. It was an incredibly safe place to grow up. We never locked the house; I never remember my father taking the keys out of the ignition. It never occurred to me that there could be ugly, mean people out there in the world. In one sense, I grew up naïve; in another sense, I grew up with a great sense of security.[21]

The security that so impressed Tom Kirkland was enforced through an unspoken code that gave every responsible adult the sanction to interfere in and report on the activities of every child in the town. Many years later, in an address delivered to the South Carolina Historical Association, Lane sardonically compared the informal surveillance network in Camden and Newberry to the secret police regime in totalitarian Eastern Europe:

> Eastern Europe had its brutal secret police and comparisons are out of order. But to boys growing up in Newberry, the surveillance system, while informal, was quite efficient. There was a whistleblower on every block. Play hookey from school and you were doomed. Your whereabouts were reported within minutes. You could get away with very little in the way of deviation from rules of deportment, as defined by the town oligarchs or by your family.[22]

In this environment of community watchfulness, Lane's father was a relaxed and easygoing presence. He liked to hunt and fish, the normal pastimes for men in that part of the country. He was a great storyteller and a man of moderate habits, the exception being a fondness for whiskey, which he usually enjoyed with a group of cotton-buyer cronies known as the Cotton Yard Crowd. He bought his refreshments from a bootlegger, a man named "Push" Schumpert, who operated outside Camden.

Recalled Lane:

> On occasion, my father would give me fifty cents, with instructions to deliver it to Mr. Schumpert. I would dutifully proceed to his house on the edge of town and rap on his screen door, which overlooked some rows of sickly looking cabbages. He would accept the money without comment and point out the particular cabbage that I was to take. Planted beneath the cabbage there would be a Mason jar filled with corn whiskey, which I would dutifully convey to my father. Mr. Schumpert, of course, was not selling whiskey. He was selling cabbages. Anything else I chanced to find there was providential.[23]

Like other middle-class white families, the Kirklands employed a few servants to look after the children, cook, and keep the house in order, even in times when money was scarce. Louise filled her days sewing, playing bridge with friends, and spending time with other women in the local garden club and in other community organizations. The Kirklands attended a small local Episcopal Church, where Louise sang in the choir. There weren't enough Episcopalians to sustain a regular minister, so a circuit-riding Episcopal clergyman conducted services once a month; on other Sundays, the Kirklands attended services at the churches of friends. Louise Kirkland retained the passion for music she had inherited from her parents; she sang and played the piano and the organ. Every Saturday afternoon quiet was enforced as the family listened to the radio broadcast of the Metropolitan Opera. Lane, too, loved those broadcasts of *La Bohème* and *The Marriage of Figaro*. He listened on a small radio in his room, puffing away on a corncob pipe. There, in small-town South Carolina, was born an appreciation for classical music that would be with him for the rest of his life.[24]

For the Kirkland children, the most important and, by the testimony of Lane's brothers, unnerving adult presence was that of their grandmother, Miss Freddie. Where Randolph Kirkland was soft-spoken and full of charm, Miss Freddie had strong convictions and an iron will. She was a woman who, in the words of Rannie Kirkland, could "strike terror in the hearts of tradesmen as far away as Sumter." Miss Freddie had never quite gotten over the financial ruin her family had suffered during Reconstruction and was determined that her children and grandchildren would develop the skills and traits of character that were crucial to moneymaking. She wanted her offspring and their children to be successful, and she had definite ideas about what constituted success.

William Lennox Kirkland, Lane's uncle, reported that his mother, Miss Freddie, taught him to swim "the hard way," by having him tossed into deep water by an older brother, "where I had to swim or else." Nor would his mother tolerate his fear of thunder and lightning, as he remembered:

> My mother . . . had no use for a coward. I recall once lightning struck a tree in our back yard about 50 feet from the house and I started for the bedroom to get under a pillow. My mother bawled me out and forced me to go out in the back yard and stand in the rain until the storm was over. I must say such treatment cured me.

William seems not to have resented his mother for her sink-or-swim techniques. "It is unfortunate," he wrote, "that none of her nine children inherited her degree of fortitude and courage."[25]

Miss Freddie had a ready supply of maxims and advice for her grandchildren. "Beauty needs no adornment," she told Katharine, Lane's sister, in explaining why a fifteen-year-old girl should not wear earrings. She taught that a Kirkland never quits and that a Kirkland always lives up to his word. It was Miss Freddie who made most of the decisions about the upbringing of her grandchildren. At one point, Miss Freddie decreed that Lane go and live for a spell in the home of his uncle, Marion Adickes, to serve as a surrogate sibling after one of the family's young children died. Adickes, as the uncle was generally known, was the manager of a local textile mill and a firm enemy of trade unions; he boasted of having kept his mills union free. Much later, after Lane had risen to a position of prominence within the AFL-CIO, he would engage in heated arguments with Uncle Adickes over the rights of workers to join unions—heated to the point where one or the other might end up leaving the room in fury.[26] Miss Freddie also saw to it that the boys were introduced to the world of culture outside small-town South Carolina. Every summer, Miss Freddie and a servant traveled to Washington, accompanied by Lane and Rannie. They stayed in a house in the city's northwest section, not far from where Lane and his wife, Irena, would settle in the 1970s. Lane spent his days visiting the historic sites and museums of the capital.

Although Lane enjoyed a normal and happy boyhood, he did not join in the traditional southern rite of passage, blood sport. Even though

Lane's father was an avid hunter and fisherman, as were Rannie and many other boys from the region, hunting held no appeal for Lane. Lane did feel the lure of football, another great pastime of southern boyhood. But Lane's physique was too slight for the pulverizing brutality of the sport, and Lane was forced to satisfy his interest as a lifelong fan. From an early age, Lane was a bookworm; he read constantly and with remarkable intensity, his passion inspired by the impressive library that his grandfather had assembled at his home in Cool Springs. In one notable incident, Lane sat on a living room couch reading a book—it might have been a novel by H. Rider Haggard or Conan Doyle—when the roof caught on fire. Despite the frenzy of family members and firemen, he went on with his reading, oblivious to the commotion going on about him until, the blaze having been extinguished, he looked up and asked, "Is something going on?"[27]

Lane's intellectual curiosity was nurtured by what all accounts suggest was a first-rate public education. "We had excellent teachers," Rannie Kirkland recalled. "The teachers picked out the best students and concentrated on them, and pretty much ignored the others." Lane was among the brightest students; his fourth-grade report card, issued by his teacher Rosabelle Thompson well before the era of grade inflation, showed all As and Bs, with an A for deportment. With a few exceptions, the teachers were women; several played bridge with Louise Kirkland and kept her apprised of her children's progress.[28]

The curriculum was standard for the time, with heavy doses of English, math, science, and history. For students who aspired to a college education, Latin was a requirement. Students also memorized long passages from works by Shakespeare and other poets, as well as excerpts from the speeches of the world's great statesmen. This proved to be good training for Lane, whose fine oratorical skills as a labor leader would give evidence of the classical training he received at Newberry High School.

Although South Carolina was a rigidly segregated state, race relations in Camden and Newberry, as in many southern towns, were more complex than northerners might have imagined. In Newberry, blacks and whites did not live in segregated neighborhoods, as later became the pattern. Tom Kirkland recalls black families living either on or next to the Kirkland property. The Kirkland boys regularly played with black children. Indeed, while no objections were raised to the boys having black friends, Kirkland's parents discouraged the children from mixing with the children of the white mill workers, the mill hands being looked on as the lowest and the least cultured of the lower classes. Tom Kirkland was occasionally taken by the family's black maid to the cinema; they sat together in the balcony, which was reserved for "colored only." Both Tom and

Katharine report that their father flatly forbade the children from using the term *nigger*. Indeed, both recall that the N word was not commonly used by adults in Camden. Tom Kirkland never heard the word used regularly until he went to the Naval Academy. "I was shocked after I went North to hear people talk that way about blacks. I had never encountered the kinds of racist attitudes in Newberry that I was regularly exposed to in the North. My family never had those attitudes and neither did my friends."[29]

There was something else that was never encountered in South Carolina: Republicans. As Tom Kirkland put it, "I never met a Republican until I joined the navy."[30] Although his parents did not have an intense passion for politics, Lane early on was alert to the consequences of economic injustice in the rural South. He was aware that for some in Camden and Newberry, grinding poverty was the central fact of life. He attended school with the children of mill hands who wore hand-me-down clothes and no shoes. The mill workers lived in the mill village, a collection of shabby houses situated near the factory. The mill owned the homes, and when times were slack at the mill, the workers faced the threat of eviction. The recollections of small-town southern poverty would have a powerful influence on Lane's political mentality. As a trade union leader, he would return again and again to the images of southern poverty in arguing for federal spending to build roads, bridges, and power facilities and pay for old-age insurance and medical assistance for the indigent.

As Kirkland entered his late teens, he developed something of a lust for adventure. He and Rannie talked vaguely about going to Spain and fighting on the Loyalist side against the fascist Franco. Although the details are unclear, his sister Katharine believes that Lane also entertained visions of enrolling in the Naval Academy. He took off to Atlanta to take the necessary admission tests, only to be told, according to his sister, that he couldn't pass the physical examination. After this setback, he set off for Canada with the intention of joining the Canadian army. When a border guard asked Lane where he hailed from, Lane, trying his mightiest to conceal his southern accent, drawled, "Dee-troit." The official didn't believe a word of the young man's story, and Lane returned to South Carolina.[31]

Although Randolph Kirkland was far from wealthy, he was determined that his children should get a college education. "He sat us all down and told us that the girls were going to get two years of college and the boys would get four," recalled Katharine. "He thought college was more important for the boys, which it was at the time." Katharine and Mollie attended small colleges in the area; Rannie graduated from

Clemson, which at the time was a military academy; Tom graduated from Annapolis.[32]

After Lane graduated with honors from Newberry High School—he and Mary Jane Grey were voted the "Most Intellectual" of the class of 1939—he enrolled in a small local institution, Newberry College. Money was an issue for the Kirklands; at Newberry, tuition was cheap and Lane could live at home. But after one year, Lane left college. War was coming, and Lane wanted to do his part. At age eighteen, he left home to go to sea. After six weeks of training in Algiers, Louisiana, across the Mississippi River from New Orleans—Lane received the highest grades of his group—he signed on as a deck cadet on the SS *Liberator*, a merchant ship owned by the Lykes Brothers Steamship Company.[33]

Many of Kirkland's stories of life at sea involve escapades in waterfront districts in exotic locales or incidents with young women. During an interlude in Cape Town, Kirkland, then all of nineteen years old, fell instantly and madly in love with a woman who had emigrated from Australia. Kirkland actually planned to jump ship to get married. He returned to his ship to get his gear; while packing, he heard a radio broadcast. It was December 7, 1941. The United States was at war, and Lane stayed on the *Liberator*. He never saw the girl again.[34]

The voyage back to the United States was terrifying for the crew of the unarmed ship. In the months immediately after the American declaration of war, German submarines stationed themselves just off the U.S. coast, primed to sink any merchant ship that came into range of their guns. Later, merchant vessels moved as part of convoys that included American warships, thus reducing the dangers from the U-boats lurking offshore. But in the early phase of the conflict, merchant vessels, which were unarmed, sailed without military escort and were easy prey for German torpedoes. Americans called this period the Great Turkey Shoot; to German naval officials, it was known as the "Happy Time" or, officially, Operation Drumbeat.

As Kirkland and his fellow crew members headed across the Atlantic, a journey of thirty-nine nerve-wracking days, they became increasingly aware of the perils that lay ahead. "The radio waves crackled with the SOS signals of allied merchant ships ahead of us, astern and abeam. For days and nights every ripple or shadow on the water brought all hands to their lifeboat stations, but we made it to port unscathed."[35]

In a letter to his parents, Lane reported his happiness in seeing several relatives in Boston and in getting together for a drunken evening with several old friends from Newberry who were studying to become wireless operators. He also noted, almost as an aside, that the *Liberator* had sailed through an area where, six hours later, the *Mornay* was torpedoed and sunk. "That's an instance," Kirkland dryly noted, "where a half hour slower and we would have been dead meat."

After unloading its cargo in Boston, the *Liberator* sailed south through a route meant to minimize danger to cargo and crew. Yet even as the ship wended its way through bays and canals, it could not entirely avoid the open sea, where prevailed conditions of "total exposure, perfectly silhouetted at night by the bright lights of every coastal city we passed on the way to New Orleans."[36]

Having emerged intact from his first wartime experience, Kirkland decided to seek promotion. In this, he benefited from the government's desperate need for merchant ship officers. The time of service required for a promotion had been reduced from four years to eighteen months. Kirkland crammed for several months and then passed the test for a third mate's license. Then, in May 1942, he enrolled in courses offered at what would become the Merchant Marine Academy at Kings Point, off Great Neck, Long Island. He was a member of the institution's first class of students and graduated a year later.

Soon after he arrived at Kings Point, Kirkland was informed that his old ship, the *Liberator*, had been torpedoed and sunk off Morehead City, North Carolina. The torpedo exploded in the engine room, and the entire watch was killed, including Kirkland's former cabin mate, Howard Payne Conway.[37]

Although in later years Kirkland delighted in talking about his life at sea, he seldom discussed his wartime episodes under enemy fire, except in the most general terms. His brother Tom said that Lane "was not the kind of person who would dwell on his war experiences."[38] Kirkland served on ships that were present in every theater of the war, from Murmansk to Luzon, Guadalcanal, and Anzio. Kirkland's ship came under attack during the beach landing at Anzio, when German precision bombers subjected American ships to heavy fire. Kirkland never went into details about that episode. But he did later write of the "hazards and horrors of night bridge watches in blacked out, zig-zagging, and ponderous convoys in the North Atlantic winter gales." A special concern was the danger of colliding with another Allied ship, loaded, like his own, "with explosives and gasoline and invisible until all too close." Added Kirkland, "The menace of proximity to other floating bombs outweighed the company of submarine wolf packs in the scale of anxieties that we lived with day in and day out." Another danger was the possibility of being hit by fire from other American or Allied ships. In Sicily, North Africa, and Italy proper, Kirkland served on ships that endured fire from every possible source: from enemy submarines, from the Luftwaffe, and, of course, from friendly fire. "The real miracle of the war," Kirkland wrote, "was the luck of surviving the good intentions and bad aim of people on your side."[39]

A half century later, Kirkland was asked by a reporter whether he was afraid that a particular decision by the AFL-CIO might prove to be a mistake, with damaging consequences for labor. Kirkland responded with uncharacteristic emotion:

> Afraid? I'll tell you what afraid is. Afraid is a four-hour night watch on the bridge of a ship in the middle of a blacked-out convoy loaded with high explosives and high octane gasoline, in a full gale in mid-winter in the North Atlantic, surrounded by wolf packs. Afraid is knowing that in another eight hours you are going to do it all over again and for many days and nights yet. That's what afraid is. The rest is just politics. Next question.[40]

Of course, not all of Kirkland's time at sea was spent in the line of fire. His letters home during the war reek of boredom, as his ships idled in various port cities. Kirkland spent considerable time reading. And it was at sea that his awareness of injustice, ignited early on by his acquaintance with the shabbily clothed sons of mill hands in Newberry, was refined into a full-blown social conscience. He was especially impressed by the stories told by veteran seamen of their treatment in prewar times, when conditions aboard ship were hard, sailors were subject to the blacklist, and seamen were compelled to live in semipoverty between voyages. It was during this period that Lane joined the ranks of organized labor by enrolling as a member of Local 88 of the Masters, Mates, and Pilots Association. He soon became convinced that union membership represented the only way ordinary workers could ensure fair treatment and a reasonable wage.

Lane was also convinced that seamen who died during Happy Time were the victims of American government indifference, just as surely as of German U-boats. Had the United States prepared for war properly, Kirkland believed, merchant ships would not have been sent forth without military escort. To Kirkland, the lesson of the war was the utter irresponsibility of playing politics with issues of national defense. As he often said later on, the United States should spend whatever is necessary to provide for a strong national defense, including enough money to ensure the maximum safety of those who do the fighting.[41]

The war was a time of intense worry for Lane's family in Newberry. The two oldest boys were under fire in battle zones: Rannie parachuted behind enemy lines in both New Guinea and the Philippines and had near-fatal encounters with the Japanese on at least two occasions; Lane faced danger from all sides aboard ship. Everyone was quiet in the Kirkland household during the evening radio news broadcast, and Randolph Kirkland kept a large map on which he charted the progress of the war. Louise read aloud the letters from the boys, letters that were, in Tom Kirkland's words, "brief and innocuous" and uninformative about the war, either due to wartime censorship or the self-censorship exercised by Lane and Rannie, neither of whom wanted to deepen the fears of their parents or siblings.[42]

Although Lane served on ships assigned to every war zone and which were often the object of enemy fire, he only once served aboard a vessel that sank. And this mishap had nothing to do with wartime conflict.

The ship, the SS *Narbo*, was an ancient "three islander" that would have been retired long before, had it not been for the necessities of war. Kirkland had just returned from a tour of duty in the Mediterranean and had only recently received his first mate's certificate. He was not unhappy to hire on as a hand aboard a ship that was scheduled for a cargo run outside the sphere of naval conflict—"where I would not be shot at by friend or foe."

The *Narbo* was to carry locomotive engines to destinations in South America and to return laden with sodium and copper from Chile. Having been involved in the loading and unloading of tanks in the European theater, Kirkland was well-qualified for a job that required experience in heavy equipment. At age twenty-two, he was the youngest member of the crew.

On the return leg from Panama to Gulfport, Mississippi, the *Narbo* steered a course that took it near Providence Island, just off the Nicaraguan coast. One night, Lane and the second mate returned to the ship after a night of port-side drinking. After a careful examination of the charts, the second mate discovered that unless the ship changed direction, it was headed straight toward a coral reef and catastrophe. He and Kirkland roused the sleeping captain and urged that he make for deep water; otherwise, the ship was likely to run aground on the reef. This proposed course was rejected out-of-hand. As Kirkland wrote years later, the captain "explained that he was the master of the ship, that when he wanted our advice he would ask for it, and in the meantime we should go fuck ourselves." The two mates, however, had the presence of mind to put their concerns in writing. They then woke up the captain a second time and had him sign their statement.

The *Narbo* thus continued on its way, straight toward calamity. At about 3 A.M., as the ship headed toward Providence lighthouse, it smashed into the reef, "and fetched up, hard and fast, in about fifteen feet of water." "Old Providence lighthouse bore dead ahead," Kirkland recalled, "shining quite brightly from the shoreline, now distinctly visible. Our position was certain and irrevocable and no bearings were necessary."

There the *Narbo* remained, "pounding and listing in the surf," for three weeks, until a salvage tug arrived to tow the ship and its luckless crew to Mobile. At the subsequent trial, the captain and the third mate lost their licenses; Kirkland and the second mate were exonerated after they presented their written objection to the captain's course as evidence. The *Narbo* was declared a total loss after it mysteriously sank while in port, and the government, as was the policy at the time, paid the steamship company a half million dollars in compensation. Lane was never asked to ship with the Lykes company again. All of which led him to ponder whether "the wreck of the *Narbo* was not altogether accidental."[43]

Kirkland made his final voyage aboard the *Contest*, a refrigerator ship out of Oakland. The *Contest* had a more formal regime than Kirkland's earlier vessels; the crew was required to wear uniforms and Kirkland was called chief and executive officer rather than first mate. The work, however, was much the same as on other ships. The *Contest* bounced around to various Far East ports—New Zealand, the Philippines, Iwo Jima, the Marianas—until returning to the United States in mid-1946. It was the last cargo ship boarded by Kirkland until 1994, when he sailed on an antiquated Liberty ship that was to take part in the celebration of the fiftieth anniversary of the landing at Normandy.[44]

After the war, the Kirkland children went their separate ways. Rannie secured a position with General Electric as an engineer and divided his time between various GE operations in the United States and Europe. Tom enrolled at Annapolis, then served at bases in the Far East before moving to Washington to work for the Defense Department. Katharine married William K. Crockett, an engineer who was involved in building factories and other facilities for the DuPont corporation, a job that led the family to move some twenty times. Mollie married William Reynolds, a vice president of the Foster Wheeler Company, which manufactured industrial furnaces. They settled in Basking Ridge, New Jersey. None of them remained in South Carolina, though Rannie would return to his hometown of Camden after his retirement.[45]

As for Lane, he now had a family to provide for. In 1942 he had married Edith Hollyday, then a student at Bennington College. Edie, as she was generally known, came from New York, where her father had made a success in the real estate business. Kirkland had met her during a leave from Kings Point. They had met whenever they could, during subsequent leaves, not all of which were officially approved. Lane and Edie liked to listen to music together and go for drives—it was Edie who taught Lane to drive. They may also have discussed politics, as Edie was a woman of strong liberal views who traced her ancestry back to a lawyer of Lord Baltimore's on her father's side and an adviser to Lincoln on her mother's (her mother was a Blair, a family that had been prominent in Maryland politics for many years). The courtship was brief, as were many during wartime, and Lane was back aboard ship soon after the wedding. Edie went to live in Camden with Miss Freddie for much of the war years.

In 1945 Edie gave birth to twin girls, Lucy and Blair, the first two of five daughters born to the couple. A year later, Lane abandoned his career as a merchant seaman. Given his new responsibilities, he felt that life at sea was no longer an option. He had hardly seen his twin daughters during their first year. He was twenty-four years old; he understood that if he were to find a career on land, now was the time to make the change. Having seen a fair part of the world and having had more than his quota of adventure, Kirkland brought his family to Washington, where he began to prepare for a radically different career.

2

EDUCATION OF A TRADE UNIONIST

ALTHOUGH KIRKLAND HAD GIVEN UP THE SEAGOING LIFE, HE DIDN'T leave the sea completely behind. Just in case things didn't work out as he sought a new career, he secured his unlimited license as a master mariner, a certificate that would allow him to serve on "vessels of any gross tons on any ocean." He also took a job as a nautical scientist at the hydrographic office of the Navy Department. The hydrographic office was one of the few places on land where a seaman could find employment and still make use of his marine training. Kirkland spent his days working on nautical charts and writing directions for seamen. It was, he recalled with typical irony, "not the most exciting place in the world."

Lane also enrolled in evening classes at Georgetown University. His choice of studies was interesting: a special program the university sponsored for students who aspired to careers in the foreign service. It isn't clear why Lane chose this particular program. He didn't want a career as either a doctor or a lawyer. We don't know whether, as a young man, he felt a strong yearning to pursue the life of a diplomat or foreign service officer.

Yet Lane was destined never to enter the foreign service. Indeed, many years later, he would turn down a presidential offer of the ambassadorship to Poland, an important post in the aftermath of Communism's fall. By that time, Kirkland was the leader of the American labor movement, a more influential position than that of any diplomatic posting and one far more congenial to Lane's political ideals and temperament. And while Lane did complete his course work and receive a degree, his principal recollection of Georgetown was of one night, one class, and one speaker—a speaker who was to change Lane Kirkland's life forever.

The speaker was William Green, president of the American Federation of Labor, the larger of the two American trade union federations of the time. Green spoke on the Taft-Hartley Act, an antilabor measure passed in 1947 that would have a major impact on labor's ability to organize workers. Green's words would have important consequences for the future course of the labor movement. He may not have won over the majority of his audience; he did, however, convince Lane—not only about the injustice of Taft-Hartley but about labor as an institution that would carry the fight for the ordinary man. Lane had already developed a strong set of convictions about the world through his experiences in the rural South and his years at sea. Green mentioned that the AFL was interested in hiring young people for its staff. Lane thereupon approached Green and mentioned that he was probably the only active union member in the class. Green urged him to apply for a job after he graduated. A year later, after receiving his bachelor's degree, Kirkland was hired by the AFL for a position on its research staff. He began his new job in June 1948 and would remain with organized labor for the next forty-seven years. Once he joined the labor movement, Lane Kirkland never looked back.

At the time, American labor was divided into two rival federations. The American Federation of Labor, founded in 1886, was the original umbrella organization for trade unions. The AFL's dominant early figure was Samuel Gompers, an immigrant, one-time socialist cigar maker who had served as the federation's president for many years and built the AFL into a reasonably powerful trade union entity. Gompers died in 1924, but his influence over the federation's philosophy was still evident when Kirkland joined the staff. Gompers was an advocate of what was called, sometimes derisively, "business unionism." He believed that the principal responsibility of the trade union leader was to provide the most effective representation for his members—to secure the best possible wages, benefits, and working conditions. Through experience, Gompers had come to distrust political radicals, whom he regarded as irresponsible utopians who treated workers as fodder for the class war rather than as living, breathing human beings. Gompers also suspected that political radicals neither understood nor appreciated the unique strengths of the American system. Gompers believed that to prosper, the labor movement must develop along lines that were compatible with American culture and the capitalist system and, conversely, that it would be suicidal for labor to adopt an antagonistic stance toward American values. While Gompers understood that labor had no choice but to involve itself in politics, he opposed the movement becoming a permanent appendage to a political party. Labor's political objectives, he counseled, should be achieved by rewarding friends and punishing enemies; it should avoid the European model, in which unions maintained formal affiliations to a party of the left. Under his leadership, and afterward under Green's, the AFL as a federation seldom endorsed a candidate for president.

The rival to the AFL was the Congress of Industrial Organizations.

The CIO was formed in 1936 as a split-off from the AFL by unions that were frustrated by the AFL's conservatism, its apathy, and, especially, its hostility to the unionization of workers along industrial, as opposed to craft, lines, a position that stood as a major obstacle to the organization in the growing heavy-industry field: steel, automobiles, rubber. In its early years, the CIO's major personality was John L. Lewis, the president of the United Mine Workers and, in his heyday, the most powerful labor leader in the United States. Because they had rid themselves of the constraints imposed by the AFL's insistence on organizing workers along craft lines, the CIO unions were able to score a series of historic breakthroughs in the auto and steel industries. The CIO also took a more aggressive political stance than did the AFL. Its leadership was strongly identified with the agenda of the New Deal—the exception being Lewis, who resigned as president after opposing Franklin D. Roosevelt's bid for a third term. CIO figures such as Sidney Hillman of the Amalgamated Clothing Workers emerged as power brokers within the Democratic Party. And where unions affiliated with the AFL were scrupulous in suppressing Communist influence within the ranks, the CIO included a number of unions whose leadership was dominated by Communist Party members, as well as other CIO unions, such as the United Auto Workers, that had powerful Communist factions that vied for internal power with non-Communist groupings.

By the time Kirkland entered organized labor, the differences over organizing, industrial unionism, political action, and Communism were less acute than had been the case ten years earlier. There were still, to be sure, two rival images of trade unionism that competed for respectability and attention. One, embodied in the craft unions of the AFL, bespoke of unions as normal participants in the American system. The labor movement that emerged from this tradition accepted capitalism, favored a bipartisan political strategy, and looked with disfavor on the domination of unions by Communists or other radicals whose first allegiance was to the party. The unions that shared this tradition could be every bit as militant as any CIO union. But the militancy of the craft unions was directed at relatively narrow goals: union recognition, more pay, better hours, the protection of jobs. The main internal problem facing AFL unions in 1948 was corruption. A number of unions from the building industry, the maritime trades, and the Teamsters would soon be the objects of federal investigations.

The CIO, by contrast, drew inspiration from the path-breaking struggles of its early years—the sit-down strikes in the auto factories; the pitched battle at the Ford corporation's River Rouge installation in Detroit, where Walter Reuther and other union leaders were battered by company goons; the bloody organizing drives of the United Steelworkers Organizing Committee (later to become the United Steelworkers of America). To liberals and the left, the early CIO exemplified a labor movement that was at once uncompromising and farsighted, with a leadership that was concerned about racial injustice and was interested in strengthening the liberal alliance within the Democratic Party. This view of the CIO was in many respects inaccurate, as its member unions were just as practical minded as any AFL affiliate when it came to providing services to the membership. But by 1948, labor in general and the large CIO unions in particular found themselves on the defensive in the wake of a series of industry-crippling strikes that had been called immediately after World War II. The strikes provoked widespread alarm at the disruption of the postwar economy. Opinion surveys showed labor unrest as the number-one concern of the American people, and the Republican Party effectively exploited the alleged excesses of labor leaders during the 1946 off-year election. The result was a catastrophe for labor. Republicans gained control of both the House and the Senate; with support from the Democratic Party's Dixiecrat wing, the GOP could look forward to formidable majorities in both houses of Congress for legislation placing restrictions on the unions.

The result was the Taft-Hartley Act. Sponsored by Senator Robert A. Taft, an Ohio senator and a leader of the Republican Party's conservative wing, and Representative Fred Hartley, a Republican, the bill set forth a series of restrictions that would have a long-range effect on unions' ability to organize workers and on their internal governance. Of particular importance to the future of labor organizing efforts, it outlawed the secondary boycott—that is, the right of unions to strike or take other actions in solidarity with a different union involved in a labor dispute or strike. The secondary boycott was a crucial weapon for unions in campaigns to organize workers en masse in a city or region; it had been used with particular effectiveness by Jimmy Hoffa during his drive to organize trucking companies, warehouses, and food stores throughout the Midwest. Second, Taft-Hartley allowed states to adopt "right-to-work" laws that effectively barred the union shop. The right-to-work provision added another obstacle to the already difficult challenge of organizing workers in the South.

The adoption of Taft-Hartley was something of a wake-up call for organized labor. It drove home the necessity for labor to expand its role in electoral politics. It also taught leaders in both the AFL and the CIO that a unified labor movement might be more effective in beating back future laws designed to curb union power. The vulnerability of a labor movement that was split along organizational and ideological lines was one of the first and most important lessons Kirkland learned as a young trade unionist. Much later, as president of a unified federation, he would make labor unity the linchpin of a strategy to counter the most serious political challenge to labor's organizational strength since the Taft-Hartley Act was passed.

Kirkland joined the AFL in the last years of William Green's stewardship. Green had served as federation president since Gompers's death and was well past the time of seeking new horizons for American trade unionism. His executive council, a governing body drawn from the leadership of the federation's major affiliated unions, included some of labor's more influential personalities: David Dubinsky of the International Ladies' Garment Workers Union; Harry Lundberg, president of the Seafarers; Dan Tobin, president of the Teamsters; and Matthew Woll, president of the International Typographers' Union (ITU). The number-two man in the federation, the secretary-treasurer, was a former Bronx plumber named George Meany.

The labor movement faced a critical moment in 1948. Like every other institution of consequence, labor experienced major changes in the immediate postwar period. Previously, American unions were primarily concerned with organizing workers and representing them in collective bargaining with management for better wages and working conditions. Unions did not maintain large staffs of lobbyists or political operatives. Nor did they sponsor medical centers, retirement homes, or adult education programs, or have on their staffs civil rights officers and experts on pensions, health insurance, Social Security, foreign trade, or international affairs. But this was about to change. In the flush of postwar prosperity and an unprecedented growth of trade union numbers and power, labor was prepared to take on new roles and responsibilities.

The AFL staff that Kirkland joined included a number of holdovers from the time of Gompers, including some whose best days of service to America's working men were well behind them. Green had a relaxed attitude toward administrative responsibilities, permitting staff members to select whatever title struck their fancy and paying no attention to such mundane matters as job descriptions or organizational charts. Kirkland was hired as a researcher, but he soon discovered that research was only part of his portfolio.

As a junior staff member, Kirkland was given the least desirable or most puzzling assignments. "You were expected to be able to bluff expertise on any subject and, in the process, you developed a role and a clientele," Kirkland recalled. Although Kirkland did not join organized labor out of ideological commitment, as a socialist might, he regarded service in labor as a calling and not simply as a job. Unlike many political radicals,

Kirkland had actually lived amid poverty in southern mill towns and had witnessed the dramatic changes that were ushered in by the New Deal. Like the New Deal, organized labor sought to better the living conditions of ordinary workers within the existing economic system. Labor also offered protection to workers from unjust treatment by bosses. Throughout his life, and especially during his years at sea, Kirkland had recoiled at acts of injustice or arrant stupidity. He thus found in the labor movement the perfect place for the fulfillment of his instincts of pragmatic idealism.

The emotional commitment to labor was present from the beginning and would grow stronger as he rose to positions of increasing responsibility. Facilitating his rise was a set of unique qualities. He was smart, curious, an omnivorous reader. The man who, as a teenager, remained oblivious to a fire a few rooms away because of his intense concentration on his book, now put those powers of concentration to good use as he read through thousands of pages of documents in order to gain expertise on one subject or another of importance to the labor movement. Kirkland never flinched if asked to draft a position paper or write a speech on an issue about which he had limited knowledge. He would go about assembling a trove of research materials, read everything relevant on the subject, consult with experts, and then distill the mass of material into a form that would prove useful and comprehensible to union officials.

Kirkland was a naturally gifted writer whose talent was immediately recognized by Green and other AFL officials, who made use of his speechwriting abilities from time to time. Kirkland occasionally faced unusual challenges in crafting speeches. He was once asked to draft a presentation for Lew Hines, the federation's legislative director and, in a previous incarnation, the Republican secretary of labor for the state of Pennsylvania. Hines had been asked to speak by the Bill Posters' Union at the annual assembly of the Outdoor Advertising Council. Kirkland was under strict instructions to include in every speech a denunciation of Taft-Hartley. He thus faced the task of relating "the case for highway billboards to the case against the Taft-Hartley Act as symbolic of the resistance to class oppression." Hines was delighted with the results of Kirkland's craftsmanship.

Kirkland's speechwriting abilities were soon noted by officials in the Democratic Party. Although the AFL boasted a substantial minority of Republican union presidents, organized labor was nearly united in its support for the ticket of Harry Truman and Alben Barkley in the 1948 election, due to the GOP's role in the passage of Taft-Hartley. Shortly after Labor Day in 1948, a representative of the Truman campaign approached the AFL. The campaign was in serious financial straits; would the AFL give Kirkland a short leave to write speeches for the vice presidential candidate?

So Kirkland joined the Barkley retinue for the final two months of the campaign. Campaigns were relatively sedate and uncomplicated affairs in those days. Barkley toured the country in a DC-6 jet chartered from United Airlines. He was accompanied by a grand total of two reporters, one from the Associated Press, the other from the *Baltimore Sun*. Aside from whatever local media decided to cover his appearances, that was the extent of the press coverage for the man who would soon be elected vice president.

As an ardent New Dealer, Kirkland was eager to do his part for the Democratic ticket. There was, however, a serious complication. Barkley had poor eyesight, to the point where he couldn't read the speeches Kirkland and another speechwriter churned out, even after the words had been hand inscribed in large letters on cue cards. Barkley finally abandoned all pretense of using the material prepared by Kirkland, falling back on the standard anti-Republican stump speech that had served him so well over the years. Kirkland continued to pound out speeches on portable typewriters during choppy flights from one city to the next. But the speeches remained undelivered, and the reporters wouldn't quote from them since they bore no resemblance to the lines delivered by the candidate at campaign rallies.

Not surprisingly, the Barkley campaign had its problems with the working press. Reporters found covering Barkley a tedious chore. He had two variations on the standard anti-Republican speech: one for city audiences, a second for country folk. An orator of the old stentorian school, Barkley delivered speeches that were emotive, long-winded, full of passion, and utterly lacking in content. The reporters grew restless; instead of writing about yet another windy address, they stirred up the embers of embarrassing episodes from Barkley's political past. Kirkland concluded that the press was "like the company of large carnivores. If they are not kept well fed, they will eat you." He then devised a new strategy. He would write a few sentences on a hot issue of the day, then sit down and implore Barkley to include a reasonable approximation of them in his speech. This ploy seemed to satisfy the press's needs for the duration of the campaign.

Once the campaign ended, Kirkland returned to the AFL, where he soon gained recognition as an authority on pensions. Pension plans emerged as an important collective bargaining issue in the immediate postwar years, due, ironically, to the government's wage-price controls that were imposed during World War II and the Korean War. With unions effectively prevented from bargaining for wage increases higher than the level set by government, other issues came to the forefront. Since employer contributions to pension and insurance plans were ruled to be noninflationary, unions chose to seek better terms through hard bargaining over fringe benefits like pensions.

The result was an explosion of private pension plans, some run along orthodox lines as company cash indemnity plans and some run by the unions themselves. Unfortunately, the expansion of the private pension system had the malign effect of opening the door to what Kirkland called a "host of opportunists, sleaze bags, shady operators from the world of commerce seeking brokerage or 'consulting' fees" and who "kindly offered to relieve untutored union officers of the complex task of deciding what to do with this money." Union officials called these pension consultants "seagulls" because, as Kirkland put it, they were like "the birds that follow ships and feed on the garbage thrown overboard." Some pension racketeers were independent operators, but soon enough the mob got involved, and there were stories of bribes, kickbacks, self-dealing, and other forms of corruption.

A committee to develop a response to the growing crisis of pension corruption was formed, and George Meany, then the AFL's secretary-treasurer, was named chairman. He in turn asked Kirkland to prepare guidelines that could be distributed to affiliated unions to assist them in protecting their members' money. Kirkland studied the subject and consulted with a number of experts, until he, too, became an expert on union pension systems. He then drafted a publication that explained the fine points of pension fund law in a vocabulary that was accessible to the layman. Subsequently, Kirkland became a pension authority. His advice was widely sought by union representatives involved in negotiating pension systems with employers, and the pamphlets he wrote were regarded within labor as the definitive statements on the subject.

Due to his knowledge of union pension systems, Kirkland was assigned as part of a team that was dispatched to Chicago to clean up a mess created by the leaders of a union called the Waste Material Handlers Local Union. The union was run by one Red Dorfman, who, along with an associate named Jack Rubenstein, was skimming money from the pension fund through a series of insurance companies operated by Dorfman's son. After an embarrassing Senate hearing, the union was placed in receivership, and Kirkland went to work reorganizing the pension fund, which he did by the simple process of placing the fund in the hands of reputable insurance companies.

Kirkland had reason to recall his experience with the Waste Material Handlers during a trip to Dallas a few years later. Kirkland; Leonard Woodcock, then a vice president and later president of the UAW; Hank Brown, president of the Texas AFL-CIO; and Oscar Mauzy, a Dallas lawyer, were having a few drinks in Woodcock's hotel room. Mauzy suggested that they visit a local club, where the star was a stripper of local notoriety who went by the name Candy Barr. Mauzy had more than passing interest in the woman. He was her lawyer and had recently won her an acquittal from a murder charge—a charge for which he was in large measure responsible. As Mauzy explained it, Candy Barr had been married to a man who regularly beat her during fits of jealous rage. She would call Mauzy and complain, "Oscar, he's beating me again." Usually, Mauzy tried to calm her down. But one night, the stripper woke Mauzy up in the late hours: "Oscar, he's beating me again." This time, Mauzy, trying hard to get his sleep-deprived brain working, blurted out, "Then shoot the bastard." Which she did.

When the men arrived at the night spot, they learned that Candy Barr wouldn't be there that night. Nevertheless, the club's owner offered the union men a round of drinks. The owner's face seemed unsettlingly familiar, but Kirkland couldn't make the identification. A few years later, after John F. Kennedy's assassination and the shooting of Lee Harvey Oswald, Kirkland realized that the club owner, Jack Ruby, was the same Jack Rubenstein whom he had helped remove from the labor movement back in Chicago.

In 1952, a few days apart, both William Green and Philip Murray, president of the CIO, died. Their successors—George Meany and Walter Reuther, respectively—were both favorably disposed toward setting aside past disputes and effecting a merger of the two federations. Meany placed the merger on a fast track; he pressed the CIO to proceed along a path that would move expeditiously to formal unity, after which the unresolved fine points could be ironed out.

By that time, practically all serious impediments to a merger had been removed. The CIO had purged Communists from its ranks and had withdrawn from the World Federation of Trade Unions (WFTU), a Soviet-dominated global labor entity. Both organizations had also given strong support to the Marshall Plan and the reconstruction of Europe. John L. Lewis had taken the United Mine Workers out of both federations, a positive development, since Lewis had proved himself as effective at wrecking organizations as he had at building them. A further inducement for Reuther was the prospect of the departure from the CIO of the steelworkers because the USW's president, David McDonald, couldn't abide Reuther. The merger of the two federations was formalized in 1955: the new entity was known as the American Federation of Labor-Congress of Industrial Organizations. George Meany was elected as the federation's first president.

While merger negotiations were proceeding, Meany set out to create some order out of the chaotic AFL staff situation. He established a Department of Social Security and placed Nelson Cruikshank as director and Kirkland as deputy director. After the merger took place in 1955, Meany launched a campaign against corruption within the labor movement. An Ethical Practices Code was adopted; Kirkland was selected to write the sections dealing with pension systems.

Although most of Kirkland's time was now devoted to pension and Social Security matters, his abilities as a speechwriter were not forgotten. In 1952, at the urging of future secretary of labor Willard Wirtz, he drafted several speeches for Democratic presidential candidate Adlai Stevenson. Kirkland also wrote speeches for Meany and for William Schnitzler, the secretary-treasurer of the merged organization.

In 1958, Kirkland left the federation to join the International Union of Operating Engineers, where he served as director of research and education. In the fragmentary memoirs he left, Kirkland is vague about his motives. One possible inducement was an increase in pay, an important matter since Kirkland was now the father of five daughters: Blair Hollyday and Lucy Alexander, the twins, 12; Louise Richardson (Rikki), 9; Edith (Holly) Hollyday, 5; and Katherine (Kitty), 2. The Kirklands had purchased a large modern house in Wheaton, Maryland, a part of Silver Spring, a major Washington suburb. With five daughters and various pets—the girls were forever adopting stray mongrel dogs, and Kirkland had purebred German shepherds—the house was often disorganized and full of commotion.

The Kirklands were a traditional family of the 1950s. Lane worked hard and provided financially for the family. Although Edie did not work, she was interested in politics and did volunteer work for various causes and candidates. Like other men of his generation, Kirkland had a haphazard attitude toward raising children. He was not particularly strict; if he became exasperated with one of the daughters, he would tell her to leave the table as punishment. But he had a quiet way of showing disapproval, and as the girls matured, he let them know that he expected them to behave responsibly, act their age, and develop the habits of independence.

Kirkland occasionally helped the girls with homework and encouraged them to read. But if one of the daughters had a serious personal problem, she went to Edie for advice. Lucy Kirkland Schoenfeld said that on the occasions when she looked to her father for help, he would listen attentively and then offer up "a one-liner that usually hit the nail on the head." On other occasions, she said, Kirkland might respond with a lecture. "But it was difficult to have a back-and-forth conversation with him."

Despite Kirkland's Episcopal upbringing in South Carolina, he was indifferent to religion as an adult. In his speeches to labor and civil rights audiences, he often injected references from the Old Testament and sometimes the New Testament. But he seldom invoked the deity in his public statements. He never attended church in his years with Edie, who, though raised Episcopalian, had embraced the Unitarian faith. Lucy recalls Lane sitting stolidly on the living room sofa, reading the Sunday *Washington Post*, while Edie dragged the girls off to Sunday school.

Kirkland loved to regale the family with stories about his boyhood in South Carolina and the exploits of his many relatives. Of his father, Kirkland spoke with both fondness and respect. Almost as a primer on personal integrity, Kirkland told the girls how Randolph Kirkland had worked much of his life to pay off every nickel he had borrowed to launch the cotton business that failed when the crop market collapsed. Like most men of his generation, Kirkland seldom permitted himself displays of emotion. But he conveyed his distress when his beloved father died in the early 1960s, although typically, his feelings were expressed through a profound silence instead of open expressions of grief. Randolph Kirkland died after undergoing what was one of the early attempts at open-heart surgery, conducted at the Johns Hopkins Hospital.

Kirkland enjoyed reading to the girls. He often selected stories where he could showcase his ability at southern dialect, such as the tales of Uncle Remus and Miss Minerva and Will Green Hill, which allowed him to mimic the voices of the various characters.

Kirkland was an intellectually curious man whose interests ranged well beyond the realms of politics and labor. He never lost the love of music that had been instilled by his mother; Edie also loved music, and the two had a large collection of opera and classical music recordings. Kirkland also liked popular crooners and was fond of the rich southern voice of Dinah Shore.

Kirkland's favorite pastimes were those that engaged his abilities as a researcher and a craftsman. He proceeded with his hobbies in much the same way he went about mastering the details of pension systems. Whether it was woodworking, chess, tropical fish, the harmonica, stereophonic equipment, gardening, or sailing sloops, Kirkland followed the same pattern. He would read books on the subject, subscribe to specialty magazines, and then gain mastery of whatever it was that occupied his fancy at the time. Kirkland approached his hobbies with the attitude that no challenge was too difficult for him to overcome if he put his mind to it. His daughter Rikki recalls that on the rare occasions when Kirkland gave vent to a fit of anger, the usual source was his frustration over a machine that wouldn't work properly or some other problem related to his hobbies.

Kirkland also had an appreciation for art; whenever one of the girls gave evidence of artistic ability, he encouraged her to pursue the talent further. But he never pushed them toward a particular career and certainly did not pressure them toward politics or labor. In a family where the father was an important figure in organized labor and both parents held strong liberal convictions, none of the children pursued labor or political careers with any seriousness. Several of the daughters were drawn to the counterculture during the 1960s and were critics of America's involvement in Vietnam. But they never directly challenged Lane's hawkish views on Vietnam. They understood that their father's commitment to the anti-Communist idea was unshakable and that an argument over the war would serve no purpose.[1]

If anything, Edie was more liberal than Lane. She particularly admired Adlai Stevenson and was proud that her husband wrote speeches for her favorite candidate. Kirkland would discuss politics with his family but seldom discussed trade union business at home. Yet he did make it clear that he was totally committed to organized labor and believed that what was good for the union movement was good for America. If a daughter questioned whether a particular strike was necessary or in the public interest, Kirkland invariably defended the union and explained why the action, though unfortunate, was important to the well-being of working people.

For two years, however, it was the well-being of operating engineers that occupied Kirkland's attention. The union represented workers who operated heavy construction equipment—cranes, bulldozers—and stationary engineers in boiler rooms. Kirkland had a modest familiarity with the engineers' craft, but since many of the boiler room men had worked aboard ship, he felt comfortable with the culture at the International Union of Operating Engineers (IUOE).

One asset that Kirkland brought to the new job was his familiarity with union corruption, a problem for the Operating Engineers at the time. Under Meany, the AFL-CIO took the issue of union corruption with the utmost seriousness. In 1957, Meany had successfully pressed for the expulsion from the AFL-CIO of the Teamsters, the federation's largest affiliate, and several other unions with records of corruption. The federation had expressed its concern about corrupt practices within the Operating Engineers, and a congressional investigation had begun to probe into its internal affairs. A friend of Meany's, Joseph Delaney, had just taken over the union's presidency, and he moved to clean up its image and quell burgeoning rebellions in some locals. Part of Kirkland's job was to work with the union's counsel, Al Woll, to develop measures that would protect the membership from the corrupt practices of union officials. To this end, Kirkland developed a system to analyze the effectiveness of contracts the union negotiated with management, and he created a central pension fund that was open to all members on an equal footing.

In late 1960, George Meany summoned Lane to his office for a talk. Would he be interested in leaving the Operating Engineers and returning to the federation, this time as Meany's executive assistant? It was an offer Kirkland couldn't refuse. Joseph Delaney tried to persuade Kirkland to remain with the IUOE and protested Meany's raiding his staff, but Meany held firm. So on January 1, 1961, Kirkland rejoined the AFL-CIO, where he was to remain for the next thirty-four years.

Just prior to leaving the Operating Engineers, Kirkland had his final experience as a presidential campaign speechwriter when he was detailed to work with a team of writers for the presidential campaign of John F. Kennedy. Kirkland wrote speeches for Lyndon Johnson, the vice presidential nominee, and for former president Truman, who had agreed to make campaign appearances for the ticket. Kirkland particularly liked writing for Truman, who read whatever words the speechwriter put before him and didn't mind a bit of hardball polemics. Without hesitation, he delivered a speech to a downstate Illinois audience in which Kirkland had written that anyone who voted against Jack Kennedy was a religious bigot.

From George Meany to Walter Reuther to the pragmatic leaders of the building trades, organized labor loved John Kennedy. The only exceptions were those unions—most notably the Teamsters—that were the targets of corruption investigations engineered by Attorney General Robert Kennedy. John Kennedy treated Meany with deference and respect; Meany, in turn, forgave Kennedy for setting voluntary wage-price guidelines that had the effect of putting a serious crimp in collective bargaining.

Kirkland, too, admired Kennedy but was also aware of the young president's shortcomings. Kennedy, Kirkland said, "had a tendency to put forward legislative proposals that were stripped of heavy substance and approached the least common denominator."

Of particular concern to labor was the omnibus civil rights legislation that the administration was preparing as its answer to the demands for the abolition of legal discrimination against blacks. From the outset, Kennedy made it clear that he preferred to limit the civil rights bill to a ban on segregation in public accommodations—restaurants, hotels, trains and buses, and the like. Kennedy was adamant in wanting to postpone consideration of a prohibition of discrimination at the workplace.

Once the administration had signaled its opposition to an equal employment opportunity provision, the AFL-CIO forged an alliance with liberal members of Congress to expand the administration's bill to embrace the workplace and to ban discrimination by both employers and unions. Meany was insistent on including bias by unions in the bill. The AFL-CIO was under harsh criticism for the discriminatory policies of certain crafts unions in the railroads and the building trades, and Meany was convinced that the only effective means of compelling change was through the force of federal law.

The prospects for including a section on job discrimination improved dramatically after labor put its muscle behind it. This dismayed Kennedy, who feared that workplace issues were of sufficient sensitivity to sink the entire package. Kennedy placed a panicky call to Meany, who was in Italy at the time on International Labor Organization business. Meany thereupon called Kirkland, told him the president wanted to meet about the civil rights bill, and instructed him to hold firm on the equal employment provision.

The subsequent meeting was, in Kirkland's words, "long and excruciating." Kirkland and Andrew Biemiller, the federation's director of legislation, listened as Kennedy listed the reasons why an equal employment provision was neither necessary nor wise. To reinforce his point that federal action was unnecessary, Kennedy had stacked on his desk a collection of reports on fair employment programs that had been developed by various state governments. As Kirkland recalled events: "Kennedy argued at length that federal action in this area was untimely and unnecessary and that this insistence on what would eventually emerge as Title VII would doom the civil rights bill. I felt the heat acutely but Meany's order impressed me more and I stuck to our guns."

When the civil rights bill was passed in 1964, it did include a strong equal employment section. For Kirkland, however, it was a source of some resentment that Meany's role was seldom recognized by those who wrote the history of the movement for racial equality. Meany is more often recalled for having refused to endorse the 1963 March on Washington, where Dr. Martin Luther King Jr. stirred the nation with his "I Have a Dream" speech. Some critics went so far as to imply that Meany lacked a commitment to civil rights, a patently untrue suggestion. It was, after all, Meany who was responsible for Title VII, the section of the Civil Rights Act dealing with job discrimination. Meany also guided the federation toward support of every other objective sought by the civil rights coalition, including such controversial issues as affirmative action at the workplace and busing for school desegregation. Other critics complained that Meany failed to recognize the march's potential significance because of an organizational conservatism. Meany, in fact, was uncomfortable with mass marches and rallies unless strictly under the control of the labor movement, out of concern that big public manifestations would be hijacked by radical elements. In the case of the march, there were other factors at work as well. One was the decision of A. Philip Randolph, the legendary leader of the Brotherhood of Sleeping Car Porters and the march's chairman, to ask for labor's endorsement through Walter Reuther. Some believe that if Dr. King and Randolph had initially approached Meany, he would have placed the federation squarely behind the event. Another was pressure from the White House, which worried that the organizers might lose control of the march and damage the chances of the bill's passage.

As he did in the meeting with Kennedy, Meany came to rely increasingly on Kirkland for the most important and sensitive assignments. Kirkland was smart and loyal and could be depended on to use sound judgment. He avoided the limelight. He was well versed on the diverse range of issues that occupied the federation, from presidential politics to the details of Great Society legislation, to international labor controversies, to jurisdictional disputes among different unions. If Kirkland wasn't an expert on an issue of importance, he would become one.

One of the qualities that Meany came to appreciate was Lane's ability to take hold of a task, study it, and then solve it himself. Kirkland came to appreciate those labor officials whose stature rested on their ability to solve problems and settle crises through a combination of intelligence, hard work, and good judgment. And he expected those qualities from members of the AFL-CIO staff. Rex Hardesty, who later worked as Kirkland's spokesman during his AFL-CIO presidency, recalls an incident involving Nat Goldfinger, the federation's director of research during the 1960s. Kirkland was enjoying a bourbon sour after hours in the Lafayette Bar when Goldfinger intruded with a problem he was wrestling with. Kirkland responded, "That's a problem that a department director of the AFL-CIO should resolve."

One job that particularly tested Lane's ability to handle sensitive issues was fund-raising for political candidates. In 1964 Meany assigned him the responsibility of raising labor money for Lyndon Johnson, who was seeking election to a full term and was opposed by the spiritual leader of Republican conservatism, Barry Goldwater. Johnson had everything going his way—peace, prosperity, the memory of Jack Kennedy—and was abetted by Goldwater, who ran a deliberately provocative campaign that stressed conservative themes at a moment in American history when liberal ideas held sway in the public's mind. Unlike moderate Republicans such as Eisenhower and Nixon, Goldwater was openly hostile to the labor movement. His views, at the time considered a reflection of right-wing extremism, propelled labor into a close working alliance with liberals; together, they mobilized a maximum effort for a man of whom neither had been especially fond in the past.

Johnson met with Meany and a delegation of labor leaders and set a goal of $1 million from the unions, no small amount by the standards of the day. Kirkland began dunning the individual unions for contributions. Dick McGuire, the Democratic Party treasurer, told Kirkland to have the unions write checks to state Democratic committees, which could legally accept direct labor contributions. Kirkland went immediately to work:

> I busied myself with this assignment, touching every conceivable base until I exceeded the goal. I would periodically deliver a bundle of checks, appropriately made out, to the grateful hands of Dick McGuire, together with lists of the contributing affiliates who wanted special consideration at party functions. We regarded this as a purely practical matter given the circumstances and choices before us at the time. We would strongly resist the notion that it in any way compromised our fierce Gompersian independence from party influence or control.

Labor had not trusted LBJ during his years as Senate majority leader. In the Senate, Johnson had been wary of labor's influence and seldom placed the weight of his considerable influence behind legislation that was of institutional importance to the union movement. Once in the White House, however, Johnson pushed for the adoption of a far-reaching agenda of domestic change with a zeal not seen since the early days of the New Deal. Labor supported the Great Society program with enthusiasm, and Meany remained supportive of the president's policies in Vietnam, a position that reflected Meany's convictions as much as it did loyalty to the president.

Kirkland paid many visits to Johnson in the Oval Office and developed a strong admiration for LBJ's political abilities and his commitment to liberal government. He was fascinated by larger-than-life southern politicians—he could quote verbatim some of Huey Long's better known lines. The wheeling and dealing that some found offensive in LBJ's way of operating didn't bother Lane at all, since the president's maneuverings were in the service of good causes. According to Kirkland, Johnson "kept strict books on who owed whom. If he went along with a request of ours, we could expect that in due course we would be called upon to balance the books by responding to a legislative or political need of his own." Johnson solicited Meany's advice on policy and personnel, and he did whatever he felt was politically prudent to advance labor's legislative program (though not enough to win passage of a measure that would have rescinded the hated section 14-B of Taft-Hartley that enabled states to enact right-to-work laws).

On one occasion, Kirkland and Meany visited the White House with a request that Johnson intervene on a piece of legislation that was dear to labor's heart but was peripheral at best to the president's program. "I don't have a dog in this hunt," Johnson told the labor officials. He noted that if he went to bat for labor by interceding with major congressional figures, he would then be vulnerable to requests for favors in return, and the labor issue was not important enough for him to expend that kind of capital. "I'll tell you what you ought to do," Johnson told the two men. "Go beat the bushes and get all your unions and your state and local groups so stirred up that they all beat me over the head with calls and letters until they just make me do it."

On another occasion, Kirkland visited Johnson during a period when criticism of his war policies was at high-water mark. Within political circles, the most relentless critics were Democratic members of the Senate Foreign Relations Committee. As Kirkland entered the Oval Office, Johnson began waving around a new attack on his policies that had just come over the news wire he kept in his office.

"It's my own damn fault," Johnson complained. He recalled that during his years as Senate majority leader, he had routinely promised to give new liberal Democratic senators the choicest committee assignments. Unfortunately, Johnson said, many of the young liberals were not smart enough or tough enough for service on the most crucial panels. To satisfy their egos, Johnson ended up dumping many of them on the Foreign Relations Committee. "They elected Frank Church, the village idiot," Johnson said, referring to the dovish Idaho Democrat. "I couldn't put him on a serious committee like finance or appropriations, so I put him where he couldn't do any real harm, the Foreign Relations Committee. And they elected Gaylord Nelson [Democrat of Wisconsin], a cigar-store wooden Indian. I couldn't put him on a real important committee. So I put him on Foreign Relations. I'm bleeding from self-inflicted wounds."

In late 1967 Kirkland joined a delegation of high-ranking Democratic operatives, including party chairman John Bailey and former Kennedy adviser Lawrence O'Brien, to discuss the reelection campaign with Johnson. Eugene McCarthy had already announced his intention to oppose the president, and a number of important figures from the party's liberal wing were already lining up behind the Minnesota senator. It was thus essential to Johnson's reelection plans that he depend on broad support from organized labor. Kirkland assured the president that labor was solid for LBJ; from the UAW to the building trades, the unions preferred Johnson to McCarthy.

Most American liberals recall the 1968 election as among the most dismal moments in twentieth-century politics. The year itself was marked by one horrifying shock after another: the assassinations of Dr. King and Robert Kennedy, campus uprisings, race riots, the tumultuous Democratic convention in Chicago, and the eventual triumph of Richard Nixon, the political figure liberals most loved to hate.

For Kirkland, the awful series of events began one evening in the spring. He was in Florida to deliver a speech to an Operating Engineers convention. He turned on his hotel room television set to listen to a presidential address, only to hear the stunning announcement that Johnson was withdrawing from the race. Kirkland immediately returned to Washington, where he found Meany similarly dumbfounded. The two then paid a visit to Vice President Hubert Humphrey, a particular favorite of labor. They urged that Humphrey get into the race quickly and promised that labor would be unstinting in its support.

Meany and Kirkland also dropped in for a talk with the president. They found Johnson in what Kirkland described as a "black mood." "He said that we lacked a full appreciation of the power of the Kennedy machine." Nor did Johnson share labor's enthusiasm for Humphrey. He proceeded to draw an obscene comparison to make the point that Humphrey would likely lose the election because "he doesn't know when to stop talking."

Meany privately shared some of Johnson's misgivings about Humphrey's toughness of character. But given the alternatives of Eugene McCarthy or Robert Kennedy, on the one hand, and Humphrey, on the other, Meany without hesitation opted for the vice president. Yet despite labor's entreaties, Humphrey declined to immediately announce his candidacy. He fretted that it was too late in the campaign season and worried that he might not be able to scare up enough delegates to carry him to the nomination. Finally, he promised Meany that if the AFL-CIO could put together a Labor for Humphrey committee that embraced the various ideological factions within trade unionism, he would make the race. Kirkland immediately went to work to get endorsements for the Humphrey committee; in the end, he got agreement from a broad cross section of the movement, from George Meany to the presidents of smallish labor federations in municipalities across the country.

With Humphrey in the race, the next challenge was the hunt for delegates. This was to be the last "boss-controlled" Democratic convention; most delegates were selected not through primaries, which Humphrey generally avoided, but through local caucus meetings that were dominated by party leaders, elected officials, and labor. As McCarthy and Kennedy slugged it out in the primaries, Humphrey methodically went about collecting delegates. Well before the convention opened in Chicago, Humphrey's nomination was assured.

To Eugene McCarthy and his supporters, there was something immoral about the tactics employed by Humphrey and his labor allies. The McCarthyites had come to believe that the campaign pitted the forces of idealism and morality against the representatives of powerful special interests and a corrupt political establishment that supported an imperialist war. McCarthy himself believed that those who spurned his candidacy operated on a lower moral plane than did his supporters; he reveled in the fact that he was the preferred candidate of the better educated. He also resented the role that organized labor was playing. During the convention, he complained that labor had denied him the nomination: "Those old buffaloes have their feet dug in and won't budge," he declared. After the convention, the AFL-CIO presented each labor delegate with a badge bearing the image of a silver buffalo.

Kirkland had already learned that despite his image as being above the grubby deal making of ordinary politics, McCarthy was perfectly willing to reach closed-door arrangements with the old buffaloes if it suited his campaign's purposes. Late in the primary season, McCarthy called Kirkland and asked if the AFL-CIO would support him in Oregon, where he was locked in a tight struggle with Kennedy. Specifically, he asked if trade unionists could be released from their support for Humphrey, who was not on the ballot in the state. In return, McCarthy promised that he would refrain from releasing his delegates to Kennedy should he fail to win the nomination. Kirkland didn't even bother consulting Meany before giving McCarthy a firm rejection. Kirkland told McCarthy, "I learned a long time ago that you can't fine-tune the masses. If it's too subtle for me, it's too subtle for them."

The election was a major disappointment for labor, and a source of bitterness, with union leaders placing the blame for Humphrey's narrow defeat squarely on the shoulders of those liberals who declined to support the Democratic nominee or did so halfheartedly, late in the campaign, and with the faintest of praise. To Kirkland, the behavior of many liberals was arrogant and irresponsible. The professors and lawyers who had scorned Humphrey could return to their offices and classrooms without suffering on-the-ground consequences from Republican economic policies. For workers, minorities, and the poor, real penalties would be paid from the change in administrations. Labor never doubted that Humphrey was preferable to Nixon. In contrast to liberalism's demoralization and confusion, the unions made a valiant effort to elect the Democratic ticket in one of their finest hours in electoral politics.

Humphrey left Chicago at a distinct disadvantage. He was the nominee of a party in disarray, and he was in dire financial straits. Meanwhile, the Republicans had fully recovered from the Goldwater debacle; in Richard Nixon, the GOP had a candidate who could unite all party factions, from the Goldwater brigades on the right to the supporters of Nelson Rockefeller, the leader of the party's liberal wing. Nixon was amply funded and had assembled a smart and ruthless campaign team that included some of the savviest media advisers in political life. Nixon also benefited from the presence in the campaign of George C. Wallace, the segregationist governor of Alabama who, running as a third-party candidate, was effectively exploiting such combustible issues as draft card burning, campus disorder, urban riots, and growing welfare rolls.

Wallace's candidacy was especially ominous because of its potential to eat into one of Humphrey's core constituencies: blue-collar, unionized workers. Labor's own polls, taken in midsummer, showed Wallace grabbing off between a quarter and a third of the union vote in such reliably liberal states as Michigan, Connecticut, and Maryland. In Flint, Michigan, a poll taken of UAW workers at a large Buick plant showed Wallace outstripping all other candidates, with 49 percent of the vote. And in some northern industrial communities, Wallace supporters in the UAW and the steelworkers union were using the presidential campaign as a springboard to mount challenges against incumbent union officials.[2]

While the AFL-CIO, through its Committee on Political Education (COPE), mobilized behind Humphrey throughout the country, it made a special effort to counter the Wallace vote within its own ranks. Unions circulated millions of pieces of literature setting forth Wallace's antilabor record in Alabama. Union volunteers rang doorbells and manned phone banks. They registered voters and dragged them to the polls on election day. In black neighborhoods, labor played a major role in getting voters registered and to the polls through a new organization of black trade unionists, the A. Philip Randolph Institute.

These were responsibilities previously handled by the Democratic Party. But the once formidable Democratic infrastructure had collapsed through years of inertia and the divisions over Vietnam and civil rights and the unraveling of the liberal consensus over the Cold War. Regarding labor's intense campaign for Humphrey, Kirkland told presidential campaign historian Theodore White:

> We had to do what we did because the party was bankrupt intellectually and financially. I reached the point where I said I'd never go into Democratic headquarters. I'd go in feeling good and come out feeling terrible. The only useful thing they did was television in the last couple of weeks and beyond that they didn't do a goddamned thing except cry.[3]

But it was not only the Democratic Party that was in disarray; liberalism itself or, to be more precise, liberal anti-Communism, was in a state of near-total collapse. To be sure, the liberal anti-Communist idea had been on shaky political ground for some time. Many liberals had come to identify anti-Communism with McCarthyism—that is, the McCarthyism of Joseph, not Eugene—and with the primitive wing of the Republican Party. As the 1960s progressed, the intellectuals whose writings had the greatest impact were those who questioned the basic precepts of the Cold War or who rejected Cold War values altogether. Vietnam accelerated the liberal flight from identification with anti-Communism; it did not provoke it.

The seminal event in this process was the endorsement of Eugene McCarthy's presidential campaign at the 1968 convention of the Americans for Democratic Action. Founded in the late 1940s, the ADA was the quintessential liberal Cold War institution, dedicated originally to the struggle against both Joseph Stalin and Joseph McCarthy. Within the ADA's ranks could be found Arthur Schlesinger Jr., John Kenneth Galbraith, Hubert Humphrey, and David Dubinsky—the leading figures behind the liberal-labor alliance. But when the ADA repudiated its old favorite, Humphrey, and opted instead for Gene McCarthy, the Schlesingers and the Galbraiths applauded while the trade unionists—Dubinsky; I. W. Abel, president of the steelworkers; and Joseph Beirne, president of the Communications Workers of America (CWA)—resigned in fury.[4] After 1968, the phrase "liberal anti-Communist" seldom figured in the political lexicon. Indeed, those who were regarded as anti-Communists were routinely described as conservatives, whether their views on the domestic order of things were patterned after George Meany or William F. Buckley. Kirkland himself was often described as a conservative because of his unapologetic anti-Communism. Kirkland had a thick skin and seldom responded directly to the barbs tossed at labor by liberal intellectuals like Galbraith. But he never forgot those who had heaped abuse on the AFL-CIO or on Meany. He had a high regard for intellectual achievement and counted among his friends many respected thinkers, writers, and journalists. Yet he had nothing but contempt for liberal intellectuals who derided anti-Communists and dismissed labor as reactionary and racist. He thought those who held such views were disloyal to the true values of liberalism. And he saw no reason to establish a "dialogue" with those who had embraced an ethic of political behavior that he could never respect.

Although it had the reputation of being the last bastion of liberal Cold War faith, the AFL-CIO was not unaffected by the crackup over foreign policy. Differences over the direction of labor's foreign policy, and

especially its attitude toward détente with the Soviet bloc, were a contributing factor in Walter Reuther's decision to pull the UAW out of the
federation in 1968. There were, of course, other motives behind
Reuther's withdrawal, notably his frustration at being consistently outma-
neuvered by Meany in the executive council. But Reuther was also disenchanted with Meany's anti-Communism, which he blamed for driving a
wedge between labor and the liberal community.

Although the merger of the AFL and the CIO was, as far as the public was concerned, a unification of two equally powerful labor federations,
in reality the AFL was clearly the dominant partner. The AFL was larger
and richer and was endowed with a leader, George Meany, who had a
more astute grasp of the internal politics of organized labor than did anyone else in the movement. Because of Meany's gruffness, his disdain for
the press, his lack of rapport with liberals, and his emphasis on the practical aspects of trade unionism, he was often underestimated by labor's
critics in the press and academe. But when it came to the techniques of
gaining and keeping power, Meany proved himself the equal of anyone in
Washington and by the mid-sixties had achieved the status of "unchallenged strongman of American labor," in the words of his biographer
Joseph Goulden.

Within a few years after the merger, it became clear that Meany could
always get the best of Reuther in disputes that came before the executive
council. On the few occasions when recorded votes were taken, the
results were typically 24 to 3 or 25 to 2, with Reuther supported by a
small core of former CIO men, such as James Carey of the International
Union of Electrical Workers, Joseph Curran of the National Maritime
Union, and Jacob Potofsky of the Amalgamated Clothing Workers.
Reuther seldom pushed the confrontations to a vote, given Meany's automatic majority. But he often complained, both within council chambers
and to the press: labor, he said, was insufficiently committed to organizing the unorganized, lacked political vision, failed to explore new horizons in collective bargaining, and lacked aggressiveness in promoting civil
rights, aid to the cities, national health insurance, and other liberal
reforms. On many of these issues, Meany and Reuther in fact shared similar positions. Meany was very much in the mold of the New Deal liberal.
But he was a traditionalist who believed that reform should be achieved
through the tried-and-true techniques of electing the right candidates to
office and then twisting arms on Capitol Hill. Meany had no use for the
big rallies, protest demonstrations, and marches that Reuther found so
appealing. Meany also worried about labor's failure to organize workers in
the South and in white-collar occupations. But he believed, as a matter of
fundamental philosophy, that organizing was the responsibility of the

unions that were affiliated with the AFL-CIO, not of the federation itself. Meany believed that the federation's role was to provide various kinds of technical assistance and, in critical situations, to make financial contributions to organizing drives. The heavy lifting of organizing, however, was the job of the individual international unions.

The differences over foreign policy, by contrast, went to the heart of American labor's worldview. And here, there was a real divergence between Meany, with his undiminished faith in the values of Cold War liberalism, and Reuther, who was in the process of distancing himself from a perspective that revolved around the conflict between Western democracy and Communist totalitarianism. Despite the CIO's active Communist wing in its early years, by the time of the merger both the CIO and the AFL were in general agreement on support for the broad objectives of American Cold War policy. Beneath the surface, however, Meany and Reuther differed over how labor should respond to the Soviet Union and to world Communism generally.

The dispute got nastier when some in the UAW expressed sympathy for the perspective, propounded by historians with a revisionist interpretation of the Cold War, that American labor was complicit in the suppression of independent labor unions that leaned in a pro-Communist direction. The left's bill of particulars against the AFL-CIO was lengthy: New Left scholars accused labor of working hand in glove with the CIA to quash labor militancy in the Third World, of receiving funds from the CIA, of supporting right-wing dictators, and of conniving with thug elements in breaking up Communist union initiatives in Europe. Meany, who made no apologies for America's hostility to pro-Communist unions, began to wonder whether his critics within the UAW shared the revisionist critique.

The differences between Reuther and Meany became more pointed as the Cold War consensus began to unravel. The UAW supported recognition of Communist China; Meany rejected the idea out of hand. Meany and Reuther also clashed over the degree to which the AFL-CIO should cooperate with the International Confederation of Free Trade Unions (ICFTU), a grouping of democratic trade unions that had been established as a rival to the Soviet-controlled World Federation of Trade Unions. Meany was disenchanted with the ICFTU because, among other things, some of its leaders had established relations with Communist bloc unions in violation of the organization's charter, which called for a policy of no contact with nondemocratic labor entities. He decided that American labor should adopt a unilateralist approach to international relations by dealing directly with unions from the developing world instead of going through the ICFTU bureaucracy. Reuther remained at heart a multilateralist, preferring that American labor act in collaboration with democratic unions in Western Europe and elsewhere.

Reuther was careful in his comments about the AFL-CIO's foreign policy. This was a prudent course, since he had voted in favor of its major policy decisions, including resolutions that supported the Vietnam War. But his brother Victor was not so reticent. Victor Reuther was the director of international affairs at the UAW; during the early years of the Cold War, he had taken bundles of money supplied by the CIA to Europe, where it was used to buttress anti-Communist union federations in France and Italy. He had come to regret those actions and blasted away at Meany and the federation, which he more or less accused of having joined the forces of reaction. Even worse, he aired his views to reporters, who duly wrote articles that spoke of a major breach in American labor over international affairs. Meany exploded; he hated the airing of differences in the press. At a tense executive council meeting, Walter Reuther said that his brother was out of line. But Meany remained unmollified, perhaps believing that Walter Reuther privately shared his brother's opinions.

Over a period of twenty months, from 1966 until the UAW's formal withdrawal from the federation in 1968, Reuther carried on what was basically a one-sided war of polemics against Meany. The UAW published a series of issues papers setting forth its sources of discontent and declared that if its demands were not met, the union would end its affiliation with the AFL-CIO. Some of Reuther's charges were wrong or inaccurate. He accused the AFL-CIO of failing to back Cesar Chavez and his farmworkers' union; in fact, the federation had ploughed considerable resources into the project. He accused the federation of opposing a test ban treaty, when the executive council had adopted a resolution supporting the agreement. Reuther also struck out in his efforts to persuade other unions to join him in exile. His old CIO friends counseled against withdrawal, contending that the UAW's departure would have no impact on AFL-CIO policy and that Reuther himself would be isolated from the rest of labor. When Reuther finally made the decision to pull out, he formed a new federation, the American Labor Alliance. It consisted of the UAW; the Teamsters, then under the caretaker presidency of Frank Fitzsimmons while James Hoffa languished in prison under a jury-tampering conviction; and a small chemical workers union. The internal contradictions of the ALA were evident from the start, and it took only a few years for the organization to disintegrate.[5]

In 1969 the AFL-CIO issued a response to Reuther. It came in the form of a White Paper entitled "To Clear the Record." The principal author was Kirkland. George W. Brooks, a Reuther admirer, called the document a "brilliant polemic" that exposed the inconsistencies in the

UAW position and made "the most of the fact that Walter Reuther is attacking the very institutions which he helped to create." Indeed, it was more than that. Until the report was released, Reuther had owned a monopoly on the debate over the state of the labor movement, and his critique of the Meany leadership enjoyed widespread credibility. Most journalists were sympathetic to Reuther, as were many of the intellectuals who wrote about labor. In addition, many labor leaders privately sympathized with Reuther's positions on labor's domestic and foreign agendas. With "To Clear the Record," the debate shifted rather considerably. Kirkland's writing may have had a polemical edge, but the report's strength came from meticulous research, rigorous analysis, and a line of argument meant to convince the core audience of trade union officials who, until the report's appearance, had been inclined to accept Reuther's side of the argument. Kirkland was especially effective in revealing the shallowness of Reuther's attacks on the alleged undemocratic nature of the executive council, in light of the thoroughly undemocratic character of the ALA.

Among other things, "To Clear the Record" solidified Kirkland's growing reputation as one of organized labor's intellectual leaders. The report was to be one of his last major projects as Meany's executive assistant. Soon, Kirkland would be elected to a position of high public visibility within the ranks of labor. His name, little known to those outside labor's inner circles, would be among those prominently mentioned as potential successors to George Meany. Others outside labor's ranks were also taking note of Kirkland's powers of mind—presidents, cabinet officials, members of Congress, business leaders. Already a key figure in labor affairs, Lane Kirkland was about to become an important participant in American political life.

3

EXPANDING HORIZONS

LANE KIRKLAND WAS FORTY-SEVEN YEARS OLD WHEN HE WAS ELECTED secretary-treasurer of the AFL-CIO in 1969.[1] He was the youngest member of the federation's executive council, a fact that caused some commentators to see in his elevation the beginning of an emerging youth movement in organized labor. Kirkland's election was by acclamation and without overt controversy, although a few council members expressed some private misgivings about placing a man from the federation staff in the number-two position. But most of Meany's brethren liked and respected Kirkland. In addition to his intelligence and sound judgment, Kirkland had a reputation for fairness in the inevitable arguments that pitted one union against another. Kirkland's credibility in adjudicating these disputes derived from the perception that he based his decisions on the merits of the case and did not play favorites. In a movement in which grandstanding was not admired, Kirkland was respected as a team player who did not engage in self-promotion. Immediately upon his ascension to the secretary-treasurer's post, Kirkland joined the labor officials regularly mentioned as potential successors to Meany; indeed, he jumped right to the head of the line, above such respected veterans as I. W. Abel, president of the steelworkers; Paul Hall, president of the seafarers; and Joseph Beirne, president of the communications workers.[2]

Meany, in fact, was still going strong and showed no interest in the life of a retiree. Physical pains that had tormented him had been alleviated a few years earlier when an arthritic hip was replaced. Meany's spirits and energy improved, and his stature as the dominant figure in American labor remained undiminished. Moreover, it became increasingly clear that the departure of the UAW had had little impact on the AFL-CIO.

The promotion to secretary-treasurer was for Kirkland less daunting than one might have expected, given that he had been carrying out many of the job's functions for much of the previous decade. Kirkland now almost automatically accompanied Meany on his visits to the White House or to briefings by the secretary of state or other high officials.

Kirkland was an advocate of racial equality; he took a strong interest in the positions the federation adopted on key civil rights issues and maintained contact with Bayard Rustin, Roy Wilkins, Vernon Jordan, and other black leaders who were regarded as friendly to labor. And he was making his mark on the higher circles of power in Washington. "When you dealt with Lane, you knew right away you were dealing with a heavyweight," said George Shultz, Nixon's secretary of labor and later the secretary of state under Ronald Reagan.[3]

One of Kirkland's personal missions was to encourage the advancement of talented labor officials whose outlook was compatible with the tradition that Meany had established at the AFL-CIO. Thus Kirkland persuaded Thomas R. Donahue to accept Lane's old position as executive assistant to Meany in 1972. Donahue had served as an official with the Service Employees International Union and had been an assistant secretary of labor during the Johnson administration. Donahue would later serve in the Kirkland administration as secretary-treasurer and, briefly, as president of the federation.

Kirkland was also responsible for the election of Albert Shanker to the executive council in 1973. This was a matter of some controversy. In general, membership on the council was restricted to presidents of international unions, though exceptions to this rule had been made in the past. Shanker was at the time the dominant personality in the American Federation of Teachers and the president of its largest local, the United Federation of Teachers in New York. But he did not serve as the union's national president; that position was filled by David Selden, a man who did not enjoy significant influence in the broader labor movement and would not have been given serious consideration for council membership. Furthermore, Shanker was a controversial figure who had led the New York teachers on a strike over community control of the schools that polarized the races in New York and led to Shanker's demonization by black extremists. But Kirkland recognized Shanker as a brilliant labor leader and a man who had important things to say about education and politics. Several influential labor leaders, including Paul Hall and Jerry Wurf, the president of the American Federation of State, County, and Municipal Workers, opposed Shanker. Meany told Kirkland it was his call as to whether to press for the election of Shanker with the executive council. Kirkland thereupon argued the case for Shanker, and his election was approved. Soon thereafter, Shanker defeated Selden for the presidency of the AFT.

Lane was still responsible for some of the more mundane and occasionally unpleasant tasks inside the federation. One of the more emotionally difficult jobs was informing David Dubinsky that he would no longer serve on the federation executive council. Dubinsky had built the International Ladies' Garment Workers Union (ILGWU) into one of America's most respected and politically influential unions. The ILGWU was a pillar of American liberalism that provided critical support to the civil rights movement and to advocates of freedom in dictatorships all over the world. Dubinsky himself was a living legend, the embodiment of the Jewish tradition in American labor. But Dubinsky had retired, and a decision had been made that retirees should surrender their seats on the federation's governing council. Meany had worked closely with Dubinsky for many decades and by all rights should personally have informed the old man of the decision. But Meany didn't relish giving his old friend the bad news, and Lane ended up with the assignment. The meeting was emotionally draining. Dubinsky responded with distress after Lane made it clear that the decision was final. Later, after he had assumed the federation presidency, Kirkland would tell his executive assistant Ken Young, "I didn't ask you to talk to Dubinsky," whenever he asked Young to take up a troublesome job.

As secretary-treasurer, Kirkland became more directly involved in labor's foreign policy work. He had already accumulated some experience in the international affairs arena; now, armed with the authority that came with his new position, he became an influential figure on the national foreign policy stage, where his opinion was sought on cabinet appointments, disarmament policies, and reform of the CIA. Kirkland and Meany had regular meetings with Henry Kissinger, first when he served as national security adviser and then as secretary of state. The labor leaders were often critical of the Nixon administration's policies—on détente, China, the Middle East. But Kissinger initiated the meetings because of his respect for both labor officials, and he later became personal friends with Lane. Kissinger was under attack from a variety of critics over détente and other administration policies. But he differentiated between the criticism that emanated from labor and that which came from neoconservative sources and from Senator Henry M. Jackson, the Washington Democrat who stood as the leading congressional voice against détente. "Meany and Kirkland were longtime anti-Communists. Some of the neoconservatives were new to the cause. Lane was broad-minded enough to understand that we had similar objectives but different strategies and that what was appropriate for the AFL-CIO was not necessarily appropriate for us. So we would meet on the basis of great mutual respect."

Meany had an ambivalent attitude toward Richard Nixon. He supported the Vietnam War because he hated the idea of another country falling to the Communists, because of the AFL-CIO's close ties to the South Vietnamese labor movement, and because he never forgot that it was working-class young men who were risking their lives in the conflict. At the same time, he was perhaps the country's most outspoken critic of détente with the Soviets and of Nixon's opening to China. On domestic affairs, Meany had major conflicts with Nixon over the president's imposition of wage and price controls and over affirmative action quotas directed at the building trades' unions. But Nixon never challenged labor's institutional interests and he appointed a secretary of labor, George Shultz, with whom Meany felt comfortable. Moreover, it was during Nixon's presidency that an impressive series of liberal domestic measures was enacted, including occupational safety and health legislation, a landmark clean air and water act, and job training and consumer protection laws.

According to Shultz, the president "really admired Meany and Kirkland as patriots and devoted anti-Communists."[4] He also harbored the hope of winning over elements of organized labor as part of a strategy to build a new Republican majority. In 1980, Ronald Reagan would make serious inroads in the blue-collar vote in his triumph over Jimmy Carter. It was Nixon, however, who made the first serious effort to expand the GOP's base by grabbing off both the once solidly Democratic South and key sections of the working-class vote. Like President Eisenhower before him, Nixon carefully wooed Meany, inviting him to regular briefings at the White House and arranging for Kissinger to keep Meany and Kirkland abreast of the administration's foreign policy moves.

In the end, however, Nixon failed to earn a passing grade on Meany's character test. Meany believed that Nixon was untrustworthy, and he also detected in Nixon an undemocratic streak. In private, Meany likened Nixon to Mussolini addressing the Roman throngs from the palace balcony.[5]

In recognition of organized labor's power, Nixon ensured that trade union leaders were appointed as members of the various blue ribbon commissions that were formed to mull over problems that were often too controversial to deal with through the normal legislative process. Increasingly, it was Kirkland who was selected to represent labor's interests on these entities.

Kirkland was the ideal commission member. As a representative of a powerful institution, his opinions counted for more than those of the various academics or policy experts who could articulate a point of view but could speak in the name of no constituency. Kirkland himself believed that in a complex democracy like the United States, organized labor had something important to say about every issue of the day, from energy policy to government funding for the arts. Kirkland took his commission assignments seriously. He was tenacious in advocating recommendations that protected ordinary people or expanded the rights and freedoms of citizens. It was not unusual for Kirkland's to be the lone dissenting vote when it came time to reach a final decision on commission findings.

Thus in 1970 Nixon appointed Kirkland to the President's Commission on Financial Structure and Regulation, which was to study private financing systems. Among his fellow commissioners was a young chief of a New York investment firm, Alan Greenspan.[6] The next year, Kirkland was appointed to the National Commission on Productivity, a body set up to recommend ways to enhance industrial efficiency by improving worker productivity.[7] In 1974, Kirkland was appointed by Nelson Rockefeller, then governor of New York, to his Commission on Critical Choices for America. Other commission members—Cold War veterans all—included the nuclear physicist Edward Teller; Leo Cherne, chairman of the International Rescue Committee; Walt W. Rostow, a former aide to President Johnson; and Daniel Patrick Moynihan, then temporarily out of government after having served as Nixon's domestic policy adviser and ambassador to India.[8]

In January 1975, Kirkland was given a more formidable challenge when he was named to a special commission chaired by Rockefeller to make recommendations on various aspects of American intelligence policy. The Rockefeller Commission was formed at the height of a furor over the conduct of the Central Intelligence Agency. The CIA had come under intense fire due to information, much of it leaked, that suggested a multitude of acts that violated its charter. Lurid stories of plots to assassinate foreign leaders, covert schemes to bring down governments, and spying and eavesdropping on radicals within the United States were reported almost daily by the press. The then CIA director, William Colby, added considerable fuel to the controversy by voluntarily releasing to Congress material documenting actions that could be interpreted as illegal or unethical.

The Rockefeller Commission was empowered to determine what abuses had occurred, to recommend remedies to ensure they did not recur, to disentangle genuine abuses from charges based on differences over policy, and to vet the "family jewels," the secret operations and plans that were coming to the light of public scrutiny through press leaks and congressional testimony.[9]

From the very outset, the Rockefeller Commission was looked on with suspicion by the CIA's liberal-left critics. The critics wanted all evidence of alleged misconduct made public; the commission intended to limit public access to certain intelligence matters. The critics wanted a wholesale transformation of the agency; the commission planned to issue proposals of a "mend it, don't end it" type. More to the point, some of the critics sought to hamstring the CIA as part of a broader strategy to force an American withdrawal from the Cold War competition. Commission members remained committed to the anti-Communist cause and thus sought to recommend changes that would compel the CIA to do its job within the limits prescribed by law but would not weaken the agency as an instrument of national security policy. The critics thus much preferred to work with two special committees established by Congress to investigate the CIA: a Senate committee chaired by Frank Church, an Idaho Democrat with strong antiwar views, and a House committee chaired by Congressman Otis Pike of New York.

Among the commission's members were Ronald Reagan, the then California governor; former secretary of the treasury C. Douglas Dillon; a retired general, Lyman Lemnitzer; Edgar Shannon, the retired president of the University of Virginia; former solicitor general Erwin Griswold; and former secretary of commerce John T. Connor.[10] Once the membership had been made public, the sniping began. For Rep. Bella Abzug of New York, the problem was a panel that, in her words, consisted of "a conservative collection of bankers, corporate officials, and a former chief of staff [who] have never shown any concern for civil liberties."[11]

For the critics, however, the real issue was not the commission's lack of concern over civil liberties, but the abiding anti-Communism of its members. Kirkland himself had strong convictions about the importance of civil liberties and democracy.[12]

The commission's report was sober, and its findings less than sensational. The recommendations primarily focused on the question of improper CIA involvement in domestic spying. The commission concluded that "the great majority of the CIA's domestic activities comply with its statutory authority," but that there had been "some activities that should be criticized and should not happen again."[13]

It was during their mutual service on the Rockefeller Commission that Kirkland had his first encounter with Ronald Reagan since the 1950s, when he had had dealings with the then president of the Screen Actors Guild. In Kirkland's recollection, Reagan attended commission sessions "rarely and then briefly." But at one session, he delivered the opinion that one of America's principal Cold War blunders was the Berlin Airlift, a "craven option," as described by Reagan. Reagan maintained that the United States should have forced a showdown and broken the blockade with troops, guns, and tanks.

It so happened that another commissioner, General Lemnitzer, had served in Germany as chief of American forces during the blockade. Lemnitzer was not impressed by Reagan's reading of history. Kirkland recalled Lemnitzer responding:

Governor, before you take that story too far, you should look at a map. Berlin is situated about 100 miles from the American zone. At the time we had, in the American zone, a half of an armored division in a poor state of readiness. The Russians had several armored divisions there in a high state of readiness. If you think we were about to send our boys into that situation to be slaughtered, you are out of your mind. We had the planes; we could do it that way. We did it and it worked. So what's your problem?

Some years later, after Reagan had been elected president but before his inauguration, the columnist George Will held a party to introduce Reagan to the Democratic Party establishment in Washington. Kirkland and his wife, Irena, were on hand, and when they shook hands, Will recounted a brief history of Irena's life as a Holocaust survivor and a refugee from Communist Czechoslovakia. The president-elect, according to Kirkland, "proceeded to deliver to her a discourse on the Berlin blockade using precisely the same words that Lemnitzer had refuted."

Lane had first met Irena Neumann in September 1956. He had traveled to London as the AFL-CIO's representative to an international labor conference. After the conference ended, Kirkland made a visit to Paris. He was alone in the city, so he decided to call a woman who had worked for the AFL and was now living in Paris. The woman told Lane that she had made a dinner date with two sisters she had met during a visit to Israel and invited him to join them. She later called again and told Lane she had had to cancel at the last minute; she wondered if Lane would solve her dilemma by escorting the two ladies for the evening.

Kirkland's expectations for the night ahead were not especially high when he arrived at the Hotel Plaza Athénée to pick up his companions. His attitude quickly changed. As Kirkland recalled years later, "At the appointed time there emerged from the elevator two visions, Irena Neumann and her twin sister, Alena. Almost immediately, I was in thrall."

The three had a pleasant evening at dinner and a nightclub. The next day Alena returned to Israel, where her husband, a South African businessman named Norman Lourie, owned and operated a resort hotel, the Dolphin House. Irena, however, was flying to New York the next day. Kirkland thereupon booked his return trip on the same flight and cajoled the reservation clerk into giving him the seat next to her.

Nothing of consequence ensued immediately from this encounter. Lane and Irena met occasionally over the next three years for dinner when he and she happened to be in New York on business. Then Irena disappeared from his radar screen; eventually, he learned that she had married a theatrical producer who had moved to Hollywood to work in the film industry. More than a decade passed until he saw her again.

Then, in 1969, Kirkland was having a business lunch with several men at one of the better French restaurants in Manhattan. As he prepared to leave, he noticed a familiar face at a nearby table: it was Irena. It had been ten years, but Lane was just as smitten as the day he saw Irena and Alena emerge from the hotel elevator in Paris. His marriage to Edie had been on shaky grounds for some time, and it wasn't long before he was seeing Irena at every possible occasion. Both Lane and Irena separated from their respective spouses in late 1971.

Irena and Alena Neumann—the sisters are identical twins—were born in Prague to a relatively prosperous, educated, and cultured family that included men who had played important political roles in the public affairs of the Czech lands. A grandfather was a member of parliament from the Czech party during the Austro-Hungarian empire; an uncle served in the government of Czechoslovakia after it gained its independence.

In their early years, the sisters led a good life in one of Central Europe's most cosmopolitan cities. Their father earned a comfortable living as an architect engineer. Both parents loved music; Irena's mother was talented enough to play the piano accompaniment during solo recitals. On many Saturdays, the twins were taken to the opera—not always willingly. When Irena met Lane, she discovered that both had spent their Saturdays listening to *Don Giovanni*, *La Traviata*, or *La Bohème*.

Then came Hitler—the threats, the takeover of the Sudetenland, then the gobbling up of the entire country, the imposition of direct Nazi rule over the Czech lands, and the horrors of occupation. In May of 1943, the Neumanns were transported to the Theresienstadt ghetto, where they lived in barracks. The girls did grueling farm labor and then worked in a factory that produced beds for the barracks. In October, they were scheduled for transport to Auschwitz as part of a group of 5,000—all of whom were immediately sent to the gas chambers. Somehow, their father managed to get their names off the list; the girls, meanwhile, came down with a dangerous case of encephalitis.

In November 1944, the twins were transported to Auschwitz while their parents remained in Theresienstadt. Again, they barely escaped a horrible fate when a woman kapo, while taking down their names and ages, mumbled under her breath a warning that under no circumstances should they both give the same birth date to the camp authorities; instead, they should tell the officials that one girl had been born at least one year before the other. The girls followed the advice and were thus spared the fate of other identical twins who were handed over to Dr. Joseph Mengele, whose experiments left his subjects dead or destroyed their health. The girls' vanity may also have played a role in their survival. They refused to wear their glasses and were thus judged healthy and suitable for work. But they survived. Of the 2,500 people in their transport, the girls were among only 200 who were directed to the right; the rest were sent directly to the gas chambers.

After a few weeks they were taken by cattle wagon to a labor camp, attached administratively to the Flossenburg complex, to work at a munitions factory near Sachsen Chemnits in eastern Germany. They were given a piece of bread and watery gruel twice a day and were overseen by a German civilian, with SS guards on constant watch.

In April 1945 the girls talked their way out of the camp and found their way back to Prague. Irena and Alena—and their parents—had survived the Holocaust, the most terrible example of totalitarian evil in history. They had endured disease, starvation diets, humiliation, and several near encounters with death. The twins were tough and resilient, and when they returned to Prague, they were determined to make up for the time they had lost during the Nazi period. They immediately took a cram course over three months in the summer and were then admitted to Charles University in the fall.

But there would be no normal life for the Neumann family. Even as the girls began their university studies, the influence of the Communist Party began to spread from one institution to another, until the Communists gained total control over society. Irena was a Social Democrat; she joined the party when Czechoslovakia was still free and served as the secretary of the party's student association. When the Communists gained absolute power, she would qualify as an enemy of the state on two counts: her political convictions and the fact that she came from a "bourgeois" background. For political reasons, Irena was expelled from the university.

Irena was a member of the Social Democrats' youth wing. At one point, Irena and other youth leaders were arrested and incarcerated in a jail where political prisoners were held for interrogation. A Soviet officer sat in on the interrogation sessions. Because of the elasticity of Communist criminal laws, Irena might have been charged with any number of offenses, due to her political convictions. But she was lucky and was released after several weeks. The authorities did, however, try to coerce her into signing a statement denouncing her friends. She flatly refused.

Irena's father tried to get the family out of Czechoslovakia. At first, he was unsuccessful. But then relations between Israel and Czechoslovakia improved, and the authorities, for a brief period, allowed the emigration of Czech Jews to the new Jewish state. The girls went first; they were permitted to take little more than the clothes on their backs. For a time, they lived in a tent city and eventually acquired jobs. Alena met and married Norman Lourie, a prosperous émigré from South Africa; Irena, after four years, went to Britain to study English, then to Paris, and eventually to the United States.

Shortly after his separation from Edie, Kirkland faced the daunting task of informing George Meany of the change in his personal situation and his intention to marry Irena. Despite their long and close association, Kirkland approached the meeting with apprehension, mindful of Meany's devout Catholicism, his views on the importance of families, and his decades-long marriage to his wife, Eugenie. After pondering for a bit, Meany responded, "You know, Lane, I've been married to the same woman all of my long adult life and never once considered divorce."

Then, after a brief pause, "Murder, yes; divorce, no."

Then, after further reflection, "It's strictly your call. Don't let anybody else live your life for you. It's nobody's business but your own."

On January 19, 1973, Irena and Lane were married in the Dickensian office of Justice of the Peace Nicholas Colasanto in Alexandria, Virginia. The only other person present was Norman Lourie, Irena's brother-in-law, who was in the United States on business. At first, Colasanto assumed that Lourie was the prospective groom and began addressing him as such. Lourie quickly demurred, telling the justice, "No, no, I already have one of those."

Kirkland held an attraction for women. Although of average height at 5 feet, 9 inches, he seemed somewhat larger because of his bull neck and thick shoulders. Lane had a trim physique when he and Irena were married. But the good food, fine wine, and a fondness for sweets took their toll, and like many of his trade union brethren, he developed something of a paunch. He seldom exercised but was an avid walker and liked especially to hike in the Swiss Alps when he and Irena visited Alena's home there. He enjoyed generally good health, despite a serious bout with cancer after the discovery of a melanoma during the 1960s. He wore glasses, which, according to observers, gave him an "owlish" or "scholarly" appearance. His principal vice was tobacco. The addiction to cigarettes that began with the rabbit weed he had smoked as a teenager remained with him the rest of his life, even as many of his friends and colleagues abandoned smoking. As a concession to health concerns, he began to use a cigarette holder, in the mistaken belief that it might help him cheat the nicotine. Eventually, the holder became part of the Kirkland persona, much as the cigar was part of George Meany's.

The wedding took place on the eve of Richard Nixon's second inauguration, so the newly married couple spent time after the wedding ceremony at an AFL-CIO reception honoring Peter Brennan, the new secretary of labor. Irena and Lane stood in the receiving line, along with Meany and Brennan, to greet the likes of Vice President Spiro Agnew and presidential assistant John Ehrlichman, who had stopped by as part of their pre-inaugural rounds.[14]

Lane's marriage to Irena came at a time when he was being asked to serve as labor's principal voice on an impressive series of controversies. One such issue was the Middle East. The American labor movement at this time was arguably Israel's most loyal supporter, after the American Jewish community. George Meany, in fact, had a special relationship with Israeli Prime Minister Golda Meir. There were a number of reasons for labor's attachment to the Jewish state. To begin with, Jews with strong bonds to Israel held a number of high leadership positions within labor. The Cold War was also a factor; Meany and others looked on Israel as America's one dependable democratic ally in an area where tyrants and despots with pro-Soviet leanings otherwise held sway. More important, though, was Israel as an example of a democratic society in which organized labor played a central role in practically all significant aspects of social and economic life. Although the power of the Israeli labor federation, the Histadrut, was to decline over subsequent years, during the 1970s its influence was pervasive. If it could be said that a labor society had been achieved anywhere in the world, that place was Israel. Furthermore, both the Histadrut and the Labor Party paid close attention to their friends in the United States; there were few high-ranking personalities in the American labor movement who had not taken part in at least one tour of Israel, during which meetings were arranged with the highest officials in the country's political life.

In the 1970s, Israel was in dire need of allies in the West. It fought off an invasion on several fronts in the 1973 Yom Kippur War and found itself confronted by hostile neighbors who exhibited no real interest in a peaceful settlement. More worrisome was the impact of the Arab oil boycott, which produced inflation and energy shortages in Western societies and, in turn, provided additional ammunition to those who contended that the United States should reorient its policies away from Israel and toward the Arabs.

Like Meany, Kirkland had a powerful commitment to the security of Israel. Kirkland admired Israel's social achievements, respected it as the lone democracy in the world's toughest neighborhood, and enjoyed close relations with various officials from the Israeli labor movement and the government. And like his friend Senator Henry "Scoop" Jackson, Kirkland respected the Israelis for their willingness to defend their achievements in the face of venomous neighbors, disdainful European elites, a malevolent Soviet bloc, a hostile UN majority, and a State Department with pro-Arab tendencies. Although Kirkland was a part of the Washington power structure and therefore acclimated to the capital's environment of accommodation and deal-making, there were certain issues on which he regarded compromise as inconceivable. Support for Israel was one such issue.

On November 4, 1974, Kirkland was a featured speaker at a huge New York rally called to denounce an invitation to the Palestine Liberation Organization (PLO) to send a representative to address a special UN session on the Middle East. Over 100,000 Israel supporters filled Dag Hammerskjold Plaza to hear Kirkland, Scoop Jackson, Moshe Dayan, New York Senator Jacob Javits, former attorney general Ramsey Clark (who later came to embrace radical Arab causes), NAACP executive director Roy Wilkins, and a lengthy list of rabbis, priests, and ministers denounce the PLO for its terror tactics and the UN for its capitulation to Arab pressure. Kirkland called the invitation "an affront to humanity at large," while demonstrators held signs declaring "PLO is Murder International" and "UN Surrenders to Murderers."[15]

Kirkland pulled no punches in his characterization of the UN's action. He called the invitation to the PLO "an outrage against the human race" and "a betrayal of every principle of decent relations among people and nations." The UN, he said, had been founded "as a citadel of freedom from fear and freedom from want" that had "sanctioned the creation of the State of Israel as a land of hope and refuge for the victims of bigotry and oppression and the survivors of genocide whom no other country welcomed or wanted."

> How far [the UN] has fallen in honor and repute. It is now about to provide a platform for the exaltation of terror, murder, extortion, and blackmail as a way of international life. . . .
>
> This act foreshadows a concerted effort, at the hands of the so-called international community, to force the PLO into the midsection of Israel, within gunshot of the sea, to bring the grenade, the torch, and the knife to the very doors of the nurseries and schoolhouses of her children. The stench of Munich is in the air, and it reeks of Arab oil.[16]

In addition to representing the AFL-CIO before pro-Israel audiences, Kirkland guided the formulation of labor's energy policy, an issue with implications regarding America's policy toward the Middle East. Kirkland was a consistent advocate of a policy to break the grip of the Organization of the Petroleum Exporting Countries (OPEC), whose oil embargo was doing serious damage to the U.S. economy and threatened to fray the bonds between America and Israel. Kirkland went so far as to urge a total ban on the import of Arab oil.[17]

Kirkland also joined the board of a new organization, Americans for Energy Independence, founded by Elmo Zumwalt, a retired admiral and a former chief of naval operations. The establishment of the committee reflected concern over the energy crisis within certain elite circles and the conviction that the United States must find a way to break free from its reliance on foreign oil.[18]

By the mid-1970s, intellectual dissent within the Soviet bloc had become a widespread phenomenon, and no institution was more stalwart in its support of the dissident cause than the AFL-CIO. Well before Andrei Sakharov and Aleksandr Solzhenitsyn became recognized throughout the world as spokesmen for the idea of freedom from Communist oppression, American labor had supported projects to inform the world about the nature of the Soviet system and undermine Communism's monopoly control over the societies of Eastern Europe. As early as the late 1940s, the American Federation of Labor had published a map that indicated the location of the various slave labor camps of the Soviet Gulag. Subsequently, the labor movement maintained close contact with anti-Communist refugees from Poland, Hungary, and other East European countries.

Each year, the AFL-CIO issued official statements denouncing Soviet imperialism and oppression. The executive council also released emergency statements to protest overt acts of repression, such as the Warsaw Pact invasion of Czechoslovakia, the 1970 shooting of Polish workers on the Baltic coast, and the trial and imprisonment of Soviet dissidents. Although these declarations received minimal attention from the American press, they were regularly broadcast into the countries beyond the Iron Curtain by the Voice of America, Radio Free Europe, and Radio Liberty. Through these broadcasts, dissidents of all ideological stripes came to recognize the AFL-CIO and George Meany as among their most reliable allies in the West. The AFL-CIO's reputation was further enhanced by the vitriolic attacks regularly directed at American labor by the Communist press. Freedom-loving Russians, Poles, and Hungarians reasoned that an organization that provoked such intense alarm at *Pravda* must be doing a great deal right.

While labor's anti-Communism was appreciated by the victims of Soviet imperialism, it was neither welcomed nor understood by liberals in the West. Meany, Kirkland, and other labor leaders were often castigated for their uncompromising stance against normalized relations with Communist regimes. Seldom did the critics undertake a serious analysis of the sources of labor's antipathy toward the Soviet system, beyond

speculating that it may have derived from the substantial presence of
Catholics within labor's ranks who were outraged over the persecution of
religious believers by Communist authorities.

As he demonstrated many times over, Kirkland was in fact an opponent of injustice everywhere, whether the regime was based on the teach-
ings of Lenin, Franco, or those who created South African apartheid. But
he treated Communism as a system that stood as a uniquely dangerous
enemy of free trade unionism. As he noted to the federation's critics,
Communists often gained power by appealing to the working classes and
capturing control of the labor movement. Once in control of things,
Communist authorities invariably destroyed the rights that unions
enjoyed in democracies and reduced unions to appendages of the party-
state. This pattern originated in the Soviet Union, after which it spread to
Eastern Europe, to China and Cuba, and to other Third World countries
where Marxist regimes seized power. Right-wing dictatorships also
destroyed independent unions and violated labor rights. But there was no
Franco or Pinochet or South African trade union model for export. The
Communists, by contrast, asserted that their trade union system was
superior in every way to the free union structure of the democracies, and
the Soviet Union's acolytes in Third World revolutionary movements
made clear that trade union rights would be eliminated and democratic
union leaders arrested once they took power.

As the AFL-CIO gained a reputation as a defender of the democratic
opposition in the Communist world, it began to receive appeals beseech-
ing help for those who had been packed off to the gulag or an East
European prison camp. First Meany and later Kirkland received heartrending letters from the mothers or wives of persecuted writers, intellectual dissidents, or workers who sought to launch a free trade union not
subject to control by the Communist Party. Meany and Kirkland passed
on their concerns to the secretary of state, and sometimes their petitions
brought results.

In 1976, the AFL-CIO was involved in a plan to gain freedom for the
Soviet dissident Vladimir Bukovsky. Bukovsky's mother had written several appeals to Meany, and Meany, who was familiar with the dissident's
insightful reports about the nature of the Soviet system, sent an especially
warm response. Subsequently, he worked with Secretary of State
Kissinger to arrange a deal whereby Bukovsky was freed from a Siberian
prison camp and allowed to come to the United States in exchange for the
release by the Pinochet regime of the jailed leader of the Chilean
Communist Party.[19]

After arriving in the United States, Bukovsky addressed an AFL-CIO
convention and was sent on a speaking tour of trade union audiences

around the country. He developed close relations with both Meany and Kirkland; when Meany was ill during the last months of his life, Bukovsky and another dissident, Aleksandr Ginzberg, paid him a visit at his Bethesda home. Later, Bukovsky met periodically with Kirkland to discuss developments inside the Soviet Union and was occasionally asked to address the executive council. He recalls one conversation with the two AFL-CIO leaders shortly after his arrival in the United States. The subject was the appointment by President Carter of Paul Warnke as America's chief arms control negotiator. When Bukovsky indicated unfamiliarity with the name, Meany explained that Warnke was a disarmament enthusiast who might even favor unilateral arms reductions in the face of a Soviet buildup. Bukovsky responded that someone holding to such a position "must either be a madman or a Soviet agent," to which Kirkland replied, "He's something in-between the two: an American liberal."[20]

An even more influential dissident, Aleksandr Solzhenitsyn, found his way to the AFL-CIO after leaving the Soviet Union. Solzhenitsyn was expelled by the Kremlin in February 1974 and came to the United States some months later. On June 30, 1975, he delivered his first public address in the United States at a dinner sponsored by the federation. The speech was a vehement denunciation of the Soviet system and a passionate call for the democracies to resist Communism everywhere. He dismissed claims that demands for change in the Soviet system of internal repression represented interference in the country's internal affairs. "Interfere more and more," he urged. "Interfere as much as you can. We beg you to come and interfere."

Kirkland didn't need Solzhenitsyn's encouragement to interfere on behalf of freedom. A few years later, as president of the AFL-CIO, he would resist pressures from the State Department and the editorial pages of the prestige media in mobilizing open support for Poland's new Solidarity trade union.

On a subsequent visit, Solzhenitsyn stayed at the Kirklands' home and was the guest of honor at a dinner that included George Meany and Vice President Nelson Rockefeller. Solzhenitsyn was not the only political dissident to find his way to the Kirkland home. Lane and Irena played host to freedom advocates from around the world. To their guests, the excellent food and conversation were important, but so was the sense that the Kirklands and the other American guests were friends who could be counted on to use their influence to advance liberty.

Kirkland did not limit his international work to high-profile dissidents like Solzhenitsyn. He was, for example, a partisan of the Kurds, a people that had been mistreated by authoritarian governments throughout the Middle East and badly dealt with by Western governments, including the United States. Kirkland and Irena became personally acquainted with General Mustafa Barzani, the leader of the Iraqi Kurds. Unfortunately, Kirkland was to have little success in mobilizing broad American support for General Barzani. He came away from the experience mistrustful of American promises of assistance to freedom movements that depended on clandestine operations implemented by the CIA without the open backing of the American people. After he was elected AFL-CIO president, Kirkland would insist on a policy of complete transparency in the federation's international work.

The AFL-CIO also worked to prevent Soviet bloc trade union representatives from setting foot in the United States. Kirkland believed that the phrase "Soviet labor leader" was an oxymoron. In his view, a labor official qualified as a trade unionist only if he functioned independently of the state or the party. But under the Soviet labor model, the trade unionist served the party and the state, whose interests were often in conflict with the workers' interests. The Soviet labor leader was, at the core, a cog in the machinery of oppression whose principal victim was the worker in whose name he spoke. Kirkland would never refer to Soviet trade unions or trade unionists; he spoke of *labor fronts* or *so-called trade unions*, or he surrounded the phrase with quotation marks. Furthermore, Kirkland believed that as long as the Soviets or East European Communists refused to permit workers who advocated for labor movements free of party control to speak out or visit the West, there was no justification for the United States giving a platform to the representatives of fraudulent labor bodies.

Within American labor, there were pockets of dissent against the AFL-CIO ban on contacts with the Communist bloc, primarily within unions that were once under the domination of the American Communist Party and had retained a strong leftist orientation. A few mainstream unions also differed with the policy—notably, the UAW and, after the election of William Winpisinger as president, the machinists. The no-contacts policy also came under criticism from liberals outside the labor movement, who regarded the refusal to meet with Soviet labor leaders as a "relic of Cold War thinking." But the AFL-CIO used its considerable influence with the State Department to prevent the issuance of visas to labor officials from the Communist world, and the United States thus lay strictly off-limits to the official representatives of the working classes from countries where Communism held sway.

There was speculation that the State Department might change its policy with the 1976 election of Jimmy Carter, who had indicated that he favored the relaxation of restrictions placed on visas for ideological reasons. But in April 1977, the State Department again acceded to the AFL-CIO's wishes and refused to issue visas to three Soviet labor officials who had been invited to attend a convention of the International Longshoremen's and Warehousemen's Union (ILWU), a union led by Harry Bridges, who was once a leading figure in the Communist wing of the labor movement. The decision was made after Meany met privately with Secretary of State Cyrus Vance to express his concern over Carter's proposed visa liberalization. When asked about the federation's policy, Kirkland replied bluntly, "There is no such thing as a Communist trade union official. They are all just rulers of labor."[21]

The AFL-CIO's power to prevent the entry of Communist bloc labor representatives was temporarily nullified by a measure adopted by Congress in 1977. Sponsored by Senator George McGovern, the McGovern Amendment removed ideology as a criterion for visa approval. As a result, several trade union delegations from the Soviet bloc visited the United States at the invitation of left-wing union organizations. But in 1979, a coalition of the AFL-CIO and Jewish organizations succeeded in convincing Congress to rescind the McGovern Amendment, winning in the Senate by a vote of 87 to 2. Jewish organizations were galvanized into action because the new visa policies were cited as justification for the admission of PLO representatives into the United States, including at least one who had been cited for involvement in terrorist actions. The rollback of the McGovern Amendment meant the effective exclusion of Communist bloc trade union officials until after the Berlin Wall came down.[22]

George Meany looked forward to the triumph of a mainstream Democrat in 1972. To be sure, the Democrats remained divided over the issues that had split party ranks in 1968. But as the election year neared, several important trends were moving in the Democrats' direction. Despite his achievements on the international scene and his decisiveness in imposing wage and price controls, Richard Nixon was not an especially popular president. In 1968, Senator Edmund Muskie had made a positive impression as the Democrats' vice presidential candidate and seemed a figure around whom the various factions of the party could unite. Meany and Kirkland were tepid on Muskie, but other union leaders, including those from the UAW, jumped on the Muskie bandwagon early on in anticipation of his inevitable nomination. Among the other leading candidates, Scoop Jackson was regarded favorably by Meany and Kirkland, as was Hubert Humphrey, back for another run at the White House. On the left were McGovern and John V. Lindsay, mayor of New York, who had recently switched to the Democratic Party. On the right, George Wallace remained a serious threat, running this time in the primaries as a Democrat but with essentially the same message as in 1968.

For the 1972 nomination process, the Democrats had approved a series of new and complex regulations that were, according to their authors, intended to open up and democratize internal party affairs and remove the taint of boss control. To chair the commission empowered to rewrite the rules, the party named Senator McGovern. McGovern hoped to inherit the mantle of antiwar leadership from Eugene McCarthy and Robert Kennedy; not surprisingly, the rules recommended by his commission—and approved by the Democratic National Committee—were designed to maximize the advantage of an insurgent candidacy. The result was a process that was not so much reformed as it was turned upside down, with a major increase in the number of states that chose their delegates through primaries and in the adoption of rules designed to ensure the openness of party caucuses.

The most controversial change mandated de facto quotas for blacks, women, and young people within each candidate's delegate slate. Although denounced as undemocratic by some within the party, labor included, the constituency quotas were approved after proponents argued that such radical measures were necessary to demonstrate to alienated electorates that the system could be made to work. McGovern and his aides on the commission staff saw the quota system as a means of inspiring the participation of the suburban liberals who had campaigned for a withdrawal from Vietnam, disarmament, feminist objectives, environmentalism, and other new causes that the party's left wing had begun to embrace. Another change eliminated automatic representation for elected officials, a measure that gave further power to cause activists at the expense of the mainstream.

A major objective of some reformers was a reduction in the influence of organized labor. Labor clearly understood what was going on; surveying the growing power of antiwar and other cause liberals in the early months of the campaign, Al Barkan, the director of the AFL-CIO's Committee on Political Education, proclaimed, "We aren't going to let these Harvard-Berkeley Camelots take over our party."[23] Barkan was wrong. For a time, at least, the left gained dominance over the party and set the tone for its increasingly radicalized agenda. Factions, like labor, that represented stability, moderation, and a program that cut across racial and gender boundaries were elbowed aside.

The impact of the rules changes became apparent almost immediately, once the campaign got officially underway. Muskie, who had scored impressive majorities over Nixon in opinion polls, proved a weak candidate and, after poor showings in New Hampshire and Florida, made an early exit. After the first round of primaries, the clear front-runners were McGovern, Humphrey, and Wallace, a classic case of two extremes against the center. Although many on the party's left interpreted the election as a sign of the electorate's yearning for change, it was not at all clear what kind of change the voters were seeking. For as the campaign evolved, the real surprise was the strength exhibited by Wallace in northern states that usually supported liberal candidates. Had he not been seriously wounded by a would-be assassin and forced to leave the campaign, Wallace may well have emerged with the largest single chunk of delegates.

With Wallace out of the picture, McGovern emerged with the nomination at a convention remarkable for the radicalism of its rhetoric and platform. Nevertheless, the forces of Cold War labor-liberalism did have their one shining moment when I. W. Abel delivered a stirring nominating speech for Scoop Jackson—a speech written jointly by George Will, Jackson aide Richard Perle, and Tom Kahn, an assistant to Meany.

Instead of uniting the various factions of the party, the convention exacerbated the Democrats' internal divisions. In response, the AFL-CIO declined to endorse the Democratic nominee. Labor was split three ways: one faction that included the Communications Workers of America (CWA); the American Federation of State, County, and Municipal Employees (AFSCME); and the machinists, along with the UAW, supported McGovern. A second faction, a group that included Meany, favored neutrality. A third group, composed primarily of the building trades—and the Teamsters—favored endorsement of Nixon.[24]

In conversations with the author Theodore White, Kirkland and Barkan traced the neutrality decision to an incident in the 1960s. Labor had launched a new campaign to repeal section 14-B of the Taft-Hartley bill. The issue was considered of sufficient importance to warrant Barkan's participation in the lobbying effort aimed at senators whose minds were not yet made up, a group that included McGovern. McGovern promised Barkan that he would support the bill and an effort to break a Republican-led filibuster designed to kill it. But when it came time for a cloture vote to end Senate debate and bring the measure to a vote, McGovern sided with the Republicans, to the amazement of Barkan, then sitting in the Senate gallery. After that performance, Meany and his lieutenants wrote off McGovern as a man whose word could not be trusted.[25]

Of course, the matter was more complex than retribution for McGovern's lapse on this one particular vote. True, Meany, Kirkland, and other labor leaders had harsh judgments for politicians who failed to deliver on their promises. But McGovern's sins were far more serious. He had been the driving force behind a project to transform the Democratic Party from an institution that derived its strength from its blue-collar base to an entity in which cause liberals predominated and in which labor's agenda had given way to a program dictated by peace activists and advocates of feminism, the counterculture, gay liberation, and the limits-to-growth wing of the environmental movement. Then there was McGovern's foreign policy, which represented an attack not merely on the Vietnam War but, as the "Come Home, America" theme he sounded at the party convention indicated, a thoroughgoing repudiation of the entire thrust of American policy during the Cold War.

Just as McGovern took one step after another to alienate labor, Richard Nixon worked mightily to detach labor from its alliance with the Democrats. He first corralled the endorsement of the Teamsters by, among other things, releasing James Hoffa from federal prison well ahead of schedule. As McGovern edged ahead of the rest of the Democratic pack in the spring, Nixon operative Charles Colson encouraged various AFL-CIO officials to give Nixon serious consideration or adopt a position of neutrality in the presidential race. Nixon then went a step further by dispatching his aide John Ehrlichman to ensure that the usual boiler-plate antilabor rhetoric was removed from the party platform. Under Ehrlichman's watchful eye, the party of Taft, Hartley, and Barry Goldwater jettisoned for this one moment its historical antipathy to organized labor. Indeed, the platform praised the nation's labor unions for "advancing the well-being not only of their members but also of our entire free enterprise system. . . . We salute the statesmanship of the labor union movement."[26]

Such unctuous formulations left Meany and Kirkland unmoved. When the Watergate scandal erupted, Meany guided the executive council in the adoption of a statement calling for Nixon's impeachment. And when Nixon's notorious Enemies' List was uncovered, Kirkland took pride in seeing his name listed with the other "enemies."

In fact, the AFL-CIO emerged from the 1972 election fortified in the conviction that its strategy had been vindicated. Organized labor helped ensure the victory of the Democrats in both the House and the Senate and was crucial in delivering victory to several liberal candidates who won by the barest of margins. At the same time, blue-collar voters opted for Nixon by 55 percent, well up from the 41 percent he had received four years earlier. The families of union members, who had given Nixon 34 percent in his contest against Humphrey, gave the president 51 percent in 1972, a much more substantial increase than Nixon's increase among white-collar voters. Clearly, George Meany and his colleagues had not lost touch with the political opinions of the labor rank and file.[27] Yet the GOP still controlled the White House, even despite Nixon's lack of popularity. For Kirkland, the lesson of 1972 was that the Democrats would remain undependable allies unless a united labor movement stepped in and restored the forces of mainstream liberalism to a position of dominance. Twelve years later, in one of the most controversial moves of his career, Kirkland would take personal command of a campaign that elevated labor to the position of the party's most powerful force.

In 1974, the AFL-CIO made another attempt to reverse the guidelines that so substantially contributed to the party's catastrophic performance in 1972. The venue was a midterm convention held in Kansas City. Barkan worked the floor to piece together a coalition of labor and regulars to undo the quotas and return more power to the Democratic mainstream. In this endeavor, labor enjoyed the support of the Coalition for a Democratic Majority, a group of party activists who favored moderate, pro-labor domestic programs; a foreign policy anchored on preventing the spread of Soviet influence; and a rollback of the party reforms. (Although Kirkland was not personally involved in CDM, he approved of COPE's providing funds for the organization's operations.)[28] A majority probably supported a plan to reform the reforms, but the effort fell apart after left-wing delegates threatened a walkout and the regulars, in typical fashion, caved in. Barkan didn't help matters with his sledgehammer approach and failure to lay the groundwork for change with potential allies prior to the convention. Party chairman Robert Strauss brokered a compromise that called for superficial changes but left the quota system intact. Barkan fumed, and Meany decreed that the AFL-CIO would no longer be involved in the internal struggles within the Democratic Party.[29]

In 1976, then, the AFL-CIO per se played no visible role in the process that resulted in the nomination of Jimmy Carter as the Democratic standard-bearer. But Meany and Kirkland did have a favorite among the announced contenders: Scoop Jackson. Jackson had run an unimpressive campaign in 1972 but had mapped out his strategy for 1976 carefully, had raised a decent war chest, and had lined up endorsements from a representative group of labor leaders and party regulars.

Jackson was by no means a consensus candidate of labor. With labor divided in its loyalties between the various Democratic contenders, a group of relatively liberal unions—UAW; CWA; AFSCME; and the Oil, Chemical, and Atomic Workers—joined together in a strategy to maximize labor's influence by placing trade union officials on the delegate slates of the various Democratic candidates, depending on which candidate looked particularly strong in a state or district. Some believe that this strategy was in part designed to deny Jackson the nomination on the grounds that as an unreconstructed hawk, he was considered unacceptable by the party's left wing.

Jackson, in fact, lost because he ran a remarkably poor campaign, in almost every aspect, from a strategy that conceded too many key states to opponents, to an ineffectual use of television, to poor management of campaign funds. The collapse of the Jackson campaign signaled the last gasp of Cold War liberalism as a factor in presidential politics in the United States.[30]

One of Kirkland's most important contributions to the 1976 election was his open encouragement of Daniel Patrick Moynihan to make the run for the New York Senate seat then occupied by James Buckley, a Republican conservative. Moynihan had recently resigned as U.S. ambassador to the United Nations, where he created a stir by engaging in open polemical war with the representatives of the Soviet bloc and radical Third World countries who at the time controlled developments at the UN General Assembly. Kirkland, in fact, was the first person of national stature to publicly call on Moynihan to make the run. He did so at a testimonial dinner sponsored by Social Democrats, U.S.A., at which Kirkland was the honoree and both Moynihan and Jackson delivered speeches. Kirkland recognized Moynihan as a political leader who would uphold the traditions of labor-liberalism that were under assault from the New Left wing of the party (epitomized by Bella Abzug, Moynihan's principal adversary in the primary), and who would reinforce the Democrats who continued to believe in an engaged internationalism. Moynihan entered the race and, with strong labor backing, scored a narrow victory over Abzug in the primary and then easily overcame Buckley in the general election. Without labor's aggressive support, Moynihan would almost certainly have lost to Abzug.

By contrast to the stolid Jackson, Jimmy Carter satisfied the electorate's demand for a fresh face and a new message. But what exactly was that message? Labor had its doubts about Carter. He had served as governor of a right-to-work state, Georgia, and had had practically no dealings with national labor leaders. On the positive side, he had governed Georgia as a progressive, was well-liked by the state's black leaders, and had not shunned relations with Georgia's labor leadership, as more conservative governors had done. Once Carter won the nomination, the AFL-CIO repressed its misgivings and moved quickly to an endorsement vote, and COPE mobilized a major campaign to secure Carter's election in November.

Having endured eight years of Republican government, organized labor had a lengthy list of items it hoped would be enacted under the new president. There was, however, some division within the movement over the tactical approach to the administration, with some advocating that labor put aside for the time being parochial issues like elimination of the right-to-work provision of Taft-Hartley. Carter, meanwhile, was emphasizing that as president, he intended to govern independently of the influence of special interests. "If labor ever asked me for anything other than to work for the control of inflation and the decrease of the unemployment rate, I would not comply with their recommendation," Carter declared a few weeks after his election.[31]

Kirkland chose to ignore Carter's strictures when he elaborated to the press on labor's expectations. Labor's agenda included a substantial tax cut to stimulate economic growth, national health insurance, more money for housing, the development of domestic sources of energy, and what Kirkland called "parochial interests" like reform of Taft-Hartley. Kirkland also plumped for the selection of John T. Dunlop as secretary of labor. Dunlop, a labor expert from Harvard University, had served as labor secretary in the administration of Gerald Ford and resigned as a matter of principle when Ford vetoed situs picketing after having promised to sign the legislation. Kirkland called Dunlop "as close to being the indispensable man as there is."[32]

In his discussions of labor's expectations from the new administration, Kirkland took time to respond to critics who asserted that organized labor was in a state of institutional decline. Labor, he asserted, was not out of step with the times or facing a crisis. He told Lee Dembart of the *New York Times* that if measured by results, "we'll stack up against any period of the labor movement." "For the first time in the history of man, a man born today can expect to spend the minor part of his life working, and we are responsible for that," Kirkland said. He claimed that the trade union movement was responsible for the great social reforms of the twentieth century, from paid vacations to the shorter work week, to unemployment compensation, to the "democratization of leisure."

In the same interview, Kirkland made it clear that he didn't think much of the new liberalism. "I would put the problem of the man who does not have a job ahead of the problem of the man who does not like his work. I would put the problem of non-work ahead of the problem of the quality of work. I would put the problem of the aged poor ahead of the problem of the unhappy young. I would deal with the problems of the unemployed, the sick, the old, and the poor before I would become very obsessed with the problems of the young, the healthy, and the affluent. And I suppose this brings us into opposition with the new politics which deals with the problems of the young and the middle class." Somewhat ruefully, Kirkland claimed that labor bore some responsibility for the youth culture that he so thoroughly abhorred. "We delayed the point of entry into the work force. We created the exemption of youth from the necessity of labor. We created the delayed adolescence."[33]

Almost from the outset, relations went badly between Carter and labor, or at least between the president and George Meany. Labor was not the only institution that had problems with the new president. Carter seemed to believe that he could govern without the traditional deal-making that past presidents had engaged in with the barons of Congress and the major Capitol Hill lobbies. But labor's disenchantment went deeper than most. Meany had hoped for a president in the Truman-Johnson mold, liberal with a solid appreciation of labor's worth as a political and economic institution. Instead, Carter revealed himself as an entirely new phenomenon: a Democrat who had liberal views on race relations, sexual equality, and other social issues, but who rejected traditional Democratic economic ideas and policies and treated labor much like he treated other groups within the party coalition. Soon enough, Meany was complaining that Carter was presiding over the most conservative economic program since Herbert Hoover. Meany was also angry over Carter's refusal to name John Dunlop as secretary of labor. Carter had rejected Dunlop out of concern that the Harvard professor would owe his primary allegiance to labor, rather than to the president, and reportedly, because organizations representing blacks and women complained that Dunlop had a weak record on equal employment issues.[34] Instead, he chose F. Ray Marshall, a southerner and a respected professor of labor economics at the University of Texas. Marshall had written several important studies of racial problems in organized labor and had actually been asked by Kirkland to serve as director of the AFL-CIO's labor studies center.

Some observers speculated that Meany and Carter were further separated by a substantial cultural divide. In fact, Meany worked well with trade unionists and political figures from the South, as witness his relationship with Kirkland, Paul Hall (an Alabamian), and LBJ. A more accurate assessment is that Meany saw in Carter a new kind of Democratic president, one who felt ambivalence toward labor and its leadership. Meany could tolerate ambivalence from Republicans; he expected something different from Democrats. Meany felt comfortable with Democratic Party professionals of the Kennedy, Johnson, and Sam Rayburn variety. Kennedy and Johnson had frequently invited Meany over to the White House for a chat; the issue could just as easily be foreign policy as something that directly affected labor policy. Carter did make a point of having Meany over for discussions from time to time and agreed that he would grant Meany a meeting on request.[35] But there was no intimacy or real friendship in the relationship, and Meany may have felt that Carter was acting out of political obligation, rather than from a genuine interest in Meany's opinions.

Carter became particularly irritated by Meany's habit in discussions with reporters of giving the new president a grade, as if he were a slow-learning student. Invariably, Meany issued his report card after a meeting with Carter at the White House. Meany would emerge, and when asked by reporters to assess Carter's performance, would respond that Carter deserved a C+ or B–; Meany was a hard grader, and the president never reached the A level.

One awful incident occurred at a meeting called by Carter to discuss the dimensions of the proposed increase in the minimum wage. The president invited the entire executive council to the White House. What ensued was later described by Kirkland as the "George Hardy Memorial Breakfast."

Hardy was president of the Service Employees International Union. He was a veteran of the navy's enlisted ranks and, Kirkland observed, "never lost the style of discourse acquired in that service." Hardy was, according to Kirkland, "literally incapable of expressing himself without compulsive use of the standard four-letter obscenities, regardless of the place or company." As Kirkland described the affair:

> [Hardy] proceeded to address the minimum wage issue, loudly and in his accustomed fashion. Carter, a world class prude, sat through his tirade with a fixed smile on his face, but not in his eyes.
>
> Later that day, I received a call from Vice President Mondale, to this effect: "That was just awful. The president is very upset. Can you get George [Meany] to call the president and apologize for Hardy's behavior?" I replied: "Fritz, the day that George Meany apologizes for any member of the AFL-CIO executive council is a day that Hell freezes over."

Kirkland later related his conversation with Mondale to Meany, who shrugged and told Kirkland, "You gave him the right answer."[36] Tom Donahue, who was working as executive assistant to Meany at the time, was of the view that Carter's "alleged sense of outrage was greatly exaggerated." Donahue said that he "found it impossible to believe that a man who had spent years in the navy had never heard those words before."[37]

The incident embarrassed Mondale, who had arranged the meeting in an effort to promote peace between Meany and Carter. "It was dreadful," Mondale recalled. "Carter expected respect and proper language, especially in the White House, and he was mad at me for setting the affair up." Mondale believed that Meany's treatment of Carter at that meeting and at others was "almost abusive." He added, "Meany had this hostility towards everything about Carter. We just couldn't break through."[38]

A special point of contention was trade policy. By the mid-1970s, the AFL-CIO was moving decisively away from its previous support for free trade, as trade-related job losses began to expand from the garment and textile industries to steel, auto, and other core sectors. In April 1977, Carter rejected a recommendation by the International Trade Commission for a sharp increase in tariffs on foreign-made shoes. Kirkland responded sharply, wondering aloud whether "our [presidential campaign] support was just another triumph of hope over experience." Kirkland's concerns went beyond the trade issue. He cited what he called the "disproportionate representation of big business" in the cabinet, a phenomenon that had been "masked" by the president's well-publicized search for minority cabinet nominees. "The process reminds us again that in national and world affairs—whether the winds blow left or right, cold war or détente, Republican or Democratic—big business adapts and comes to winning terms. When the Republicans are in, big business wins because it owns the party. When the Democrats are in, business wins because it exacts the price of business confidence."[39]

Kirkland complained of an inadequate stimulus package and Carter's retreat on a minimum wage increase: the administration proposed an increase from $2.30 to $2.50, while labor wanted $3. "The message is simple and clear," Kirkland said. "Inflation is to be fought at the expense of its primary victims, and the poor will always be with us." Kirkland also had a strong message for those who cited cost as a justification for trade with low-wage countries. With a candor unusual for those involved in the trade debate, he asserted that fairness for American workers might mean somewhat higher prices for consumers. "A word needs to be said on the emerging principle of consumer sovereignty as it affects trade issues— that is, the proposition that the consumer has an inalienable, top priority right to $4 Korean shoes, regardless of the conditions under which they were made, the human and economic cost of lost American jobs, and of who really gets the $4. The principle is mostly expounded by those who get their shoes at Gucci."[40]

Then there was foreign policy. Although Meany generally restricted his criticisms to domestic matters, it was no secret that he and Kirkland were disappointed by some of Carter's foreign policy appointments and policy initiatives. During the campaign, Carter had rather brilliantly suc- ceeded in convincing both hawks and doves that he shared their values and worldviews: to the hawks, he was the former naval officer who got his advice on the state of the world from former Secretary of State Dean Rusk and Zbigniew Brzezinski, a hard-line anti-Soviet academic. To the doves, he promised to rethink America's commitment to Cold War ortho- doxies, and he hinted at appointments for Cyrus Vance and Paul Warnke, both Cold War skeptics.

Carter did appoint Brzezinski as national security adviser but other- wise filled his administration with men whose careers had been defined by their opposition to the Vietnam War. Although the AFL-CIO did not formally oppose any of the foreign policy or national security nominees, Kirkland worked behind the scenes toward the defeat of several choices. Warnke was one. He had served as assistant secretary of defense during the Johnson administration; since leaving government, he had been a biting critic of the basic precepts of American policy under both Republican and Democratic administrations. Kirkland also supported James Schlesinger, who had served as defense secretary under Ford, for the same post in the Carter administration. In the end, Schlesinger was named secretary of energy, while Harold Brown got the defense job.[41]

Kirkland also opposed the nomination of Theodore Sorensen as director of the CIA. Although Kirkland was undoubtedly unsettled by Sorensen's worldview, which increasingly tended toward a thoroughgoing criticism of America's postwar foreign policy course, there was another, more fundamental, factor at work. Whether fairly or otherwise—and he always denied the charge—Sorensen had been linked in press accounts to Ed Sadlowski, an insurgent from Chicago who was seeking the presidency of the steelworkers' union.[42]

Sadlowski was one of two candidates vying for the job that had been held by I. W. Abel, a respected union leader, who was retiring after having reached the steelworkers' mandatory age. Sadlowski came out of the fabled South Works steel mill in Chicago and served as district director of the Chicago area. He identified as a leftist; promised a get-tough, adversarial policy toward the steel industry management; attacked the trade union establishment; and spoke with derision of labor's anti-Communist foreign policy orientation.

On the surface, the Sadlowski campaign involved nothing more than a highly competitive struggle for ascendancy in one of America's more important unions. But for those who cared about the future political orientation of organized labor, the ramifications of the steelworkers' election were huge. The left believed that victory for an avowed leftist like Sadlowski in an important union like the steelworkers could drive the entire trade union movement to the left and pave the way for further radical incursions in other unions. "The left's attitude was—'Capture the steelworkers and then take over the rest of labor,'" recalled Bruce Miller, a labor lawyer who served as an adviser to the anti-Sadlowski slate. Organized labor was the only significant element within the Democratic Party that maintained a commitment to Cold War values; Sadlowski's supporters from outside the labor movement clearly hoped that his victory would trigger a process that would detach the AFL-CIO from its anti-Communist commitments and move it toward a position of neutralism. While the left's vision of a transformed and radicalized labor movement was a bit grandiose, it had every reason to believe that Sadlowski might capture the USW leadership. The steel industry was entering troubled times; there had been layoffs, and jobs were in jeopardy because of foreign trade and technological advances. There was thus an audience within the union for Sadlowski's vow to challenge the big steel corporations.

The Sadlowski campaign had provoked a furious reaction within the labor movement because of Sadlowski's contemptuous treatment of mainstream trade unionists and, especially, because of the extensive involvement of radicals and liberals in funding his insurgency. Cocktail parties were held in the liberal salons of Manhattan, Berkeley, and Cambridge to raise money for Sadlowski; the roster of contributors ranged from Jane Fonda to John Kenneth Galbraith to Victor Reuther, brother of Walter and recently retired as international affairs director of the UAW. According to Bruce Miller, the Sadlowski campaign raised over $400,000 from outside the union. According to some reports, Sorensen had been among those who gave money to the Sadlowski campaign. Joseph Rauh, a liberal mainstay who had moved progressively to the left in the post-Vietnam period, served as Sadlowski's chief ambassador to the monied world outside the labor movement. At the same time that Sadlowski was raising campaign money from what Meany referred to as "so-called limousine liberals," he was utilizing the services of activists from various leftist sects, including those that sympathized with Communist tyrannies, as campaign workers.

Ultimately, Sadlowski was defeated by the candidate of the union establishment, Lloyd McBride. An important factor was McBride's having added a prominent Canadian steelworker official, Lynn Williams, to his slate. Canadian steelworkers voted overwhelmingly for McBride; Williams, who was elected union secretary, succeeded to the presidency a few years later, when McBride died unexpectedly.[43]

The Sadlowski campaign would be the first experience in a trade union factional struggle for a number of veterans of the New Left. Their involvement in labor affairs would deepen over the years, and some would eventually serve in important staff positions in key international unions, although not within the federation. Kirkland regarded avowed leftists much as Samuel Gompers had looked on an earlier generation of radicals as irresponsible ideologues whose first loyalty was to the revolution and not to organized labor and who, given the opportunity, would like nothing better than to seize control of the union movement. The left, in turn, treated Kirkland with unconcealed animosity. Years later, when Lane was forced to retire from his post as AFL-CIO president, left-leaning union staff members were the first to celebrate. If the left had not actually captured the federation, Kirkland's departure enabled political radicals to gain a degree of influence that was unprecedented in the history of the AFL-CIO.

As for Sorensen, he withdrew his name from nomination for the CIA post in the face of heavy opposition in the Senate.

In addition to its problems with Carter, labor was facing a series of organizational problems. There was, to begin with, membership decline. Each year, the percentage of the workforce represented by unions had declined slightly, from a high of around 35 percent in the mid-fifties to a bit over 20 percent in the mid-seventies, although the raw numbers of trade union members did increase from year to year. In 1977, however, the Department of Labor released a report that showed a drop of 767,000 union members in the period 1974–1976, the first such decline in years. The survey also showed unions losing a steadily growing percentage of representation elections, winning only 46 percent in 1977.[44]

Part of the problem was an increasingly tough stance taken by employers during unionization drives. The construction unions were especially hard hit, as contractors in the large northern and midwestern cities—until recently, bastions of building trades strength—marshaled an array of sophisticated legal tactics to thwart unionization. At the same time, large corporations that had traditionally enjoyed good relations with their unions began to relocate operations to the antiunion South and West or to low-wage countries of Asia and Latin America.

The organizational problem was compounded by a decline in the AFL-CIO's lobbying influence in Congress. If ever there were a lobbyists' Hall of Fame, Andrew Biemiller would no doubt win unanimous election as a charter member. But Biemiller was in the last years of a legendary career, and like a basketball player who entered the game in the era of Bob Cousy and ended it in the time of Julius Erving, Biemiller had lost touch with a faster and more complex game. He had flourished when lobbying was a simpler affair, requiring above all a rapport with the relevant committee chairmen. Biemiller was a product of the schmooze and booze school of lobbying. He knew the congressional barons by their first names, knew their brands of whiskey, and understood the pressures that tugged at them from various directions. Biemiller was at his best in an era when a chairman had the means to impose discipline on junior members; that era, alas, had passed, and many of the old liberal-labor Democrats had been supplanted by young men and, increasingly, women, who were put off by Biemiller's lobbying techniques.

Biemiller and his cohorts found that the old methods didn't work with the post-Watergate new Democrats. Many came from suburban districts where unions lacked members and clout. Although the new Democrats were not antilabor, they were inclined to regard unions as yet another interest group—a Democratic interest group, to be sure, and thus worthy of support most of the time, but a group whose motives were more suspect than, say, Friends of the Earth or the National Organization for Women. Many of the new Democrats were what were called *process liberals*—reformers whose passions focused on such issues as the system of campaign finance rather than the minimum wage. Rachelle Horowitz, the political director of the American Federation of Teachers, recalls the Watergate Democrats as having "no sense of history and no real ideology." They had, she said, "won election by an accident of history and, because they lacked core beliefs, were obsessed with the shifting views of their constituents." Ken Young, who succeeded Biemiller as legislative chief and then went on to serve as Kirkland's executive assistant, called the new Democrats "thumb-suckers"—politicians who wet their fingers in order to more easily tell from which direction the winds were blowing. The fact that labor was for or against a particular piece of legislation left these new Democrats unimpressed; they needed to be convinced that it was in the public interest or in the interest of their political careers. They did not reflexively support an issue because it carried the imprimatur of an AFL-CIO endorsement. If small business or corporate interests from back home inundated their office with postcards urging a "no" vote on an issue of importance to labor, they took those views seriously.[45]

The first shock came with the common situs picketing bill. Adoption would have enabled building trades unions to shut down an entire project site in cases where only one out of several unions was involved in a job action against the contractor. The bill had passed Congress during the Ford administration, only to fall victim to a presidential veto. In 1977, a supremely confident labor movement had revived the measure. In the meantime, however, builders' groups, assisted by newfound allies from the political right, launched a massive lobbying campaign to turn the measure back. Labor was unprepared for this game of hardball, and when the bill came before the House, it went down to a stunning defeat, with 217 votes against the measure, as compared with just 178 two years previously. The president's position didn't help; Carter adopted a stance of strict neutrality toward the measure, promising only to sign the bill if it reached his desk. But his operatives made it clear in private that they were not unhappy to see situs picketing defeated.[46]

The fate of situs picketing was a clear signal that corporate America was no longer content with the business-as-usual attitude that had prevailed in labor-management affairs through most of the postwar period. Labor took note and was thus better prepared for the next, and more significant, struggle over labor law reform.

The AFL-CIO had initially planned to launch another attempt to roll back section 14-B of the Taft-Hartley law. But after talking things over with the administration and congressional leaders, labor decided to offer a compromise measure. The revised proposal sought to deal with a new and growing problem: the violation by employers of the spirit and some-times the letter of existing labor legislation in order to prevent the unionization of their workforce. A specific problem was the stalling tactics that corporate lawyers resorted to when confronted with a representation vote that was likely to favor the union. Another problem was the inability of union activists to obtain timely justice for acts of reprisal from management; it took, on average, two years for a worker to win reinstatement after a finding of illegal dismissal for union activity. Furthermore, when found guilty, companies were compelled to do nothing more than provide back pay, a slap-on-the-wrist penalty that failed to discourage management from summarily firing union supporters. The bill called for an expansion of the National Labor Relations Board (NLRB) in order to expedite hearings on cases of alleged violations, permitting two NLRB members instead of the full board to adjudicate routine cases, and the establishment of strict time limits for a recognition vote once the union had gathered enough authorization cards from the workers. To deal with the growing inclination of employers to flout labor laws because of the modest penalties involved, the bill called for double back pay for workers fired for union activity, the denial of federal contracts to employers who repeatedly violated labor laws, and tougher penalties for employers who refused to bargain in good faith, and it gave the NLRB the power to seek injunctions in cases where workers were dismissed for union activities.[47]

Labor law reform would have had little effect on corporations that enjoyed harmonious relations with their unions. But for companies that sought to employ rough tactics to prevent union representation, the proposed law was a serious matter. If labor law were adopted, companies could no longer pile on one delaying tactic after another in the hope that eventually union supporters within their workforce would simply give up the fight. Nor could they fire with impunity workers who were agitating for a union. The section calling for a loss of federal contracts was especially ominous for any company that hoped to do business with the government.

Although some labor officials grumbled that a president who was more forceful and shrewd in his relations with Congress might have ensured victory for labor law reform, most acknowledged that Carter put his administration fully behind the measure. In a speech before the Texas AFL-CIO, Kirkland had nothing but praise for the president. Kirkland called Carter "a big man in a big job—big enough to change his mind when a strong case is presented to him." Kirkland added that Carter had "placed his administration on the side of hard-pressed working people, pursuing a just cause, against the pressure and propaganda of the Chamber of Commerce, the right-to-work movement, and the other components and fronts of the anti-labor lobby."[48]

On October 6, 1977, the House gave the measure overwhelming approval, 257 to 163. This brought the bill to the Senate, where a majority clearly supported passage. In the Senate, however, labor confronted the challenge of an almost certain Republican filibuster. Filibusters had been used before to thwart labor law changes, especially efforts to eliminate section 14-B. But a significant change had been made in the Senate rules: instead of the previous two-thirds majority to invoke cloture, or sixty-six votes, the bill's supporters needed only sixty senators willing to cut off debate.

Although labor law's strategists understood that the bill would draw strong opposition from the corporate community, they were not prepared for the total war declared by big and small business alike, assisted by their new allies in the right-wing universe. In this particular fight, the role of the right was crucial. As the labor law campaign demonstrated, the right could no longer be written off as a marginal element of primitive anti-Communists, racial bigots, and opponents of water fluoridation. The organized right—or, as it was now known, the New Right—was smarter, more mature, and interested in attaining power, instead of maintaining ideological purity at all costs. The right had produced a battery of operatives who were expert at the new technology of political warfare. They had perfected the techniques of mass mailings to raise money for candidates and causes and to galvanize the faithful into action against laws they deemed objectionable. Just before the labor law struggle heated up, the right had mounted a huge campaign against ratification of the Panama Canal treaty. The treaty survived despite an intense lobbying campaign, but everyone agreed that the New Right had proved itself a force to be reckoned with.

The major antilabor organization on the right was the National Right-to-Work Committee. Previously, its main purpose had been to encourage campaigns in various states to adopt right-to-work measures and to mobilize the troops to beat back labor campaigns to revoke existing right-to-work provisions. The committee's director, Reed Larson, had recognized the potential for a major expansion in the organization's revenues and influence in the new mass-mailing techniques and, over a three-year period, had expanded the group's list of contributors from 27,000 to 360,000. With a base centered among small businessmen, Larson played a central role in organizing business opposition to situs picketing. The White House had described the amount of mail opposing this rather obscure piece of legislation as "unbelievable." Having tasted blood in the situs picketing campaign, the New Right moved on to the next challenge: beating back labor law reform.

The role of the right did not bother Kirkland as much as did the participation of major corporations and business lobbies in the campaign. The Business Roundtable, composed of blue chip corporations with histories of decent relations with unions, decided to join the fight against labor law reform, as did the Chamber of Commerce and the National Association of Manufacturers. Mainstream business channeled its lobbying campaign through the National Action Committee, an entity originally called the National Action Committee Against the Secondary Boycott that had been established to beat back situs picketing. The Chamber of Commerce issued dire and transparently exaggerated warnings about "compulsory unionism" and predicted that passage would lead to a three-fold increase in union membership.[49]

As the debate intensified, labor leaders grew enraged at the business community's tactics. "There is a word for the kind of campaign that American industry has launched to kill the hopes of the most oppressed and deserving in this country," Kirkland declared. "It is class warfare." Kirkland delivered these words not to a labor pep rally, but to a conference of businessmen on labor-management relations. Kirkland saw the all-out campaign against the labor bill as an ill omen for the future of industrial accord. "Much progress," he said, "has been made under a system of sometimes cooperative, sometimes adversary relations between parties with a shared set of values." But he added that further progress is "not likely to survive the bitterness that would be engendered by the blind obstruction of this measure. . . . I for one would be most reluctant to continue to participate in labor-management committees or symposia engaged in high-minded discourse. A certain amount of hypocrisy, of course, helps to make the world go round. But I would not know how to carry out a serious and constructive dialogue with split-level, double-breasted management." He added:

> It is class warfare. And there is a filibuster, organized, promoted, and sustained not just by some primitive sections of industry but by all of corporate America through its major organs of influence. The circle is unbroken. No voice of compassion for the plight of a worker stripped of his livelihood for having the character to overcome fear and exercise his legal rights has been heard from any official of a major corporation. I confess that I am not all that comfortable to be here engaged in earnest reminiscences about the future of industrial society with the convivial

Dr. Jekylls of corporate enterprise while their Mr. Hydes are busy in Washington preserving the power of certain companies to add to their profits by breaking the law.[50]

Kirkland called the right-to-work groups and other New Right organizations "a windfall blessing" for the respectable elements of the business community. "They do all the dirty work, slanderous advertising, the name calling and the business community keeps its hands clean and gets the job done."[51]

In July 1978, matters came to a head in the Senate. Labor easily got its majority, and indeed got as many as fifty-eight votes, two short of the magic sixty mark needed to cut off debate and bring the matter to a vote. In fact, Senator Russell Long, a "no" vote, privately promised to support the measure if his vote was required to break the filibuster. But try as they might, labor's lobbyists and its supporters in the Senate could not find that one additional vote.

The failure of labor law reform was a critical juncture for labor, and it played an important role in shaping Kirkland's attitude toward cooperation with corporate America as the time neared when he would succeed George Meany. He had been involved in a series of discussions with major business executives over ways to enhance labor-management cooperation, both at the workplace and in the setting of national economic policy. It was Kirkland's fondest hope to forge a kind of social contract in the United States between business, labor, and government. Kirkland did not give up on his ambition. Henceforth, however, he regarded business with a wary eye, and his references to business in subsequent speeches focused less on the opportunities for cooperation than on corporate greed and corporate treatment of workers as disposable items.

In the 1978 off-year elections, the Republicans made important gains in both House and Senate, destroying whatever chance there might have been to revive the legislation in subsequent years. Although no one could have predicted it at the time, 1978 was the last year in which the Democrats would have commanding control of both Congress and the presidency. Never again in the twentieth century would the political alignment in Washington be as propitious as in that year.

There was, in fact, increasing evidence of a gathering conservative tide in the United States. Out in Middle America, a backlash was gaining strength against the ideas and changes that were spawned by the movements of the 1960s: radical feminism, the antigrowth strains of environmentalism, racial quotas and busing for integration, the notion that American foreign policy was rooted in racism and neocolonialism. In addition to discontent over these hot-button issues, a companion grassroots movement was on the rise against growing local property tax rates, with public employee unions very much in the crosshairs of the sponsors of local referenda that sought to roll back tax rates and place limits on government's ability to tax and spend.

The collapse of labor law reform also led to a renewal of the cold war between George Meany and Jimmy Carter. Relations reached a new low at the end of 1978, when Carter struck Meany's name from a list of presidential appointees to the board of directors of the Communications Satellite Corporation, a position Meany had held since 1964. This provoked Kirkland to immediately resign from presidential appointments to the advisory committee to the Arms Control and Disarmament Agency and the National Advisory Commission for Women.[52]

By now, however, some in labor's higher ranks were growing exasperated at Meany's feud with Carter. The most outspoken was Glenn Watts, president of the Communications Workers of America. Watts, a relatively soft-spoken and low-key union chief, charged that Meany's carping at the president was doing "a disservice to the country and the labor movement." Watts refrained from urging Meany to step down, but he made it clear that he would be pleased if Meany took the hint. He noted that he would like to deliver a nominating speech for Kirkland as Meany's successor. But he added that in six years he would be sixty-five, the mandatory retirement age at his union. "I don't think I'll have the opportunity to nominate Lane," he declared.[53]

4

CAPTAIN OF THE SHIP

"LANE'S RELIGION," A FRIEND ONCE COMMENTED, "WAS THE LABOR movement." By the end of 1979, he would have the opportunity to place his own unique leadership stamp on the movement to which he had dedicated his life.

Although closing in on his eighty-fifth year, George Meany had lost none of his intellectual edge. A story was circulating that Meany was writing his memoirs. The working title: *The First Hundred Years*. Whether denouncing the latest Soviet outrage or fulminating against President Carter's latest policy zigzag, Meany remained a commanding presence in American public life. Commentators dwelt obsessively on his age and speculated endlessly on the impending succession. But when Meany spoke, it was as the authoritative voice of American working people.

Yet even as Meany continued to issue challenges to presidents, oil barons, OPEC sheiks, and Soviet commissars, his ability to function as the day-to-day leader of organized labor was slipping away. For twenty years he had endured the rumors, the editorials, the cartoons, and the jokes about his age and retirement. A famous *New Yorker* cartoon showed a man peering into a mirror; his wife observes, "You may be crusty, but you're not as crusty as George Meany." But by 1979, Meany was giving evidence that what some had come to doubt was after all true: George Meany was mortal. He was afflicted with aches and illnesses, and these in turn affected his mood. Then Eugenie, his wife of many decades, died, an event that seemed to accelerate his physical deterioration. Increasingly, it was Kirkland who acted as the AFL-CIO's spokesman in appearances before the press and Congress and as its official representative in private meetings with the White House.

A further sign of decline in Meany's iron grip was an ever-so-slight increase in the willingness of union leaders to call publicly for his retirement. Bill Winpisinger, the new president of the Machinists and a self-described socialist, was—take your pick—the most assertive or the most obnoxious critic, calling Meany "too goddamn old." In a more circumspect comment, Sol "Chick" Chaikin, president of the International Ladies' Garment Workers Union, said that Meany's age was an image problem in a youth-oriented society like the United States. Various proposals were floated for the creation of an emeritus or a chairman of the board post to enable Meany to play a role in federation affairs, all of which Meany studiously ignored.[1]

Lane Kirkland emerged as the de facto leader of American labor at the August meeting of the executive council, which Meany failed to attend because of his infirmities. The meeting took place in the midst of a mood of national discontent and growing signs of international crisis.

Two important steps were taken at the August council meeting. The first was the passage of a resolution urging the nationalization of the oil industry. The proposal was far-reaching, calling for a government agency to import oil, negotiate its price, and "allocate it throughout the society to best meet the needs of all segments of society." It then went even further, urging legislation that would prevent oil companies from acquiring or merging with companies in other energy-producing fields, in order to forestall the oil giants from dominating the burgeoning renewable energy sector. Never in its history had the AFL-CIO called for the federal takeover of a major segment of the economy; to do so would have violated labor's long-standing acceptance of America's commitment to the market economy. But many labor officials had come to believe that the OPEC cartel was primarily responsible for an energy crisis that was in turn driving up the rate of inflation; furthermore, they were convinced that American oil companies were in connivance with OPEC and acting against the American national interest. The statement carried a strong Kirkland imprint. He was certain that the oil industry was playing an insidious role by pressuring the United States to support the Arab cause. He also held a visceral dislike for giant American corporations that consistently disregarded the country's national interest in their dealings with foreign governments. He regarded these corporations as unpatriotic and believed it was essential that the federal government regulate their behavior lest they do damage to American workers and consumers and to national security. This was particularly important, he believed, in a critical sector like energy. At a press conference, Kirkland said that American unions were "not mad advocates of nationalization. But in this situation where you have ironclad control of a vital resource that is deeply imbued with the public interest . . . where they become energy companies, not just oil companies, it begins to take on . . . a wholly different coloration."[2]

The second major policy decision was to support the Strategic Arms Limitation Talks, or SALT II, the arms control agreement that stood as the linchpin of the administration's policy toward the Soviet Union. The council's endorsement of SALT II was something of a news item, since the previous February Kirkland had denounced the agreement as a "colossal failure of arms control." Kirkland, in fact, was generally unenthusiastic about arms control treaties that failed to demand serious cutbacks in weapons of mass destruction and saw little reason why labor should give its imprimatur to agreements whose real-world impact was minimal. During the intervening months, however, the administration had engaged in a relentless campaign to persuade a number of the more politically potent international unions to support the treaty. Once the Steelworkers had been brought on board, Carter's people were confident that Kirkland would adjust his stance in order to maintain peace within the ranks.

But labor's endorsement was less than wholehearted. In an early display of his political savvy, Kirkland ensured that the resolution was predicated on a series of demands for a strengthened defense that the administration was not likely to fulfill, including the modernization of American strategic forces, the development of the MX missile, and goals and timetables for the mutual reduction in nuclear warheads. Kirkland spoke for forty minutes on the issue, and when a vote was taken, only two of the council's more dovish members—Winpisinger and Murray Finley of the Amalgamated Clothing and Textile Workers Union—dissented. Both objected to linking SALT to the MX.[3]

And to remind the world that the AFL-CIO retained its view of the Soviet Union as dangerous and evil, the council issued a sharp declaration about the dangers of selling advanced technology to the Communists. This, too, was a theme that Kirkland often returned to in speeches about business morality. Just as oil company executives would cut deals with Middle East despots whose policies were inimical to American interests, so, he believed, corporate chiefs from high-technology sectors would gladly sell the Soviets and other adversaries the computers and other advanced goods that might prove critical to the modernization of their militaries. The resolution noted that recent Soviet high-tech acquisitions "would make Lenin's statement that the Western democracies would 'sell us the rope for their own hanging' seem like a prophecy."[4] At Kirkland's urging, the council also passed a statement rejecting the Transfer Amendment, a perennial favorite of the peace movement, which called for the shift of $15 billion from the military budget to social programs. The resolution noted that the country was rich enough to support both a robust defense and the common welfare.[5]

In late September 1979, Meany formally announced his retirement. Kirkland conveyed the decision to a hushed audience of reporters and AFL-CIO staff on September 28. Kirkland almost never displayed strong emotions in public, but on this occasion his voice quavered and, for one of the few times in his public career, he was unable to express his thoughts: "There is so much I feel I want to say . . . I cannot say anything." In answer to a reporter's question, however, Kirkland made clear that he intended to seek the federation presidency.[6]

At home, Kirkland drew up a list of executive council members on a yellow note pad, checking off the names of likely supporters, likely opponents, and those whose loyalties were unclear. Kirkland was the obvious favorite; indeed, as events were to prove, he was the only serious candidate. But even though Kirkland had often been described as the heir apparent by the press, he had never been so designated by Meany. Despite the closeness of their relationship, Meany had never spoken to Kirkland about the presidency, never discussed retirement, never dropped a hint to friends on the executive council that Lane was his choice for the succession.

Meany's silence on the subject encouraged the short-lived candidacy of J. C. Turner, the president of the Operating Engineers. Turner regarded Kirkland as lacking in charisma; he also professed to believe that the presidency by right should be passed down to another representative of the building trades. If Meany were genuinely neutral, Turner believed that he might succeed in putting together an opposition bloc among the construction trades unions. First, however, he and Martin Ward, the president of the Plumbers Union and a Meany friend, visited Meany in his Bethesda home, where he was convalescing. Asked for his blessings, Meany informed his guests that Lane was his choice for the job. Turner then withdrew from the competition, enabling Kirkland to be elected by acclamation.[7]

Why had Meany designated Lane as his successor? Quite simply, he saw in Kirkland someone who could assume the leadership role of all aspects of the labor movement. On one level, there was Lane's broad expertise, on matters ranging from pensions to electoral politics, to foreign policy, to the state of the individual unions that belonged to the federation. At the same time, as Jack Joyce, president of the Bricklayers' union, observed, Lane "had qualities that Meany respected: toughness, inner-directedness, thoughtfulness, sound judgment." "Lane was a good card player," Joyce said. "You never knew what he was up to. There was some of the way he played cards in his leadership style." Bob Georgine, the president of the federation's Building and Construction Trades Department, frequently played gin rummy with Lane. "Lane remembered all the cards that had been played, and he kept his own hand close to the vest. He knew his own strength, and he had a pretty good idea of his opponents' strength. And that pretty well sums up his relations with people as a trade union leader." Kirkland seldom displayed emotion at cards, though Irena and a few others who were sensitive to his moods could detect excitement or anger in the way his mouth worked or in his eyes. He seldom allowed himself open displays of temper. He told Irena that during his years at sea, his temper had been responsible for brawls in which he had come out second best. He subsequently directed his emotional energy into political work. Kirkland used his considerable powers of memory in relations with others. He catalogued important biographical information—achievements, problems, incidents. He even remembered to the date when they occurred and would remind the person about the incident to drive home a point. He was, Joyce said, "quiet when he was supposed to be and forceful when he had to be." Another quality Joyce admired was Lane's honesty in personal dealings. "I was around Washington for ten years and hardly ever encountered anyone who would say 'no.' They would say: 'We'll see about it,' or, 'I'll see what I can do.' Lane would say 'no.'" Added Joyce, "Lane never allowed the media or the intellectual class to define him. He was completely rooted, he knew who he was, and he was comfortable with it."

Lane's marriage to Irena was an important source of strength as he moved into a position of national political leadership. Irena was devoted to Lane and to labor. She marched with Lane in picket lines and cheered on his favorite political candidates. The two shared the same domestic political perspective, and both were unapologetic anti-Communists and strong advocates of the proposition that the promotion of freedom should be the centerpiece of American international policy. Both also believed that America should remain a haven for the persecuted and the scorned of the globe. Shortly after the two were reacquainted in 1969, Lane cited Irena (though not by name) in a speech he delivered to the American Trade Union Council for Histadrut. The subject of the speech was "Labor and Freedom," and Kirkland was dealing with the question, widely posed at that particular time, of whether the nature of a society's political system was important to the average citizen—that is, as Kirkland put it, would "the life of work, family, and small pleasures [remain] much the same, regardless of the condition of those abstractions, freedom and democracy?" He went on to relate that he had posed this question to a friend, an Israeli of Czech origin who had endured both the Holocaust and the oppression of Communism.

I was told that this was exactly the rub—that the oppression of plain people was precisely the most devastating and inevitable consequence of totalitarian rule. The most common trait of tyranny, I was informed by this voice of experience, is acute paranoia. They fear nothing so much as the rank and file of the people—and among the people, their greatest apprehensions and suspicions are directed toward the native instincts and aspirations of workers.

Irena was Lane's wife, partner, and confidante for the rest of his life. They were devoted to each other, genuinely enjoyed being together, and were mutually protective. In one of the very few instances in which he showed public anger, Lane circulated a letter he had sent to Robert Reich, the former secretary of labor under President Clinton, which expressed outrage over a description of a dinner party at the Kirklands' that was highly inaccurate and, Lane believed, insulting toward Irena.

With Irena as his wife and having attained the federation presidency, Lane Kirkland was a complete man.

Tom Donahue was elected to succeed Kirkland as secretary-treasurer. There were some mutterings about elevating a member of the staff to a leadership position, and several building tradesmen—including Martin Ward—were reported to have an interest in the post. But most international presidents were convinced that Donahue was the best man for the job. Smart, gregarious, and hard working, Donahue enjoyed the confidence of all factions within the labor establishment and was popular with mainstream Democratic liberals. He would prove to be the perfect complement to Kirkland.[8]

Upon Meany's retirement, Daniel Patrick Moynihan wrote Kirkland that given the choice between being able to name either the president or the chief of the AFL-CIO, he would choose the labor position, since it was "in institutional terms . . . the more important job."[9]

Kirkland probably agreed with Moynihan's assessment. He certainly harbored a deep love for the American labor movement. Like other men in politics, Kirkland disdained public expressions of emotion over political matters. But Kirkland had an almost sentimental attachment to organized labor. "He saw service to labor as a calling," recalled Jack Joyce. Kirkland not only agreed with Moynihan's appraisal of the importance of his new job—he often said that a cabinet appointment or an ambassadorship would represent a demotion—he held the conviction that the best possible society would be one guided by the values of American labor. He saw labor as the driving force behind liberal change in postwar America and believed that the great men of the movement—the Meanys, the Gomperses, the Dubinskys, and the Paul Halls—were as crucial to the country's success as was any group of politicians and adhered to a higher standard of ethical behavior than did elected officials. Kirkland's attitude was summed up in an interchange with Rachelle Horowitz, the political director of the American Federation of Teachers. Horowitz, one of labor's most effective political operatives, had been offered a position on the staff of Senator Edward Kennedy, and out of courtesy she had asked for Kirkland's blessing for the move. Kirkland said the decision was entirely hers; if she genuinely wanted to make the change, she should go ahead. But as she prepared to take her leave, he offered a final thought: "Rachelle, you will be theirs, not ours." Horowitz stayed with the teachers' union.

One area where Kirkland and Meany certainly differed was in their speaking style. Meany was earthy, entertaining, and sometimes insulting. He was at his best at press conferences; reporters were an appreciative audience for his caustic appraisals of the adversary of the moment, whether it was Nixon, McGovern, Carter, or Arthur Burns, the chairman of Nixon's Council of Economic Advisers and a favorite target of Meany's barbs. Although not particularly fond of the press, Meany liked to banter with reporters, and while he seldom said anything about federation policy that wasn't common knowledge, his one-liners kept the labor beat reporters satisfied. If they didn't have a real story to report, they at least had a quote or two from crusty George Meany.

Kirkland had an impressive voice dominated by southern cadences and a baritone pitch that sometimes dropped down to the bass level. He spoke with confidence and authority, qualities that were accentuated by the low richness of his tone. Kirkland was not as agile with the one-liners as was Meany. But there was never any ambiguity in his speeches; no listener ever doubted which side Kirkland was on. At press conferences, Kirkland's responses never included an ungrammatical sentence or an imprecise thought. In answering reporters' questions, he concentrated deeply, chose his words with careful deliberation, and often spoke quite slowly. As a result, he did not make a strong impression on television talk shows. "I am looking into my brain," he explained to Irena when she once suggested that his television appearances would be improved if he looked directly at the interviewer. By this, Kirkland meant he was devoting his considerable powers of concentration to giving an intelligent and accurate reflection of his and organized labor's views and could not focus on his on-air image.

Kirkland took great pride in his speeches. Although he always had a speechwriter on staff, he basically wrote his own drafts. The more important the occasion, the more attention Kirkland paid to the speech and the more of Kirkland's individual cadence was highlighted. Kirkland himself drafted his inaugural speech, writing it by hand the night before it was delivered. He took particular pride in the keynote speech he gave at each federation convention. He waited until the night before the speech was to be delivered, then wrote long into the night, banging out the sentences on an aging manual typewriter or by hand on yellow note paper. He kept a special folder in his desk that contained newspaper clippings with information Lane thought relevant to labor's condition. The material from these clippings would then find its way into the convention speech. David St. John, who wrote for Kirkland from 1988 until his retirement in 1995, had perhaps the most success of any of Lane's writers in capturing the texture of his voice. But even St. John found the work intimidating. "Writing for Lane was a challenge because he was such a good writer himself and because he did not speak a normal vocabulary. He wanted well-reasoned arguments and hard-hitting sound bites at the same time." St. John and his predecessor as writer, Tom Kahn, agonized over their boss's more significant addresses. Kirkland appreciated their efforts, even as he redid large sections of their craftsmanship. "He never asked me to do anything that he didn't regard as a personal favor, even though I was really just doing what I was paid to do," St. John said.

"Lane never gave a bad speech," said Bruce Miller, a Detroit labor attorney. "Every one of his speeches was evocative of trade unionism's highest ideals, appealed to humane values, and was well crafted. He was not a table thumper. His speeches were somewhat understated. I think workers appreciated that he was not talking down to them, but talking directly to them."

The Kirkland style was on display on November 19, when Lane addressed his first AFL-CIO convention as president of the federation. Lane worked especially hard on what amounted to his inaugural address. This would be the first time he would be presenting himself to the members of organized labor as their leader. It was on this occasion that he laid out his intention to bring back into the House of Labor the Teamsters, the UAW, and other independent unions that had departed, been expelled, or remained independent from the federation. "All sinners belong in the church," Kirkland said. "All citizens owe fealty to their country, and all true unions belong in the American Federation of Labor-Congress of Industrial Organizations. Their pride and pelf do not equal what they are missing because—to borrow from the *New Yorker*'s alleged view of the world—everything outside the AFL-CIO is really Hoboken."[10]

It has never been recorded how many reporters understood Kirkland's reference to "pelf"; anticipating an endless round of questions, the AFL-CIO public relations staff prepared special bulletins that informed reporters that according to the *Webster's New World Dictionary*, *pelf* meant "ill-gotten gains, booty; money or wealth regarded with contempt." Nor did Kirkland's reference to Hoboken go unnoticed; that city's mayor, Steve Cappiello, complained publicly about the perceived slur, as did John Grogan, a former Hoboken mayor and at the time president of a shipbuilding workers' union. Kirkland, who scorned political correctness, eventually issued a half-hearted apology.[11]

One sad event marred what was an otherwise triumphant occasion for Lane. During the convention, Paul Hall, president of the Seafarers, suffered a terrible fall, was rushed to the hospital, and was diagnosed as suffering from a serious brain tumor. Hall was a mentor and a confidant to Kirkland. A southerner—he was from Alabama—Hall was instrumental in forging the Seafarers into a powerful and modern labor organization. Kirkland was fascinated by Hall's habits of work: he could labor around the clock for days on end to resolve a crisis and then spend days of seeming idleness. Hall was exceptionally intelligent; he was also a well-read man who could quote the classics to make a point. He was a legendary master of creative profanity as well. "Chaucerian" and "literary" is how acquaintances described his use of four-letter words. Lane respected Hall's judgment; during his years as secretary-treasurer, he often sought the older man's counsel on matters of federation policy.

Both Hall and Meany—Lane's closest friends and beloved mentors— died within a few months of his election as president.

Kirkland did not deviate from trade union tradition in his dealings with the federation staff. The AFL-CIO was divided into separate departments for political affairs, legislation, international affairs, civil rights, organizing, education, and so on. Under Meany, the principal directorships were occupied by men who were loyal to the president, devoted to the institutional interests of the AFL-CIO, and in some cases, legends in their own right. Andrew Biemiller, Meany's chief lobbyist, was personally responsible for the passage of innumerable pieces of liberal legislation and the deep-sixing of many bills regarded as antilabor or just plain reactionary. Al Barkan, the COPE director, was the major architect of a powerful political machine. During most of Meany's tenure, the international affairs department had been run by Jay Lovestone, a mysterious figure who had shifted from Communism to anti-Communism and was the target of much rumor and conspiracy theorizing. Lovestone had been eased out in 1975; his successor was Ernest Lee, a marine veteran and Meany's son-in-law.

Kirkland, like Meany, believed that a trade union should not fire staff members unless they were guilty of disloyalty, corruption, or extreme incompetence. If a staff member was not measuring up, Kirkland's usual solution was to move him to another position within the federation or find him a job with some allied institution. Kirkland's fair treatment of subordinates reflected his own character. But it also derived from his notion of the proper behavior of a trade union leader. As David St. John put it: "Lane believed in living according to a trade union code of conduct. That meant you never sucked up to those above you and never mistreated those below you. And that you always treated people honestly. He really believed that the trade union code was superior to the way other institutions operated." Kirkland did not want yes-men in his inner circle, and he encouraged his associates to speak up if they differed from his proposed course of action. But he did not believe the federation should be run as a participatory democracy. "I have the final vote," he would tell his staff when decision-making time came.

Kirkland preferred to hire staffers who had actual trade union experience, either as elected officers or as staff. His staff had no one as colorful as Biemiller or Barkan. But Kirkland staffers generally shared a quiet competence, were hard working, and were comfortable with the latest techniques in conducting political campaigns or waging an organizing drive. Kirkland had a relaxed attitude toward staff supervision, much of which was carried out by Tom Donahue. Like Meany, Kirkland treated department directors as if they possessed a franchise on their operation. Kirkland gave the principal staff members their marching orders and let them determine how best to get the job done. The better staff members appreciated the Kirkland approach. "Lane was a great boss; he really treated you like a man," recalled John Perkins, who was appointed to succeed Barkan as director of COPE. But Kirkland's attitude toward staff performance could be a problem if the person in question was not producing quality work. "Lane had a nuanced way to letting you know he was disappointed in your work," recalled Adrian Karatnycky, who worked as an assistant on international affairs issues. "If you had a tin ear to his subtleties, you might miss the point altogether."[12]

Despite his reputation as being somewhat standoffish, Kirkland was responsible for many acts of kindness, acts that even close associates were unaware of. Once, during the Carter years, Lane received a call from the wife of a staff representative of one of the railroad unions, a man who had raised considerable amounts of political money over the years. The man was in prison on a corruption conviction. The wife told Lane that her husband was dying of cancer and asked if he could use his influence to have the man released to be with his family for his final months. Kirkland thereupon asked Hamilton Jordan, Carter's chief aide, to pay a visit to federation headquarters. "I know that what this man did was wrong," Ken Young recalls Kirkland telling Jordan. "But he's dying, and the administration should do something for him." Young recalls that Kirkland went out of his way to help trade unionists or others who faced personal troubles, much as he went out of his way to help political dissidents under repression from tyrants. That his generosity is at all known is due to the testimony of close associates like Young. Kirkland himself seldom spoke of his acts of personal kindness.

As his executive assistant, Kirkland chose Ken Young. Young had spent practically his entire life in the labor movement. He had started out with a union that represented insurance salesmen, worked for the International Union of Electrical Workers, and joined the AFL-CIO staff in 1965. Young had succeeded Biemiller as the legislative director and was thus well-connected with both the labor leadership and members of Congress. Young was proud of his CIO heritage and had the soul of a labor activist; he loved public manifestations of all kinds—rallies, picket lines, demonstrations. He was, at the same time, a man of sound judgment who knew everything there was to know about the AFL-CIO and its personalities.

The first thing Kirkland told Young was that he would never say or do anything that would sully the reputation of George Meany. "Lane told me: 'I will make no changes that George Meany would not have made. I was part of all the decisions that Meany made, and I agreed with them.'" Young took this stricture as signifying that Kirkland did not want the labor movement or the press to interpret the changes that he intended to make as a departure from the Meany tradition or a betrayal of the Meany legacy. If Kirkland's policy differed from the course that prevailed under Meany, Lane would explain that this was a different era and that Meany himself would have adapted to new times and new challenges.[13]

Kirkland did not make decisions on impulse. Confronted by a major challenge, he might ponder the problem for several days before deciding on a course of action. "He would sit and read and think," recalled Ken Young. "But when he finally reached a decision, he knew exactly where he was going. He had total confidence in the decision; he didn't second-guess himself."

Among the first issues facing Kirkland was the question of labor's role in the Democratic Party. By the time he was installed in the presidency, it was already too late to do much about the 1980 election except to stand aside and watch Carter and Senator Edward Kennedy slug it out for the nomination. But Kirkland could see serious troubles for the Democratic Party on the horizon. He also understood that Kennedy's challenge probably spelled doom for whichever man won the nomination. He was convinced that unless a unified labor movement exerted its muscle in party matters, the Democrats would remain divided and impotent in the face of the mounting challenge posed by a united, confident, and increasingly conservative GOP.

An immediate problem was Al Barkan. Under Meany, Barkan had run COPE with little interference from the president's office. Barkan was a man of strong convictions: he hated Goldwater Republicans, McGovernite Democrats, radical feminists, the peace movement, and the gay lobby in about equal degrees. And he loathed the constituency quotas for blacks, women, and for a time, young people that had been adopted by the Democratic Party. While other traditional Democrats suffered in silence, Barkan was voluble in denouncing the militant feminists, gays, and New Leftists—groups that were increasingly influential in party affairs. He blamed these new constituencies for the Democratic Party's troubles; they were, he believed, bent on displacing mainstream liberal forces like labor and on imposing an extreme agenda that alienated the party's working-class base.

Kirkland shared many of Barkan's misgivings. But he had decided that the party's drift to the extremes would only worsen if labor did not take action, and if this meant a coming to terms with affirmative action in internal party structures, so be it. Kirkland also decided that he, and not Barkan, would be making the key decisions about labor's political role. Barkan resisted; eventually, there was a showdown over the selection of trade unionists for the seats on the Democratic National Committee reserved for labor. Barkan wanted to appoint a group of international union presidents, all white males, who gave substantial contributions to COPE. When Kirkland told him to put together a list that included women and minorities, Barkan objected and told Kirkland that under Meany, he, Barkan, would have been allowed to make the decision. Kirkland responded with a full-scale dressing down, and Barkan emerged shaken from the meeting. The subsequent relations between the two were professional but never close, and in 1982, Barkan retired.[14]

It is worth noting that while Kirkland wanted diversity, he was strongly opposed to the appointment of women and minorities as token representatives. Those named to the DNC included a number of assertive female political operatives: Evelyn Dubrow, the long-time political director of the International Ladies' Garment Workers Union; Rachelle Horowitz, political director of the American Federation of Teachers; and Joan Baggett, political director of the Bricklayers. Dubrow later received a presidential Medal of Freedom; Baggett moved on to serve as executive director of the DNC and later as the White House political director under President Clinton; Horowitz served as chair of the DNC's rule committee.

The Barkan episode had a ripple effect through the federation staff. It conveyed the message that while Lane did not intend to micromanage department directors, he expected them to meet certain standards and to carry out the federation's, and his, policies.

The institution that Kirkland inherited was entering troubled times. This being the era of Carterite national malaise, the same could be said of just about every important segment of American society, business included. In some respects—the political arena, in particular—labor remained vigorous and influential. Labor's most serious problem was a failure to recruit new members to compensate for the loss of those whose jobs in core industries were disappearing. During the mid-fifties, trade unions enjoyed close to saturation representation in the heavy industries that stood as the backbone of the American economy. As the economy evolved and grew more diffuse, the percentage of jobs in basic industry declined in favor of jobs in white-collar and service sectors and in the ranks of management. Although labor retained its strength in steel, auto manufacturing, machine tools, and other traditional industries, unions failed to make serious inroads in the growth areas of the economy. Nor had labor made much headway in the solidly antiunion South, a region that was showing steady growth, just as the labor heartland of the Northeast and the Midwest showed accelerating signs of deterioration.

Labor had, of course, experienced recession before and had always regained strength once the economy picked up. But labor had a new phenomenon to cope with in the mid-seventies—new, that is, in the postwar environment: an aggressive business campaign to discourage the unionization of nonunion companies and eliminate union representation in companies where unions already had a foothold. Naturally enough, the determination of corporate America to resist unionization was reinforced by the defeat of labor law reform. By the decade's end, a cottage industry of lawyers, publicists, and strategists had sprung up, its energies devoted single-mindedly to the war against unionization. The impact was recorded in statistics reported by the National Labor Relations Board. In 1978, unions won slightly over half of union representation elections; the comparable figure for the fifties was 80 percent. There was also an increasing number of decertification initiatives brought by management—decertification barely existed in the fifties and sixties—and unions were losing three out of four of these procedures.[15]

Finally, because of what would later come to be known as a diversity gap, labor faced something of a public relations problem. At fifty-seven, Kirkland was among the younger members of the executive council. There were no women on the board and only one black, Frederick O'Neal, the president of a small actors' union. In a country and in an era in which youth, the participation of women, and racial integration were respected values, the labor movement seemed out of step with the times.

One of Kirkland's first significant moves as president was to address the diversity problem by bringing a woman onto the executive council. To accomplish this, Kirkland had to break with long-standing tradition, which held that only presidents or, in a very few cases, secretary-treasurers should occupy council seats. No woman served in either capacity in an AFL-CIO union at the time, so Kirkland had to persuade the council to approve the selection of a lower-ranking official, as well as to accept the fact that the new member's union would have two representatives on the council, while other major unions would have just one member.

At the time, women accounted for 30 percent of the federation membership; blacks for 25 percent. Blacks did hold a number of important-sounding staff positions in various international unions. But even in the most liberal unions, blacks seldom held positions of real influence. As for women, they occupied only 19 of the 324 important elected union positions and 144 of the 2,170 seats on union executive councils.[16]

Although a few union presidents opposed the breaching of tradition, the majority accepted Kirkland's arguments for the change. Kirkland then proposed Joyce Miller as the first woman council member. Miller was an official of the Amalgamated Clothing and Textile Workers and served as president of the Coalition of Labor Union Women, the principal women's organization within the ranks of labor. Miller, who was voted onto the executive council in August 1980, was well-known and respected by her male colleagues, and the choice was a popular one.[17]

Kirkland's next attempt to advance diversity proved more troublesome. Kirkland wanted a "two-fer," that is, a black woman, in order to satisfy two diversity slots. There was no dearth of candidates, as articulate black women held reasonably high staff positions in a number of unions. But Kirkland required that the candidate's union president give his assent before the choice would be placed before the council, and this proved an obstacle. Kirkland called one union president after another to inquire about the credentials of the black women among their leadership and in each case was urged to make another selection, usually on the grounds that the proposed candidate might embarrass them by voting differently on a crucial issue and sometimes because they regarded the candidate as a troublemaker. Finally, Kirkland settled on Barbara Hutchinson, a vice president of the American Federation of Government Employees and a member of the federation's civil rights committee. Once Ken Blaylock, the AFGE president, signaled his approval, Hutchinson's election was apparently assured. Some black labor officials, however, objected to Hutchinson and to the fact that the five candidates they had put forward were not considered by the nominating committee (federation officials contend that the concerns of the black union critics had never been conveyed to them). In the end, Hutchinson was given approval to join the executive council at the AFL-CIO convention in November 1981.[18]

Kirkland also brought a new style of leadership to federation affairs. Meany had a reputation of smothering debate through intimidation. As Jack Joyce put it: "There was a real lack of dialogue under Meany. He had been sitting as a federation leader since the 'thirties, and the council members felt intimidated by him. I think they misread his attitude to differences of opinion. But they wouldn't take him on. Most of the union presidents who boasted to the press about how they had challenged Meany in fact hadn't said a thing during the meetings." Kirkland actually encouraged union presidents to participate in council affairs, serve on committees, and speak their minds at meetings. "It was remarkable how a person with his powerful mind could be so patient with union leaders who were less articulate," was how Joyce put it. To Joyce, Kirkland's leadership style was an important model for the labor movement generally. "If you believe that the participation of the union is important on the job, then you are obliged to believe that participation is important within the union. Unions aren't by nature anti-democratic, but union leaders don't as a rule encourage the members to participate. But this is precisely what Lane tried to do on the executive council." To be sure, after everyone had had his or her say, Kirkland reserved the right to the final summing up. Kirkland was a master summarizer. He would pull out the essence of the discussion and then point his audience to the proper conclusion. Almost invariably, debate ended after the Kirkland summary.

Kirkland believed that a major role of the federation was to shape a common vision of labor's mission among union officials at every level. A second objective was to inspire the participation of union activists in political work. He sought to transform the federation from a Washington-oriented organization focused on lobbying to something that was capable of influencing political affairs from the grass roots as well.

To this end, he encouraged a revival of activism among the lower ranks of labor officialdom. The vehicle was a series of regional meetings where he, Donahue, and other federation officials would make presentations on the issues of the day and then open the floor for questions. This was a new experience for lower-level union officials. Initially, local activists were often reluctant to ask pointed questions or air complaints. Eventually, Kirkland convinced his audience that no subject was out of bounds, that local officials should openly air their concerns, even if it meant challenging the national AFL-CIO or embarrassing their own unions. He also made it a practice to walk a picket line with a striking union in whatever city the meeting was held.[19]

According to Jack Joyce, Kirkland was a man "who did not suffer fools gladly." This comment pretty well sums up Kirkland's attitude toward certain members of the working press who covered labor affairs. Kirkland did respect a few labor beat journalists, those who were knowledgeable about unions and were modest enough not to assume that they knew more than Kirkland did about how to lead the labor movement. But

Kirkland was offended by some of the younger reporters, who treated labor leaders with condescension and believed that they were better qualified as labor experts than were the movement's elected leaders. Another pet peeve was the press's treatment of labor as something of a backwater. Many newspapers assigned coverage of labor affairs to young reporters who were ignorant about the movement and not particularly keen on educating themselves about it. In the old days, at the time of the AFL and CIO merger, labor was a coveted assignment on big city newspapers and national magazines. Serious intellectuals had started their careers as labor journalists, the best example being the eminent social critic Daniel Bell, who covered unions for *Fortune* during the 1950s. By the time of Kirkland's presidency, high-profile journalists and intellectuals were assigned to cover race relations and the culture wars but not labor, and reporters treated the labor beat as a way station on the road to a plum assignment covering the White House or international affairs. Many press outlets had abolished the labor beat and treated union developments as part of overall coverage of the business community.

Kirkland had certain principles in dealing with the press. Bruce Miller had recommended that Kirkland grant an interview to Tony Snow, at the time a young but obviously talented journalist who had just moved from the *Detroit News* to the *Washington Times*. Snow called Miller and told him that Kirkland wouldn't return his calls; when Miller asked Lane why he was snubbing the reporter, he was told, "I'm not about to give an interview to a reporter from a nonunion paper."

"My problem with journalists is much the same as my problem with academics," Kirkland once told Rex Hardesty, his spokesman. "By dint of their profession, they are forced to ask questions to which any intelligent person would respond: 'I don't know.'" Kirkland hated the "I don't know" questions, such as: "Has labor hit bottom?" Or: "Can labor recover from this latest defeat?" "I'm not going to give a seminar in Labor 101," Kirkland would tell aides who beseeched him to be more forbearing. Kirkland had occasional run-ins with Irving R. Levine, the bow-tied, pedantic television correspondent. Levine once arrived late to a press conference and missed a juicy Kirkland quote. He thereupon pestered Kirkland with questions, repeating again and again that he didn't "have a clear understanding." Kirkland finally responded, "Irving, I can dispense information; understanding you'll have to get on your own." Levine did not get his sound bite.[20]

No one greeted Lane Kirkland's elevation to the AFL-CIO presidency with more enthusiasm than Jimmy Carter. The president and his aides were relieved that there would be no more report cards with C– grades.

But Carter's people viewed the change at the federation's headquarters as not merely the removal of an especially prickly critic; they had high hopes that under Kirkland, organized labor would forge a partnership with the administration as the election season drew near. Some theorized that as a fellow southerner, Kirkland might feel a special kinship for the president from Plains, Georgia. Although disappointed by some of Carter's policies, Kirkland remained hopeful that the administration would embrace a course that would focus on job creation and energy independence. He also respected various Carter aides and cabinet members. Finally, Kirkland recognized that whatever Carter's deficiencies, he was infinitely preferable to any of the Republican hopefuls, especially given that party's sharp lurch to the right.[21]

A few months before Meany's retirement, Kirkland had gotten a close-up view of the Carter team in action as a participant at the Camp David "summit" meeting to which the president had summoned a number of leading personalities from government and the private sector to mull over the nation's problems. The meeting, dubbed the "malaise summit" by the press, did not reinforce Lane's confidence in the president's leadership qualities.

The summit consisted of a series of informal sessions with eminent figures from government and the private sector. It took place in the midst of the administration's "national malaise" period, and Carter, by Kirkland's account, seemed torn between seeking honest advice or elite reinforcement for decisions he had already reached. Along with Kirkland, the meeting included, among others, Jesse Jackson; Sol Linowitz, a prominent diplomat; and Clark Clifford, the Washington gray eminence.

After dinner the first evening, everyone gathered in the president's lodge. According to Kirkland, Clifford—"ever the courteous courtier"—opened the meeting with a sycophantic tribute to Carter's leadership skills, all delivered in "mellifluous, honeyed tones."

As Kirkland later recalled the event, Clifford's introduction went something like this:

> Mr. President, you are without doubt the most thoughtful, the most qualified and the most dedicated person to serve in the White House during my long years of service in Washington, and I have known many presidents. Your problem, sir, is this: Why is it that those fine qualities, which I perceive so clearly, are not fully appreciated by the public at large?

Carter, Kirkland recalled, "dutifully wrote these remarks down on a pad." Next, a discordant note was sounded by Jackson and Linowitz who,

Kirkland said, advanced the proposition that Carter's woes could be traced to the disloyalty of certain cabinet members, specifically Joseph Califano, Health, Education, and Welfare; W. Michael Blumenthal, Treasury; and James Schlesinger, Energy. Carter demurred on the question of Schlesinger, noting that the energy secretary had offered to resign if doing so was deemed expedient, but he was noncommittal on the other two. Kirkland, however, disagreed with the proposed dismissals, calling the three cabinet secretaries "able public servants following a rather uncertain trumpet." Kirkland added that the officials in question, "if given solid backing rather than being undercut by White House staff, could perform their duties well." No one seconded Kirkland's objections, and Schlesinger, Califano, and Blumenthal were duly dismissed following the summit.

The next morning, they all met around a conference table to hear from First Lady Rosalynn Carter, who reported on her soundings around the country. A discussion of energy policy ensued, with Kirkland pressing hard for the AFL-CIO's preference for strong controls on the oil industry, stressing the overriding objective of gaining American energy independence. Carter subsequently emphasized the importance of energy "freedom" for America but ignored the substance of the AFL-CIO position.

On the helicopter ride back to Washington, Kirkland sat next to Jesse Jackson, at the time best known as the head of Operation PUSH, the Chicago-based organization that pressed major corporations to hire minority workers. Jackson began chewing Kirkland's ear about the labor movement's relations with the civil rights movement. Jackson, according to Kirkland's account, said, "You know, Lane, the AFL-CIO shouldn't keep giving money to outfits like the NAACP and the Urban League. They can't help you when you get harassed on civil rights. You ought to support me. I can cover your ass."

Kirkland responded that labor "had a strong tendency to stick by our friends, which I shared. That we were closely allied to the two organizations, that that is the way it had been and that is the way it was going to be."[22] Having been rebuffed by Kirkland, Jackson would in a few years be attacking organized labor for its alleged lack of racial diversity.

The "malaise summit" was followed by the entry of Senator Edward Kennedy into the presidential race. Under ordinary circumstances, labor might have opted for Kennedy in a primary clash. Kennedy was a friend of labor who embraced the agenda of labor almost down the line, spoke the language of labor, and could inspire the labor rank and file as could few other politicians of the time. But Carter had the advantage of incumbency and thus had reason to believe that he could prevent a consolidation of labor support around a Kennedy candidacy. To this end, Carter had supported policies of interest to different unionized industries—trade restrictions to help garment manufacturers and steel companies and support for several measures of particular importance to the building trades.

As early as the summer of 1979, several important union leaders were assembling a Labor for Carter Committee. The driving force behind the initiative was Glenn Watts of the CWA. Other unions quickly signed on, including the United Food and Commercial Workers, the Steelworkers, and the National Education Association, a large teachers' organization that functioned outside the AFL-CIO. A majority of the building trades unions also backed the president.

But Carter's base of support within labor was unimpressive for a sitting Democratic president. The UAW, the Machinists, AFSCME, and the American Federation of Teachers—big unions with political clout— mobilized behind Kennedy. Internal union polls gave Kennedy the clear edge, not only in the unions that were backing the challenger, but in unions where the leadership had opted for Carter, including the CWA and the Steelworkers. At some union gatherings, the criticism of Carter grew so intense and angry that Al Barkan, who was privately for Kennedy, was compelled to warn labor officials to keep their misgivings to themselves, lest the president be weakened further.[23]

Through all this, Kirkland remained publicly noncommittal. While there was considerable speculation about his personal preference, no one could say with certainty which candidate he privately favored, so close to the vest did he play it. In all likelihood, Kirkland preferred Kennedy's unambiguous liberalism to Carter's indecisiveness and economic centrism. But he appreciated Carter for his willingness to endorse the National Accord. And he was privately unhappy with Kennedy's candidacy. "The voters will never forget Chappaquiddick," he told Irena. Furthermore, Kirkland believed that although Kennedy could not win a general election, he could so thoroughly divide the Democratic Party as to ensure a Republican victory.

Kirkland had another reason for seeking to heal labor's rift with the administration. He was at the time deeply involved in negotiations for an unprecedented agreement—dubbed the National Accord—that he hoped would usher in a new era of cooperation between the administration, labor, and the business community and would give labor a role in the formulation of important elements of national economic policy.

To Kirkland, the National Accord represented the first step toward a much more ambitious goal: a tripartite system under which business, labor, and government would collaborate in the formulation of policy and the establishment of overall goals for the economy. Within policy circles, John Dunlop was the principal supporter of tripartitism; he had promoted the idea, without success, in the early days of the Carter presidency. Ray Marshall was another supporter of the concept. Kirkland, despite his firm grounding in the traditions of American labor—with its preference for an adversarial relationship between labor and management—had been impressed by the European system, in which cooperation was emphasized both in relations on the shop floor and in the higher circles of economic decision-making. Kirkland saw problems on the horizon for his movement: the decline of basic industry, the impact of trade with low-wage countries, and the determination of management to create a "union-free environment" in wide swathes of industry. After the failure of labor law reform, Kirkland looked to the tripartite model as an instrument for labor's revival.

The National Accord germinated from a series of summer 1979 meetings involving Kirkland and Landon Butler, the Carter administration's liaison to organized labor. In Kirkland's account, Butler had initiated discussions by asking what it would take to get labor on board in support of a national policy on wages. Kirkland responded that labor "would have to be a part of the wage-policy decision-making process." He added that "if the government wanted us to voluntarily waive some of our legal rights—such as free collective bargaining—we, in turn, had several issues with the government that we wanted favorably resolved."[24]

The two then embarked on a series of lunch meetings at a Washington restaurant, Jean-Pierre. At the first meeting, Kirkland drew up a list of seven labor demands while Butler took notes on a laundry receipt. A few days later, on July 11, Kirkland met in a more formal setting with several Carter aides, including Vice President Mondale. Kirkland spoke for a full ninety minutes, laying out his philosophy of what he called "shared austerity." This was Kirkland at his eloquent best—a tour de force performance during which, as one Carter assistant put it, Kirkland "put each one of those parochial labor issues into a framework on the state of the economy."[25]

The terms of the accord required labor to acknowledge that "the war against inflation must be a high priority" and to participate in a Pay Advisory Committee that was to chart the course of the next phase of the administration's campaign for wage restraint. In return, the administration agreed to labor's proposals on a series of issues of special concern to unions. The accord also spelled out in some detail how the administration would shift away from a strategy dictated by the needs of the business sector in the fight against recession. According to Kirkland, the accord included several verbal commitments agreed to by the administration that were not set forth in the formal document but that were "crucial to the unanimous agreement" of the executive council.[26]

Negotiations continued through the summer under ultrasecret conditions; Kirkland kept even key members of the executive council in the dark until talks were well along the way. In early September, an obstacle emerged in the person of Charles Schultze, the chairman of Carter's Council of Economic Advisers. At a September 14 White House meeting, Schultze proposed that the pay board operate under a tight set of principles that would be set down by the administration—a "fettered board," in the parlance of the negotiators. Kirkland, supported by Ray Marshall, opposed Schultze's scheme as a deal-breaker. Debate raged between Carter's economic advisers, on one side, and his political aides, on the other; in the end, Carter decided that labor's political support in an election year trumped the apprehensions of his economic team, and he opted for the unfettered board.[27]

The National Accord was unveiled at a press conference at which both Kirkland and Carter spoke. Among other things, it was announced that John Dunlop would serve as the chairman of the pay board, a reassuring choice for labor. But while the National Accord was billed as a partnership between labor and government toward conquering the recession, the agreement did not, in fact, give the unions a serious role in the economic policy process. It was rather a vehicle to allow the Carter administration to claim the cooperation of labor in an election year. Kirkland, however, was not discouraged. He was a realist and recognized that the accord was an essential part of a long-range process to revitalize American industry and organized labor at the same time. He interpreted the agreement as the first step toward a new paradigm for economic policy—"an American version of a British-style 'social contract'" is how he put it. It would take time, and possibly a different administration, to achieve full implementation of what would be, for the United States, a new way of determining national priorities. The National Accord was the first step in what Kirkland saw as a protracted struggle. As long as the Democrats held the White House, Kirkland was optimistic about labor's chances of prevailing in that struggle.[28]

The president and other administration officials wrapped themselves around Kirkland during a media event in the Old Executive Office Building on September 29. Not only were Carter and Ray Marshall present, but Charles Schultze and Alfred Kahn, another member of the president's economic team, both of whom were skeptical of the wisdom of the National Accord, tagged along in an effort to upstage Kennedy. To reinforce his credentials with labor, Carter took several additional steps, including signing an order giving the go-ahead for the completion of the

Tellico Dam, a Tennessee project that had been held up by the supposed danger to the snail darter, an obscure fish, and by the strong opposition of the environmental movement.[29]

On the surface, then, the advent of the Kirkland leadership seemed to augur an era of collaboration and warm feelings between labor and the administration. In practice, labor and the administration had lingering differences over the direction of the antirecession strategy and other issues. It became clear early on that forging a workable consensus on the pay board would prove a monumental challenge. Signs of rancor between Kirkland, on the one hand, and the representatives of business and the administration, on the other, were already present at the board's first meeting, on October 18. Kirkland was adamant that workers should make every effort through collective bargaining to compensate for wages lost through OPEC price hikes. He also made clear his dislike for a one-size-fits-all guideline, such as the 7 percent figure set down by the administration the previous year. The only agreement to emerge was that it would be a long, slow road to progress for the pay board.[30]

Although Kirkland spent much of his time criticizing budget cuts and price gouging by Big Oil, he recognized that the long-term prospects for reindustrialization—and for the revival of the labor movement—could not be achieved through a strategy that focused solely on the domestic economy. As early as 1980, Kirkland was what might be described as a premature critic of globalism. He had become convinced that as long as multinational corporations could shift resources from one country to another with no obligation to their home land, there would be unchecked pressure on employers to depress wages because of increased competition from businesses around the world. Multinational corporations, he said, "can make their separate peace with whatever barriers or incentives exist in the world." He contended that free trade could not exist as long as multinationals were free to practice "rampant mercantilism."[31]

A resolution of the trade dilemma was a long-term proposition. Kirkland's immediate challenge was to unify labor behind the Carter reelection effort. This was no easy task, since even Kirkland could not hide his disappointment in the administration's economic course. Prior to the Democratic National Convention, Kirkland told a reporter that the AFL-CIO would support the president "with some enthusiasm and considerable peace of mind," not exactly a ringing endorsement. But Kirkland preferred to dwell on Carter's negatives, noting with disappointment that the president had succumbed to the "hysteria" of a balanced budget and was showing signs of joining the "tax-cutting hysteria" that was being spread, with some effectiveness, by Reagan.

Kirkland urged Carter to eschew across-the-board tax cuts—he called them "wasteful windfalls"—in favor of targeted assistance to troubled industries like steel. He endorsed a "period of shelter" for the auto industry to provide time for an adjustment to the "predatory practices" of foreign competitors, especially the Japanese who, he said, "move in like tiger sharks." "I think we have one of the more ruthless systems in the world in terms of relations between the worker and the job," he said. "By and large, we still hire workers by the hour and lay them off by the hour."[32] Kirkland also urged Carter to scrap other aspects of the 1980 budget, which he saw as undermining any chance of setting the National Accord in motion. Ken Young and Rudy Oswald, the AFL-CIO's director of research, spent an entire morning remonstrating with key administration economics officials, to no avail. Young came away believing that Carter's people gave no more than lip service support to the agreement.

But while Kirkland may have harbored misgivings about Carter, he saw in Reagan an unapologetic champion of what from labor's perspective were the worst features of the American system. Aside from an economic philosophy that stressed a free market system with minimal government restrictions, Reagan was on record as favoring a number of measures that unions regarded as particularly objectionable. Reagan or his aides were prone to muse about the application of antitrust laws to labor-management issues, a prospect that alarmed labor leaders, since such a change might place in jeopardy such long-standing practices as industry-wide bargaining, strikes, product boycotts, and agreements between unions to resolve jurisdictional disputes. Reagan had opposed labor law reform, favored a subminimum wage for teenagers, and called for repeal of the Davis-Bacon Act, under which wages are set on federally assisted construction projects. Unlike Nixon and Ford, who had been satisfied with opposing the expansion of union power, Reagan seemed intent on rolling back laws and practices that had been embedded in the American labor-management system for years. Labor thus feared Reagan as it had not feared previous Republican candidates; its attitude was summed up by a COPE statement that said, "No presidential candidate in modern times—including Barry Goldwater—has gone so far in urging the demolition of unionism as it is practiced in America."[33]

Yet not even the looming presence of Reagan could impose a disciplined and united stance among the various institutional and constituency factions within the Democratic Party. A minifuror erupted at the August Democratic convention over a Kennedy proposal for a platform endorsement of a $12 billion jobs-for-the-unemployed program. Carter, through his chief aide, Hamilton Jordan, rejected the proposition; in response, Kirkland and Doug Fraser weighed in strongly in favor of the Kennedy plan, and labor delegates, including those committed to Carter, pressured their state party leaders to line up behind the proposal. After the labor leaders made their displeasure known, Carter issued a meaningless clarification in which he supported the goals, but not the means, of a high-price-tag jobs scheme. This response failed to satisfy Kennedy, who asserted that the party should take the opportunity to advance a Democratic solution to one of the country's more serious problems. Jordan responded that it would be a mistake to advocate a major spending item when the American people were demanding fiscal restraint. Carter then agreed to a fuzzy formulation that could be interpreted as indicating his intention to ignore the jobs plank. This, too, was rejected by Kennedy's people, who passed along their misgivings to Kirkland. It is unclear what happened next, but within a half hour Jordan placed a frantic call to Kirkland with the message that there had been a rethinking by the president. Ten minutes later, new language was put forward in which Carter gave halfhearted endorsement to the jobs proposal's "spirit and aims." With this, Kennedy gave formal support of Carter, and labor remained on board.[34]

On August 20, the executive council gave formal endorsement to the president. But instead of providing a desperately needed boost to the beleaguered Carter, the AFL-CIO action was further evidence of the lack of enthusiasm for the incumbent by a key member of the Democratic family. Bill Winpisinger was the only no vote; he announced that he would support the candidacy of Barry Commonor, a radical environmentalist running as the nominee of the Citizens Party. Two other union presidents—Fred Kroll of the Railway Workers and Captain J. J. O'Donnell of the Airline Pilots—abstained; both had differences with administration proposals for the regulation of their industries. Five council members were absent, and several of these were known to have serious reservations about the wisdom of supporting the president. Some union leaders had even urged postponement of the council decision, proposing instead that each union negotiate concessions from the administration in return for campaign support; this group included a number of Kennedy supporters. They dropped this idea after Kirkland forcibly reminded them that whatever his shortcomings, Carter was clearly preferable to the Republican candidate.[35]

Once the AFL-CIO's endorsement had been made formal, COPE launched an aggressive campaign both for the president's reelection and for the reelection of a long list of endangered Democratic incumbents. Barkan called the fall COPE drive "the most intensive, costly, expensive political operation in our history." But the challenge was daunting; at the time of the council endorsement vote, polls showed rank-and-file union members preferring Reagan. In tacit acknowledgment of

Carter's unpopularity, the COPE campaign stressed Reagan's conservatism rather than the president's record. In some states—Michigan, Ohio, Pennsylvania, New Jersey—unions comprised the only organized force behind Carter, as local party organizations concentrated on congressional and Senate races.[36]

In the end, the results were far worse than Kirkland or other labor officials had anticipated. Reagan not only rolled over Carter by an impressive margin, he carried with him enough Republican Senate candidates to give the Republicans control of the upper house for the first time since the Eisenhower years, thus ensuring that Reagan would have a working majority to push through much of his program. Many of the new GOP legislators were deeply conservative and hostile to labor; after 1980, the pro-labor, Rockefeller wing of the party barely existed. As for the labor vote, it went for Carter, but just barely, 47 percent to 44 percent— well short of the 63 percent Carter had earned four years earlier.

Some labor officials consoled themselves with the notion that the shift in the political winds was only temporary, a product of Carter incompetence and bad luck. Once the Republicans failed to restore economic health and Reagan was revealed as an extremist, the country would again look favorably on liberal ideas and liberal candidates. Sol Chaikin said publicly what other labor officials believed privately: that many workers had voted "against their own self-interest." But polls conducted by the AFL-CIO and other unions showed that union members had embraced Reagan out of a complex series of motives. Many, in fact, agreed with Reagan's position on a number of the hot-button social issues that the Republicans had exploited so effectively during the campaign: abortion, welfare, affirmative action, gun control. For justifiable reasons, organized labor declined to come down on one side or the other on certain issues: the AFL-CIO took no position on abortion or gun control, questions on which the rank and file were divided. But the poll results did suggest that convincing those who came to be known as the "Reagan Democrats" to return to the liberal fold would demand a more subtle strategy than simply offering an alternative to Reaganomics.[37]

Meanwhile, a sign that difficult times were ahead came with the announcement that Orrin Hatch, the Utah Republican who had spearheaded the campaign against labor law reform in the Senate, would assume the chairmanship of the Senate Labor and Human Resources Committee. Hatch immediately announced his intention to seek a rollback of the minimum wage for teenagers.

In keeping with his respect for the presidency, Kirkland's initial comments were conciliatory toward Reagan. He noted that there were "elements of reality and of good will and of the judgment of history that will work against running, administering, and operating a presidency that is in the pocket of or wholly identified with narrow segments of American life." He added that while Reagan's economic philosophy might lead to conflict, "we're not going to start on the assumption that what might turn out to be bad already has."[38] But Kirkland understood that the election results had cost labor dearly. Not only were the White House and the Senate in firm conservative control, but labor's hopes of gaining a role in the economic policymaking process had been dashed, possibly for years to come. Under Reagan, there would be no National Accord, no tripartite arrangements, no consultation on "shared austerity," and no schemes for government-supported reindustrialization.

As 1980 neared its dreary end, Kirkland saw his mission as making sure that the Reagan interlude lasted only four years. He had already held a series of meetings with the three most powerful Democrats in the post-Carter period—Mondale, Kennedy, and Speaker of the House Tip O'Neill—to devise a strategy to bring the party together and prevent another debacle similar to those in 1972 and 1980.[39] Even before the election, he had emphasized the necessity of the return of a unified trade union movement to the Democratic fold, and he had already decided that labor should not simply participate in party affairs but should play a leading role in the party's revival.

5

LABOR VERSUS REAGAN

AS THE YEAR 1981 BEGAN, LANE KIRKLAND PREPARED TO MEET FORMIDABLE challenges on a number of different fronts. Ronald Reagan was soon to be inaugurated, and while the details of his economic program were yet to be spelled out, everything he had said during the campaign indicated a radically different economic course than that followed by Jimmy Carter. With prospects for the National Accord in ruins, Kirkland would need to move quickly to devise a labor strategy to counter the budget cuts that were surely in the offing. Within a few months, he would assume de facto leadership of a broad coalition that was opposed to Reagan's domestic policies. On the international scene, Kirkland was in the midst of a project to mobilize international labor support for Poland's Solidarity union, whose formation the previous August had shaken the very foundation of the Communist world. Kirkland also faced a volatile situation in Central America; in early January, three men who worked for the American Institute for Free Labor Development (AIFLD), the AFL-CIO's Latin American arm, were murdered at the instigation of right-wing military officers. Kirkland was also in the midst of sensitive negotiations to convince the United Auto Workers to rejoin the federation as the first step toward his goal of labor unity.

An in-depth look at Solidarity, Central America, and labor unity will be found in subsequent chapters. For Kirkland, at the beginning of 1981, the most critical issue of the hour was Reagan, Reaganism, and Reaganomics. Although Reagan had run as an unabashed conservative, Kirkland and other labor leaders hoped that once in office, he would behave pragmatically and treat labor with the same respect as had previous Republican presidents. This meant, at minimum, refraining from a frontal assault on labor's parochial interests. It also meant the appointment of a secretary of labor whom the trade union leadership could trust. Labor leaders recalled that Dwight Eisenhower, a business-oriented president whose closest friends were drawn from the highest circles of corporate America, had appointed an outstanding—from labor's perspective—secretary of labor, James Mitchell. Likewise, the AFL-CIO had respected Richard Nixon's secretary of labor, George Shultz, and regarded Gerald Ford's labor secretaries, John T. Dunlop and William Usery, as friends.

A sign that rough times were ahead came with the process followed by the Reagan transition team for the selection of a labor secretary. In the past, the general practice for new Republican presidents was to submit a list of potential candidates to the president of the AFL-CIO to determine if any of those under consideration were deemed unacceptable. Reagan, however, chose not to consult Kirkland during the cabinet selection process. Nor did he follow the advice of those in the Republican Party who had experience in dealing with labor issues, such as Orrin Hatch. Hatch, though no friend of organized labor, promoted the candidacy of Betty Southard Murphy, a moderate who had put in a term as chairman of the National Labor Relations Board. Murphy had served as a liaison between the Reagan campaign and the top labor leadership; she had helped arrange a meeting between Kirkland and Reagan adviser Ed Meese and had also played a role in securing the Teamsters' endorsement for the Republican candidate. She was considered acceptable by the AFL-CIO, the Teamsters, and the U.S. Chamber of Commerce.[1]

But Reagan eschewed the usual practice of choosing a Republican who enjoyed the confidence of both organized labor and the major organizations representing corporate America. He instead chose Raymond J. Donovan, a partner in the Schiavone Construction Company, one of New Jersey's largest building contractors, whose specialty was highways and other large government-funded projects. Donovan had been a major contributor to the Reagan presidential campaign and had played an important role in the president-elect's efforts in New Jersey. Aside from his having represented Schiavone in negotiations with building trades unions and having gained a reputation for maintaining labor peace in the rough-and-tumble of the New Jersey construction industry, there was nothing in Donovan's biography to suggest that he was qualified to run the Department of Labor. That he boasted neither credentials nor stature suggested that Reagan regarded the labor department as a policy backwater.

Kirkland was irritated at being excluded from the selection process and puzzled by the choice of a complete unknown. At the same time, he was willing to give Donovan the benefit of the doubt. Nothing in his resume suggested a hostility to unions, and building trades officials from New Jersey who had dealt with Donovan described him as a man of his word and a "stand-up guy." There was, however, one discordant note: the National Right-to-Work Committee and other antilabor organizations greeted Donovan's selection with undiluted enthusiasm; they were especially pleased that he had been selected, instead of a moderate figure like Betty Murphy. Carter Clews, an official of the National Right-to-Work Committee, reported that his organization had submitted a series of questions to Donovan and that the new secretary had answered every one to the right-to-workers' satisfaction.[2]

Donovan quickly demonstrated that the high expectations of the right-to-work movement were well-grounded. He was wont to tell interviewers that he intended to be a secretary of all labor, not just organized labor. Other labor secretaries had expressed similar sentiments, but Donovan also seemed to find it difficult to say anything positive about the role of unions in the economy or at the workplace. More disturbing was that some proposals for cutbacks in regulations and programs for workers and the poor began to filter out from the labor department. Under the decentralized system that prevailed under Reagan, Donovan had considerable latitude in setting the tone for the administration's labor policies. From the beginning, he established the department's priorities without seeking the counsel of Kirkland or other mainstream labor leaders.[3] When Donovan announced plans to reorganize his department, he credited the Heritage Foundation, a conservative organization deemed unfriendly to labor, the Business Roundtable, and "some unions" with having supplied worthy ideas.[4]

Donovan had promised Kirkland early on that he would not blindside labor by issuing new regulations without first notifying the AFL-CIO. But Kirkland was neither notified nor consulted when, with monotonous frequency, cutbacks and changes in regulations were announced by Donovan and his deputies. Thus the department proposed rules that would relax protections for workers from cotton dust and lead as well as the rules governing homework—garment work done by workers from their homes on a piece-rate basis, a practice that, among other things, made unionization efforts almost impossible. Kirkland accused Reagan of using the labor department "to dismantle programs that have been in place and that have been fundamental to the modern and civilized industrial society." Nor was Kirkland amused at an anonymous administration official's statement that labor should be grateful "for the things we are not doing," such as interfering in the collective bargaining process or imposing controls on wages.[5]

Donovan further alienated Kirkland by his behavior at the federation's February executive council meeting in Bal Harbour. As was customary, the federation asked the labor secretary to brief the labor leadership on relevant administration policies. Donovan explained some of the initiatives planned by the Reaganites; then, at a subsequent press conference, he claimed that the proposals had received strong backing from the trade union leadership and said that he had received a standing ovation at the end of his presentation. At his press conference, Kirkland corrected the record: there had been no enthusiastic expressions of support for Donovan's ideas and absolutely no standing ovation. Kirkland had strong feelings about men who, he believed, had behaved dishonestly, and after the Bal Harbour incident (although not solely because of that incident) he began to treat Ray Donovan as a nonperson. Kirkland refused to utter Donovan's name at press conferences, declined to meet with him, and dealt with the administration through other figures, such as Vice President George Bush.[6]

About this time presidential adviser Ed Meese and William Casey, the director of the CIA and a Kirkland acquaintance, paid a visit to Kirkland. The two Reagan officials said they understood that the AFL-CIO and the administration would be at odds on some issues but hoped that labor would support the administration on issues of mutual interest. As the meeting wound up, Kirkland asked Meese and Casey to come to his window and enjoy the view of the White House, clearly visible across Lafayette Park. Kirkland then said, "The best thing is that after you're gone, we'll [meaning labor] still be here."[7]

In fact, Reagan's people well understood that they had but a limited window of opportunity to effect the kinds of broad policy changes that candidate Reagan had promised. Reagan set the tone in his inauguration address: "In the present crisis, government is not the solution to our problem; government is our problem. . . . It is my intention to curb the size and influence of the federal establishment." Reagan then proceeded to propose major cuts in the budget he inherited from Carter and sizable reductions in federal taxes. By the end of May, four months into his term, he had succeeded in pushing through his first budget by winning enough Democratic votes in the House to defeat a Democratic alternative. Reagan then proposed a whopping 30 percent tax cut, eventually compromising on a 25 percent reduction over three years.

At its annual February session in Bal Harbour, the executive council denounced the president's economic package as a "high risk gamble with the future of America." Kirkland told reporters that the Reagan plan was based on "exceedingly dubious and esoteric theories."[8]

On March 4, Kirkland had several testy exchanges with Republican lawmakers during testimony on the budget before the House budget committee. Unlike other witnesses, who praised the budget's overall thrust while differing on certain details, Kirkland adopted a position of down-the-line attack. He said that the president's program was "based on an untested theory, unrealistic projections, and questionable logic" and called the budget "the most costly roll of the dice ever proposed for this

country by economic policymakers." Kirkland contended that
Reaganomics would lead to more joblessness, less energy security, and a
deepening crisis for cities and basic industries. When Rep. Ed Bethune,
an Arkansas Republican, asked whether Kirkland planned to "undermine
and obstruct the president," Kirkland shot back, "If we have convictions
. . . we do not intend to set them aside and march lockstep. We're exer-
cising our rights as citizens, and I make no apology, sir." As to charges that
the voters had given Reagan a mandate for change, Kirkland asserted that
"no presidential candidate has a right to cut black lung benefits unless he
campaigned on that platform in West Virginia," a reference to a proposed
benefits reduction for a chronic disease of coal miners.[9]

Kirkland was also concerned about the general tenor of the administration, which seemed intent on changing the informal rules that for
decades had governed relations between organized labor and the federal
government. The Donovan appointment was Exhibit Number One.
Another source of concern was the flurry of regulatory changes that
removed burdens from the business community while relaxing protections for workers, minorities, and consumers. Reagan was packing his
domestic agencies with appointees who, in many cases, were openly hostile to the declared mission of the agency. Whether it was the Justice
Department, the Equal Employment Opportunity Commission, the
NLRB, or OSHA, the watchword was a more user-friendly regulatory
environment and, where possible, a reduction in agency budget and personnel. Many appointees came from the corporate world and seemed
ignorant of the workings of their agency or the issues with which it dealt.
Some came from businesses that were subject to the agency's regulation,
suggesting a conflict of interest. Labor was unsettled by the appointment
of a building contractor, Thorne Auchter, to head the Occupational
Safety and Health Administration (OSHA); one of his first acts was to
eliminate health and safety warnings to textile workers. Like other
Republicans of the past, Reagan had run on a platform that promised a
less adversarial regulatory regime; unlike the others, Reagan took his
promises seriously. It was, as E. Pendleton James, Reagan's director of
personnel, put it, "a whole new ball game."[10]

In these early months of the Reagan administration, organized labor
was practically alone in its disapproval of each and every new domestic
initiative. Kirkland was critical of proposals for a special subminimum
wage for teenagers, a favorite project of conservatives. Kirkland opposed
legislation introduced by Senator Charles Percy, an Illinois Republican,
that called for a subminimum wage for younger workers during a six-
month initial period on the job, a measure that included special protections for older workers. Among other things, Kirkland regarded the

Percy proposal as a camel's nose in the tent for more radical tinkering by conservatives, some of whom advocated outright abolition of any minimum wage whatsoever.[11] Kirkland also headed up a coalition of thirty-seven groups that protested cutbacks in affirmative action regulations in the workplace.[12] And on March 27, Kirkland joined in a protest rally organized by the United Mine Workers to oppose the proposed cutbacks in the black lung program. Several thousand took part in the rally outside the White House—men with gnarled or missing fingers, weather-beaten faces, and other tell-tale emblems of hard lives spent in the pits of Pennsylvania, West Virginia, and Kentucky.[13]

Kirkland was also disturbed by the administration's trade policy. In early July, the White House issued a white paper on industries facing decline because of foreign competition. The report spoke of low-wage countries that have a "natural competitive advantage" and said that American industry "must find a way to upgrade its capabilities" or shift its resources to other, nonmanufacturing, areas. To Kirkland, this bespoke a "sink or swim" philosophy that justified the virtual abandonment of the country's basic industry capacity. He accused the Reaganites of viewing "the world as it appears in a book, but not as it really is." "Other nations do not apologize for pursuing their national interest," he said. "Yet the U.S. is under constant assault when suggestions are made to move in the U.S. national interest."[14]

By midyear, then, relations between the White House and the AFL-CIO had deteriorated to the point where communications between the two sides were minimal. Presidential aides groused about the polemical vocabulary employed by Kirkland; they urged labor leaders to be "respectful and civil and stop using excessive rhetoric." In truth, Reagan's inner circle was uninterested in organized labor's perspective on the state of the economy. Reaganomics stood for everything labor opposed: tax cuts skewed toward the upper-income brackets, less spending, deregulation, free trade, a survival-of-the-fittest attitude toward America's declining industrial base. To some of Reagan's hard-bitten lieutenants, a dialogue with the AFL-CIO made no sense as policy, given the wide gap between the two sides, and even less sense politically, given the administration's strategy of treating critics as special-interest pleaders. In a July 1 memo to chief of staff James A. Baker III, presidential adviser Lyn Nofziger asked, "When are we going to quit trying to be nice to Lane Kirkland?" Reagan officials often noted that Kirkland was regarded as an ally on national security and foreign policy issues. Such comments betrayed a misunderstanding of the distinct international role labor had adopted—a role that was independent of any party or president. They were also cold comfort to Kirkland, who felt that labor's preference for a policy anchored by a commitment to roll back Soviet power was being undermined by Reagan's lack of respect for the AFL-CIO's views on domestic matters.

In this environment of one grim development after another, an incident at the White House provided a brief moment of levity. The occasion was a meeting with Reagan's economic team, led by Donald Regan, the secretary of the treasury, and Murray Weidenbaum, chairman of the Council of Economic Advisers. Kirkland was accompanied by Doug Fraser and Frank Fitzsimmons; the three labor leaders listened while Regan outlined the administration's program to stem inflation and stimulate the economy. Then Weidenbaum twitted the trade unionists by asking if there were items in the budget that they would propose for spending reductions. Kirkland and Fraser had nothing special to offer, but the usually inarticulate Fitzsimmons had an immediate and animated response. As Fraser recalled it, Fitzsimmons, his voice rising with genuine anger, blurted out, "I'll tell you one reduction you can make. You can get rid of the witness protection program. You're wasting millions of taxpayer dollars to support these stool pigeons and their families." Fraser later asked Kirkland what he was doing during the Teamster's diatribe. "I was looking at the floor," Kirkland said. To which Fraser replied, "I was looking at the ceiling."[15]

On August 3, the Professional Air Traffic Controllers' Organization (PATCO) launched what proved to be one of the most disastrous labor actions in the history of American trade unionism. Although the controllers' strike temporarily damaged commercial air traffic in the United States, it was the controllers' union and organized labor generally that were to suffer the most devastating long-term consequences. The strike— or, more precisely, Reagan's response to the strike—cost over 11,000 controllers their jobs and destroyed PATCO. It enhanced the stature of the president at a time when many Americans were beginning to doubt the wisdom of his economic course. It emboldened government at every level to deal more firmly with public employees. It also encouraged private employers to take a tougher line in dealings with unions. The PATCO episode even had international reverberations. In Europe, where illegal labor actions were more common—and more likely to be tolerated—than in the United States, government officials and corporate leaders looked on in wonderment at the display of presidential resolve; special note was taken by the British prime minister, Margaret Thatcher, then just embarking on a campaign to curb the power of militant unions that was to drastically shift the balance in labor-management relations in the United Kingdom. The *Economist* of London summed up European attitudes in its headline: "The Sacking Bomb."

When Kirkland arrived in Chicago in early August for a meeting of the federation's executive council, his overriding concern was to forge a unified labor strategy to counter Reagan's domestic policies. He was aware that the air controllers' union was locked in tense negotiations with the government. Indeed, in June Kirkland had sent Reagan a telegram expressing concern about the lack of negotiating progress between the union and the Federal Aviation Administration (FAA) and voicing sympathy with PATCO's demands.[16] But PATCO had not notified Kirkland or other AFL-CIO officials that a strike was imminent, had not sought the advice of more experienced union leaders, and had not indicated that it might need the support of other unions. When Tom Donahue put in a call to the union to see how negotiations were progressing, he was informed that everything was under control and that PATCO knew what it was doing.[17]

Like most federal worker unions, PATCO enjoyed collective bargaining rights but was forbidden to strike under U.S. law. When hired, air controllers had to sign a statement agreeing not to strike on pain of a fine and possible dismissal. In addition, the controllers were still subject to a nonstrike pledge made in the aftermath of a brief job action, a "sick-out," in 1970.[18]

Yet while public worker strikes were illegal almost everywhere, unions that represented government workers were increasingly treating strike prohibitions as a nullity. In the one previous major strike by federal workers, President Nixon had declined to seek harsh penalties against 200,000 postal workers who struck nationwide in 1970. Instead, Nixon ordered National Guard and Reserve units to handle the mail in New York and directed his postmaster general to resume collective bargaining with the union. Union officials were occasionally given brief jail sentences, but sanctions were rarely, if ever, taken against the rank and file. Given this history, it is not surprising that the air controllers believed that the administration was unlikely to impose draconian penalties for defying federal law.[19]

The union had another reason to suspect that it could act with impunity. During the 1980 presidential campaign, PATCO, whose membership included a substantial number of young, white, Republican veterans of the military, had broken ranks with the rest of labor and supported Ronald Reagan. Reagan, in fact, had sent a friendly note of greeting to the union's convention in May that thanked PATCO for its support during the campaign and expressed appreciation for the "important and complex job PATCO members perform."[20]

The union had been working without a contract for several months. In late July, transportation secretary Drew Lewis put forward an offer centered on an 11 percent pay hike per year over the three years of the contract, but which did not meet PATCO demands for changes in working conditions and hours. The union's president, Robert Poli, urged acceptance, but the membership voted to reject the proposal by a whopping margin of 20 to 1. PATCO's counteroffer called for a $10,000 increase across the board, a shorter work week, earlier retirement, and other items. When Lewis turned the proposal down, PATCO gave the administration seventy-two hours to come up with an acceptable offer or face a strike.[21]

In its confrontation with the administration, PATCO thought it had a trump card: air safety. "If passengers are killed," Poli warned Lewis, "it'll be your responsibility." But Reagan didn't blink. Faced with the air safety issue, the prospect of a crippled air travel system, and a serious setback to an airline industry already in difficult straits due to deregulation, Reagan adopted a firm position. At 11 A.M., four hours after the strike began on August 3, Reagan met reporters in the Rose Garden, where he announced that the controllers had forty-eight hours to return to their posts or face immediate and permanent dismissal. An aide described the president as "emphatic," regarding the strike as "desertion in the line of duty."[22]

Two days later, the administration launched a massive campaign against PATCO that made use of every punitive measure available under federal law. Dismissal notices were sent to the striking controllers. The administration moved against PATCO's finances with fines and seizures. The Justice Department filed criminal charges against the union leadership—twenty-two PATCO members were booked on felony counts in the strike's first few days. The administration impounded the union's strike fund and decertified the union as bargaining agent for the controllers.

Poli insisted that the union would not yield to government pressure and said the controllers would "stay on strike as long as it takes." But only a few days into the strike, it was apparent for all who cared to see that PATCO had been thoroughly beaten. In addition to the dismissals, the arrests, and the fines imposed on PATCO and its members, the administration was moving to rebuild the air control system. By August 7, the administration had pieced together a workable air control system, utilizing managers, nonstriking controllers, and some five hundred controllers ordinarily used by the military.[23]

Lane Kirkland learned of the strike on the morning of the first day of the executive council meeting. His initial response was to support PATCO's right to strike. "I respect the law," he told reporters hours after the strike began. But he added that when working people "feel a deep sense of grievance, they will exercise what I think is a basic human right, the right to withdraw their services, not to work under conditions they no longer find tolerable." He added that the union's demands were reasonable and compared the administration's actions to the government's response in the Danbury hatters' case in the first decade of the twentieth century, a legendary labor conflict in which workers' homes and bank accounts were seized. "Harsh and brutal overkill" is how Kirkland described the government's measures.[24] Privately, he regarded the strike as an act of civil disobedience that, as Ken Young recalls, "might result in punishment but certainly not the death penalty."

Kirkland was also concerned about the strike's impact on the trade union movement. As president of the federation, Kirkland had no power to order PATCO back to the bargaining table or to compel the union to accept the government's offer. The cards he had been dealt, principally by the controllers' union, were limited.

Kirkland placed on the table a proposal for broader labor action to support the controllers and directly challenge Reagan's hard line on the dismissals. Almost immediately, it became clear that the unions that would be crucial to an escalation of the confrontation—whether in the form of a strike, a refusal to cross picket lines, a work-to-rule, or some other form of protest—were unwilling to do anything beyond offering moral support to the controllers, and some wouldn't even go that far. A solidarity strike by the pilots and the machinists would have effectively brought air travel to a halt. Kirkland turned first to the Machinists' president, Bill Winpisinger. Winpisinger responded that he would consider a sympathy strike if the pilots would join in, knowing already that the pilots were strongly opposed to a job action.[25] The pilots' union president, Captain J. J. O'Donnell, said bluntly that his members would not honor PATCO picket lines, explaining that pilots looked on the controllers as adversaries rather than colleagues. He added that his members would vote him out of office if he tried to persuade them to engage in a sympathy strike. He also threw cold water on PATCO's contention that Reagan's actions jeopardized passenger safety. His members, he said, might consider a strike if flying conditions were unsafe, but he added that reports from unionized pilots indicated that the risk of accidents was no greater than normal. Winpisinger then said that mechanics at several airports had refused requests to observe PATCO picket lines; if anything, rank-and-file workers were less supportive of PATCO than was the machinists' leadership. Left unstated was a pervasive resentment of PATCO among other airline industry unions because of the controllers' failure to support job actions they had initiated in the past.

According to the *New York Times*'s veteran labor writer A. H. Raskin, the word most often employed by union leaders to describe the strike was *suicidal*. Doug Fraser, attending his first executive council meeting since the UAW reentered the federation, said publicly that the strike could do "massive damage" to organized labor. In contrast, when asked whether the controllers' strike could "destroy" the labor movement, an exasperated Kirkland responded, "The labor movement has been [described by you as] destroyed and destroyed and destroyed. Yet we survive. We serve a basic human need."[26]

On August 6, Kirkland acknowledged that the American people were supporting Reagan. He also put a damper on calls for a general strike, something that he recognized as totally incompatible with American history and culture. "It is all very well to be a midnight gin militant to stand up and call for general strikes," he told the press. "But member unions will have to make their own appraisals. I am not going to make that appraisal."[27]

It was already clear, a day or two into the strike, that Reagan saw the conflict as an opportunity to demonstrate his resolve. The president's behavior belied his reputation as poorly informed and disengaged from key policy decisions. Several cabinet members who favored less draconian punishment than permanent dismissal decided against putting forward alternate solutions in the face of Reagan's obvious strong feelings on the matter.

The strike's outcome had a chilling effect on public worker unions, which now feared that every governor, mayor, or county administrator harbored the desire to emulate Reagan's tough line. And the collateral damage was not restricted to the public sector unions. In the private sector, management was emboldened to take a tougher line in contract negotiations and to demand union concessions. And companies that were intent on remaining union-free became even more willing to violate federal labor laws, convinced that their tactics enjoyed the tacit approval of the White House. As Donald Devine, Reagan's director of personnel management, put it, the president's handling of PATCO "put some spine in the private sector executives in their dealings with labor."[28] Reagan's adamant insistence on firing the controllers also had important international repercussions. Richard V. Allen, Reagan's first national security adviser, called PATCO "Reagan's first foreign policy decision." Not only did PATCO encourage foreign leaders in their dealings with unions, it sent a message that this was a president who was capable of bold, unpredictable moves and who was not bound by the old ways of doing things.[29]

Whatever his private reservations, Kirkland never uttered a critical word about the strike or the union leadership in public. Immediately after the executive council, he, Irena, and other AFL-CIO leaders returned to Washington by bus, stopping along the way to join PATCO picket lines in various cities. Asked whether Americans should travel by air during the strike, Kirkland said that to do so would be "highly imprudent": he charged the administration with trying to enforce a yellow-dog contract, a once-common practice whereby employers demanded that workers agree to foreswear union membership as a condition of employment. In a speech to union leaders, he accused Reagan of breaking the "implicit social contract" whereby the state recognizes unions as the legitimate representatives of workers. In a passage triggered by administration assertions that the president and not the unions was best qualified to speak for working people, Kirkland accused Reagan of trying to "conceal the radical nature of his policies by claiming the support of those who would suffer the most" from them. Privately, he also urged union leaders to stop criticizing PATCO in public.[30]

Kirkland reached out to his contacts within the Republican Party, most notably Howard Baker, the Senate majority leader, to piece together a solution that would provide penalties for both the union and the workers but would also offer the prospect of eventual reinstatement for individual controllers. The contours of the compromise included the following: Poli and other union leaders would resign, admit the strike was illegal, and acknowledge that the union members had been misled by them; the administration would agree to rehire the air controllers, except for Poli and his lieutenants and various union "troublemakers"; the controllers would agree to sign documents acknowledging the strike's illegality; a prominent citizen such as George Shultz would be appointed to conduct a fact-finding study with recommendations for future federal policy; and finally, Kirkland would issue a statement indicating that the strike was illegal, that the president had acted properly, and that the solution was not amnesty but a fair resolution, given the union leadership's role in misleading the membership.[31] Baker reportedly signed on to the plan and agreed to present it to officials in the White House. In the end, however, Reagan himself vetoed any compromise over PATCO. Reagan's willingness to ruin the lives of American workers appalled Kirkland. Rex Hardesty recalls overhearing his boss telling Ed Meese over the phone, "We're not talking about five-letter words like PATCO and union; we're talking about going on the battlefield and shooting the wounded. We're talking about amnesty for brothers and sisters who have lost their lifetime work."[32]

Reagan's men were deaf to such emotion-laden entreaties. For the time being at least, the administration believed it could roll over any and all adversaries, labor included. Its confidence was buttressed by the release of a Harris poll that showed 39 percent of union members supporting the president's handling of the controllers' strike and by polls that indicated that, overall, Americans regarded PATCO as the most signal achievement of the president's first nine months.[33]

Kirkland stepped up his rhetorical attacks on the president. He began comparing Reagan's actions in the PATCO case to the attempts by the Communist authorities in Poland to destroy Solidarity, the independent Polish trade union that was in the process of being formally established after a wave of strikes forced the regime to participate in negotiations. In a Labor Day statement, Kirkland declared, "What remains to be established is, Where's the rest of him?" an allusion to the movie *King's Row*, in which Reagan played a man whose legs had been amputated. "Where's the heart? And where's the understanding of people's problems that will make it possible to have a decent resolution" of the strike. Originally, Kirkland planned to deliver this statement on CBS Radio. But the network, perhaps skittish over Republican complaints of liberal media bias, claimed the text was overly political and canceled the broadcast. Kirkland retorted that the action was "strikingly similar to the dispute in Poland between the Solidarity union and the government controlled media," in which the Communist authorities denied the independent union access to radio and television.[34]

Unlike many of his fellow labor leaders who would have been happy never to hear the word *PATCO* again, Kirkland never abandoned the controllers. Kirkland, to be sure, had no use for Poli. "It stuck in Lane's craw that Bob Poli ruined that union," recalled Rex Hardesty. "Lane felt that Poli had struck a deal [with the transportation department] and then abandoned the field after it became clear that the rank and file would not accept it." But Kirkland spent years trying to gain a measure of justice for the controllers. He established a relief fund, chaired by Msgr. George Higgins, a Catholic theologian with strong ties to organized labor, that distributed over $750,000 to unemployed PATCO members. He and Ken Young worked closely with the new union that was formed to replace PATCO after it was decertified. And he continued to press behind the scenes for the controllers' reinstatement, using his contacts in the media and the Republican Party to try to persuade Reagan and, after him, President George Bush to show a bit of magnanimity and lift the blacklist. Kirkland finally succeeded, though not until the election of Bill Clinton.[35]

Even before the air controllers' crisis, Kirkland had decided to hold a rally in the nation's capital as an act of protest against the administration's domestic policies and as a response to Reagan's declaration that labor leaders did not speak for or reflect the views of their members. Kirkland announced the rally after a number of local labor leaders suggested a march on Washington during a series of regional meetings in 1981. The march was dubbed Solidarity Day, a name inspired both by the Polish union and the old labor song "Solidarity Forever."

The great protest rallies of the civil rights movement provided the organizational model for Solidarity Day. Although Kirkland understood that holding a rally against Reagan's domestic agenda did not enjoy the same moral stature as the campaign to overcome legal segregation, he did hope that the coalition model that the civil rights movement had embraced in its most successful phase could provide a blueprint for Solidarity Day and perhaps beyond.

As a warm-up to the big rally, Kirkland served as the grand marshal at a huge Labor Day parade up New York's Fifth Avenue. It was an impressive event, drawing some 160,000 trade unionists and featuring a procession of fire trucks, heavy construction equipment driven by building tradesmen, and moving vans driven by Teamsters. A battalion of several thousand air controllers and their families were among the marchers; they chanted, "Strike, strike, strike." One of their number, Steve Wallaert, a member of the Norfolk unit, who had been photographed being hauled off to jail with his hands manacled, marched with a chain around his neck.[36]

Solidarity Day proved to be a stunning success, drawing either 250,000 marchers (according to the park service) or 400,000 (labor's estimate), figures that either equaled or exceeded the assemblage for the 1963 March on Washington for civil rights and exceeded the big antiwar rallies of the 1960s. Virtually every significant union brought members from around the country, as did organizations representing blacks, Hispanics, women, environmentalists, the disabled, the elderly, and various organizations of the political left.

Kirkland believed that to build a movement powerful enough to defeat the Republicans at the polls and in Congress required a broad-tent approach to coalition building. He thus invited to serve as rally sponsors a number of liberal-left organizations, including some whose names had not been traditionally linked to trade union causes and a few who had occasionally lined up against labor during policy debates. At the same time, Kirkland wanted to maintain control over the proceedings and to keep the rally's message focused on Reaganomics and its victims. Participants were asked to use only the official march slogans on their banners. Gay and lesbian organizations were also permitted to march, though they, too, were asked to use march slogans and to eschew the pink triangle, out of fear that it might offend blue-collar workers.[37] The speakers, however, were chosen from the mainstream of the labor and civil rights movements.[38]

Kirkland's remarks touched on the anti-Reagan themes that he had been sounding since the first round of social spending cuts had been announced. But he did strike a powerful cadence in linking the rally to the American values of fairness and equality. "If you reject the notion that only the state, through its chief executive, faithfully expresses your will—look about you, you are not alone. If you believe that governments are raised by the people, not as their enemies but as their instrument to promote the general welfare, look about you, you are not alone." As for the administration, Kirkland said that "those who have risen to power in this city have set out to strip the government of any capacity to serve your needs and aspirations. They have set out to cancel and dismantle the safeguard of a humane society and to commit us to the economic jungle."

In preparation for Solidarity Day, John Perkins, the march organizer, met regularly with a battery of law enforcement and intelligence agencies: the Capitol police, the Secret Service, the metropolitan police, the park police, and the Treasury Department. "We tracked every [radical] group," Perkins recalls. Perkins also placed several bands at strategic places within the march route. He had been informed about the various points at which radicals might be waiting, in the hope of bursting in on the march. To forestall this possibility, Perkins had the bands march on the curb in such a way as to prevent any intrusion on the peaceful flow of events.[39] The march went off without disruption.

Abetting the day's success was an unintended conspiracy of events on Wall Street and within the administration. The previous day, a Friday, the stock market fell to its lowest level in two years. Around the same time, Reagan's budget director, David Stockman, had been on the air almost daily with announcements of new cuts in politically sensitive programs, including a proposal to defer a scheduled increase in Social Security benefits that produced howls of disapproval from Republicans and Democrats alike. Reagan himself spent a quiet day at Camp David, while advisers kept him apprised of the goings-on at the Solidarity Day rally. While some aides had urged the president to aggressively attack the rally as a naked Big Labor power grab, Reagan was content to issue a statement expressing sympathy with the frustrations of working Americans and blaming their woes on the sick economy he had inherited.[40]

For Kirkland, Solidarity Day was an unalloyed success. He was given widespread credit for an event that gave promise of a reinvigorated labor movement. Labor had been routinely derided as a spent force, a movement, in the words of more than one headline writer, that was "in disarray," that lacked aggressiveness, creativity, and daring. Solidarity Day put these criticisms to rest.

Furthermore, Solidarity Day was one among several signs that the honeymoon between Ronald Reagan and the white working class was on increasingly shaky grounds, as unemployment figures continued to head toward double-digits and joblessness replaced inflation as the major preoccupation of the American people.

One sign that Reagan was concerned about his standing with working Americans was an attempt to forge a détente with the AFL-CIO leadership in the fall of 1981. First, in late November, Reagan hosted the leadership of his favorite union, the Teamsters. The meeting was uneventful, except for Reagan's promise to Roy Williams, the new (and already indicted) Teamster president, that he would oppose further deregulation of the trucking industry and a statement that was interpreted as indicating that Reagan might soften his stance on the dismissed air controllers. After the Teamsters departed, the president's aides scrambled to assure the press that Reagan's remarks about PATCO had been misinterpreted and that he in fact continued to hold fast to his determination to bar their reinstatement.

On December 1, Kirkland came to call, flanked by members of the executive council. Prior to the meeting, the *New York Times* columnist William Safire, a Reagan supporter and a personal friend of Kirkland's, urged the president to reach a compromise on the controllers' fate. He reminded Reagan that politics was not "total war" and that it was alien to the American political tradition to "demand blood" in clashes with adversaries.[41] Reagan, in fact, was generally conciliatory; he was reported to have said, "I never anticipated I would be estranged from labor with all the years I put in as a union member" with the Screen Actors Guild. Reagan then asked whether the two sides could "consider starting over." But when Kirkland and Fraser broached the air controllers' fate, Reagan, according to Fraser, "told a ridiculous story about his father bringing home a pink slip on Christmas Eve, the point being that he understood the plight of the controllers."[42] Nor was Reagan willing to compromise on the elements of his anti-inflation program to which labor objected. Kirkland told Reagan that "deep principled differences" divided labor from the administration, and little of substance was accomplished. After the labor delegation departed, Reagan's spokesman, Larry Speakes, described the session as "frank" and "businesslike," two terms that in diplomatic parlance usually indicate that things didn't go terribly well.[43]

What did Kirkland actually think of Reagan? For one thing, he never forgot that as president of the Screen Actors Guild, a much younger Reagan had embraced positions that were consistently to the left of the American Federation of Labor. In private conversation with Irena and others, Kirkland often harked back to his experiences with Reagan, then governor of California, during their service on the Rockefeller Commission, at which Reagan was notorious for making assertions that betrayed serious lapses in judgment. Now, ten months into the president's first year in office, Kirkland had reached even gloomier conclusions. In an interview with William Serrin, the labor reporter for the *New York Times*, Kirkland described the president as both out of touch with the lives of ordinary Americans and something of a bully in his dealing with the air controllers. Noting the president's frequent descriptions of a happy youth spent in an America uncorrupted by big government, Kirkland declared that his own boyhood in South Carolina had led him to quite different conclusions. "I remember when farm houses were lit by kerosene lamps—the good old days before government got on our backs with the Rural Electrification Administration. I remember the days when malnutrition, pellagra, hookworm, were widespread—the good old days before government got on our backs with the Public Health Service. I remember the days when the county poorhouse was the sure destination of destitute senior citizens—the good old days before government got on our backs with Social Security." As for the controllers, Kirkland complained that Reagan had mobilized "all the instruments of public relations and propaganda against these working people and their families . . . including arresting some of these working people in shackles, nice young men hauled off to jail."[44]

One consequence of the standoff with Reagan was a slight pulling back from labor's support for the defense budget. For years, Winpisinger, Jerry Wurf, Murray Finley, and a few other labor doves had lobbied for a less hawkish defense stance, without effect. But at the August 1981 executive council meeting, a phrase was inserted in an official resolution declaring that "our support for national defense . . . is not to be taken as a blank check for the Pentagon."

This innocuous formulation was followed by stronger words in a resolution adopted at the February 1982 council meeting. The statement declared that "labor's long-standing support for a strong national defense does not oblige it to support a defense budget that is unfairly financed." The Reagan defense buildup, it said, was being paid for by the working classes; as an alternative, the AFL-CIO proposed a progressive surtax on individuals and a tax on the gross profits of corporations. Kirkland told reporters that the government is obligated to sustain the common welfare, as well as the national defense. "It does not suggest trade-offs," he added. "This strong country, properly led and managed, ought to be able to do both. But this administration has imposed an intolerable trade-off, imposing it on those who have the least to give and who have gained the least from the fruits of our democratic society." Kirkland recalled the criticism directed at Lyndon Johnson for having refused to request a tax increase to pay for the Vietnam War; now, he added, Reagan was proposing a major defense increase at the same time that he was implementing a "$750 billion rich man's tax giveaway," a measure Kirkland called "the most irresponsible fiscal act of my memory." He worried that Reagan's policies would "split the country over defense issues" and destroy "the element of consensus that had been slowly built up that we ought to do something to enhance our defenses."

To Kirkland, the issue of the defense versus domestic spending trade-off was a matter of first principles. Like other Cold War liberals, he had engaged in a long and ultimately losing fight for the soul of liberalism that centered around the trade-off question. He and like-minded liberals had long argued that it was politically and morally irresponsible to oppose defense spending on the grounds that the federal budget was a zero sum document, in which any money devoted to guns meant less resources for social needs. Kirkland was confident that the United States was rich enough to deal with both domestic and defense priorities. He also believed that as put forward by the left, the guns-versus-butter thesis was fundamentally dishonest, since the peace movement cared little about budget priorities but cared a great deal about forcing the United States to withdraw from its global commitments and retreat to a position of neo-isolationism. Along with others among the steadily shrinking band of "Defense Democrats," Kirkland had long foreseen that the party would remain in crisis as long as it was perceived as antidefense or even as ambivalent about the nation's military needs. The Defense Democrats had the satisfaction of being proved right, but of little else, as the post-Vietnam, antidefense mindset plagued Democrats even after the collapse of the Berlin Wall.

There had always been a minority wing of dovish-minded union leaders within the AFL-CIO, even in the heyday of George Meany. With Reagan in power, however, the equation shifted somewhat. Committed doves were emboldened to argue their case for a critical stance toward defense matters; other labor leaders were so enraged at Reagan's domestic policies that they concluded that a stance of opposition to Reaganism on all fronts was the only appropriate response.

While Kirkland believed that the administration was undermining popular support for defense by its reductions in the domestic budget, he was determined that the AFL-CIO maintain its historic commitment to an internationalist perspective that supported both a robust defense and American engagement in the struggle for global freedom. He therefore created a special defense committee within the executive council with the mission of making recommendations for labor's future policy toward long-range defense needs. While some observers interpreted the committee as a concession to the federation's left wing, a more accurate assessment would be that the committee was a vehicle to deflect nascent antidefense sentiment. The committee's first chairman, Jack Lyons, the president of the Ironworkers, was a certified hawk, as was his successor, Jack Joyce, the Bricklayers' president; the committee was dominated by supporters of a strong defense; and the staff member assigned by Kirkland to work with the committee, Tom Kahn, had strong anti-Communist views.[45]

In addition to its divisions over international affairs, the Democratic Party was giving evidence of growing confusion over a response to Reaganomics. Kirkland was particularly disturbed by the willingness of Democratic members of Congress to support critical aspects of Reagan's domestic program. He was vexed by Democratic support for the balanced budget amendment, a favorite of conservatives, that called for a constitutional requirement for a balanced federal budget. Kirkland pronounced the Senate's approval of the measure as "the greatest act of political cowardice and chicanery in modern political history." Twenty-two of the Senate's 46 Democrats voted for the amendment, including 11 incumbents who were up for reelection that fall.[46]

By mid-1982, the national focus was no longer on Reagan's boldness as a leader. It was, instead, trained squarely on the unemployment rate, which climbed inexorably. It finally reached the magic 10 percent mark—10.1 percent, to be precise—a month before the off-year elections. This represented a higher rate of unemployment than the United States had registered when it entered World War II. Other economic indicators also pointed to a deepening recession. The poverty rate reached 14 percent, the highest in fifteen years, and the trade deficit was at an all-time high as well. The press regularly featured human-interest items centered on struggling American workers who had suffered the double blow of a layoff and cutbacks in the social safety net ordered by Stockman, Donovan, or other Reagan officials. Reagan's approval ratings sank below the 50 percent mark; it seemed as if the message that Kirkland had been pounding home ever since Reagan assumed office—that Reaganomics were meant to further enrich the wealthy at the expense of all the rest—was beginning to register.

The results of the congressional elections only reinforced the perception that Reagan was on the defensive and also provided further evidence of a labor revival. Although the Republicans managed to retain their margin of 54 to 46 in the Senate, they suffered a major setback in the House, losing 26 seats, enough to deprive the president of the working majority of Republicans and moderate Democrats that had supported much of the administration's legislative package. Polls showed labor union families returning to the Democratic fold by a two-to-one margin and indicated that union families made up a huge 40 percent of the Democratic vote. In the Senate, twenty of the thirty COPE-endorsed candidates triumphed; in the House, the figure was 63 percent. The Democrats did especially well in Rust Belt states, winning back a number of seats that had previously gone to Republicans.[47]

In December came yet more bad news for the president: the unemployment rate shot up to 10.8 percent. With over 12 million out of work, Kirkland called on Congress to enact job legislation immediately rather than wait for the new Congress to be sworn in. "If it takes riots in the streets to bring about movement, I would regret that," he announced. "I think we have a democratic society that is supposed to be responsive. If all else fails and then people come to the conclusion that the only way they can get people's attention is to create turmoil in the streets, well, then, I guess we have to go out and organize some turmoil in the streets, if that's what it takes to convince people."[48]

6

ALL OUT FOR FRITZ

THE 1982 MIDTERM ELECTIONS REINFORCED KIRKLAND'S CONVICTION that Reagan was vulnerable if a united Democratic Party put forward a strong candidate and a prudent platform. He also understood that if recent history was any gauge, the party would find some way to squander whatever advantage it might enjoy. The Democrats were still burdened with their post-Vietnam torpor; the party stood as a fragile and undependable ally to its traditional working-class base. Given the direct impact the Democrats' enfeeblement had on the prospects for the revival of organized labor, Kirkland decided to take matters in hand. If the party was incapable of fixing itself, it would fall to labor to take the necessary steps to return the Democrats to their mainstream liberal roots.

Having won by landslide proportions in 1964, the Democrats lost three of the next four presidential elections, and these three setbacks were attributable as much to internal party divisions as to the popularity of the Republican standard-bearers. Kirkland was particularly concerned about the reforms that had transformed the rules for selecting presidential nominees. Labor had initially opposed the reforms because they were meant to dilute the influence of union officials in internal party affairs. Labor, however, had adjusted to the constituency quotas by going out and recruiting women and minorities from its own ranks and placing them on the delegate slates of competing presidential contenders. Kirkland now believed that the reforms were seriously weakening the party's ability to nominate a candidate with a sufficiently broad appeal to win the presidency. For it was not labor alone that had been targeted by the reformers. Labor, members of Congress, governors, local party officials—the very forces that formed the crucial link between the party and the electorate and were therefore sensitive to the opinions of the rank and file—these representatives of traditional political authority had been supplanted by the advocates of liberal causes and by the avatars of what came to be called identity politics. The result was the nomination of George McGovern, a man clearly outside the mainstream, and of Jimmy Carter, a political unknown whose lack of national seasoning was central to the collapse of his presidency.

Through bitter experience, Kirkland had learned that labor could not depend on the traditional leadership to take the initiative in restoring equilibrium to internal party affairs. Confronted with nonnegotiable demands and walkout threats from left-wing stalwarts like Bella Abzug, the congresswoman from Manhattan's Upper West Side, and Ron Dellums, the congressman from Berkeley, party leaders inevitably caved in or agreed to compromises that reinforced the reform machinery. Kirkland never forgot his experience in the 1968 Humphrey presidential campaign, when party regulars seemed paralyzed by division and self-doubt. He recalled the AFL-CIO's campaign to thwart George Wallace in his effort to win over blue-collar workers as a heroic chapter in labor's political history. The anti-Wallace drive had been organized in a few weeks; in 1982, Kirkland had two years to marshal his forces against Ronald Reagan.

Kirkland was also influenced by his experiences during the 1980 election, when as the newly elected AFL-CIO president he had engaged in some plant-gate campaigning for President Carter. At a factory in Washington state, a worker told Kirkland, who had just handed him a Carter leaflet, that he "wouldn't vote for that SOB if he was the last man on earth." "Put that brother down as undecided," Kirkland quipped.

In fact, Kirkland was disturbed to find that many local union officials wouldn't support AFL-CIO-endorsed candidates out of fear that their plant-floor credibility would suffer. The lesson, for Kirkland, was that it mattered little if labor had the most technically sophisticated political machine if the rank and file simply rejected labor's candidates. He was determined that in 1984 there would be no repeat of the Carter experience.[1]

Kirkland's first target was the reforms. In the past, the AFL-CIO had focused on eliminating the quotas that guaranteed levels of representation to women, blacks, and other minorities. Those efforts had failed, and while Kirkland no doubt found the gender and race quotas obnoxious, he decided to make peace with affirmative action in party affairs. Instead of trying to undo the constituency quotas, Kirkland and Charles Manatt, the chairman of the Democratic National Committee, quietly pushed through a series of changes to enhance the power of elected officials, labor, and party regulars at the expense of liberal cause groups and of hitherto unknown politicians who ran as outsiders unbeholden to "special interests," à la Jimmy Carter. First, the schedule for primaries and caucuses for 1984 was frontloaded so that most took place in the election season's early months. The primaries were tightly compressed in time but geographically dispersed to benefit candidates with large campaign coffers, strong field operations, and the ability to mount a serious effort in every region of the country. In addition, five hundred convention slots were reserved for "superdelegates" (elected officials and party officers), mainstream elements who would be reluctant to mortgage the Democratic future by nominating another unknown quantity.[2] The goal was not simply to secure the nomination of a mainstream liberal but to do so relatively early in the primary cycle. John Perkins, who had succeeded Al Barkan as COPE director, served as a member of the commission that was rewriting the nominating procedures. His objective was to have the nomination wrapped up by Super Tuesday—March 13, when a half-dozen or so important primaries would be decided—well before the end of the nomination process.[3]

Step by step, then, rules that were tailored to enhance the power of political outsiders and McGovern-style liberals were changed to reinforce the authority of insiders and the old New Deal coalition of blue-collar workers, unions, mainstream liberals, blacks, and immigrants. To be sure, the strategy did represent an acknowledgment that the center of gravity within the party had shifted to the left. Nowhere was this more apparent than in the realm of international affairs. By 1982, practically everybody had abandoned the pretense that a Scoop Jackson wing of the party existed in sufficient numbers to nominate a candidate with a hard-line anti-Communist perspective. In fact, the litmus-test issues for aspiring presidential nominees remained under the firm control of the party's doves: opposition to Reagan's policies in Central America, a freeze in the deployment of nuclear arms, criticism of the administration for its alleged inflexibility in arms negotiations with Moscow.

Having dealt with the rules of the game, Kirkland turned to the two most critical issues: selecting an electable, pro-labor candidate and determining precisely what labor's role would be in the campaign. In all his political maneuverings, Kirkland's overarching objective was to forge a unified labor position on the nominee and on an election strategy. He was determined to avoid a repeat of 1976, when labor was split between various candidates, or 1980, when unions were divided almost down the middle between Kennedy and Carter.

Although a number of prominent Democrats were giving consideration to entering the 1984 campaign, two names stood out from the rest of the pack: Senator Edward M. Kennedy and former Vice President Walter F. Mondale. Both men remained faithful to the traditional Democratic creed: they believed in strong doses of government intervention in economic matters; voted down-the-line for the expansion of civil rights, worker benefits, safety and health measures, and the rights of unions; and were willing to support labor's trade agenda some of the time. These were not Atari Democrats—a reference to the early video game company and a label attached to Democrats who were fascinated by high-technology solutions to social problems. They preached an updated version of New Deal, Fair Deal, and Great Society ideology and voted consistently for issues that were of institutional relevance to the union movement. Unlike the new Democrats, who often seemed uncomfortable at labor gatherings, Kennedy and Mondale actually drew inspiration from labor audiences and maintained personal friendships with Kirkland, Donahue, Doug Fraser, and other labor leaders.

There were, of course, questions about Kennedy's electability, because of doubts both about his character and about voter resistance to his aggressive brand of liberalism. That concern was resolved on December 1, 1982, when Kennedy announced that he would not stand for the presidency.

Kennedy's withdrawal greatly simplified matters for Kirkland. With the prospects of an intramural labor clash pitting Mondale supporters against Kennedy partisans eliminated, labor could unite around one candidate, Mondale, and do so well in advance of the primary season. Although Kirkland stayed studiously neutral in public comments and invited any and all Democrats to seek labor's endorsement, behind the scenes he was lining up members of the AFL-CIO executive council for an early Mondale endorsement.

Kirkland's strategy entailed some risk for organized labor and for him personally. Although labor had a long tradition of involvement in American politics, its leaders had refrained from becoming intensely involved in internal party affairs. Labor leaders from Gompers on down had deemed it unwise for unions to become integrated into the party structures because, unlike in Europe, where workers voted overwhelmingly for social democratic parties, American workers divided their loyalties between the two major parties. Dwight Eisenhower could always count on the support of a segment of organized labor in his presidential campaigns, mainly craft unions from the building trades. And in the 1972 general election, labor had divided its support three ways, with about one-third of the unions endorsing McGovern, another third supporting President Nixon, and another third remaining neutral.

But conditions had changed with the triumph of Reaganite conservatism. With a few lonely exceptions, moderate, pro-labor Republican officeholders had passed from the scene, often replaced by conservatives with low opinions of unions. Unlike Eisenhower and Nixon, Reagan had no strategy to win over a segment of the trade union leadership, with the exception of the Teamsters, whom the administration assiduously courted.

Even if Kirkland succeeded in forging labor unity behind Mondale, he faced the opposition of those Democrats who were concerned about the party's being too closely identified with the unions. And, of course, there was the question of how Reagan would deal with labor issues should he win reelection in the face of all-out AFL-CIO opposition. On this score, Kirkland was convinced that the effort was worth the risk, having concluded that the administration's policies couldn't get much worse than they already were.

In light of subsequent developments, especially the charges that Mondale was the captive of special interests—"Big Labor," in particular—it is worth noting that the former vice president was hardly alone among presidential aspirants in seeking labor's support. John Glenn, Alan Cranston, and Gary Hart made it clear that they would welcome the AFL-CIO's money, manpower, and goodwill. The most desperate suppliant was Cranston, a labor-liberal with close ties to the union leadership. Cranston spent an entire week pleading his case at the annual Bal Harbour executive council session in February 1983. As one union official noted, unkindly, "When you needed a towel at poolside, he was there to hand you one; when you needed your laundry done, Cranston was there." Kirkland and others assured their old friend that the endorsement had not been locked up for Mondale, though it was evident to all that preparations for a Mondale endorsement were well underway.

In any event, Cranston received a much warmer reception than did John Glenn, the former astronaut. According to early polls, Glenn, a moderate, held the greatest potential among the probable Democratic candidates to appeal to the electorate across party lines. But the labor leadership treated Glenn coolly. Each year, COPE issued a scorecard that rated members of Congress on their voting record on issues labor thought important. Glenn's score was relatively low for a northern Democrat.[4] To Kirkland, Glenn resembled a Democratic office-seeker who, in an appearance before the executive council, declared that he was a friend of labor who would support the union movement "when it was right." To which Kirkland responded, only partly in jest, that "a true friend is someone who will support you when you're wrong." Clearly, John Glenn fell well short of that standard.

Initially, Kirkland planned to convene the executive council for an endorsement decision in December 1983. But in August, he moved the day of reckoning up to October, when the AFL-CIO convention was scheduled. At the time, Glenn took his rejection with good grace and promised that he would refrain from attacking Mondale as the candidate of the labor bosses. An aide spoke with awe of the political machine the unions had assembled for the campaign, commenting that it would be "brilliant and overwhelming" if the unions were "able to do half of what they're describing."[5]

The formal endorsement came at the AFL-CIO's biannual convention, held in Hollywood, Florida, in early October. Support for Mondale was nearly unanimous. Only one maritime union, the Marine Engineers Beneficial Association, stood in opposition, while the longshoremen and seafarers remained neutral. Otherwise, the convention was awash in enthusiasm for Walter Mondale, with delegates standing on tables, chanting refrains of "We Want Fritz," and singing raucous choruses of "Solidarity Forever" and "Happy Days Are Here Again." Mondale delivered a speech effusive in its praise of labor's contribution to the common man, and he aligned himself with the most controversial aspect of labor's agenda, trade restriction, by pledging to press American corporations to create jobs in the United States instead of exporting them abroad and promising to impose trade restrictions on countries that practiced protectionism. "I will match other countries' export subsidies product for product and dollar for dollar," he vowed.

In his address, Kirkland lauded Mondale as carrying forth the tradition of Hubert Humphrey and Scoop Jackson and asserted that labor had made a "commitment to be at your side at every primary and every caucus in every state of the union." Kirkland made a withering attack on Reagan and his policies, damning the president's shining city on a hill as a place where "steel mills and cotton plants stand idle, bridges are falling down, streets are riddled with potholes, the water system is rotting, and parks are being stripmined and logged." Under Reagan, he added, "schoolteachers are vilified," "laws are selectively enforced," and "derelicts and bag ladies huddle" in doorways and "expire in alleys."[6] Kirkland also hit back at those who derided labor as just another special interest whose support should be avoided lest a candidate's independence be compromised. "Candidates are advised by the public soothsayers to spurn or even go out of their way to avoid or offend various elements of the electorate in order to win," he declared. "As far as I can figure, that would leave only a handful of prosperous, middle-aged white males to run the country as they see fit—and the model sounds suspiciously like . . . James Watt," a reference to Reagan's gaffe-prone secretary of the interior.[7]

Walter F. Mondale has not been treated kindly by those who have chronicled the history of recent American politics, having been lumped in with George McGovern, Michael Dukakis, and the Jimmy Carter of 1980 as weak nominees who were out of step with the mood of America and presided over badly run campaigns. Yet in late 1983, Kirkland and his labor brethren had every reason to believe that in Mondale they had a candidate with a reasonable chance of defeating Reagan. There was, to begin with, Mondale himself, a mainstream liberal who commanded respect throughout the party. Mondale drew the enthusiastic support of the most influential black politicians, who stuck by him even after Jesse Jackson entered the contest. On the other end of the ideological spectrum, Mondale was considered an acceptable candidate by the tattered remnants of the party's Scoop Jackson wing. After a meeting with Mondale, Ben J. Wattenberg, chairman of the Coalition for a Democratic Majority, praised Mondale for his openness to different perspectives, a trait that, Wattenberg added, had been notably lacking in President Carter.[8] And hard-liners appreciated the fact that despite the shift in party sentiment, Mondale still spoke with pride of having worked with Hubert Humphrey to purge the Minnesota Democrat Farmer Labor Party of Communist influence. Had the Democratic Party been molded in the tradition of European social democracy, Mondale would have been the obvious choice for party leader.

Just as Mondale seemed electable, Reagan appeared vulnerable to a strong Democratic campaign. Although Reagan has subsequently been widely proclaimed as one of America's most successful presidents, in 1983 his election to a second term was hardly a foregone conclusion. While inflation had been brought under control, the country was mired in recession, with unemployment climbing to a peak of 10.2 percent. The argument—repeatedly struck by Kirkland over the previous three years— that the president's policies favored the rich over everybody else had resonance in the country, to the point where polls showed Mondale with a clear lead in a head-to-head contest against the president.

Nor could Reagan depend on divisions within Democratic ranks to boost him to an easy victory, as had been the case in 1980. To be sure, the Democratic primary field was crammed with candidates: Mondale, Glenn, Cranston, Hart, Jesse Jackson, Governor Reubin Askew of Florida, South Carolina Senator Ernest Hollings, and former Senator George McGovern. Yet once Glenn's campaign failed to catch fire, it seemed reasonable to conclude that Mondale, who enjoyed the support of an impressive list of party leaders, in addition to labor, was headed for a relatively easy victory.

Unlike John F. Kennedy, Mondale could not rely on local Democratic machines to man the phone banks and ferry voters to the polls, since big city organizations had deteriorated to the point of near uselessness. Here, however, the AFL-CIO proposed to fill the organizational vacuum. COPE had undergone major changes since Kirkland assumed the presidency. In 1982, Al Barkan retired after issuing a parting blast at the radicals and ultra-liberals, who, he believed, had ruined the Democratic Party. John Perkins, his successor, was by temperament and style Barkan's antithesis, a man who shunned the limelight and concentrated on the nuts and bolts of labor's political operation.

As early as 1982, Perkins and his two deputies, David Jessup and Dick Wilson, were hard at work perfecting labor's campaign machinery in preparation for a Mondale campaign. In modernizing the COPE apparatus, Perkins borrowed extensively from techniques developed by New Right fund-raisers like Richard Viguerie; at the heart of the operation was the development of a computerized list of 12 million rank-and-file union members. Studies had demonstrated that a Democratic candidate who won 65 percent of the labor vote stood an excellent chance of winning the presidency, and it was Perkins's goal to inundate those 12 million trade unionists with letters, appeals, and fact sheets, all explaining why their future depended on electing labor's proven friend, Fritz Mondale, to the presidency. As a further step, the AFL-CIO hired the pollster Peter Hart to conduct surveys and train affiliate unions on the techniques of conducting their own membership polls.[9]

As labor moved inexorably toward a Mondale endorsement, Kirkland anticipated that the candidate would be subject to charges of being the puppet of "special interests," "Big Labor," and "trade union bosses." During his 1980 campaign, Reagan had used the special-interest theme with considerable dexterity, and ever since, Reagan and his strategists had ascribed opposition to the administration's policies as little more than interest-group whining. Reagan, in fact, had achieved the impressive feat of transforming the very meaning of the phrase *special interest*. Originally employed as a pejorative description for large corporate entities, *special interests* were now perceived as referring to civil rights organizations, feminists, environmentalists, the consumer lobby, and, of course, labor. The Democrats, for their part, had opened the door to this line of attack by encouraging the rise of single-issue and identity politics. To ensure party unity, a Democratic nominee was forced to run a gauntlet of special pleaders, ranging from pro-abortion groups to coalitions pressing for an American pullout from Central America to feminists pushing for a women's agenda, blacks demanding a black agenda, gays pressing for a gay agenda. Among their demands were policies that were highly unpopular with the electorate, such as racial preferences, unilateral disarmament, civil rights protections for homosexuals, and so forth.

Kirkland assumed that Reagan would depict Mondale as the special-interest candidate, no matter what the degree of labor involvement in the campaign, and concluded it made little difference whether labor backed Mondale early and with enthusiasm or later and with more circumspection. In either event, the Republicans would claim that the Democrat was the instrument of the labor bosses. As Kirkland put it in his speech to the

AFL-CIO convention, "If we do not do what we propose to do, we shall be reviled as toothless and irrelevant. If we succeed, we shall be condemned as daring to aspire to a share of power in our society. Given that choice of slurs, I much prefer the latter."[10] Kirkland also believed that the AFL-CIO was behaving responsibly toward the Democratic candidates. Unlike other cause groups, labor had not advanced nonnegotiable demands or litmus-test issues and did not insist that Mondale or other candidates endorse unpopular legislative measures. Like Meany before him, Kirkland was a passionate believer in labor as the people's lobby and felt certain that a Democratic candidate who aligned himself with labor's broad agenda would enhance, not damage, his election chances.

What Kirkland did not anticipate was the willingness of Mondale's *Democratic* rivals to pound away at the special-interest theme to the point where the former vice president was permanently identified as a man beholden to the interests. Front and center in this regard was Gary Hart. While Glenn was the first to raise the special-interest theme, it was Hart who proved the cleverest at exploiting the issue.

Hart was the quintessential Atari Democrat. He had originally gained notoriety as George McGovern's campaign manager in 1972. While that campaign ended in shambles, Hart escaped with his reputation for tactical brilliance undiminished. Hart returned to his native Colorado and, with labor's support, won election to the Senate in 1974 and then again in 1980. Like most Big Sky states, Colorado was tilting increasingly to the GOP; thus Hart's success was due in part to his having rid himself of the odor of McGovernite liberalism. Indeed, Hart carved out a blurry ideological reputation made up of doses of libertarianism, traditional liberalism, New Politics dovishness, and the Atari Democrat's fascination with technological advancement and new economic trends. His ratings from COPE and the liberal Americans for Democratic Action were distinctly lower than Mondale's, not to mention Cranston's or McGovern's. He voted against gun control and for a balanced budget. In 1978, Hart proposed a whopping 20 percent tax cut; the measure was tilted toward the poor but at the same time called for a slowing in the growth of spending for Social Security, Medicare, and food stamps. Hart had once expressed interest in a consumption tax, an idea Kirkland had denounced as regressive. Hart was among eight Democrats to oppose Jimmy Carter's windfall profits tax on the oil industry and had opposed Carter's program to develop synthetic fuels. He had further irritated labor by opposing the loan guarantee to the failing Chrysler Corporation, asserting that under free enterprise principles, "the federal government cannot assume responsibility to prevent the failure of individual firms, no matter how large."

Despite these departures from labor-liberal orthodoxy, Hart remained firmly within the liberal camp on most critical issues of the day. But labor still yearned for a liberal leader in the Humphrey mold, and its leaders had not forgotten that Hart had boasted upon entering the Senate that he had not been elected as just another Hubert Humphrey. Kirkland's suspicions about Hart's loyalty to the labor movement were reinforced by a remark Hart dropped to Chris Gersten, the political director for the operating engineers union, in 1980. Hart was running for reelection, and Gersten was responsible for collecting labor contributions to the campaign. During a meeting, Hart asked Gersten, who had a vaguely countercultural appearance, whether there was an "alternative" to the Meany-Kirkland leadership within the AFL-CIO. Gersten subsequently passed Hart's remarks along to Kirkland.[11]

Kirkland was convinced that Hart would try to depict Mondale as a tool of the special interests. As a precautionary measure, he asked Ken Young to pore over Mondale's record and make a list of issues on which he had adopted positions different from labor's. Young dug up seven or eight issues, including several that would provide the candidate with solid ammunition to use in televised debates when the inevitable questions were hurled at him. Young sent the list along to Bernard Aronson, a Mondale aide with roots in organized labor, with the suggestion that the candidate make use of the list if Hart or Glenn began raising the special-interest charge. Kirkland's common sense strategy to defang the special-interest theme was stymied not by Hart or Glenn, but by none other than Fritz Mondale. Mondale adhered to a strict code of political ethics that forbade attacks on allies and friends. Under no circumstances, Young was told, would Mondale trash his friends at the AFL-CIO, not even when it was Lane Kirkland himself who was encouraging him to make his differences with the unions public.[12]

The 1984 Democratic nominating process opened with party caucuses in Iowa. For months, labor had been mobilizing its forces to produce a decisive first-round triumph for its candidate, and by January COPE had assembled a well-oiled machine whose reach extended throughout the state. John Perkins had dispatched some 100 COPE operatives to the state, and another 95 were assigned to full-time duty by various international unions—each and every one committed to Mondale. The campaign was built around a pyramid principle, in which COPE operatives and representatives of international unions would mobilize a larger group of Iowa trade union officials, who in turn would organize several thousand union town wardsmen.[13] The objective was to reach, through mailings or by telephone, every trade union member in the state who was not already committed to another candidate. Labor had established phone banks in every major community, and since it was the unions, and not the Mondale campaign, that paid for the phones, the cost did not count against Mondale's campaign spending ceiling. By contrast, Hart, Glenn, and the other candidates had to use scarce resources to rent office space and telephone lines.[14]

Mondale scored a smashing triumph, gaining 49 percent, with Hart finishing a distant second with 16 percent. The AFL-CIO executive council, meeting in its Bal Harbour retreat, assumed a low profile; there was no gloating from Kirkland or other labor leaders. They didn't need to gloat, since leading Democrats and the press spoke in awed tones of Iowa as labor's—and Kirkland's—triumph fully as much as it was Fritz Mondale's. The respected columnist George Will saw in Iowa powerful evidence that the Democratic Party had completed its recovery from the Vietnam Syndrome, with Mondale in secure command of a united party, reinforced by a revived labor movement under the skilled leadership of Lane Kirkland.[15]

For Mondale, the only sour note was the repeated question raised about his relations with organized labor and other constituency groups. An increasingly desperate John Glenn was the most relentless in accusing Mondale of being labor's pawn. But it was Hart who landed the most damaging blows. On February 11, during a televised debate in Des Moines, Hart, as Kirkland had predicted, pressed Mondale by asking him to "cite one major domestic issue where you have disagreed with organized labor." Having disdained to make use of the AFL-CIO's special list of Mondale-labor differences, Mondale made no attempt to respond to Hart's question. "Labor came to me in support of my proposals," Mondale insisted. "It was not a deal. They wanted a candidate they could trust, not one they could run."[16]

To Mondale, the refusal to respond directly to the special-interests question was a matter of principle. The labor movement had supported him through the years; unions had been a critical part of his electoral coalition in Minnesota and labor officials like Kirkland had lobbied to secure his selection as vice president. Moreover, he shared with labor a commitment to an activist and caring government. Why, then, given this history, should he be expected to distance himself from a movement whose values he respected and whose leaders he regarded as personal friends? Mondale was also rankled by the hypocrisy of the whole affair. After all, Glenn, Hart, and the others had wanted labor's support every bit as much as he had and had placed great value on labor's backing during earlier political campaigns. Kirkland and other labor officials were more realistic; they understood as soon as he stumbled during the Iowa debate that Mondale would face further charges of being a wholly owned subsidiary of the AFL-CIO, and they wanted desperately for him to take the necessary action to put the issue behind him.[17]

After several days of nonstop hectoring by the press, Mondale released a list of three items where he and labor had parted company, including the MX missile and an issue that pitted the environment against union jobs. But the damage had been done. Shortly after Iowa, a poll taken by the *New York Times* gave Mondale the largest primary lead in history. But the momentum generated by his victory in Iowa was quickly and dramatically shattered in New Hampshire where, in the campaign's first primary, Hart cruised to an easy victory. There were, of course, mitigating circumstances. New Hampshire was an untypical state, with a weak labor movement and an election system that permitted independents to vote in the Democratic primaries, all of which strengthened the hand of insurgents like Eugene McCarthy, George McGovern, and Gary Hart—politicians who made a fetish of independence from the special-interest lobbies and the "Establishment." But the press interpreted Hart's success as due in large measure to his pounding away at the special-interest issue, and an ABC exit poll showed that Hart had benefited from the growing perception that Mondale promised too much to too many interest groups. Furthermore, post–New Hampshire polls showed Hart pulling to within a few points of Mondale nationwide, a development that suggested that Mondale's problems were not restricted to states like New Hampshire with unpredictable and quirky voters.[18]

The special-interest charge was not Mondale's only problem. The steady recovery of the economy and the dwindling of the unemployment rate robbed Mondale of a major theme and played well into Hart's strategy of depicting the campaign as between the past—Mondale and labor—and the future, as represented by Gary Hart and his legions of suburban liberals. Even more damaging was the entrance into the campaign of Jesse Jackson. Given Mondale's many years of devoted service to the civil rights cause—a far more impressive record than Hart's or Glenn's—he had every reason to anticipate overwhelming support from black Democratic voters. Indeed, even with Jackson in the race, Mondale still gained the endorsement of most black elected officials and, due to the hard work of the A. Philip Randolph Institute, retained the backing of black trade unionists in key states. But Jackson proved a dynamic presence in the campaign, and he hurt Mondale severely by monopolizing the black vote in northern industrial states and in several southern states as well. Jackson also joined in on the frenzy of labor bashing that marked the latter stages of the primary campaign. The man who, a few years earlier, had asked Kirkland if he, and not the NAACP, could serve as labor's principal liaison to the black community, now attacked "labor bosses" and derided the trade union leadership as "old wine" that needed to make way for "new wine skin." And he complained of the lack of black leadership within the unions, asserting that "A black or a woman will clearly be president of this country before one will even be able to run for president of the AFL-CIO."[19]

Rather quickly, the campaign narrowed to a two-man race, Mondale versus Hart, with Jackson grabbing off the black vote and what remained of the left. Under the most intense pressure of his political career, Mondale surprised most observers by fighting back with considerable effectiveness. He won several important southern states, scored a close victory in Illinois, and then won by a wide margin in New York, leaving Hart badly wounded. Not only was Mondale winning in crucial industrial states, he was also rolling up a substantial lead in the delegate race, in part due to the changes in the party rules that Kirkland and others had engineered to bolster the chances of mainstream liberals and weaken the prospects of outsiders like Hart. Contributing to Mondale's comeback were growing questions about Hart's character. In the middle of the campaign, it was revealed that Hart had fudged his date of birth and changed his name from Hartpence to Hart. Hart also found himself on the defensive when Mondale and others began to demand that Hart explain just what his vaunted New Ideas would mean in practice.

Kirkland took quiet satisfaction in Hart's setbacks. Kirkland was capable of issuing a withering attack on a Republican official one day and sitting down to a pleasant lunch with the very same conservative the next day to discuss areas of mutual interest. Kirkland, in fact, could respect a conservative who voted his principles but was flexible enough to cooperate with labor when it was beneficial to both parties. But Kirkland believed that a special place in hell should be reserved for Democrats who during election campaigns accepted labor's money and manpower and then proceeded to blast away at greedy labor unions and power-hungry trade union bosses. After a drink or two, Kirkland liked to amuse friends by quoting verbatim from John L. Lewis's 1937 radio address, in which Lewis declared, "It ill behooves one who has supped at labor's table and who has been sheltered in labor's house to curse with equal fervor and fine impartiality both labor and its adversaries when they become locked in deadly embrace." In fact, Kirkland believed that Lewis's sentiments could be appropriately applied to those who, having accepted campaign money from labor, proceeded to distance themselves from the "special interests" or to speak of Big Labor and Big Business as equally responsible for society's ills. By this standard, Hart qualified as the worst kind of political ingrate.

Kirkland's coolness toward Hart predated the primaries. "Lane saw Hart as one of those politicians who put their finger in the air to see which way the winds were blowing," recalled Ken Young. "And Lane identified Hart as one of the new Democrats who trumpeted the end of the New Deal. Lane was a New Dealer to his dying day, and therefore he thought Hart was a bad Democrat."[20]

After the New Hampshire primary, Kirkland became personally involved in the campaign. This was an unprecedented step for an AFL-CIO president. But Kirkland felt it was important to remind the rank and file about labor's stake in the election. He was, as well, viscerally opposed to the prospect of a Democratic ticket with Hart at the top. In speaking of Hart, Kirkland employed polemical language he seldom resorted to in referring to labor's Republican adversaries. He attacked Hart as the "self-appointed spokesman for the younger generation" and as someone who "has given hypocrisy a bad name." In an unkind jab, Kirkland compared the choice between Hart and Reagan to "two Liberaces at the same piano." He urged Hart to "at long last, vote your age. Peter Pan politics is passé." He told a conference of construction trades unions that Hart "belongs to that familiar breed of politician who profess to love workers but insult their organizations." He dismissed Hart's New Ideas theme: "Have you ever noticed on television how the weaker and more insipid a project is, the more they plug it as 'new' and 'improved'?" Kirkland added that Mondale "is not some Masked Marvel or Mystery Man. He is not made of silicon or microchip flames. He is made of flesh and blood and brains."[21] Kirkland also taunted Hart by requesting that he return the contributions that unions had made to his 1980 Senate campaign. "I have a question for Mr. Hart," Kirkland said. "When you sought and accepted more than $135,000 in labor contributions to your 1980 Senate campaign, did you become an indentured servant to labor?" borrowing a phrase Hart had used to describe Mondale's relationship to the labor movement.[22]

Kirkland was also the apparent originator (others have claimed authorship) of a line that summed up growing misgivings about Hart's capabilities. Speaking on March 11 to a labor audience in Rosemont, Illinois, Kirkland said, "You can apply the burger test to Hart: It's a big bun, but where's the beef?" a reference to a popular ad slogan for Wendy's, the fast-food chain. Shortly thereafter, Mondale included the "Where's the beef?" line in his stump speeches; eventually, "Where's the beef?" became for Hart what "special interests" was for Mondale—a phrase that seemed to sum up all the weaknesses of his candidacy.[23]

In the end, the New Deal alliance prevailed. Mondale won the nomination by a margin that was deceptively large, given the obvious appeal of Hart's message to certain elements of the party. Organized labor's vote-pulling machine made a critical difference in a number of pro-Mondale states, including Alabama, Iowa, Michigan, Illinois, New York, and Pennsylvania. In Georgia, which Mondale won by 1 percent, he won the labor vote by 38 percent to 22 percent. Labor's role was almost as critical in Alabama, where union members preferred Mondale over Hart by 48 percent to 15 percent, while Mondale won the state by 13 percent. The labor vote went for Mondale by 48 percent to 32 percent in Illinois, 48 percent to 22 percent in New York, and 48 percent to 32 percent in Pennsylvania.[24]

Kirkland was prompted to chastise those who had predicted that labor support would be "albatross, millstone, burden, affliction" to the Democrats. He was right; it was not labor that had damaged Mondale but Hart, with his charges that the Democrats were being transformed into "the American Labor Party," an unkind comparison to the British Labour Party, then in ill repute because of its lurch toward socialism and pacifism. But there was no denying that Hart had drawn blood with the special-interest theme, as polls showed that this particular issue represented Mondale's most vulnerable point.[25]

Kirkland had no regrets. Labor had produced as promised for its candidate and demonstrated that within the Democratic Party the AFL-CIO was a potent force. As for Hart, Kirkland noted that "the first stone wasn't cast from our side" and declared himself ready for a détente with the senator, though he added that improved relations would depend on the degree of "pettiness and vindictiveness" on the part of Hart and his people.[26] In fact, John Perkins told a reporter that Kirkland was prepared to support Hart as the vice presidential choice if he believed it would help secure a Mondale victory. Perkins quoted Kirkland as saying that if Hart were chosen, "we would find qualities in Senator Hart that even his mother didn't know about."[27]

Meanwhile, Kirkland and other labor officials maintained a distinctly low profile within Democratic Party internal affairs, a policy that stood in sharp contrast, for those who cared to notice, to the behavior of other constituency groups, which began to press their demands on the nominee in a loud and very public manner. Feminists were insistent that Mondale name a woman as his vice presidential running mate; the National Organization for Women threatened to disrupt the convention if Mondale refused to add a woman to the ticket. Jesse Jackson was pressing his own agenda, including a prohibition on run-off primaries, a demand that could hurt the party in the South. Hispanics, for their part, made vague hints of boycotting the convention if the candidate did not repudiate legislation to reduce illegal immigration. The highly visible demands by women's groups especially hurt when, in the end, Mondale selected Rep. Geraldine Ferraro as his running mate, since it made Mondale's gesture appear as much a capitulation to an interest group as a daring move to broaden the party's appeal.

If labor was not the noisiest constituency group at the party convention in San Francisco, it was by far the largest. Labor boasted 752 delegates and alternates, fully one-fifth of the total number, and formed, with delegates from the National Education Association, one-third of Mondale's delegates. Though Kirkland was not a delegate, he was on hand in San Francisco to function as a behind-the-scenes field general of labor's forces. Before the formal opening of the convention, Kirkland led some 100,000 trade unionists in a festive march for the Mondale candidacy. Marchers pushed baby strollers and rode in wheelchairs, fire trucks, bulldozers, and construction cranes, as well as on horseback. Spirits were high, though the event lost some press attention to a competing, and more flamboyant, parade of San Francisco's gay community.[28]

Soon enough, Kirkland's counsel was required due to a Mondale blunder of substantial proportions. Just before the convention was slated to open, Mondale stunned everybody by announcing that he intended to replace party chairman Charles Manatt with Bert Lance. The move bordered on the bizarre. Lance, a Georgia businessman, had resigned as treasury secretary in Jimmy Carter's administration under a cloud of scandal rumors. Lance, it turned out, had been treated unfairly; nevertheless, he was never able to shed the reputation of wheeler-dealer, and his credentials as a national party leader were limited. Kirkland was unsettled by the move, first, because Mondale had rejected his advice (he told Kirkland that Lance was essential to the campaign's chances in the South) and, second, because Lance was prominent among the Democrats who were pressing Mondale to distance himself from his labor base. Indeed, one of Lance's first acts was to urge the nominee to steer clear of labor's endorsement. While Kirkland remonstrated with the candidate, Ken Young and John Perkins lobbied against Lance with high party officials. After a firestorm of criticism, Lance graciously withdrew.[29]

The Lance affair was all too indicative of a campaign that felt a desperate need to make bold gestures in order to regain momentum. Similarly, the selection of Ferraro represented another dramatic maneuver that eventually backfired when questions were raised about her husband's business dealings. And finally, there was Mondale's acceptance speech, in which, during prime time, he announced a platform based on cutting the federal deficit and raising taxes. In phrases designed to impress Americans with their blunt candor, Mondale proclaimed:

> We are living on borrowed money and borrowed time. . . . Whoever is inaugurated next January, the American people will pay Mr. Reagan's

bills. . . . Taxes will go up, and anyone who says they won't isn't telling the truth.

I mean business. By the end of my first term, I will cut the deficit by two-thirds. Let's tell the truth. Mr. Reagan will raise taxes, and so will I. He won't tell you. I just did.

That the message was unusual, even daring, is beyond question. The consequences, however, were disastrous. Kirkland and other labor people immediately understood the magnitude of the blunder. Dick Wilson, who had invested hundreds of hours over two years in the cause of a Mondale presidency, watched the address in horror. "As soon as Mondale made his promise to raise taxes, I knew it was all over; I was crushed."[30] Kirkland was also disturbed. He said later that he had not been consulted about the speech. He complained that it required something akin to "a diplomatic mission" to crack the Mondale inner circle. If his opinion had been asked, Kirkland would have reminded the candidate that two state senators in Michigan had been recalled after voting for a tax increase proposed by Governor James Blanchard, a Democrat. Labor wanted a campaign centered on jobs and growth, not tax hikes.[31]

Other labor leaders left San Francisco in a hopeful frame of mind, ready to do battle despite the odds. William Wynn, president of the food and commercial workers, likened the election to 1964, when trade unionists and liberals joined together in unprecedented unity to defeat the Republican nominee, Barry Goldwater, in the belief that Goldwater was a dangerous extremist. Sam Fishman, president of the AFL-CIO in Michigan, also saw the election in stark ideological terms: "I don't think Reagan represents fascism in the country," Fishman told a reporter, "but I think he represents a very anti-labor, reactionary attitude. And it's not just him. It's the atmosphere and the way those election results will be read." Kirkland took a less alarmist perspective, but, like the others, he was worried that labor would incur serious losses should Mondale go down to defeat.[32]

Yet as the polls began to filter in during the weeks after the convention, it became obvious that the events in San Francisco had actually weakened Mondale's standing, and that Reagan was building an insurmountable lead. Probably no Democrat could have defeated Reagan in 1984. At home, the misery index—the combination of the inflation, unemployment, and interest rates that Reagan had exploited to great advantage in his race against Carter—was now tilting in the incumbent's favor, with inflation in dramatic decline and the unemployment rate dropping from over 10 percent to 7.5 percent over the past year. Reagan also scored well on foreign policy issues; despite division over arms control and Central America, the president had succeeded in placing America's adversaries, especially the Soviet Union, on the defensive.

Throughout the final dreary weeks of the campaign, Kirkland adhered to a code of conduct that rejected defeatism, blame placing, and whining as unworthy of a trade unionist. Yet Kirkland was not invulnerable to the claustrophobic atmosphere in Washington, and he was thoroughly weary of listening to the complaints of mournful labor officials and fielding questions from reporters asking—again and again and again—what he thought of the latest poll results.

From past experience, Kirkland had come to believe that when the air in Washington became oppressive, the best antidote was a visit to the real America beyond the Beltway. Kirkland grew to hate sitting passively in his office while the rest of the Democratic Party seemed mired in finger-pointing and self-pity. And he felt it important to remind the labor rank and file that there was still a campaign going on and that their candidate, Fritz Mondale, needed their support.

So in mid-October, a little more than two weeks before Election Day, Kirkland set out in what was dubbed the Solidarity van, a large recreational vehicle festooned with Mondale posters, on a two-week tour of the trade union heartland in the Northeast and the Midwest. He was accompanied by Irena; Ken Young; Murray Seegar, the AFL-CIO's spokesman; Tom Kahn, Kirkland's speechwriter; and Bob McGlotten, a federation lobbyist.

The Solidarity van traveled from one industrial center to the next: big cities like Detroit and Cleveland and smaller towns like Sandusky, Ohio. Kirkland and his small entourage stayed in motels and then, each morning, set off to a tape of Willie Nelson's "On the Road Again." Despite his reputation as a gourmet, Kirkland preferred eating most meals in fast-food restaurants, and he decreed that to amuse themselves, the Solidarity tour members conduct an ambiance survey of each McDonald's and Dairy Queen they visited, answering such questions as whether the plastic plants really looked like plastic. He often spoke at several rallies in the course of a day, addressing labor audiences in sometimes shabby union halls or occasionally in large arenas. He had a set stump speech that he varied at each stop in accordance with local conditions. The rhetoric was more direct and hard-hitting than was usually the case with Kirkland; it included lines like, "Republican flags and Republican jobs are all made in Taiwan." Local Democratic candidates often appeared with Kirkland; Paul Simon, then in a close contest for the Senate in Illinois, was so impressed by his reception at a union rally in Chicago that he turned up, unannounced, at a Kirkland rally the next day at a downstate venue four hours away.[33]

In the general election, Reagan rolled up one of the most over-whelming majorities in American history, 59 percent to 41 percent, with Mondale winning only his home state of Minnesota and the District of Columbia. Mondale fared well among union members and their families, receiving 57 percent among trade union members and 53 percent among union households, according to a CBS–*New York Times* survey. This was still below the 65 percent union vote threshold that experts claim Democratic candidates need to ensure victory. Nevertheless, the labor leadership seemed satisfied with its efforts. "I don't think we could have done anything more or anything better than we did this campaign," said John Sweeney, president of the Service Employees International Union. Nor was the news entirely bad for labor. Despite Mondale's crushing defeat and Reagan's obvious popularity, 63 percent of the labor-endorsed congressional and gubernatorial candidates emerged victorious.[34]

For labor, though, the legacy of 1984 was decidedly mixed. The Mondale campaign certainly elevated Kirkland's stature. He had person-ally taken hold of a movement that had looked weak and divided in the 1980 election and transformed it into the single most powerful force within the Democratic coalition. He had pressed as a first priority the strengthening of labor's political machine, he had used his powers of per-suasion to convince the rest of labor that the movement's future depended on political unity, and he had rallied his forces when the Mondale candi-dacy came under threat from Gary Hart.

At the same time, Sam Fishman's fears about how the pundits would interpret a Reagan victory proved altogether prescient. Walter Mondale was fated to go down in history as the candidate of the special interests. It didn't matter whether such a reading of the election was unfair or over-drawn. Kirkland told a reporter that it "is a strange argument that the ones who produced the greatest margins for their candidates are the ones who are not effective." But the conventional wisdom decreed otherwise. In the election's aftermath, high Democratic officials asked Kirkland to forgo an early endorsement in future elections, a request he politely rejected, asserting that if labor could unite around a candidate in the future, it would do so. Meanwhile, the political machine that Kirkland had assembled was intact, and labor remained one of the most powerful entities in national politics. Kirkland had taken a labor movement that was politically divided and lacked confidence and transformed it into a force that combined a commitment to a set of ideas, political unity, and a high degree of technical competence. That achievement would endure the defeat of a single political candidate.

Randolph Kirkland, Lane's father

Louise Kirkland, Lane's mother, in her wedding dress

Two members of the Greatest Generation: Lane (right) and brother Rannie, in uniform

Mary Withers Kirkland, Lane's great-grandmother, who lived in seclusion after the death of her husband during the Civil War

Lane admired Israel for its courage under duress and its social welfare system. He and Irena were friendly with a number of leading Israeli politicians, such as Prime Minister Golda Meir, shown here with the Kirklands during the 1970s.

Lane had high hopes for President Clinton, though his opinion of Labor Secretary Robert Reich (right) was less positive. Vice President Gore and Alexis Herman, who succeeded Reich as secretary of labor, were also on hand.

Lane with President
Carter during the
Camp David "malaise
summit"

Lane was a regular presence on picket lines of major strikes. Here he joins striking hotel
workers in Las Vegas.

Kirkland denounces Reaganomics at a Solidarity Day rally, 1981.

Lane and Douglas Fraser (second from left) shortly after the UAW rejoined the AFL-CIO. Tom Donahue is at right.

Lane and George
Meany during the
1970s

The torch passed from Meany to Kirkland at the AFL-CIO's 1979 convention.

Lane's dachshund, Stanley, would sing along to harmonica renditions of *Amazing Grace*. Irena sits at right.

Lane (front row, third from right) led a delegation of labor leaders in civil disobedience for the striking Pittston mineworkers in 1989. The United Mine Workers subsequently rejoined the AFL-CIO, but its president, Rich Trumka (with mustache) later joined the faction that pressed for Kirkland's retirement.

A triumphant moment with Lech Walesa at the 1989 federation convention

Lyndon Johnson was one of Kirkland's favorite politicians.

Lane and Irena with Egyptian President Anwar Sadat and his entourage

Irving Brown (center) was Kirkland's chief international affairs adviser. He played a central role in labor's Cold War policies from the beginning until his death, just before the collapse of the Berlin Wall.

7

SOLIDARITY FOREVER

IT ALL BEGAN ON AUGUST 14, 1980, WHEN WORKERS AT THE LENIN Shipyard in Gdansk, a Baltic port city, launched a strike against the enterprise management. On one level, the strike was a response to the Communist regime's announcement of major increases in the price of basic foods and the dismissal of several popular workers. But in a broader sense, the strike's target was Communism itself: Communism's elaborate system of control; its endemic corruption and favoritism; its identification with Poland's historic enemy, Russia; its atheism; the lies of its press; and, ultimately, its denial of basic worker rights, a denial that the authorities justified in the name of the working class.

Lane Kirkland had long been convinced that ordinary working people, and not diplomats, would bring about Communism's demise. Now, in Poland, his faith was seemingly being vindicated in ways that he himself could not have foreseen. In Poland, the working class was the agent of revolutionary change. But where Marxist theorists had predicted that workers, under the tutelage of educated elites, would rise up against capitalist oppression and pave the way for Communist society, in Poland it was Communism itself that was the target of worker anger. The instrument of revolution was a trade union, albeit a totally unique union, one that combined the traditional function of worker protection with the broader mission of national liberation. And to the astonishment of almost everyone—but not Kirkland—Poland's workers won. They won despite domestic repression, saber-rattling by the Kremlin, and predictions of failure and chaos from Western foreign ministries. Throughout it all, Kirkland was to serve as a redoubtable champion of Polish freedom. He used the influence of his position, his powers of persuasion, his clout in international circles, and the organizational capabilities of the AFL-CIO to promote Solidarity, defend its activists, and punish those who vowed to destroy it. He pressed the cause of Polish workers in Congress, kept the heat on three presidential administrations, enlisted the aid of labor movements from other democratic countries, and coordinated a wide-ranging program of material assistance that supported beleaguered union activists and enabled Solidarity to maintain an underground press that amounted to hundreds of newspapers and bulletins. When, in 1989, Solidarity scored an overwhelming triumph over the Communists in democratic elections, it triggered a chain reaction that within months brought down the entire apparatus of Communist oppression in Eastern Europe. It would be a great victory for Poland, a marvelous triumph for freedom, and total vindication of Kirkland's leadership and vision.

This was not the first display of worker unrest in People's Poland. In 1956 an uprising by industrial workers in Poznan had led to major changes in the Communist Party, including the elevation of Wladyslaw Gomulka, at the time regarded as something of a reformer, to the party leadership post. In 1970, it was Gomulka who was forced to step down after the military fired on strikers at Baltic coastal ports. At least forty-four workers were killed by troops under the command of General Wojciech Jaruzelski in that episode, but the new party chief, Edward Gierek, was cautious in his dealings with the industrial working class, and the price increases that had ignited the troubles were rolled back.

Then, in 1976, workers in large industrial installations in Radom and Ursus went on strike over government price policies. Again, the regime backed down for fear of wider disruption but at the same time carried out reprisals against the strike ringleaders, jailing some, firing others. On this occasion, however, the democratic intelligentsia responded to the acts of official repression by forming a new entity as a means of defending workers who had suffered at the hands of the state. The new organization was called the Committee to Defend Workers and was generally known by its Polish acronym, KOR. The founders of KOR included a number of the country's leading dissidents, writers, and academics who, for the most part, had devoted little previous attention to the problems of the working class. KOR forged links to the working class by organizing legal and material assistance for worker activists who had lost jobs or been packed off to prison. At the same time, KOR members began to build alliances with worker dissidents who gave evidence of leadership qualities, in anticipation of the inevitable next round of labor unrest. Of particular importance was the establishment of the Flying University, a movable classroom sponsored by KOR members to provide an alternative to Communist falsehoods on matters of history and culture. The Flying University shifted its meeting places from apartment to apartment; when Solidarity emerged, it counted many of the Flying University students and teachers among its leadership.

Lane Kirkland was an interested observer of these developments. He was regularly briefed on the state of the Polish opposition by Leo Labedz, the editor of *Survey*, a journal of Soviet bloc affairs, who had wide contacts among dissident groups in Eastern Europe. Labedz was a friend of Carl Gershman, who became president of the National Endowment for Democracy in the 1980s. Gershman introduced Labedz to Lane. Kirkland was well-versed in East European developments—Lech Walesa, the leader of Solidarity, described him as more knowledgeable about Communism than he himself was—and immediately recognized the alliance between workers and intellectuals as a unique and potentially powerful threat to Moscow's domination of the satellite countries. Kirkland was sufficiently impressed with KOR to give the approval for a modest amount of assistance for its worker defense activities.[1]

Kirkland was also among the first to grasp the significance of the burgeoning strike movement in August 1980. As the strike spread from Gdansk to other Baltic port cities and then to steel mills, tractor factories, and textile enterprises, he noted the high degree of organization, the shrewd tactical instincts, and the self-discipline of the workers. Where in the past Polish workers had given vent to anger through indiscriminate protests and riots, they now acted like veteran trade unionists in a developed capitalist society, occupying factories, mobilizing the support of the broader community, selecting leaders and negotiating committees through democratic processes, and putting forward demands that ranged from issues of workplace safety to broader questions of civil rights for the entire Polish population. Kirkland was intrigued with descriptions of Lech Walesa. An electrician who had been fired for his labor activism at the Lenin yard, Walesa seemed the epitome of the charismatic working-class hero, a man with little formal education and lacking in strong ideological passions, outside a devotion to the Catholic Church and an instinctive love of freedom.

Finally, Kirkland took especially careful note of the Communist regime's seeming impotence in the face of what was fast becoming a movement for worker rights, free expression, and civil liberties that embraced practically the entire Polish nation. The authorities carefully refrained from violence, there were few arrests, and when it became clear that the strike leadership intended to ignore the regime's pleadings and bluster, the government did the unthinkable: it sat down and bargained with its workers and in the end agreed to most of the strikers' demands.

One week into the strike, and well before the settlement with the regime had been announced, Kirkland made clear the federation's intention to provide assistance to the Polish workers. At an August 21 press conference during an executive council meeting in Chicago, Kirkland was asked whether the regime might be "antagonized into taking some further action against the strikers" in response to assistance from the

AFL-CIO, a question that reflected a concern that was widespread among Western foreign policy elites, including high officials in the Carter administration. In diplomatic circles, a consensus view prevailed that the Soviets were determined to thwart all challenges to their domination of Eastern Europe and that anti-Communist movements like Solidarity were doomed to fail. The foreign policy establishment also believed that the West should refrain from giving assistance to forces that posed a threat to the East European status quo, on the grounds that Western "intervention" would provide Moscow with a pretext for military response. Kirkland, however, flatly rejected the proposition that aid from Western trade unions would provoke official repression or a Soviet invasion. His credo in such matters was summarized in his answer to the press:

> I believe that the Soviet Union and its vassal Polish government will take such actions as it deems in its interests. I believe that the main deterrent to such action would be (a) the hope they might have that the strike would simply collapse and the workers revert to a condition of servitude and exploitation; (b) that such action would not be cost-free.
>
> Every spokesman for freedom in Iron Curtain countries with whom we have had contact . . . has strongly asserted the proposition that their survival and inspiration depend very heavily on support and attention and publicity from the Free World. I have never heard one of them . . . suggest that the strongest possible expressions of support, publicity and attention did them harm. . . . I'm unable to convince myself that better deeds are going to be done in the dark than will be done in the broad daylight of attention and vocal and public support.
>
> They are our brothers and sisters and we owe them that support. . . . We would feel a little bit like dogs if we failed to do it out of some apprehension as to what the Soviet government might do, particularly if we believe . . . that if the world sits silent and is incapable of responding appropriately, these powers will be encouraged to brutally repress the strike.[2]

Even before Kirkland made these remarks, the American labor movement had taken action to support the Polish workers. The day prior to Kirkland's press conference, Teddy Gleason, president of the International Longshoremen's Association (ILA), announced that his union, which represented 110,000 dockworkers at ports on the East Coast and Gulf of Mexico, would launch a boycott of Polish shipments and named as initial target a cargo of Polish hams headed to the United States. Kirkland, meanwhile, dispatched letters to the International

Confederation of Free Trade Unions and the International Transport Workers' Federation, requesting support for the ILA action.[3]

Although high officials in the American government continued to pay lip service to the liberation of Eastern Europe from Communist rule and Soviet domination, it had been many years since the United States had welcomed the destabilization of Moscow's satellite empire. Some, recalling the tragic fates of anti-Communist uprisings in East Germany and Hungary and the nonviolent Prague Spring, had concluded that efforts to change the settled order of affairs in Eastern Europe were foredoomed by the certainty of Red Army intervention. In Europe, diplomats seemed to resent the Polish workers for complicating relations with the Kremlin.

Kirkland's forthright endorsement of the strikers' objectives and his unapologetic vow to involve the AFL-CIO in the Polish dispute by dispatching assistance to the workers made him unique among influential Americans. On August 31, both Kirkland and Douglas Fraser, whose UAW had yet to reaffiliate with the AFL-CIO, made separate announcements of their intention to send aid to the embattled Polish workers. Fraser revealed that his union had already made a donation of $25,000, the money being channeled through the International Metalworkers Federation. Fraser was reluctant to dwell on the UAW's action out of fear that the Soviets might seize on American labor's involvement to label the strike an "imperialistic, capitalistic plot," and added that he did not want to give the "Communist hierarchy" the opportunity "to say that this was not really a workers' revolt." By contrast, Kirkland told reporters on *Meet the Press* that the Polish strike was "an exciting and inspiring event" and asserted that the international labor movement would impose a massive transportation blockade on Polish goods if matters were not soon resolved. But Kirkland was already looking at Polish developments from the perspective of the long and arduous struggle to liberate East Europeans from the Soviet maw. "For the first time a pluralistic institution has been accepted within a Communist regime," he noted, "with consequences that could be quite far-reaching."[4] Few others could claim to share Kirkland's prescience.

From the very outset, then, Kirkland regarded the Polish workers' movement—soon to be formally constituted as a union and given the name Solidarnosc, or Solidarity—as a phenomenon altogether different in character and potential from the samizdat manifestoes and dissident protests that had emerged throughout the Soviet bloc during the 1970s. Intellectual dissidents wrote brilliant polemics and displayed remarkable personal courage in the face of Communist brutality. But until Solidarity, the authorities had shown themselves fully capable of smothering the small, atomized, and factionalized opposition. If the influence of a

particular dissident reached a level that the higher circles deemed dangerous, the apparatus of control had the option of packing him off to prison
camp or forcing him into exile, as was done to Solzhenitsyn and Vladimir
Bukovsky. Poland's Communists, however, did not have the option of
exiling or jailing an entire working class.

Kirkland's embrace of Solidarity brought him into immediate conflict
with the Carter administration. Despite the administration's avowed commitment to human rights, Edmund Muskie, secretary of state, decided
that quiet diplomacy was the most prudent course to follow in the Polish
crisis. He summoned Kirkland to his office for a September 3 lunch, during which he gave a "negative assessment" of the Polish aid fund that the
AFL-CIO had just launched and declared that the federation's open support for Solidarity could be "deliberately misinterpreted" by the Kremlin
in order to justify military intervention.

Kirkland was unimpressed by these arguments. He told Muskie that
while it might not be wise for the American government to provide direct
support to Solidarity, the labor movement, as an independent institution
with ties to free unions around the world, had the obligation to assist its
fellow unionists. He added that the aid fund would enable American
workers to make personal contributions to the Solidarity cause and was
consistent with labor's actions on behalf of workers in Chile.[5]

Muskie was not alone in deploring labor's Polish initiative. In a *New
York Times* column, Flora Lewis called the workers' aid fund "most unfortunate" and compared the impact of Kirkland's action to a putative Soviet
decision to provide assistance to striking New York subway workers (a
strike of the New York transit system had recently been lost) or to the
farmworkers' union led by Cesar Chavez.[6] Nevertheless, the administration decided against exerting further pressure on Kirkland to abandon the
aid fund.[7]

Soon enough, the Communist bloc press ignited a drumbeat of criticism aimed at Kirkland and the federation. The more sophisticated arguments were voiced by anonymous "moderates" within the Polish party in
discussion with Western correspondents. Regime figures praised the
restraint of the American government; in contrast, they criticized the AFL-
CIO's initiatives as acts of "interference" that might have the effect of
emboldening hard-liners within the party.[8] The Polish press agency, PAP,
published a more vituperative commentary; it condemned the AFL-CIO
for its "rabid anti-socialist program" and accused American labor of trying
"to intrude on the new Polish trade union with a line of action that is inimical to the Polish sociopolitical system and Poland's alliances."[9] Not to be
outdone, TASS denounced "trade union bosses in America" for "exerting
every effort to support subversive, anti-social forces in Poland."[10]

While the anti-AFL-CIO diatribes published by TASS and other official Communist sources could be dismissed as boilerplate bluster, unofficial Kremlin sources—the sorts of "moderates" that diplomats and journalists looked to for hints about the Kremlin's thinking on the issue of the day—were insinuating a message designed to reinforce the State Department's concern about the AFL-CIO aid fund. The American embassy in Moscow sent a cable to Muskie that quoted Genrikh Trofimov, an analyst for the Institute for the Study of the USA and Canada, to the effect that Kirkland's move "was the kind of action that could cause problems." Polish officials were also telling American diplomats that the AFL-CIO's action "could certainly be used as a pretext for Soviet intervention." Although American officials understood that the Soviets were fully capable of "discovering" evidence of foreign mischiefmaking to justify an invasion, Muskie decided to inform the Soviet chargé d'affaires, Vladillen Vasev, that the Polish workers' aid fund had been launched as an independent venture by American labor and was done without the sanction of the administration. Whether directly or otherwise, Muskie was telling the Soviets that the government not only had nothing to do with the AFL-CIO action, but disapproved of it as well.[11]

Solidarity did not share the State Department's apprehensions about American labor's involvement in Polish developments. On September 12, Walesa said that outside assistance was welcomed, given the union's lack of resources inside Poland. He pointedly added, "Help can never be politically embarrassing. That of the AFL-CIO, for example. We are grateful to them. It was a very good thing that they helped us. Whenever we can, we will help them, too."[12]

Although Kirkland and Walesa were not to meet until 1989, there was, from the beginning, a strong bond between the two leaders that transcended their inability to speak to one another directly. Both were committed trade unionists; both believed that international labor solidarity was a powerful force against dictatorship and that Communism, despite its brutal and totalitarian character, was vulnerable to opposition movements that enjoyed mass popular support. Kirkland admired Walesa's audacity—his willingness to ignore the threats of Polish Communists, the rantings of the Soviet Politburo, and for that matter, the polite advice that emanated from the American embassy in Warsaw. Although Kirkland was unaware at the time, Communist officials had gone to Walesa and urged that Solidarity avoid ties to the AFL-CIO on the grounds that the federation was an instrument of the CIA. "I simply ignored them," Walesa said years later.[13] Kirkland's resolve was reinforced by Walesa's expressions of gratitude. Kirkland told *U.S. News and World Report* that labor would help the Poles "in any way we can, including financially." He again dismissed the proposition that the delivery of aid to the Poles would trigger a Soviet invasion. "I don't believe that the cause of trade unionism was ever advanced on little cat feet. We are a movement of free trade unions, and freedom of expression is the only way we know to conduct our affairs." Besides, he added, the Soviet Union "will act on the basis of its own appraisal of its own interests, not on the basis of anything we might say."[14]

The administration again had occasion to fret over the AFL-CIO's role in Poland on September 29. During a meeting of senior foreign policy officials, Warren Christopher, then deputy secretary of state, asked whether anything could be done to convince Kirkland to take a low profile on assistance to Solidarity. Zbigniew Brzezinski, national security adviser, said he would talk to Kirkland and drive home the sensitivity of the Polish crisis.[15] But when it became evident that Kirkland could not be dissuaded from establishing a fund-raising project for Solidarity, government officials and other members of the foreign policy elite adopted a new tack. They suggested that rather than give assistance directly to Solidarity, the AFL-CIO send contributions through "discreet" or clandestine routes. Kirkland found the notion that labor should operate secretly through intelligence channels ironic, given the criticism heaped on the federation for its alleged past involvement with the CIA. Kirkland, of course, did not share the Left's disdain for the CIA. But he was skeptical of the CIA's more adventurous operations, questioned the agency's judgment at times, and believed that successful movements for freedom required the support of the masses rather than military action by CIA-backed surrogates. More important, he was committed to the proposition that on his watch, labor's involvement in international affairs would be completely transparent.

Kirkland was also aware that in taking on the role of Solidarity's chief Western backer, the AFL-CIO was assuming a unique set of responsibilities. While Kirkland was rocklike in his support for the Polish union, he was never reckless in his comments or actions. He and his aides scrupulously refrained from issuing commentaries on the evolving political situation in Poland. Kirkland also made it a foundation of AFL-CIO policy that in relations with Solidarity, the Americans would adhere to the wishes of Walesa and his advisers and avoid efforts to impose anything that could be construed as an American agenda. "Our policies will be guided by Solidarity's needs," he declared.[16]

Among Carter's top officials, the figure most sympathetic to Kirkland's stance on Poland was Brzezinski. Brzezinski was impressed by the lines of communication that the federation had opened to Solidarity and regarded Kirkland's influence within the international labor movement as an important asset in the event of a crackdown against the union.

In December, Brzezinski told Kirkland that American intelligence believed that a Soviet invasion of Poland was imminent; to forestall a catastrophe, Brzezinski was putting together a list of retaliatory measures the United States would take, with the intention of sending it along to Soviet leader Leonid Brezhnev as a reminder that intervention would not be without consequences. Kirkland told Brzezinski that should the Soviets intervene, a worldwide boycott on the shipment of Polish and Soviet goods—by air, sea, or rail—could be organized, given Solidarity's popular standing with unions around the globe. Brzezinski subsequently added the boycott threat to his list.[17]

By mid-January 1981, the AFL-CIO reported that it had raised $160,000 for Solidarity, the money coming from contributions from individual unions, collections at plant gates, and the sale of T-shirts and other Solidarity paraphernalia organized by a youth organization established specifically to raise money for Solidarity and to mobilize pro-Solidarity events on college campuses. The AFL-CIO was not alone in supporting Solidarity; unions from West Germany, France, Japan, and other countries were helping the Polish union with material contributions; the bulk of the money was used to purchase printing equipment and other instruments of communication.[18]

Kirkland's commitment to the Solidarity cause was reinforced by a report he received from Bayard Rustin, who visited Poland in April 1981 at the invitation of a Solidarity group in the city of Kielce. Rustin, a legendary civil rights leader and president of the A. Philip Randolph Institute, had visited Warsaw two years previously and at that time thought the city gray, somber, and fearful. Now, however, he found the Polish capital transformed, marked by "a sense of straightforwardness, honesty, and new-found freedom," a place where "everyone speaks without restraint." A perceptive observer of social revolutions, Rustin was impressed by Solidarity and cautiously optimistic about its long-range prospects. He seemed to concur with a Solidarity official who described the union as a "national movement in trade union form" and quoted approvingly declarations that identified Solidarity as the initial event in a broad movement for freedom in East-Central Europe. Rustin described Solidarity as "unprecedented" in his long experience with revolutionary movements, in that it was "the first not led by a small educated elite" but rather one whose "engine is what can probably be characterized as society's most potent force for social change—workers."[19]

By the summer of 1981, Kirkland was confronted by challenges on several different fronts, as described in chapter 5. President Reagan had announced a series of domestic initiatives that labor opposed, had appointed officials who seemed committed to undoing regulations that unions deemed essential to working people, and had fired the air traffic controllers. Kirkland was also preoccupied with plans for Solidarity Day, the first major step in his campaign to reverse the conservative direction of American domestic politics. But Kirkland was determined to maintain his involvement in the unfolding developments in Poland. He was by now recognized as Solidarity's most resolute supporter in the Free World. Poland's Communist authorities gave recognition to Kirkland's role as a source of financial and ideological sustenance for the new union by denying him a visa to attend Solidarity's first congress in September 1981. Kirkland was disappointed and angry; he accused the authorities of "a vicious and slanderous propaganda attack on the AFL-CIO delegation."[20] Kirkland then gave a text of the speech he had planned to deliver to Msgr. George Higgins and sent another to the congress through the normal channels the AFL-CIO used to get material in and out of the country. Higgins was traveling to Poland on a tourist visa; he gave the text to the organizers of the congress, who then had it read to the delegates.

Kirkland was one of the few foreigners barred from the congress, a fact that did not escape the Solidarity delegates. "We figured that if the Communists prohibited Lane Kirkland from attending our congress, he must be our best friend," noted Wiktor Kulerski, a union leader from Warsaw.[21] The speech itself stressed Solidarity's role as a motor force of freedom for workers everywhere, which the delegates interpreted to mean the Communist world. Solidarity, Kirkland wrote, had "renewed the spirits of workers around the world. Polish workers still continue to teach the world." He added that there was "no task more urgent than unlinking human rights and freedom from the question of who owns the means of production. Respect for workers' rights does not automatically flow from any economic system."

Kirkland's remarks can be looked on as a coded version of the controversial resolution adopted later by the Solidarity delegates that pledged solidarity with working people throughout the Soviet bloc, a statement that was widely deplored as provocative, but that reflected the anti-Communist and internationalist sentiments shared by the union leadership. The delegates certainly understood the subtleties of Kirkland's message; his speech received a stormy ovation.

It had always been clear that Polish authorities had tolerated the existence of Solidarity because of their own weakened condition, and not from genuine commitment to change. The new Polish leader, the same General Jaruzelski who had put down the worker rebellion in 1970, was under intense pressure from the Soviets, who, although unwilling to launch an invasion of Poland, were privately issuing demands that the Polish party take measures to restore order and eliminate Solidarity. The year 1981 was marked by a series of clashes between Solidarity and the regime; as the year drew to a close, American intelligence officials received urgent warnings that a major act of repression was imminent.

On December 13, 1981, the regime gave its answer. That night, members of the ZOMO, a special security unit formed to put down manifestations of political opposition, arrested the bulk of the union leadership, including Walesa, as they left a conference in Gdansk. Jaruzelski imposed a series of martial law measures and banned Solidarity. The ZOMO and other security units scoured the country, breaking into apartments and stopping travelers in a nationwide dragnet for members of the union leadership who had eluded arrest in Gdansk.

When martial law was declared, Kirkland was in Paris attending a meeting of the Organization for Economic Cooperation and Development. Before heading back to Washington, he stopped off in London to attend a dinner at the English Speaking Union, where he could meet with a group of high officials from the Labour Party, the Social Democratic Party (a recently formed split-off from Labour), and British trade unionists. The Labour Party was in a state of disarray, with a growing cleavage between the party's moderate wing and the forces of the left, which included a substantial representation of pacifists, neutralists, and Marxists. But even though those attending the dinner were drawn from the moderate Atlanticist faction, Kirkland found the evening an exercise in frustration. Asked to say a few words, Kirkland reminded his hosts of the serious nature of the Polish crisis and urged the Free World to respond with a full range of penalties against the Polish and Soviet regimes. This brought a pointed rejoinder from Denis Healey, an important Labour Party figure who at one time was considered a prospect for the leadership post. "I think we should all pray for the success of General Jaruzelski," Healey told the stunned Kirkland. "There is no possibility of there being a democratic labor movement in Poland and the best we can hope for is stability and General Jaruzelski represents stability." Kirkland was infuriated, and a loud argument ensued. In fact, Healey's views, though crudely expressed, did reflect the lack of enthusiasm for Solidarity that was widespread in the Labour Party; Solidarity veterans recall Labour as among the least stalwart European parties during martial law.[22]

Upon returning to the United States, Kirkland issued a statement that blamed the Polish government for the country's ills and accused the regime of "consistently dealing in bad faith with the Polish people." "[Solidarity's] battle is ours, and we shall not let them down," he concluded. He also called on Western governments and the ICFTU to immediately plan measures to punish the regime.[23]

On December 15, Kirkland was summoned to the White House to discuss the Polish crisis with President Reagan. Reagan was flanked by several top aides, including secretary of state Alexander Haig; chief of staff James Baker; presidential counselor Ed Meese; and James Nance, acting head of the National Security Agency. Prior to the meeting, Nance had asked an aide to prepare a briefing paper for Reagan; the paper observed that the AFL-CIO "claimed that we had not been strong enough in our reaction to the Polish government's imposition of martial law."[24]

This was Kirkland's second meeting with the president; the first, two weeks earlier, had ended without labor and the president having reached common ground on the air traffic controllers or economic policy. With this past difficulty in mind, Reagan opened the meeting by declaring, "Well, at last we have something we can agree on." Kirkland, however, demurred. He told Reagan that the administration's response to martial law was inadequate. Asked how he would have the government respond, Kirkland went directly to what he saw as the heart of the matter: the billions in outstanding loans from Western governments and banks that had been extended to Poland over the years in support of unsound development schemes, money the Poles were now unable to repay. Kirkland proposed, in effect, a declaration of economic war. He urged "the toughest possible sanctions . . . and you should start by declaring our loans to Poland . . . in default, which in fact they are. You should declare them formally in default." Such action, Kirkland added, should be taken with the goal of destroying Poland's credit and making it impossible for the regime to receive further loans. Kirkland also told Reagan that the AFL-CIO intended to get material into the hands of Solidarity's surviving structures through the networks it had developed over the previous year. "We have the contacts . . . to do it, and we'll use whatever resources we can, but whatever resources could be provided would be [helpful]." Reagan said he would take Kirkland's views into consideration, and the meeting ended. The next day, Kirkland had a similar session with Vice President George Bush at Bush's residence. Among those present was William Casey, CIA director.[25]

While Haig was firmly opposed to Kirkland's plan for wide-ranging sanctions, he hoped to forge a cooperative relationship with the labor leader. Haig respected Kirkland for his toughness, patriotism, and commitment to America's Cold War objectives. Haig also thought highly of Irving Brown, the AFL-CIO's European representative (and soon to be appointed as director of international affairs), with whom he had worked while serving as America's ambassador to NATO.[26] Haig planned to ask Kirkland to use his powers of persuasion to enlist the support of European trade unions to support the administration's Poland policy.

Kirkland was already pressing the Europeans to mobilize behind Solidarity; if anything, he would likely encourage his international labor contacts to support stronger countermeasures than Reagan planned to initiate.[27]

For the duration of the Polish crisis, Kirkland remained critical of the Reagan administration for what he regarded as a consistently inadequate policy toward the Jaruzelski regime. Kirkland believed that the administration was fixated on Central America, a region he saw as of secondary importance to the outcome of the Cold War, while giving low priority to a struggle that held forth the possibility of rolling back Soviet power in its East European backyard. Kirkland was convinced that the Soviets, already bogged down in their Afghanistan quagmire, were unlikely to intervene in Poland, thus opening the way for the United States to devise creative measures to prevent Jaruzelski from consolidating the kind of "normalized" regime that the Soviets and their Czechoslovak subalterns had imposed rather quickly after the Prague Spring had been crushed in 1968. Kirkland also believed that the administration's Poland policy was dictated in large measure by the Republican Party's ties to the world of finance, which vigorously opposed Kirkland's prescription of calling in the debt and forcing the Polish government into default.

After martial law, then, Kirkland invariably included a swipe at the Reagan administration in speeches and interviews about Poland. Thus, at a January 30, 1981, rally in Chicago—one of a number held in various American cities to protest martial law—Kirkland took both the administration and other Western governments to task for permitting "a steady flow of credits to those who keep Lech Walesa in prison, Andrei Sakharov in exile [the Soviet dissident had been sentenced to internal exile in Gorky for protesting the invasion of Afghanistan], thousands in psychiatric clinics, countless more in labor camps, and whole peoples enslaved."[28]

To be sure, the administration did adopt a series of sanctions directed against the Polish regime. But these measures were largely symbolic in nature: the cancellation of landing rights for Lot, the Polish national airline; the denial of commercial fishing permits in American waters; the cancellation of Export-Import Bank insurance for deals with Poland. Reagan took no steps against the Soviets and refused to call in the debt and declare Poland in bankruptcy. Kirkland fumed, as did hard-liners within both parties. But within policymaking circles, the business community, and the foreign policy establishment, there was no support for a sanctions regime that went beyond the modest measures imposed by the United States. Although the Polish-American community was divided over sanctions, its most influential circles were opposed to the strong measures favored by Kirkland. Within the administration, the influence of anti-Communist hard-liners, substantial on policy toward Central America and arms control, was insignificant regarding Poland. At a meeting to hammer out a recommendation for administration action on Poland involving officials from the State, Commerce, Defense, and Treasury departments and the National Security Council, only Fred Ikle, undersecretary of defense for policy, argued for default.[29] Finally, America's European allies were unenthusiastic about any measures designed to punish the Polish regime and were appalled at the idea of economic warfare. West Germany, then governed by the Social Democrats, argued that the time was not right for an "overreaction" to Polish events, while British Labour Party leaders declared that Poland's troubles were in part due to extremists within Solidarity and called for restraint by the West.[30]

The absence of broad support for a bolder response to martial law did not deter Kirkland. In late December 1981, the AFL-CIO unveiled an even more ambitious sanctions formula that lumped the Soviets in with the Polish Communists as targets. As explained by Tom Kahn, aide and speechwriter to Kirkland, the plan called not only for economic measures against the Communist bloc, but for penalties against West European countries that undermined the sanctions through economic arrangements with Warsaw or Moscow. Kahn said that wherever possible, the United States should coordinate its Poland policies with its NATO partners. "But given the current state of confusion in European thinking," Kahn added, "this is not the time for the United States to follow or to seek the lowest common denominator of actions." In addition to calling in the debt, the AFL-CIO proposal demanded the denial of future credits to the Soviets and their Warsaw Pact satellites, the suspension of export licenses for American corporations involved in a Siberian gas pipeline deal, the placement of technology to the Soviet Union under strict national security scrutiny, and the withdrawal of the American delegations from arms control negotiations and from the conference in Madrid to review progress in the Helsinki Accords.[31]

Kirkland had another opportunity to lay out his sanctions proposal during a meeting with Reagan on February 3, 1982. The administration's response came two weeks later, when Secretary of State Haig addressed the executive council at its annual Bal Harbour retreat. After listening to Kirkland criticize Reagan as lacking fortitude on Poland and urge the United States to act unilaterally if its allies balked at sanctions, Haig argued that a go-it-alone strategy would have no impact on the Soviets and that a ban on exports to the USSR would in effect amount to an embargo on grain, by far the most important American export to its Cold War adversary. Reagan, in fact, had ended the embargo on grain shipments to the Soviets that Carter had imposed after the invasion of

Afghanistan as fulfillment of a campaign promise to farm interests. Haig contended that to reinstate the embargo would be politically difficult and would have limited effect, since the Soviets had the option of buying grain from other countries.[32]

Although he sometimes criticized Reagan's policies, Kirkland enjoyed good working relations with Haig and his successor as secretary of state, George P. Shultz, and regarded Lawrence Eagleburger, undersecretary of state, as a friend. Kirkland, however, was convinced that where Poland was concerned, it was Reagan's buddies in the banking community who were calling the shots. He accused Reagan of caring more about the impact of default on bankers in the United States than on the suffering of the imprisoned Solidarity leadership. "The bankers are calling the tune, and the tune is business as usual," he declared. Before the West German labor federation, however, Kirkland concentrated on the nature of the Polish regime, calling the Jaruzelski government a "fascist junta."[33]

Kirkland issued another attack aimed mainly at the administration on Labor Day in 1982. "Stop the flow of credits to the Soviet bloc," he implored. "Stop financing Lech Walesa's jailers." Kirkland also had a sign erected on the outside portico of the federation's headquarters. It contained two messages. One message read: "AFL-CIO Remembers: This is 262 Days for Solidarity prisoners." The second message focused on domestic concerns: "U.S. Unemployment Over 10.8 Million—9.8 Percent." The sign was changed daily; it was taken down a year or so later, after martial law was effectively ended and the unemployment rate began to decline.[34]

Reagan did, in fact, strengthen the sanctions by stripping Poland of its Most Favored Nation trade status in response to the vote by the rubber stamp Polish parliament to outlaw Solidarity. Under normal economic conditions, this action would have weakened Poland diplomatically and economically—it was the only Communist country to enjoy MFN status—by adding layers of duty onto imports from Poland. But given the collapse of the Polish economy, the withdrawal of MFN had little practical political effect. Kirkland dismissed the initiative as "relatively weak" and renewed his demand for an end to the rollover of Poland's external debt. "It's the only way we know to stop this constant financing of the Eastern bloc, the financing of the buildup of military power, and the enforcement of police state measures." To the administration's assertion that default would have damaging consequences for American banks, Kirkland responded, "If it hurts us now, all the more reason to do it before it hurts us even more in the future." Kirkland expressed the fear that by continuing to extend credit to economically weak Communist countries, the West could wind up in a position where the debtors could actually dictate terms to the lenders. "We've got ourselves into the position where, virtually, they own us in terms of the banking connection. If we're going to sell them the rope by which they're going to hang us, at least we should make them pay cash for it."[35]

But by this time, the issue confronting Kirkland was not whether the administration would stiffen its stance toward Poland, but whether it would retain the relatively modest measures already in place. Few within the State Department supported sanctions to begin with, and there was practically no inclination on the part of those responsible for policy toward Eastern Europe to tighten the screws on Jaruzelski. Reagan himself paid little attention to the Polish crisis once it appeared that the regime had gained the upper hand over Solidarity; he devoted far more time to relations with the Soviets and with Central America. Likewise, the State Department had no settled, consistent policy toward Eastern Europe and did not believe that Solidarity had the capability of bringing down the Communist system.

Yet even though Poland was not a high item on its agenda and despite the lack of consistency in its policies during the Poland crisis, the administration did support Solidarity. Unlike the leaders of the principal West European allies, Reagan was not committed to a status quo that forever ceded domination over Eastern Europe to the Soviets. Reagan, in fact, actually believed that Communism was destined to collapse, and his policies were designed to move that process along. Within the State Department, the expectations of change were less ambitious. According to Thomas Simons, deputy assistant secretary of state for European affairs, the goals of American policy were threefold: to keep the Soviets on the defensive, to "soften up Communism," and to increase the liberty of the Polish people by pressuring the authorities to make concessions. These objectives were pursued, Simons says, "without the expectation of overthrow."[36] Kirkland believed that the administration did not care whether Solidarity reemerged as a legal trade union. He told Jonathan Kwitny, "It was our government's policy during that underground period to find some way out that did not involve the reemergence of Solidarity." He claimed that Undersecretary of State Eagleburger asked him to recognize the government-created and -controlled trade union that had been set up to supplant Solidarity. Kirkland replied with the slogan: "No democracy without Solidarity."[37]

About one year into martial law, Jaruzelski announced his intention to lift the restrictions imposed on Polish society, the exception being the ban on Solidarity. But when on July 22, 1983, the regime announced the formal end to martial law, Kirkland spoke out against a relaxation of sanctions. Instead, he called Jaruzelski's actions a "sham" and aligned himself with Solidarity's demands for the release of all political prisoners, the restoration of trade union rights, and adherence to the Gdansk accords, which gave Poles the right to form independent unions. Kirkland added that the regime had failed to grant an amnesty to high-ranking union officials, retained special powers to curb unrest, and had insinuated into the legal code martial law's most repressive features.[38]

On October 3, Kirkland was presiding over the federation's biannual convention in Hollywood, Florida, when it was announced that Walesa had been awarded the 1983 Nobel Peace Prize. Kirkland was delighted with the news and happily read a note from Walesa that lauded American labor for its stalwart support. "The good will and solidarity, as well as the moral and concrete assistance extended to us . . . is received by Polish trade unionists with joy and gratitude," Walesa wrote. Responded Kirkland, "In solidarity, we shall triumph."[39]

Within a month, the administration announced that it was formally easing the sanctions regime. Kirkland heard the news while attending an exhibition of Solidarity art in the Russell Long Senate Office Building. He reacted sharply: "As we assemble here, to rededicate to Solidarity, bureaucrats in other buildings are straining to find excuses for relaxing the modest sanctions on Poland by our government. We must hope they do not succeed. If we falter in our resolve with regard to Poland, our demonstrations of force elsewhere in the world will not suffice to restore credibility to our declarations of support for freedom fighters around the world." Kirkland's allusion to "demonstrations of force" referred to the administration's operation in Grenada, executed the previous month. Kirkland supported the removal of the pro-Soviet New Jewel Movement from power but, again, believed that Grenada, like Nicaragua, was a Cold War sideshow; the real target of opportunity, he felt, was on the Soviet Union's doorstep, in Poland.

The most important of the concessions involved what, for Kirkland, was the most critical issue: Poland's external debt. According to the announcement, the United States would work with other Western nations to allow Poland to renegotiate its debt of $11 billion that was owed to governments. Poland would also be able to negotiate new fishing rights in American waters. Left unchanged were the denial of landing rights for Lot, a prohibition on the sale of high technology, the revocation of Most Favored Nation status, and the denial of new economic assistance. In justifying its actions, the administration cited the regime's having released most of the Solidarity leaders seized in the first weeks of martial law. But two thousand political prisoners remained behind bars, and the authorities were about to place eleven activists on trial for treason.[40]

Throughout the period of Solidarity's underground existence, Kirkland maintained a policy of synchronizing the federation's actions with Walesa and his leadership. In practice, this meant that if Solidarity supported the relaxation of sanctions, Kirkland would go along. Although Solidarity leaders were kept well informed about the shifting currents of Poland policy in the United States and understood the different approaches of the administration, Congress, labor, and the Polish-American community, they seldom distinguished between Reagan and Kirkland as advocates of Polish freedom. Likewise, both were perceived as supporters of sanctions and were applauded for it. Sanctions could be a delicate issue for the better-known Solidarity figures. "We could not openly support sanctions," said Janusz Onyszkiewicz, Solidarity's principal spokesman, "because then the authorities could charge us with treason." Onyszkiewicz said Solidarity supported a "stick-and-carrot approach," whereby sanctions could be eased in return for improvements in human rights or tightened in times of crackdown. Onyszkiewicz himself was a beneficiary of this approach; he was among a group of political prisoners who were released after the United States announced one of its periodic rounds of sanctions lifting.[41]

Some of Lane's aides were convinced that the American government exerted pressure on Walesa to endorse the administration's decision to lift sanctions. Solidarity officials acknowledge that diplomats from the American embassy did discuss the sanctions question with them and occasionally encouraged Walesa to support their easing but deny any arm-twisting. Tom Simons acknowledges that Walesa's blessings were regarded by the administration as crucial to any sanctions-lifting decision but expresses the belief that Walesa's approval of an easing of the sanctions regime was "sincere" and not the result of American pressure.[42] In fact, Solidarity veterans respected the American ambassador, John Davis, who was described by Bronislaw Geremek, an adviser to Walesa, as "a man who supported Solidarity without violating the norms of diplomacy." Geremek supported sanctions, as did other Solidarity officials, "even though we understood the penalty they were exacting from Poland." "I never doubted that in the long run the sanctions policy helped Poland. In this regard, Kirkland expressed the sense of our expectations."[43] Another Solidarity leader, Zbigniew Romaszewski, recalls that at one point Walesa prepared two letters: one supporting the maintenance of sanctions; the other calling for their lifting. Reagan eventually announced a compromise by which some sanctions were left in place.[44]

By 1986, the administration began serious consideration of lifting all remaining sanctions. Although Kirkland and a few hard-liners lobbied for the status quo until Solidarity was given back its legal status, the antisanctions position had mushroomed into a broad coalition in the United States and abroad, ranging from the Polish Catholic Church, European governments, influential Polish-Americans, important elements of the American Catholic Church, and a number of the Democratic Party's leading voices on international affairs. Shultz went along, although with some misgivings; he worried that in the absence of serious economic reforms, Poland was likely to seek yet another round of loan extensions, something that would achieve little beyond further burdening the country with debt.

When, in early 1987, the administration decided to lift the remaining sanction measures, Tom Simons traveled to New York to inform Kirkland of the decision face-to-face. Kirkland was attending an exhibit of Fabergé eggs at the museum in the Forbes publications offices. The news angered Kirkland; he assented to the decision, grudgingly, after a French trade union delegation passed a note to Walesa during a visit (it was assumed that Walesa's home was bugged), asking whether he supported the administration's move. Walesa indicated that he did support the Reagan policy.[45]

Kirkland, however, did not surrender the sanctions fight. In large measure due to lobbying by the AFL-CIO, legislation that set the terms for the General System of Preferences—under which poorer countries were allowed to export commodities to the United States at favorable trade terms—called for a denial of GSP status to countries that violated internationally recognized worker and trade union rights. Reagan had already invoked the worker rights' provisions in denying GSP privileges to Nicaragua, Chile, Hungary, and Paraguay. On August 22, 1988, Kirkland announced that the federation intended to issue a formal complaint against Poland, citing its suppression of Solidarity.[46]

Kirkland's GSP action would almost certainly have been successful, given Poland's widespread violation of the International Labor Organization's (ILO) freedom of association conventions. But before the case worked its way through the system, a series of remarkable events transformed the political landscape of Poland, Europe, and the world. Within a year, Solidarity had not only regained its legal status, it had become the ruling party of Poland, and Communist rule, as that concept was generally understood, had ceased to exist in the satellite countries.

Kirkland's contribution to Solidarity's triumph went well beyond his relentless campaign to push the administration toward a policy of robust support for Solidarity. There was the example of his resolve, his loyalty, his refusal to compromise basic principles, and his unique grasp of Solidarity's potential as an instrument of revolutionary change. There was the influence he wielded within the international labor movement toward a stance of support for the Polish union. And, of course, there was the money and material that the American labor movement provided to Solidarity from its inception right up until it achieved power, support that was crucial to the union's ability to survive during the dark days of martial law.

Kirkland began putting in place the structure of a distribution network linking American unions to the Solidarity underground almost immediately upon the declaration of martial law. The most important channel ran through a Solidarity office in Brussels that had been established, at Walesa's direction, to represent the union's interests during martial law. Jerzy Milewski, a Solidarity activist who had left Poland for a visit to the West two days before martial law was imposed, was selected to direct the office. Another veteran of the democratic opposition, Miroslaw Chojecki, took on the responsibility of developing routes into Poland by which money, printing presses, computers, and other materials could be shipped to underground sources.

To administer the federation's Poland project, Kirkland relied on a small cadre of dedicated assistants who shared his passion for the Solidarity cause. Tom Kahn, an assistant to Kirkland, coordinated the undertaking. Kahn had come to the AFL-CIO during the 1970s after years as a political radical and civil rights worker, having served as an aide to Bayard Rustin and then as executive director of the League for Industrial Democracy. Kahn was to succeed Irving Brown as director of international affairs upon Brown's death in 1989. Joining Kahn in the mid-1980s was Adrian Karatnycky, an American of Ukrainian descent who was fluent in Polish, Russian, and Ukrainian and who had been involved in various anti-Soviet protest campaigns. For reliable information from inside martial-law Poland, Kirkland relied heavily on the Committee in Support of Solidarity, whose principal figures—Irena Lasota, a Polish émigré who came to the United States after meeting with persecution for antiregime involvement as a university student, and Eric Chenoweth, a young political activist—had developed a wide range of contacts within the Solidarity structure.

Solidarity's principal needs were threefold: money to support the families of imprisoned activists and sustain the underground structure, printing presses and other equipment for an underground press, and financial aid to enable the union to conduct strikes and other nonviolent actions meant to weaken the regime's grip.

Getting money through the border control to Solidarity presented few problems since it was relatively simple to conceal cash in clothing or luggage or to squirrel it away in automobiles. But getting shipments of printing equipment into the country posed a number of tricky problems. To begin with, there was always the risk that ultra-diligent officials in

Western Europe might complicate matters, since the methods of shipment often violated the laws of the country of origin, as well as those of Poland. A more serious challenge was getting the shipments past Polish border control. To outwit the authorities, Chojecki developed transport networks originating from a number of European countries—principally, Sweden and France.[47] But while most shipments reached their intended destination, there were some notable failures as well. The Brussels office was sometimes criticized for sending large shipments into Poland on big, over-the-road trucks with false bills of lading. On one occasion, three trucks were stopped in Gdansk; authorities confiscated 14 duplicating machines, 5 copying machines, 9,500 duplicating machine matrices, 17 sets of light-sensitive matrices, a radiotelephone, and printed material. The equipment was unloaded and laid out in a sports stadium and then shown on television news as evidence of the subversive maneuverings of the enemies of Polish socialism. While these failures were dismaying at the time, veterans of the period contend that the seizure of some of the material was inevitable. "A certain amount of failure was expected," says Bronislaw Geremek, an adviser to Walesa who later became Poland's foreign minister. "They were strong; we were weak. The really important challenge was to determine if there were people within Solidarity who were informing the police about the shipments."[48]

Irving Brown came to believe that additional lines in and out of Poland were needed. He reasoned that given the decentralized nature of the underground, the more channels of distribution, the better. He also believed that the effectiveness of the Brussels office was hampered by the contradiction between its role as Solidarity's representative to the Free World and its responsibility for clandestine deliveries of equipment into Poland. He and Kirkland agreed that a second distribution route would be established; to run the operation, Brown chose Miroslaw Dominczyk, a Solidarity activist from Kielce who had been forced into exile after a year of martial law internment. Dominczyk had become acquainted with Karatnycky when Karatnycky accompanied Bayard Rustin to Poland in 1981. After his arrival in the United States, Dominczyk was asked to take responsibility for a smuggling operation and was given the code name "Coleslaw."[49]

Dominczyk's principal mission was to get into the hands of the underground printing equipment similar to that which had been seized during the first weeks of martial law. He soon moved his operation to London because of the availability of used and therefore inexpensive printing equipment that was compatible with the technology available to Poles. His initial success came when he persuaded a Polish bus driver to smuggle in printing equipment during his monthly trips to Warsaw (the passengers

were elderly Poles returning to the homeland for a visit). The driver did
not deliver the equipment to its destination; instead, he left his keys at a
prearranged spot. The shipment would then be off-loaded by members of
the underground, and the keys returned to the driver's room. Dominczyk
arranged alternative routes as well, using trucks and automobiles. He even
concealed printing equipment in a shipment of refrigerators.

Dominczyk then hit on an idea that greatly simplified his work. He
arranged for members of the underground who were responsible for
printing operations to visit London as tourists. There, he taught them
how to take apart and reassemble a printing press. Afterward, he began
shipping the equipment part by part, a much less risky smuggling method
than trying to get an entire press past the border. He also persuaded
yachtsmen from Denmark and Sweden to take equipment on trips around
the Baltic coast; the equipment would be transferred to boats manned by
Solidarity members, who would then bring it to shore.

There were failures as well. He once cried in frustration after a shipment of offset machines was returned; apparently, underground activists
feared that the authorities were watching the shipment and decided
against claiming it. Dominczyk's worst calamity occurred in 1987, when
a large shipment, encompassing seven offset machines, plates, ink, and
spare parts, was confiscated in East Germany.

Although the AFL-CIO was by far Solidarity's largest supplier of
material aid, it was not the only source of assistance. Trade union federations from all over Europe were sending equipment to the underground.
The most generous, according to Solidarity veterans, were the French,
including the CGT, the Communist-led federation. Likewise, both
Communist and non-Communist unions from Italy made contributions.
The least helpful were the union movements from West Germany,
though the German unions were more sympathetic than were the country's political leaders, who regarded Solidarity as an impediment to Bonn's
increasingly close ties to the Soviet Union and East Germany. Joanna
Pilarska, who worked with Milewski in the Brussels office, recalls that
while West German union officials were helpful in bringing Solidarity's
complaints before the ILO, they preferred that their role not be publicized back home. And where the AFL-CIO gave total and uncritical support to Solidarity, European union leaders frequently lectured the Poles
about the dangers of moving too far, too fast, to the point where
Solidarity officials stopped listening to them.[50]

That Solidarity received assistance from European union federations
with ties to social democratic and Communist parties carried important
propaganda value for the underground. "We didn't hide the fact that we
got money from abroad," recalls Janusz Onyszkiewicz. "The fact that we

got money from trade unions, including Communist federations, was not embarrassing for us. Rather, it was embarrassing for the authorities."[51] While the AFL-CIO and European labor disagreed on a number of geopolitical issues—Central America, for example—these differences were largely set aside when the goal was keeping Solidarity a viable force, though Onyszkiewicz recalls that the Swedish federation, the LO, was unhappy with the Polish union's close ties to American unions.

For Solidarity, contributions from abroad meant, above all else, the ability to maintain an underground press. In the vivid description of Wiktor Kulerski, "The printing presses we got from the West during martial law might be compared to machine guns or tanks during a war."[52] The publications ranged from mimeographed factory newsletters to intellectual journals to newspapers with a wide popular audience. Western assistance financed the entire publications structure, from the printing presses to the people who operated the presses, to the journalists who wrote articles, and on down to those who distributed the publications.

The importance of the press cannot be overemphasized. With Solidarity declared illegal, its activists could not perform their functions as union officials or as members of the democratic opposition, except through periodic strikes and protests, the impact of which diminished considerably as Polish society sank into a state of exhaustion. The press thus was the sole means of communication with Polish society, really the only way Solidarity could keep hope for the future alive and remind the authorities that no peace was possible as long as Solidarity was illegal. Irena Lasota summed up the critical role of the press thus:

> The press quite simply allowed Solidarity to survive during martial law. It kept people informed. It also gave Solidarity activists a sense of unity and comradeship and a purpose. If you couldn't write, you could contribute as a printer. If you couldn't write or print, you could help in the distribution. For some in Poland, the only sign that Solidarity was alive came through the press. And in some regions, it was the only source of real news. Even the worst newspapers played a unifying role in society, and the best ones played a role similar to the great newspapers of the past.[53]

To a certain extent, the press functioned as a surrogate trade union, taking on the responsibilities that Solidarity would have shouldered had it been legal. The press reported instances of workplace injuries and management corruption and told of families who had suffered through tragedy or official repression and were thus in need of help. The impact of its reports was magnified when selections were read over international broadcast services sponsored by Western governments, particularly Radio Free Europe.

Among the publications issued by the underground press were books long banned by the Communists, such as George Orwell's antitotalitarian classic *Animal Farm* and philosophical treatises by Hannah Arendt and Karl Jaspers. There were also journals targeted to those involved in the apparatus of repression. Czeslaw Bielecki, director of an underground publishing consortium, published a journal entitled *Dignity*, which was aimed at the police and included militia members among its writers. Another of Bielecki's publications, *Redoubt*, was meant for members of the military; most of the writing was done by three lieutenant colonels.[54]

As is often the case with opposition movements that challenge the authorities in totalitarian settings, Solidarity was awash in rumors of spies, double agents, and infiltrations by internal security. The Brussels office was the target of some of these rumors. Kahn and Karatnycky maintained a careful eye on Milewski's operation but never found reason to doubt the honesty of its staff, despite at least one major breach in security. In 1985 it was revealed that an agent of the regime had been functioning as a liaison between Brussels and the underground. The agent, Jacek Knapik, had lived in Austria for ten years and was in contact with various Solidarity support offices in Europe. In 1984, Knapik provided the police with information that led to the arrest of Bogdan Lis, one of the few Solidarity leaders to have eluded the police dragnet. When they arrested Lis, the police found letters addressed to him from Milewski that included the names of Solidarity's Western contacts, including Kirkland, Brown, and Brzezinski, and the amounts of money given Solidarity by the AFL-CIO's Free Trade Union Institute. Colonel Zbigniew Pudysz, the chief of the Interior Ministry's investigations office, called Kirkland "CIA-connected" and claimed that Brown was an actual agent. The main evidence against Brown was an accusation leveled by the renegade CIA agent Philip Agee in his book *Inside the Company*. "Contacts between Brown and Milewski are a classical pattern," declared Pudysz. "They prove how deep the CIA can penetrate."[55]

When years later Bogdan Borusewicz served on a parliamentary commission that investigated the tactics employed by the state security against Solidarity, he concluded that while the regime had recorded some successes in infiltrating the underground structures, the authorities had not succeeded in preventing the delivery of money and equipment from Western sources. Borusewicz believes that virtually all of the money sent to the underground reached its intended destination and that 70 percent of the equipment got through the border control. One of the early Solidarity leaders from Gdansk, Borusewicz says that the major worry for the underground was not the infiltration of the union's structures inside Poland, but the intelligence service's ability to insinuate agents among Polish communities in the West. "I was most concerned that Polish security might get to us through our contacts abroad," he recalls. For this reason, Solidarity preferred to deal with non-Poles rather than with émigrés in the United States, Great Britain, France, and other countries. While Solidarity leaders appreciated the political support the union received from Poles abroad, they sometimes refused to meet with Polish émigrés for fear they might have been recruited as informants for the regime.[56] The accusations of CIA involvement only reinforced Kirkland's credibility with the Polish people, who automatically assumed that those who came under attack by the official media were their allies in the cause of freedom and national sovereignty.

Despite Kirkland's insistence to the contrary, there were occasional rumors that the intelligence agency was the source for some of the AFL-CIO's Polish money. No evidence has ever been advanced to support this charge. Indeed, beginning in 1984, the AFL-CIO received a series of large grants from the new National Endowment for Democracy specifically for work on behalf of Solidarity; this money was supplemented by two $1 million allocations given to labor directly by Congress in 1988 and 1989. Further evidence comes from Robert M. Gates, a high-ranking CIA official under William Casey and later the agency's director. Gates reports that prior to martial law, Casey opposed CIA involvement in Poland in part because, in Casey's view, the AFL-CIO was doing a better job than the CIA might do in Poland; if the agency got involved, Casey said, it might "screw it up."[57]

By 1988, the struggle between Solidarity and the regime had reached a stalemate. On one level, the regime had clearly gained the upper hand in the political realm. Jaruzelski felt sufficiently confident of his power to lift martial law, release political prisoners, and ease restrictions on foreign travel. These measures had burnished his international stature; increasingly, he was regarded as a patriotic Pole who had reluctantly adopted a course of repression in order to prevent a Soviet invasion, rather than as an East European version of Chile's Pinochet. (The more charitable view of Jaruzelski has proved unwarranted; documents uncovered during the 1990s showed that Jaruzelski was actively seeking Soviet intervention and not, as was widely believed, arguing against invasion with Moscow.) But though Jaruzelski could claim to have gained dominance over Solidarity, he continued to preside over a critically ill economy, a condition that was not likely to improve until the government enjoyed the support of the people.

Solidarity then called a series of strikes in a determined effort to revive its fortunes and convince the regime that social peace required a settlement that included Solidarity. Foreign assistance, particularly from the AFL-CIO and the National Endowment for Democracy, was critical; without a strike fund, miners and other workers would not have agreed to make the financial sacrifices demanded by a work stoppage. Although the strikes did not succeed in crippling the government, they served an important purpose by convincing the regime to open talks with the opposition toward some sort of national accord. The result was an agreement to hold national elections in which the opposition, though unable to run as a Solidarity party, could put forward candidates for parliament and the regime would accept the election results.

This was a settlement of historic proportions. Nonetheless, many observers reckoned that it was the regime and not Solidarity that had gotten the better part of the bargain. Some doubted that Communists would ever permit a fair election, while others predicted that Poles would opt for the strong leadership of Jaruzelski rather than gamble on the undisciplined forces of Solidarity. Kirkland, however, was confident that unless the regime falsified the returns, Solidarity would easily triumph. He reasoned that given the option of voting for oppression or freedom, Poles—indeed, any people—would choose freedom.

Years later, he explained his faith in Solidarity's eventual victory:

> I still believe and I believed then that history moves when civil society reaches a critical point. It is not decided in the foreign ministries or the palaces of power but in the streets and the work places. And when critical mass is reached, there is nothing you can do unless you are willing to kill and slaughter and put the whole country in chains.[58]

Whatever his crimes, Jaruzelski was not inclined to kill thousands of his own countrymen to retain power. But like any autocrat, he enjoyed immense advantages over his adversaries, which he exploited to the hilt. The official press trumpeted the achievements of Communist candidates and studiously ignored the opposition. The party made liberal use of its patronage power. The police hovered over Solidarity rallies, checking identification papers and recording the names of those on hand. Bronislaw Geremek remembers that American government officials expressed pessimism about Solidarity's prospects, while Communists were certain they would win. "They had the apparatus of power, they had money, and they knew how to use it, especially in the press."

To help ensure a more level playing field, the AFL-CIO and the Polish American community gave Geremek, who was traveling in the United States, $100,000 for Solidarity's election campaign. The money was in cash, and when Poland's future foreign minister went through customs in Warsaw, he was searched, and the money was taken, laid out, and photographed, with the result that the media were full of accounts of the attempts by foreign interests to influence the Polish elections. But

Geremek was allowed to keep the money, a sign, Geremek believes, that the authorities were confident of victory.[59]

The regime's confidence could not have been more misplaced. When the elections were held in June, Solidarity scored an overwhelming victory, winning all but one of the contested seats in the lower house of parliament and 99 out of 100 in the upper house. While the accord with Jaruzelski had called for a power-sharing arrangement with the Communists, even in the event of a Solidarity electoral triumph, the results meant the effective end of Communist rule in Poland. By the end of the year, Communist dictatorships had been routed in every Soviet bloc country of Eastern Europe.

In the end, the AFL-CIO was responsible for channeling over $4 million to Solidarity. Prior to martial law and during martial law's initial period, some $500,000 was raised for the AFL-CIO Polish workers' aid fund. But with the establishment of the National Endowment for Democracy in 1984, the amount of money available to the AFL-CIO for Poland purposes rose dramatically. In all, $1.7 million was given to Solidarity by the Free Trade Union Institute, using NED grants. Money for Poland rose yet again when Congress approved special $1 million allocations to the federation for use on behalf of Solidarity in 1988 and 1989.

When Solidarity veterans are asked to select the people from abroad who made the most enduring contributions to their country's freedom, two names are invariably mentioned at the top of the list: Ronald Reagan and Lane Kirkland. These veterans are aware of the irony of linking a Republican who had free market convictions with a labor leader known for his strong liberal beliefs. They are also aware that the two held different positions on sanctions. But the nuances of the sanctions debate seem to have resonated more loudly in the United States; in Poland, the fact that Reagan was the only world leader to support any kind of sanctions regime was more important than the fact that he resisted Kirkland's demands for tougher penalties.

The Solidarity leadership respected Kirkland as their most loyal friend and as a man of power in Washington. As Onyszkiewicz put it: "We understood Kirkland's position in American politics. We knew that presidents come and go, but Kirkland would still be there."[60]

Czeslaw Bielecki, who visited Washington during particularly dark days in 1988, found his meeting with Kirkland something of an antidote to the environment of exhaustion and hopelessness back home:

> I was surprised by how well informed Kirkland was about Polish developments, about how much he knew about Poland, a small country in Central Europe. He was warm and friendly, but he also came across as a

man with a strategic vision. He was certain that what we were going
through was a battle, a campaign, with different stages, and not simply
an event. And he understood that we had a strategy for freedom.[61]

For Andrzej Celinski, a key Solidarity official, Kirkland's significance
derives from his grasp of European politics, his belief in the possibility of
radical change in Communist Europe, and the power he wielded as leader
of American labor. Celinski actually met Kirkland prior to martial law,
during a visit in which he sought to convince influential Americans "that
there was a chance to achieve democratic change in Central Europe."
Celinski added:

> We believed that this would require the active participation of the
> United States, since political leaders in Europe were comfortable with
> the division of Europe that had been reached in the agreements at Yalta
> and Potsdam. But I also had to convince Americans that policy towards
> Central Europe need not be viewed through the prism of relations with
> Moscow.
>
> Kirkland was one of the very few who understood what we were say-
> ing. He also understood that America was the only country that could
> make its policy on the basis of fundamental values and was not inhibited
> by the complacency that prevented serious initiatives by Europe.
>
> With Kirkland, there was no need to explain the context of things.
> He understood European history, he knew the complexities, he recog-
> nized the difference between dreams and realities. He knew why certain
> things are best left unsaid. A twenty minute meeting with Kirkland
> could be more productive than two hours with someone else. He was the
> only American whose language and way of thinking were on the same
> wave length as ours.[62]

In April 1990, Lane, Irena, and a delegation from the AFL-CIO traveled to Warsaw and Gdansk to attend the second Solidarity congress—a
triumphal gathering of those who had forged the democratic revolution
from inside Poland and those who had sustained the revolution from
abroad. During the visit, Lane and Irena stopped at the grave of Father
Jerzy Popieluszko, a priest murdered by the secret police for his uncompromising support for Solidarity. The Kirklands placed flowers at the
gravestone; as they turned to leave, a church caretaker approached. "You
should know something," he said. "At each mass during martial law,
Father Popieluszko included the name of Lane Kirkland in his prayers."

"I could not reply," Kirkland wrote later. "On Judgment Day, I would
be willing to settle for that account in my book of life."[63]

8

CENTRAL AMERICA
Fighting the Good Fight at Home and Abroad

AROUND 8 O'CLOCK ON THE NIGHT OF JANUARY 4, 1981, THREE MEN—
two Americans and one Salvadoran—sat down to dinner in the main dining room of the Sheraton Hotel in San Salvador. All three were key
figures in El Salvador's ambitious—and controversial—land reform program. Michael Hammer, an official of the AFL-CIO's American Institute
for Free Labor Development (AIFLD), had spent years building peasant
unions, promoting land reform, and irritating the elites in Latin America.
Hammer had flown to El Salvador that morning on an emergency mission after hearing that the land reform effort was in jeopardy. The second
American, Mark Pearlman, had been hired as a contract worker by
AIFLD and had been sent to San Salvador to assist in the development of
a legal framework for the reforms. The third man, Rodolfo Viera, was a
Salvadoran campesino union leader who was serving as the head of the
Salvadoran Institute of Agrarian Transformation, the agency that admin-
istered land reform policies.

Hammer had been dispatched to El Salvador rather suddenly because
of difficulties the program was encountering and reports that Viera was
about to resign his post at the land reform institute over frustration at the
government's inaction on land reform and the murders of campesinos by
the regular military and paramilitary death squads. Hammer was
endowed with immense energy and considerable physical courage—a
quality that had been repeatedly tested during seventeen years of service
in the often dangerous environment of Latin American labor affairs. He
believed in the land reform project, which he saw as the key to solving El
Salvador's endemic rural poverty and restoring political stability to the
country, then in the early stages of a civil war that would drag on for the
next decade. His faith in land reform was shared by American government officials, who were alarmed at the growing power of a leftist guerrilla insurgency and feared that El Salvador might share the fate of
Nicaragua, where the Somoza dictatorship had been overthrown by the
Sandinista Liberation Front in 1979. Nicaragua had been a wake-up call

for the United States; despite early promises of pluralism and democracy, the Sandinista regime had taken on an increasingly anti-American and Marxist-Leninist coloration. Without economic change and democratization, the State Department worried that the entire region might succumb to a revolutionary tidal wave.

Hammer, Pearlman, and Viera understood the dangers associated with involvement in the land reform program. Between them, Viera and his assistant, Leonel Gomez, had been the targets of assassination attempts on no fewer than eight occasions. Viera had been wounded in the most recent attempt, after which he stayed with Pearlman out of safety concerns. AIFLD had actually purchased an armored car after the assassination of the head of a construction workers' union; the car was given to Viera after he was wounded.

Seated at another table in the restaurant was Hans Christ, a San Salvador businessman who was prominent in right-wing political affairs. Christ immediately recognized Viera and reportedly blurted out, "There's that son-of-a-bitch Viera; he has let his beard grow. I wish he were dead." His two companions, Rodolfo Lopez Sibrian, a lieutenant in the National Guard, and Eduardo Avila, an army captain, immediately left the hotel to make preparations to murder the three trade unionists. In the street outside the hotel, Lopez Sibrian and Avila rounded up two young soldiers, a private and a corporal, and informed them they were to kill the head of the land reform program and two gringos. When one of the would-be killers balked, he was told that higher-ranking officers had approved the operation. The two shooters were provided with submachine guns and a jacket to conceal the weapons and were sent into the hotel. The killers waited until the AIFLD group was alone in the dining room, then calmly entered and murdered all three in a hail of bullets, gangland style. Afterward, the shooters were driven away by Sibrian Lopez and Avila.[1]

Hammer's body was placed in a flag-draped coffin and flown to Washington, where it was met in a National Airport hangar used by cargo planes by Lane and Irena and William C. Doherty Jr., the director of AIFLD. Hammer was given a funeral usually reserved for those killed in the line of military or diplomatic duty, with high officials from both the Carter administration and the incoming Reagan administration on hand. Edmund Muskie, secretary of state, delivered a eulogy; he was accompanied by Vice President Mondale; Patt Derian, assistant secretary of state for human rights; and Robert White, ambassador to El Salvador. Jeane J. Kirkpatrick, who had been designated as the new ambassador to the United Nations, and Richard V. Allen, who had been selected as the new national security adviser, represented the Reagan administration. After the funeral service, Hammer was given a hero's burial at Arlington National Cemetery.

Until the murders of Hammer, Pearlman, and Viera, Kirkland had devoted little attention to Central America. His consuming international interest was the emergence of Solidarity in Poland, a development he believed would play a central role in determining the outcome of the Cold War. At the time of the murders, Solidarity was moving ahead with the creation of a nationwide structure that would make the union a presence in every community and every workplace in the country. Clearly, Solidarity needed Kirkland's help. But the AIFLD murders made the fate of Central America a personal, as well as a political, issue. To Kirkland, Hammer and Pearlman were killed for carrying out trade unionism's noblest mission—seeking justice for the poorest of the poor.

Kirkland was to exert an important influence over the course of events in Central America. Although he maintained a generally low profile on issues in the region, he was responsible for a wide-ranging project that would provide financial and security support for democratic trade unions that were under siege from both the right and the left. From his position as the leader of American labor, he also helped shape the domestic debate over the United States' role in Central America, a controversy that reached a level of rancor and bitterness that rivaled the polarization American society experienced during the Vietnam War.

Although Central America was a divisive issue for labor, it never seriously threatened the unity Kirkland had forged. This is largely because he framed the debate as revolving around basic trade union rights, in which democratic union leaders were under constant threat from the violent Marxist left and the death squad right. Furthermore, Kirkland emerged as one of the leading figures who advocated an American policy that concentrated on the construction of democratic institutions in the countries in conflict, instead of simply treating Central America as a contest of East versus West. Given the obstacles arrayed against him—Salvadoran death squads, weak Central American allies, an emboldened and violent Marxist left in the region, an unfriendly domestic environment, a relentless and energized left opposition within the labor movement—Kirkland's eventual victory ranks as an impressive achievement.

The AFL-CIO had been deeply involved in Latin American labor affairs throughout the postwar period. Through AIFLD, American labor sought to build strong unions that were independent of the control of both government and the Marxist left. This was no mean task. In many countries, the indigenous unions faced adversaries at every turn: hostile business elites, suspicious military juntas, pro-Communist movements intent on capturing control of more moderate unions. AIFLD was founded in 1962 as part of the Kennedy administration's Alliance for Progress project to build democratic institutions as a way of countering

Communist influence in Latin America in the wake of the Cuban Revolution. Its board was something of an anomaly, consisting of both international union presidents and a number of America's most powerful businessmen, including several who presided over corporations that had less than stellar labor-management records.[2] AIFLD derived the bulk of its budget from the federal government, specifically from the U.S. Agency for International Development (USAID).

One of Kirkland's first acts as AFL-CIO president was to remove from the AIFLD board its chairman, J. Peter Grace, the head of Grace shipping lines and the only member of the business community left on the body.[3]

AIFLD had endured some troubled times in El Salvador even before the murders. In 1973, its mission had been expelled by the country's military leaders, after which Hammer, having relocated to Venezuela, continued to administer a program by working through local peasant union leaders, including Viera. The ruling junta permitted AIFLD to reopen its headquarters in 1979; soon enough, AIFLD began an aggressive campaign to develop a land reform policy and to popularize the idea of land redistribution among the country's campesinos. As its local partners, AIFLD chose to work with the Union Communal Salvadorena (UCS), a campesino union, and the Confederation of Salvadoran Workers (CST), a labor federation with a Christian Democratic orientation. The UCS was an affiliate of the International Confederation of Free Trade Unions, and both were firmly opposed to the imposition of a Marxist regime in the country.[4]

Meanwhile, polarization between violent forces of the right and the left was accelerating. Inspired by the Sandinista example, the Farabundo Marti Liberation Front (FMLN) opened a campaign centered in the countryside and aimed at undermining the economy and recruiting peasant supporters through persuasion or, if necessary, intimidation. Aligned with the FMLN was a coalition of the country's exiled left-of-center political leaders, who had joined together to form the National Democratic Front, or FDN. Arrayed against the left was a loose right-wing network that included the country's leading conservative political party, the National Republican Alliance (ARENA); influential factions within the military and security apparatus; and the paramilitary death squads.

During the Carter administration, the American government looked to AIFLD and the democratic Salvadoran unions as crucial to land reform's success. In March 1980, Robert White, ambassador to El Salvador, cited an "urgent" need to provide AIFLD with $5 million to promote the reform process. "Agrarian reform is moving extraordinarily well," White wrote in a memo to Cyrus Vance, secretary of state, in an outburst of optimism that was, one suspects, not warranted by events on the ground. Land reform, White stressed, entailed both economic and political dimensions. He noted the importance of "moderate and democratic" forces and the "continued independence" of campesino unions, presumably from domination by the guerrilla left. White described the UCS as having a "proven record on productivity and payback" and added that assistance from the United States would help ensure that the union enjoyed "continued full independence as a democratic and responsible voice ensuring land reform promises are fully implemented." According to White's memo: "This is probably [the] best opportunity in this hemisphere we have seen in [the] past two decades to promote a democratic model of reform, and any further delay on this crucial first step element of support would be, in my opinion, most unwise."[5]

Within a year, the optimistic tones that pervaded White's memo would be replaced by more sober assessments from American diplomats, as political conditions in El Salvador deteriorated and the forces of the democratic center grew increasingly isolated. For AIFLD and the beleaguered Salvadoran labor movement, simply staying alive became the paramount priority. In the wake of the Hammer-Pearlman-Viera murders, AIFLD hired a former FBI agent, Gordon Ellison, to shore up security at its San Salvador mission and to advise Salvadoran unions on security matters.

Ellison was also asked to assist in the investigation of the AIFLD killings, an issue that remained a high priority for Kirkland. Ellison's initial dealings with local police and military officials left him confident that the case could be solved rather quickly, and that not only the killers, but the men behind the killers, could be brought to justice. There was, he would later say, "simply too much evidence for us not to succeed."

At Ellison's recommendation, the AFL-CIO offered a $50,000 reward for information leading to the capture of the killers, set up a hot line in Washington to receive tips, and advertised the reward in Salvadoran newspapers. Soon enough, witnesses began to come forward: a waitress from the Sheraton provided useful information, as did a cab driver who had been parked outside the hotel when the shooting took place. Six weeks into his investigation, Ellison believed he had accumulated more than enough evidence to prove that the real culprits were Avila and Lopez Sibrian, and not the two hapless triggermen.

Unfortunately, Ellison did not take into account the unwritten code that no Salvadoran army officer be punished for crimes against civilians. Just when it seemed as if a solution to the case was in sight, the police began to place roadblocks in Ellison's way. He was convinced that a major breakthrough had occurred when the two shooters made confessions that implicated Avila and Lopez Sibrian. Under El Salvador law, however, a confessed criminal's testimony against a confederate was inadmissible in court. Even after this avenue was foreclosed, Ellison believed that the testimony of the cab driver, who could place Lopez Sibrian at the scene, might prove conclusive, especially when combined with failed lie detector tests by both officers. Once again, the authorities connived to thwart the prosecution. A man with a striking shock of red hair, Lopez Sibrian was permitted to dye his hair black, grow a beard, and use makeup before appearing in a lineup. After the cab driver failed to identify the suspect, Lopez Sibrian was set free.[6]

As Ellison learned more about the Salvadoran judicial system, he reached the conclusion that the two officers could never have been convicted, no matter how ironclad the evidence. Both had ties to the right; in May 1980, the two had been arrested with the notorious Major Roberto D'Aubuisson, the leader of the paramilitaries, on charges of plotting a coup and then quickly released.[7] Moreover, Lopez Sibrian's uncle was a ranking member of the ARENA party and a judge on the Supreme Court, the body that would have ruled on appeals had there been a conviction. Finally, Ellison says he eventually discovered that the judge in the case had been promised $1,500 and a new refrigerator if the pair were released; if they were convicted, the judge was told he would be killed.[8]

Although AIFLD officials were never again to be the target of assassination attempts, the safety of both the Americans and, especially, the Salvadoran trade unionists remained a problem. Despite the beefed-up security arrangements introduced by Ellison, AIFLD felt in jeopardy as long as it was treated as a hostile entity by D'Aubuisson and his henchmen. If D'Aubuisson chose to be circumspect in his comments about the American trade union advisers, he was direct and often menacing when he spoke of the Salvadoran trade unionists who cooperated with the AFL-CIO in land reform projects. In 1983, D'Aubuisson made veiled threats against Samuel Maldonado, a peasant union leader who at the time was in Miami being interviewed by the Kissinger Commission, the special body empaneled by President Reagan to make recommendations on American policy in Central America. Maldonado remained in the United States after D'Aubuisson described him as a guerrilla sympathizer in the course of a television interview; D'Aubuisson, for his part, was unrepentant. Summoned to the embassy in San Salvador for a talk, the ARENA leader called UPD-UCS initiatives "intolerable and infuriating" and characterized the unions as "an arrogant interest using unacceptable pressure tactics on the National Assembly for their own narrow purposes." D'Aubuisson made it clear that if El Salvador's unions continued to press for the implementation of land reform, they would do so at their own peril.[9]

In El Salvador, then, the AFL-CIO found itself in the classic position of supporting a reformist program that was rejected by both the left and the right. In Nicaragua, American labor's problem was much different.

Having defeated the dictatorship of Anastasio Somoza in 1979, the Sandinistas moved rapidly to consolidate power and impose a series of revolutionary changes on Nicaraguan society. Although the Sandinistas initially promised a government committed to democratic reform, they soon set about creating a Marxist-Leninist regime patterned loosely on Castro's Cuba. The AFL-CIO had enjoyed a close relationship with a democratic labor federation with anti-Somoza credentials, the Unified Workers Federation (CUS), an affiliate of the ICFTU. The Sandinistas, however, treated the CUS with undisguised contempt, harassed its leaders, and used menacing tactics to pressure workers into joining the rival Sandinista federation, the Sandinista Workers Central (CST). At the same time, as part of a campaign to minimize American influence in the country, the Sandinista government prevented AIFLD from establishing a project in Nicaragua.[10]

To Kirkland, developments in Nicaragua bore an unmistakable similarity to the traditional pattern of totalitarian takeovers in which democratic leaders were squeezed out and, step-by-step, the institutions of government and of civil society were folded into the revolutionary party structure. In an echo of declarations by countless Soviet and East European Communist trade union apparatchiks, Sandinista labor officials asserted that strikes were no longer a necessary weapon of the working class, since the strike was a tool "used by the workers against their class enemies, the capitalist exploiters." "There is no room for this type of struggle in Nicaragua because power is in the hands of the workers," a CST resolution declared. Kirkland also took note of the decision of the Sandinista labor federation to affiliate with the World Federation of Trade Unions (WFTU), the Soviet-dominated entity that was headquartered in Prague and saw itself as a rival to the ICFTU.[11]

There was thus no doubt in Kirkland's mind of the Sandinistas' true character. But unlike in El Salvador, where the AFL-CIO had a direct influence on events through its AIFLD mission and partnership with democratic Salvadoran unions, in Nicaragua American labor's role was limited by its inability to establish a direct presence in the country. The AFL-CIO thus focused its energies on providing, to whatever degree was politically prudent, support to the CUS and its leader, Alvin Guthrie. Since the Sandinistas looked askance at Nicaraguan institutions that received funds from the United States, American labor's most important contribution came in the form of political and moral support. Kirkland regularly issued protests to Sandinista leader Daniel Ortega over specific cases of trade union repression, publicized Sandinista acts of brutality, and sent information to the administration and Congress about the plight of Nicaragua's trade unions.

There were no objections within the AFL-CIO to Kirkland's assistance to the CUS or his anti-Sandinista declarations. The issue over which labor divided was contra aid. The Reagan administration had embraced a policy of support for the Nicaraguan contras, or counterrevolutionaries, a guerrilla force that was creating havoc inside Nicaragua without actually threatening to overthrow the Sandinistas. American liberals, meanwhile, were not simply opposed to contra aid; they treated it as a litmus-test issue.

In keeping with the consensus view within the AFL-CIO leadership, as well as with his personal convictions, Lane Kirkland remained neutral on the question of contra aid throughout the period of Sandinista rule. His stance was motivated by his apprehensions about American-financed and CIA-administered projects to overthrow foreign governments. In the early 1960s, Kirkland had been placed in charge of an AFL-CIO campaign to acquire and ship tractors and other goods to Cuba as part of an American ransom for the exiles who had been captured during the Bay of Pigs fiasco. The experience had taught Kirkland a lesson about the bad consequences that good intentions sometimes produced. Kirkland often commented to friends that the suburbs of northern Virginia were littered with the human casualties of failed American adventures in Southeast Asia and other parts of the world, and he feared that the main result of the contra war would be to enlarge this sad population of political exiles.[12]

On July 18, 1983, President Reagan announced the appointment of Kirkland to the National Bipartisan Commission on Central America, a body popularly known as the Kissinger Commission for its chairman, Henry A. Kissinger. The commission's formation was made public in a speech to the annual convention of the International Longshoremen's Association, one of a handful of unions to have endorsed the president in 1980. Reagan had formed the commission in an effort to build political support for his policy of defeating Marxism in the region. That policy was under immense pressure—from Democrats, from a growing protest movement, and from influential segments of the foreign policy establishment. It survived only because the Democrats, however much they disliked Reagan's assertive moves in Central America, had a greater fear of being blamed for an American Cold War setback. Reagan hoped that the Kissinger Commission could emulate the success of two previous bipartisan panels whose recommendations had won widespread acceptance: a commission on the financing of Social Security, chaired by Alan Greenspan, and one on the development of the MX missile, headed by Brent Scowcroft. Kirkland had served on both of these commissions.

Along with Kissinger and Kirkland, the panel consisted of a collection of centrist political figures, academics, and civic leaders: Henry Cisneros, mayor of San Antonio; Carlos Diaz-Alejandro, a professor of economics at Yale; Richard Scammon, a prominent political scientist; John Silber, president of Boston University; Potter Stewart, a retired Supreme Court justice; Robert S. Strauss, an influential figure in the Democratic Party; Dr. William B. Walsh, the founder of Project Hope; Nicholas Brady, a former Republican senator from New Jersey; and William P. Clements, former governor of Texas.

Next to Kissinger, Kirkland was to play the key role on the commission. Kirkland's participation came despite the stirrings of opposition to the AFL-CIO's Central America policies from within labor's ranks. Or, at least initially, from its left-wing margins. By the time Kirkland was named to the Kissinger panel, a growing network of trade union committees had sprung up with the express purpose of building a mass movement of radicals, peace advocates, feminists, and union officials that was dedicated to the defeat of the Reagan administration's Central America policies. Initially, these committees consisted of left-wing cause activists who used their positions as union members or staff as a base for the promotion of a broader political agenda.

Kirkland patiently explained his views to serious critics from within the labor movement and ignored the others. He justified his involvement in the Kissinger panel on the grounds that it was essential to have a trade union perspective in a report that might determine the direction of American foreign policy. He also believed that by participating in the Kissinger Commission, he might be able to accelerate the process of Salvadoran justice in the matter of the AIFLD murders. Whatever their personal views on Central America might be, Kirkland's colleagues on the executive council found his reasoning convincing, and the sniping was restricted for the moment to labor's left fringes.

Kirkland's patience and temper were sorely tried on more than one occasion during a mission to the Central America crisis zone taken by the commission. There was a meeting with a defiant Daniel Ortega, whose swaggering attitude ensured that the commission would entertain no recommendation for a major change in policy toward Nicaragua. Kissinger said Ortega was "very stupid because he was so provocative. He helped us make our case with the soft-liners on the commission." Kirkland had a testy exchange with Ortega over the principles of free trade unionism; according to John Silber, Kirkland "had the manners of a southern gentleman, but he was a tough cross-examiner." Kirkland also had a tense confrontation with Major D'Aubuisson, during which D'Aubuisson blamed the murders of Salvadoran civilians, the AIFLD officials, and six

American nuns on regular military forces and not on the paramilitaries under his control. D'Aubuisson's assertions of innocence were less than convincing, given that the previous week he had made threats against Samuel Maldonado while Maldonado was meeting with the commission.[13]

The commission also had an interesting meeting with General Manuel Noriega, at the time the leader of Panama. "Why don't you occupy Nicaragua and get it over with?" Noriega asked his visitors. This provoked one of the Democratic members to respond, "But then you'd call us the colossus of the North." To which Noriega replied, "But you are the colossus of the North."[14]

According to Silber, Kirkland's role on the commission was "absolutely critical." "I doubt that we would have held that commission together without Lane's participation." Silber said that Kirkland's views carried a high degree of authority because he was a trade union leader and a liberal Democrat. "Because Lane was a committed trade unionist, he knew exactly what the Sandinistas were up to. For the same reason, he could talk to the leadership of the Democratic Party and explain what was wrong with the Sandinistas." Henry Kissinger credits Kirkland with bro-kering the agreement that enabled the commission to unanimously endorse the final report. At one point during the negotiations over the report's language, Kissinger became bogged down in a lengthy argument with a Democratic member, who was demanding the inclusion of anticon-tra formulations as the price for his endorsement. Kirkland sat doodling while the debate continued for an hour or so. Finally, he looked up from his pad and said to the recalcitrant commissioner, "You wouldn't want to do a chicken-shit thing like that, would you?" thus ending the discussion.[15]

The recommendations bore a clear Kirkland imprint, insofar as they reflected the AFL-CIO's perception of Central American developments. The report endorsed most administration policies, implicitly backed aid to the contras, and rejected negotiations over power-sharing with the guerrillas in El Salvador. It agreed with President Reagan's assertion that Soviet and Cuban support for the Sandinistas posed a threat to American security, and it insisted on progress toward democracy in Nicaragua as a precondition to normal ties.

At the same time, the report called for a massive infusion of Marshall Plan–type aid to the region—$8 billion in economic assistance alone from 1985 to 1989. It also urged that future assistance to El Salvador be tied to progress toward human rights and democracy issues; the commission majority, including Kirkland, insisted that military aid "should, through legislation requiring periodic reports, be made contingent upon demon-strated progress toward free elections, freedom of association, the estab-lishment of the rule of law and an effective judicial system, and the termination of the activity of the so-called death squads, as well as vigorous prosecution to the extent possible of past offenders."[16]

The report satisfied no one. The administration resisted the recommendation that tied aid to El Salvador to progress on democracy; Democratic liberals, meanwhile, persisted in their adamant opposition to contra aid. Economic assistance was not forthcoming, at least not in the amounts urged by the report. Yet in light of unfolding developments in the region, the commission's recommendations come across as both realistic and shrewd. In El Salvador, American pressure led to political reforms, including free and honest elections that paved the way for the eventual reintegration of the left into the country's political life, while continued American military support eventually convinced the guerrillas that war was futile. And in Nicaragua, it was pressure from the contras, combined with the withdrawal of support by the Soviet Union, that convinced the Sandinistas to allow the elections that ended their rule.

Although the Kissinger Commission recommendations differed in some respects from the AFL-CIO's formal position on El Salvador, Kirkland convinced the executive council to give unanimous endorsement to the findings. The council statement said the recommendations "represent a comprehensive and long overdue approach to Central America's urgent need for massive social, economic, and political reform and lay the basis for constructive bipartisan action to meet that need."

To some extent, the divisions were encouraged by certain left-wing cause groups that aspired to a greater role within organized labor. Some on the left had long believed that the key to enhancing their influence lay in controversies over international affairs. By the 1980s, radical theorists had concluded that the burgeoning split over Central America could be exploited to challenge, and possibly even reverse, the fundamental orientation of the AFL-CIO's foreign policy. Charles Kernaghan, a staff member of the clothing and textile workers' union, circulated a memo in which he outlined a strategy to use the differences over Central America as "an underpinning for progressive forces within the AFL-CIO." Kernaghan, who once made the patently false accusation that Doherty was responsible for "large numbers of deaths in South America," urged that the left "directly confront the AFL-CIO" in a campaign to "realign labor's foreign policy" and proposed a "struggle to control AIFLD."[17]

The first challenge to AFL-CIO policy came in the form of exchange visits between American trade unionists and officials from unions aligned with the El Salvador left and the Sandinistas. Officials from international unions were free to participate in these meetings. But according to a formal AFL-CIO policy, state labor federations and county or municipal union bodies that were subsidiaries of the federation were forbidden to participate in or sponsor exchanges involving unionists with ties to the Communist-dominated WFTU. Kirkland insisted on a strict enforcement of the policy; he was determined that no structures under his control be allowed to establish relations with unions that were part of a global alliance that was hostile to democracy. When a labor solidarity committee organized an American tour for a delegation of WFTU-affiliated Latin American union officials, Kirkland sent a letter to federation affiliates reminding them of the policy of no-contacts with Communists. He sent a more sharply worded letter to state federations in August 1985, denouncing another tour of Central America by an American labor delegation scheduled for that fall. He noted that the Sandinista unions function as instruments of government policy and had renounced the right to strike, and he pointed out that the WFTU had cheered on the suppression of Solidarity in Poland and supported the Soviet invasion of Afghanistan.[18]

Initially, the exchange visits and other manifestations of opposition to the AFL-CIO's policies were organized by small committees consisting of avowed radicals who enjoyed little influence within their unions. Of more direct concern to Kirkland was the formation of the National Committee on Human Rights and Democracy in El Salvador. The labor committee boasted the endorsement of a number of labor's leading personalities, including Doug Fraser, former UAW president; Bill Winpisinger; Gerald McEntee, president of AFSCME; Kenneth Blaylock, president of the American Federation of Government Employees; William Bywater, president of the International Union of Electrical Workers; and James Herman, president of the West Coast longshoremen. The committee's guiding spirit was Jack Sheinkman, at the time the number-two man at the clothing and textile workers union. Sheinkman gave hours of his time to the committee's activities, allowed the committee to operate from his union's headquarters, and gave the committee staff support by putting several of its activists on the union payroll.

Aside from Sheinkman, the committee's leading personality was Ken Blaylock. A tall, rangy southerner, Blaylock had a political outlook that was equal parts trade union consciousness and southern economic populism. Blaylock's hold on power within his union was less than secure; he had narrowly beaten back challenges to his presidency on several occasions and faced perpetual problems of declining membership rolls and budget deficits.

Although Kirkland never answered Blaylock's jibes at federation policy or AIFLD directly, colleagues described him as irritated by what he regarded as Blaylock's self-righteous tone. Blaylock's comments seemed to suggest that those who supported American policy lacked a humanitarian core, were oblivious to the crimes of the death squads, or had

McCarthyite tendencies. In a 1986 interview in *Labor Report on Central America*, Blaylock ridiculed AIFLD's claims that Communists had infiltrated El Salvador's unions. "There are some who see Communists behind every rock," Blaylock commented. "We have them in our society; we have them in the labor movement. McCarthyism is still very much alive in some people's minds."[19] Kirkland was also disturbed by the behavior of a delegation of American trade unionists led by Blaylock that visited Nicaragua in 1985. Either Blaylock or other members of the delegation had made favorable remarks about political conditions under the Sandinistas, leading a Sandinista newspaper to publish an article under the headline: "AFL-CIO: Freedom Alive in Nicaragua."[20]

Kirkland believed that for an American labor leader to adopt anything but the most critical stance toward the Sandinistas had the effect of undermining Alvin Guthrie and his beleaguered band of democratic unionists. After the Blaylock delegation's visit to Managua, Guthrie wrote to Kirkland to express dismay "when certain groups of North American trade unionists, often working in cooperation with Nicaraguan government agencies or government supported unions, try to extract statements from us that support their own stated view of Nicaraguan reality." Guthrie noted that in Nicaragua at the time, it was illegal to criticize the government or the Sandinista revolution while abroad and that attempts to organize a political opposition were met with violence by Sandinista mobs. He asked Kirkland to inform American unions of his union's "special circumstances."[21]

While Blaylock, Sheinkman, and Winpisinger frequently spoke to audiences of Sandinista sympathizers and attacked AFL-CIO policy in press interviews, they never criticized Kirkland personally. Nor did they challenge federation policy at executive council meetings. The reason may have been unease at going head-to-head in debate with Kirkland. Although collegial and patient during executive council meetings, Kirkland could be intellectually intimidating when under challenge. Furthermore, in any debate over Central America, Kirkland could be expected to ask pointed questions about the democratic credentials of the Sandinistas and the Salvadoran left. On this score, the critics had no credible answer.

While Kirkland remained publicly aloof from much of the factionalizing over Central America, he was privately incensed by some of the tactics employed by the critics. He was distressed to learn that those who opposed federation policy were exploiting differences over labor's Central America policy within the family of Mike Hammer. Hammer's brother Frank, a UAW member, had denounced the AFL-CIO's Central America policy at several labor venues; his words could be interpreted as suggesting that his brother had died for an unworthy cause. This prompted a letter from

Michael Hammer Jr., the son of the slain AIFLD official, to Arthur Osborne, president of the Massachusetts AFL-CIO, whose convention was to be addressed by Frank Hammer. The letter disavowed Frank Hammer's views and praised AIFLD for having "incessantly pursued all channels in an effort to achieve justice" in the case of his father's murder.[22]

Although Kirkland did not engage in direct debate with international union presidents, he did look for opportunities to express his own strongly felt views. In October 1985, Ronald Fortune, an official of the Northwest Oregon Labor Council, wrote to Kirkland to urge support for a resolution that would drastically alter labor's Central America policy along lines favored by the left. Kirkland's response represented a succinct statement of his views on the issue.

Kirkland took issue with the resolution's assertion that no improvement in El Salvador's human rights record had occurred and pointed out that the statement, in setting forth atrocities committed by the right, failed to take note of the assassinations of Christian Democratic mayors by the guerrillas. A permanent ban on military assistance, as proposed by the resolution, would strengthen both left and right extremes "at the expense of the democratic center." As for the idea of bringing the left into the government in a power-sharing arrangement—a popular idea among critics of American policy at the time—Kirkland noted acidly that the guerrillas had opposed the elections that had elevated Jose Napoleon Duarte, a Christian Democrat with liberal credentials, to the presidency. "We do not support giving the guerrillas a share of political and military power without the consent of the Salvadoran people simply because they continue to wage guerrilla war," he wrote. And he accused the guerrillas of carrying out a "war of attrition against the people and economy of El Salvador, blowing up trucks, bridges, and power lines, creating hundreds of thousands of refugees, and resulting in death and destruction for campesinos and workers."

Kirkland was equally scathing in his evaluation of the Sandinistas, whom he accused of having "betrayed their promise of democratic pluralism from the moment they took power." He explicitly differed from the resolution's depiction of the Sandinistas as neither repressive nor totalitarian, describing Nicaragua as a country in which a Marxist party "controls the armed forces, virtually all the media, has established its own state-run 'trade union' organizations, set up 'neighborhood defense committees' to regulate political activity of individuals and control their access to food, through rationing, has built up the largest army in Central America, an elaborate state security and police apparatus with the assistance of Cuban, East German, and Bulgarian advisers, and conducts a foreign policy that supports the Jaruzelski regime in Poland and brands Solidarity an enemy of the state."

Kirkland noted that the AFL-CIO supported the Contadora process, a scheme advanced by several Central American countries to promote a peaceful transition through negotiations and democratization. As to contra aid, Kirkland indicated that the federation took no formal position. But he added that he personally was skeptical "about the CIA's reliability as a force for sustaining movements for democratic change" and added that he had "historically opposed the use of surrogates to fight U.S. battles." At the same time, Kirkland expressed strong opposition to American involvement in a Central America Yalta Pact, whereby the Nicaraguan government would be allowed to consolidate domestic power in return for a pledge to refrain from assisting guerrilla movements in neighboring countries.[23]

Kirkland's response was a powerful exposition of the liberal Cold War idea. Kirkland emphasized human rights and democracy and abhorred the extremes of left and right. At the same time, in his comments about the Sandinistas, Kirkland demonstrated an instinctive grasp of the nature of the Marxian project, especially the step-by-step campaign to consolidate control over the key institutions of power without killing thousands upon thousands of campesinos. Kirkland believed, as did other anti-Communists, that democracy could never be attained as long as pro-Communist forces held the reins of authority or were trying to "shoot their way into power," as Secretary of State Shultz put it.

Kirkland's approach to the Central America crisis had an impact on the evolution of the Reagan administration's Central America policies. While the Reaganites had entered office convinced that the solution to the Central America problem lay through military power, they were compelled to adjust and readjust their policies in response to a skeptical public mood and congressional opposition. By the mid-eighties, the administration had adopted a dual-track approach, pressing for democratic change, while at the same time arming the contras and the El Salvador military. Kirkland was prominent among those who pressured for a policy anchored on the promotion of democracy, the result of which was the 1985 election of Jose Napoleon Duarte to the presidency. In turn, Duarte's election had the effect of considerably reducing congressional opposition to the administration's policies.

By 1985, Kirkland's lieutenants had become sufficiently concerned about the mounting criticism of labor's foreign policy to propose a counterattack. They developed a strategy that emphasized the building of a base of support among international union presidents and lower-ranking officials for the AFL-CIO's policies.

To carry out this campaign, AIFLD hired Dave Jessup, who had served as an assistant to John Perkins at COPE. Jessup carried a deep

passion for the democratic cause in Central America and was a strong
supporter of the AFL-CIO's policies in the region. Indeed, Jessup was a
figure of some controversy among those involved in the debate over
America's course in Central America. His interest in Central America was
provoked when he learned that the Methodist Church, to which he
belonged, was engaged in various collaborative projects with Communist
governments and movements. A committed anti-Communist, Jessup
responded by forming the Institute for Religion and Democracy, a small
advocacy organization. The IRD's principal mission was to present an
alternative foreign policy voice to the mainstream Protestant denomina-
tions, practically all of which were supporting and often providing financial assistance to Marxist movements in Central America, Asia, Africa, and
other parts of the world.[24]

Once at AIFLD, Jessup worked with Doherty and Tom Kahn to
develop a program to build grassroots support for the federation's policies. The principal vehicle was a series of exchange visits between
American union members and their counterparts in Central America—
the very same strategy employed by the AFL-CIO's left-wing critics.
Over the next five years, Jessup organized some twenty trips in which
more than two hundred American trade unionists conducted study missions to El Salvador, Nicaragua, Guatemala, and other regional countries.
For the most part, the participants were drawn from the ranks of midlevel
officials from international unions, state federations, and local labor bodies. In El Salvador, the delegations met with trade unionists, government
officials, and American embassy officials. In Nicaragua, Jessup tried to
arrange audiences with Archbishop Obando y Bravo, the spiritual leader
of the anti-Sandinista movement, and Violetta Chamorro, the anti-
Sandinista widow of a prominent newspaper editor who had been slain by
Somoza's gunmen. Jessup also made sure to include a meeting with officials from Sandinista unions. "The Sandinista union people always shot
themselves in the foot," Jessup recalled. "They were so doctrinaire and
strident that they almost always alienated whomever they talked to." But
just as the Sandinistas gave negative reinforcement to the AFL-CIO's
policies, democratic union officials from El Salvador and Nicaragua made
the most compelling witnesses for AFL-CIO policy. "It was impossible to
speak with these labor officials without your heart going out to them,"
Jessup recalled. "They were completely sincere, and at the same time they
were under attack in the most vicious way by both the left and the right.
Decent trade unionists from the United States inevitably identified with
their plight. As a result, I don't recall a single person who participated in
our exchanges returning to the United States and criticizing AFL-CIO
policy."[25]

The counteroffensive was launched at a propitious time, since Kirkland's critics planned a major effort to reverse the federation's Central America policy at the 1985 convention in Anaheim. Ken Blaylock was the leadoff speaker. He urged the convention to demand a cut-off in military aid to the government in El Salvador and an end to contra support. In a line that was much-quoted in the press, Blaylock declared, "Now, I don't know about the rest of you people here, but when I look at Iran, I look at Vietnam, I look at Nicaragua, I look at El Salvador, Guatemala, I would like for one time for my government to be on the side of the people, not on the side of rich dictators living behind high walls."

Among those following Blaylock to the microphone was Ed Asner. Although known to millions for his portrayal of Lou Grant on the Mary Tyler Moore sitcom, Asner had emerged as an outspoken advocate of liberal-left political causes. Ironically, Asner's base of support was the Screen Actors Guild, in which he, like Ronald Reagan many years before, served as president. Unlike Blaylock, who—whatever his differences with federation policy—regarded himself as a loyal team member, Asner had a dim regard for the AFL-CIO. He once said that the American federation was "like a rock in the shoe of the international labor movement"; at Anaheim, he directly attacked AIFLD, which he accused of abandoning Central American unions that had become "too liberal, too uncontrollable." Asner also charged that the AFL-CIO was behaving like a "global vigilante."[26]

Asner and Blaylock were answered by a diverse group that included influential union presidents like Al Shanker and Jack Joyce and midlevel officials who had taken part in the AIFLD exchanges. Shanker weighed in against those who supported the state-controlled Sandinista unions and referred to "government puppet unions . . . sent here from time-to-time to try to justify the suspension of freedoms in their own country." Ed Cleary, president of the New York State AFL-CIO, denounced the delegations of left-wing Central American unions that made periodic tours of the United States as an "enemy within floating around the United States under the guise of representing workers." Leon Lynch, a vice president of the steelworkers' union and an officer of the A. Philip Randolph Institute, declared that he had been persuaded by the testimonies of persecuted Central American labor officials he had encountered on a mission to the region, a view that was endorsed by several other veterans of AIFLD trips who took the microphone.[27]

In the end, the convention approved a resolution that represented a victory for Kirkland. It denounced Reagan for overreliance on the military but was scathing in its description of the Sandinistas and, in the key section, refrained from criticizing contra aid. Yet even as a statement that represented a reaffirmation of Kirkland's policies won approval, there were signs that the Central America controversy was not about to disappear. A voice vote on the resolution showed the convention about evenly divided between supporters and opponents of federation policy (the nays were amplified by shouts from leftists in the gallery); when Kirkland, who was chairing the session, declared the leadership position to have prevailed, no one sought a roll call tally. (Two years later, the AFL-CIO would in fact adopt a formal position condemning contra aid.) Kirkland, however, was pleased, not only with the result but with the eloquent support for his policies that had come from the floor. Dave Jessup recalls Kirkland telling him afterward that the sight of the trade unionists lining up to argue against the left's position was "one of the sweetest sights I've ever seen."[28]

Kirkland's Central America problems were not limited to challenges by Ken Blaylock and Ed Asner. Elements of American conservatism were also irritated at the AFL-CIO for its support of Duarte. During a Senate hearing, Jesse Helms criticized AIFLD for its "interference" in Central American policy and linked the labor institute to the Konrad Adenauer Foundation (an institution affiliated with West Germany's Christian Democrats), the CIA, and USAID, as forces that had joined together to ensure the election of the Christian Democrats at the expense of the senator's favorite party, ARENA. Here, Helms was echoing the ARENA press: the April 26, 1988, edition of *Latino* reported that ARENA favored AIFLD's expulsion because of its close ties to Duarte.[29]

In fact, Kirkland had reason for disillusionment with the Christian Democrats and Duarte. Once in power, Duarte balked at a major expansion of the land reform program and, more disturbingly, issued a blanket amnesty for those who had committed human rights abuses, guerrillas and death squad members alike. This meant that not only would the killers of Hammer, Pearlman, and Viera go free, but the possibility of prosecuting those who ordered the murders would be foreclosed. Kirkland responded with a pointed letter to Duarte and a request to Secretary of State Shultz that military aid be suspended because of El Salvador's "flagrant violation of the condition requiring judicial reform."[30]

Although Kirkland maintained pressure on the administration over the AIFLD killings, the domestic debate over El Salvador had nearly run its course. The election of Duarte and the gradual improvement in human rights conditions—meaning that death squad murders had declined, not ended—were sufficient signs of progress to convince moderate Democrats to support the continued provision of military assistance to the government.

Nicaragua, however, remained a source of domestic strife. Having adopted a position of neutrality on the contentious issue of contra aid, Kirkland concentrated on the protection of Alvin Guthrie and other democratic union leaders. AIFLD dispatched delegations to meet with Guthrie and the democratic opposition in Managua and mounted letter-writing campaigns reminding members of Congress of the persecution of union members by the Sandinistas. Protest letters were also sent to the Sandinistas, including one, in October 1986, addressed to Daniel Ortega and signed by Joyce, John J. Sweeney, and Gene Upshaw, the president of a union of professional football players. The AFL-CIO also sponsored a tour of workers from *La Prensa*, the newspaper edited by Violetta Chamorro, that had been shut down by the Sandinistas.[31]

In the spring of 1987, the left was to mount yet another major demonstration that would create divisions within the labor movement. Designated as the April 25 Mobilization, it consisted of large rallies planned simultaneously in Washington and San Francisco at which tens of thousands were expected to call for major changes in American policy toward Central America and South Africa. In a letter to state federation presidents, Kirkland discouraged labor participation in the April mobilization. He noted that the AFL-CIO was a strong critic of the administration's policy of constructive engagement in South Africa, instead urging Reagan to pressure the Pretoria government to introduce majority rule. Nor had labor followed the administration's course in Central America; labor emphasized land reform and democratization, rather than the military option. Finally, he noted that the April 25 event included among its roster of speakers a representative of a guerrilla movement that was seeking to undermine democratic unions in El Salvador as well as a representative from the Sandinista government that was persecuting unions.[32]

Jack Joyce circulated a memo on the April 25th event that was less politely formulated than was Kirkland's note. The bricklayers' president pulled no punches in describing the mobilization as a sign of a "reemergence of radical left-wing groups dedicated to putting unions, as well as religious organizations, to those groups' purposes." He added:

> Anyone who knows or remembers the popular fronts put together by the Communists in the 1930s will know precisely how the April mobilization works and what it is about. . . . Fifty years ago the issues were the Spanish Civil War or the Scottsboro boys, the enemy was fascism and racism, the Communist Party was the organizing force and the agenda was that of the Soviet Union. Now the issue is Central America, the enemy is the Reagan Administration and the Central America oligarchies. The organizers come from the Committee in Support of the

People of El Salvador [a leftist cause group] and the agenda is that of the
Sandinistas and of various Central American Marxist-Leninist revolu-
tionaries. Having seen prior efforts by outsiders to play the puppet master and have the labor movement play the puppet, [the bricklayers'
union] doesn't intend to participate in the April Mobilization.[33]

Joyce's letter was reviled as an example of updated McCarthyism, as
was an accompanying analysis, prepared by Joyce's assistant, Joel
Freedman, that dissected the radical roots of the various organizations
sponsoring the April Mobilization. But Joyce clearly grasped the essence
of the mobilization's agenda: the collapse of Duarte's democratically
elected government and its replacement by the left through force of arms
and the consolidation of Sandinista authority in Nicaragua. To be sure,
the mobilization organizers valued the participation of mainstream trade
unions. In a concession to John Sweeney and Morton Bahr, president of
the Communications Workers of America, who had threatened to withdraw money and support from the event, a decision was made to cancel
plans to have the rally addressed by a Sandinista official and a representative of a guerrilla-backed union in El Salvador. But this minimal gesture
did not change the mobilization's political complexion or its basic goal of
a Central America ruled by Marxist movements that drew their inspiration from Cuban Communism and not from the Founding Fathers.[34]

Kirkland faced a new set of problems in El Salvador with the 1989
electoral triumph of ARENA. ARENA had unburdened itself of some of
the death squad taint; the new president, Alfredo Christiani, was Harvard
educated and a relative moderate. But ARENA had never concealed its
hostility to land reform, trade unions, and AIFLD. On November 1,
Kirkland wrote to Christiani to protest an attack on the headquarters of
FENESTRAS, a union with a reputation of guerrilla ties and hostility to
AIFLD. Kirkland sent Christiani a second letter three weeks later to
object to "what appears to be a pattern of increasing violations of human
and trade union rights against trade unions who share our commitment to
democratic values." Kirkland said he was "alarmed about reported
attempts to impose new leaders on campesino cooperatives by members
of your government, abusive behavior on the part of local civil defense
officials, and increasing reprisals by employers against union members
engaged in legitimate organizing and bargaining activities." As a consequence of the deterioration in labor rights' conditions, Kirkland informed
Christiani that the AFL-CIO intended to file a protest against El
Salvador's continued access to duty-free trade privileges under the
General System of Preferences. Kirkland's threats, however, failed to alleviate the pressure against El Salvador's unions. In 1990, the government

threatened to clamp down on the UNOC union, on the grounds that the union was abetting the AFL-CIO in its GSP case. The minister of agriculture called UNOC traitors, "sell-outs of their country" and "fronts for the FMLN," and the entire UNOC executive committee was threatened with arrest.[35]

The Central America debate came to an abrupt conclusion on February 25, 1990, when, to the shock of practically all observers, Violetta Chamorro defeated Daniel Ortega for Nicaragua's presidency, and her opposition slate swept the Sandinistas from power. One of the few observers who was not surprised by the outcome was Kirkland. Kirkland had an abiding faith in the democratic sensibilities of ordinary people; if given the option of repression or freedom, he believed that voters would always choose freedom. In a free and fair election, the Polish people had dealt their Communist persecutors a massive defeat, and now the Nicaraguan people had done the same.

Kirkland made a congratulatory call to Bernard Aronson, the assistant secretary of state for Latin America in the Bush administration, whose support for the contras had made him persona non grata among liberal Democrats.[36] But Kirkland himself could enjoy a measure of satisfaction, since his AFL-CIO had been a stalwart supporter of Nicaraguan democracy from beginning to end. During the election campaign, the AFL-CIO made a $100,000 contribution to the CUS to assist in its electioneering activities. The American labor movement dispatched several delegations of monitors and provided other forms of material assistance to the democratic camp. On election day, some thirty-five American trade unionists were on hand as monitors and advisers. They reported that while there were massive campaign violations by the Sandinistas, the election itself was relatively fair, probably the fairest in the country's history. They took particular pride in the fact that among those who won parliamentary seats on the Chamorro ticket was Alvin Guthrie, a democratic stalwart who had fought the good fight throughout the long decade of Sandinista rule.[37] Although the Sandinistas' American supporters grumbled that the vote represented a capitulation to American pressure by a war-weary and hungry people, rather than a repudiation of Ortega and the other commandantes, most Americans were pleased that the specter of Marxism in Central America had been eliminated, hopefully forever, and that the domestic arguments over contra aid had come to an end.

Kirkland never gloated over Central America, although he must have privately felt that his commitment to the democratic center had been vindicated. Although Kirkland had to adjust and compromise to forestall major conflict in the labor movement, he had steered a course that kept the AFL-CIO on the side of the region's democratic forces and in opposition to the revolutionary left and the death squad right throughout the period of crisis.

The left clearly understood Kirkland's role in the Central America crisis and hated him for it. A number of those who had gotten their first taste of political involvement through the movement for American withdrawal from Central America later moved to staff positions within various international unions. When in 1995 Kirkland was pressured into retirement, the loudest cheers came from those who had been demanding a reversal in labor's foreign policy. But by that time, the foreign policy priorities of the AFL-CIO had undergone a transformation. No longer focused on the Cold War, the federation's foreign policy apparatus was mobilized to meet the challenges of the global economy, and its programs concentrated on trade, the antisweatshop movement, free trade areas, worker rights in developing countries, and similar issues.

As for the democratic unions of Central America, the aftermath of the Cold War was at once sweet and bitter. In El Salvador, the left finally abandoned its revolutionary aspirations, rejoined civilian society, and participated in electoral politics as relative moderates. Land reform, however, was judged a failure by most neutral observers. Trade unions in both El Salvador and Nicaragua were permitted to function without fear of death squads or *turbas divinas*—the divine mobs employed by the Sandinistas against their enemies. But unions did not play a particularly important role in the new democracies, whose economic policies were geared toward finding a niche in the global economy.

In 1988 Ken Blaylock was defeated for the AFGE presidency by John Sturdivant, a black man who had served as the union's executive vice president. Although there is no evidence that Blaylock's outspoken positions on Central America contributed to his reelection failure, Blaylock himself concedes that his intense focus on foreign policy at a time of internal union crisis—the government workers were losing members and suffered a budget deficit—may have alienated some members.[38]

As for John Sweeney, the future president of the AFL-CIO maintained friendly relations with both factions in the Central America debate. Sweeney signed on as a member of the Sheinkman-Blaylock labor committee and endorsed the April 25th Mobilization, while at the same time participating in an AIFLD exchange trip and signing a subsequent report that strongly endorsed Kirkland's perception of Central American developments. Both sides in the debate could justifiably believe that they enjoyed Sweeney's loyalty.

But after Sweeney brought in his new, post-Kirkland regime, a purge and a reorganization of the international affairs department were among the first orders of business. AIFLD, along with the institutes for Africa and Asia, were abolished and their functions merged into a single entity, the American Center for International Labor Solidarity. Those placed in charge of international affairs included a number of activists who had backed the left in Central America.

By that time, of course, the Cold War had ended, and Kirkland's legacy as one of America's foremost advocates of freedom was secure. His ability to keep the AFL-CIO on a steady course during the Central America crisis is an important part of that legacy. In Central America, Kirkland was driven by the same liberal principles that dictated his actions on Poland, South Africa, and other areas of conflict. To the end, Kirkland was driven by the conviction that true liberalism was defined by a firm opposition to tyranny everywhere. As John Silber, Kirkland's colleague on the Kissinger Commission, put it, "Lane just couldn't understand how we had reached the point where to be liberal meant you had to be accommodating to the Sandinistas."[39]

9

MR. DEMOCRACY

IN THE EARLY 1980S, KIRKLAND HELD A SERIES OF MEETINGS WITH influential diplomats and political figures to hammer out plans for an instrument that would ensure a permanent role for the United States in the promotion of democracy around the world. The objective was to create an institution that was amply funded, had the flexibility to provide assistance quickly and without the burden of extensive bureaucratic oversight, and was free from interference from official Washington. The result of these discussions was an entirely new organization, to be called the National Endowment for Democracy (NED).

The founding of the NED—the story of its establishment will be addressed later in this chapter—was an important dimension of Kirkland's foreign policy record. The other crucial part of that record was labor's role in the Cold War triumph of the democratic world. With Communism's collapse at the end of the 1980s, Kirkland could take quiet satisfaction in the vindication of labor's commitment to freedom. Kirkland himself was accorded due honor for his steadfast support of the democratic movements that had emerged victorious in Eastern Europe during 1989. In the months after freedom's triumph, a lengthy roster of former "enemies of the state" lined up to shake Kirkland's hand and convey their appreciation for the statements of support he had issued, the urgent calls he had placed to free a dissident or save a condemned opposition politician, and the material sustenance that American labor had contributed to the cause of freedom.

The beneficiaries of Kirkland's interventions were not limited to the dissident giants of the Communist world. They ranged from obscure Salvadoran and South African labor leaders to future prime ministers in countries like Argentina and South Korea. Kirkland made time for them all, including those whose dissident efforts were quixotic or ineffectual. Personal courage and a commitment to democracy were enough to win Kirkland's admiration. And when Kirkland visited the countries of the former Soviet bloc, he was treated as a brother-in-arms by the leaders of the new, democratic governments.

Kirkland's achievements were all the more impressive, considering that his anti-Communist convictions were regarded as out of step with prevailing liberal opinion right up to the very end of the Cold War. When Kirkland was elected as president in 1979, organized labor stood as the only major political institution that rejected détente in any form with any country that adhered to the Communist system. Labor was accorded no tributes for this display of principle; its anti-Communism was regarded as an anachronism by editorialists, liberal politicians, and businessmen who were eager to make deals with the Soviet Union, China, and other Communist countries.

Kirkland succeeded in keeping the AFL-CIO true to its core values, in part because he defined the struggle not as one pitting East against West, America against Russia, or capitalism against Communism, but instead as a contest of democracy against all forms of despotism. To be sure, Kirkland drew his greatest inspiration from Solidarity, the movements for Baltic independence, and Czechoslovakia's Charter 77. And the opposition figures he most admired were the great figures of the democratic opposition in the Soviet bloc: Lech Walesa, Andrei Sakharov, and Vaclav Havel. But he also cared about the fate of freedom in countries oppressed by military juntas and right-wing authoritarians. When he spoke publicly about the state of the world, he seldom used the term *Communism*; he spoke instead of tyrants, dictators, and totalitarians. Kirkland was a prominent member of what came to be called the democracy movement, which consisted of a small group of elected figures and civic leaders who pressured the government to enshrine the promotion of freedom as a fundamental objective of American foreign policy. Kirkland was uniquely effective as a spokesman for the democracy movement. Because of his anti-Communist orientation, he commanded attention when he insisted that the United States embrace the struggle against apartheid in South Africa and support a transition to democracy, and not merely the military defeat of the Left, in Central America. And because he was the leader of American labor, an unabashed domestic liberal, and a partisan of freedom everywhere, Kirkland enjoyed the respect of all but the most isolationist elements of the Democratic Party coalition.

Among the most important personnel decisions Kirkland made upon succeeding Meany was to appoint Irving Brown as the AFL-CIO's director of international affairs. Brown worked in several union positions prior to World War II and then, after the war, was given an assignment by the AFL to assist in the rebuilding of a democratic trade union movement in Western Europe. Brown achieved near-legendary stature, due to his efforts to prevent a takeover of the labor movements in several countries by Communist parties that were under firm Moscow control.

It was in France that Brown won his most notable victory. There, unions under the control of the Communist labor federation, the CGT, were planning actions to sabotage the delivery of American goods sent to France as part of the Marshall Plan. Brown determined that countermeasures had to be taken to ensure that control would be wrested from Communist hands at the port in Marseilles, the entry point for Marshall Plan goods. Brown thereupon hired a man with wide contacts on the docks; the man, in turn, enlisted a group of street toughs to assist in clearing the port of CGT influence. The mission was quickly accomplished, there were no more political strikes directed at American policy, and Irving Brown's reputation as a hero of the early Cold War was firmly established.

Brown stayed on in Paris as the AFL-CIO's European representative. His role in preventing Communist control of the French unions had earned him widespread respect among the architects of the West's Cold War policies. For much the same reason, Brown was hated by the Left, which depicted him as a CIA stooge or an outright intelligence operative. In fact, the AFL (and the CIO, for that matter) accepted substantial sums of American government money, some given publicly through the Marshall Plan and some covertly through intelligence channels, to advance the cause of free trade unionism and limit Communist inroads in Europe during the Cold War's early years. Because Brown's name, and the AFL's, were linked to the defeat of Communist designs in France and, to a lesser degree, in Italy, they became favorite targets of left-wing journalists whose particular bent was the unmasking of American "spies."

Brown was a dedicated labor man who was convinced that the most effective way to spread freedom was through the institutions of free trade unionism. After the war, he played the key role in carrying out an AFL policy to support anticolonial movements in the Middle East and Africa. During much of the 1950s and early 1960s, Brown directed a project to help create independent unions in the countries of North Africa and in a few black African nations as well. Brown believed that the new unions would serve as the cornerstone of a stable, postcolonial democratic system and that their leaders would constitute a crucial element of a democratic governing class. Unfortunately, Brown's African venture did not end well. Once the old colonial masters had been supplanted, in country after country the new rulers, a group that included men Brown had trusted and collaborated with, moved quickly to suppress the unions Brown had helped nurture.

Kirkland had gotten to know Brown during the 1950s, during the time Kirkland served on the federation's research staff. During his visits to Washington, Brown often made time to talk to Kirkland about international issues, even though Kirkland's job at the time focused on domestic problems like Social Security. The two got along well. Kirkland respected Brown's judgment and was impressed by the respect he was accorded in European political circles and the intellectual community—Brown knew Raymond Aron and other Cold War thinkers. Kirkland also liked political gossip, and there was no better source of information—whether it was about shifting alignments in the Kremlin, the factional struggle within Britain's Labour Party, or the latest on Communist Party prospects in Portugal—than Irving Brown.[1]

Kirkland did not have the same high esteem for Jay Lovestone, the man who had served as international affairs director through most of Meany's presidency. Lovestone was a man of myth and mystery. He had started his political career as a Communist and at one point served as general secretary of the American Communist Party. Lovestone was deposed by Stalin himself, who acted after Lovestone naively challenged the Soviet leader's authority to determine policies for the American party at a meeting in Moscow. Lovestone was lucky to get back to the United States alive and afterward embarked on a career of fighting Communist influence within the American labor movement, working for a time for the International Ladies' Garment Workers Union, which was then led by the fiercely anti-Communist David Dubinsky. Lovestone was involved in a number of undertakings launched by the CIA in the early years of the Cold War, ranging from Radio Free Europe to the Congress for Cultural Freedom. His main job, however, was as director of international affairs for George Meany, in which capacity he was a figure of much controversy. Walter Reuther and other CIO veterans mistrusted Lovestone and tried to prevent his appointment as international affairs director when the AFL and the CIO merged. Others, Kirkland most likely among them, believed that to the degree that labor's foreign policy was treated with respect, it was because of Irving Brown and not Lovestone, whose opinions were becoming crankier as he aged and whose secretive methods were out of place in an institution that was in the American mainstream.[2]

In the mid-1970s Meany finally forced Lovestone to step down, replacing him with Ernest Lee, a Marine veteran and Meany's son-in-law. To pave the way for Brown's promotion, Kirkland shifted Lee to a position at the George Meany Center for Labor Education. Brown was formally named director of international affairs in June 1982.

Even before elevating Brown to the top foreign affairs position within the federation, Kirkland worked with him toward bringing the AFL-CIO back into the International Confederation of Free Trade Unions. The ICFTU owed its existence to the anti-Communist forces within a number of Western trade unions, which broke away from the World Federation of Trade Unions because of its domination by the Soviet Union.

From the outset of the founding of the ICFTU in 1949, there were tensions between the American labor leadership and the European trade union federations that comprised the majority within the ICFTU. Initially, the major source of difference was colonialism; later on, contacts with labor organizations from the Communist bloc emerged as a thorny issue. The ICFTU charter contained a prohibition on meetings between member unions and labor organizations from Communist countries. But unions from various European countries—in particular, West Germany and Great Britain—ignored the provision and held occasional conferences with trade union officials from the Soviet Union and various East European countries. As the years passed and Cold War tensions eased, unions from West European countries increasingly ignored the no-contacts provision and conducted regular meetings with their East bloc counterparts. Finally, in the late 1960s, the ICFTU adopted a policy over AFL-CIO objections that in effect eliminated the no-contacts rule.

West European labor leaders understood the fraudulent character of Soviet bloc labor organizations; they justified their actions on the grounds that contacts might promote détente between East and West. Meany, however, did not share their appraisal of the usefulness of a détente with the Communist bloc. He had consistently refused to dignify what he considered to be labor fronts with the term *union*, and he could not understand why legitimate trade unionists would lend credibility to bogus entities by inviting them to formal conferences. Meany was also exercised by the ICFTU's dealings with Walter Reuther following the UAW's withdrawal from the AFL-CIO. Many European union leaders found Reuther's views on the international labor movement more to their liking than were the positions adopted by Meany. The ICFTU's general secretary therefore held private discussions with Reuther with a view toward the UAW's affiliating with the international body, independent of the AFL-CIO. Meany was infuriated when he learned that talks with Reuther had been going on behind his back. In 1969, he pulled the AFL-CIO out of the ICFTU.[3]

The withdrawal from the ICFTU was followed in 1978 by a U.S. withdrawal from the International Labor Organization, a step that was taken at the urging of the AFL-CIO. The ILO had been regarded as one of the more successful international bodies, much more so than the United Nations itself. This was due to its unique tripartite structure, in which representatives from business, labor, and government participated in the establishment of global worker rights and labor standards. Increasingly, however, the ILO's credibility was being undermined by a growing politicization, driven by an alliance of the Soviet bloc, the Arab states, and various other leftist Third World regimes. This loose coalition of dictatorships offered resolution after resolution attacking Israel and a handful of other pariah states and prevented discussion on any report that was critical of labor practices in Communist countries or in much of the Third World. Each session became a showcase for denunciations of South Africa, Chile, Greece (during the reign of the colonels), and of course, Israel—while blatant abuses in Uganda, Syria, and Cuba went unmentioned. In 1975, Brown and Kirkland led a walkout of the American delegation when the ILO granted formal observer status to the Palestine Liberation Organization. The United States thereupon announced its intention to withdraw unless reforms were instituted. In 1978 secretary of state Cyrus Vance, after vigorous remonstration by Kirkland, made the withdrawal official. Among the steps taken by Vance was the suspension of America's financial contribution, a full 25 percent of the ILO's total budget.[4]

Kirkland made a return to the ICFTU a major early priority of his presidency. By the time the formal reaffiliation took place, on January 1, 1982, he had already moved to enlist European unions in the support of Solidarity and, more generally, to reassert American leadership in international labor affairs. Likewise, Kirkland advocated a return to the ILO by the United States, a step that was formally taken in 1980. He believed that the American withdrawal had had a salutary effect on the delegations from other democracies. Without the Americans around to lead the fight against extreme Soviet-Arab bloc initiatives, the Europeans had mustered the courage to resist Moscow's provocations and to build an effective alliance with moderate Third World countries. The result was a restoration of political balance on most pressing issues; for the first time in years, reports critical of Communist bloc countries were winning approval, and while Israel was still singled out for abuse, the Middle East conflict no longer occupied center stage in the body's deliberations.[5]

By the early 1980s, Kirkland had emerged as among the most eloquent spokesmen for the proposition that democracy promotion should be a centerpiece of American foreign policy. In a 1983 speech before the National Strategy Information Center, a hard-line group that had conducted research into the Soviet Union's international labor strategy, Kirkland argued that for labor, the question of democracy was a matter of both core values and self-interest:

The American labor movement does not recognize the split between ideals and self-interest that has plagued the foreign policy debate in this country. Simply stated, we have a vested interest in the promotion of free trade unions and the elevation of labor standards throughout the world. Experience teaches us that trade unions can prosper only in a climate of respect for human rights. Absent freedom of association, of assembly, and of expression, free trade unions independent of the state can neither be created nor sustained.

He then proceeded to attack the business community for its willingness to underwrite "the hare brained economic schemes of the Communist Party" in Poland and other Soviet bloc countries and he criticized the Reagan administration for allowing its policies to be dictated by the priorities of corporate America. Finally, he identified trade unionists as prominent among the ranks of patriotic Americans who placed the defense of freedom above narrow self-interest:

> We consider irrelevant, even if we do not dispute, the argument that a given expenditure for defense creates fewer jobs than the same expenditure for non-defense programs. We have opposed so-called "transfer amendments" that would transfer funds from the defense budget to social programs. Social spending should be driven by social needs. Defense spending should be driven by the external threat to our security.[6]

His views on transatlantic issues carried weight, given the respect he was accorded by the political leaders of European social democratic parties. A firm supporter of NATO and other Atlanticist institutions, he could be brutal with Europeans like Denis Healey who expressed sympathies with General Jaruzelski and sharp with those who refused to acknowledge the dangers posed by the actions of the Soviets and the Cubans in Central America. Nor did Kirkland have patience for the European attitude of tolerance toward radical Arab states or their refusal to accept a share of the defense burden in the Middle East. Kirkland was especially concerned that the unwillingness of Europe to spend more on its own defense would encourage American politicians to exploit isolationist tendencies, as, he believed, Gary Hart was doing in the 1984 presidential campaign.[7]

Kirkland had a traditionalist view of human rights that emphasized the freedoms of press, speech, assembly, the right to free and fair elections, and the right to be free from torture, arbitrary imprisonment, and state meddling in the personal affairs of citizens. It was notable that as a trade unionist with liberal social and economic views, Kirkland rejected what he called "the fallacy that political rights can be subordinated to 'economic and social rights' or to 'basic human needs.'"[8] At the same time, he had strong convictions about the obligation of the United States to behave with generosity toward political refugees. Both Lane and Irena were active in the International Rescue Committee, an organization that gave assistance to political refugees. Kirkland spoke with pride of the AFL-CIO as a "receiving station for visits, information, and appeals from the dispossessed, the wretched of the earth, the refugees, the losers, the victims of oppression from every corner of the earth. . . . One seldom hears in the West today as eloquent or moving expressions of the mean- ing of freedom or of the basic innate hunger for the rights of man as one hears from these victims of the consequences of their denial."[9]

Despite his firm Atlanticist convictions, Kirkland was well aware of Europe's tendencies toward compromise and accommodation with the Communist bloc and other dictatorships. He therefore believed that the spread of political freedom required American leadership. Having expe- rienced the policy lurches from Nixon to Carter to Reagan, Kirkland was convinced that the United States should create a permanent mechanism that would encourage the spread of freedom with a minimum of intrusion from presidents, the State Department bureaucracy, and Congress.

The United States was not without past experience in what would later be called democracy promotion. During the early years of the Cold War, the CIA channeled millions of dollars to a lengthy list of publica- tions, radio stations, and private organizations that raised the banners of both anti-Communism and political freedom. The best known of the agency's intellectual properties was Radio Free Europe, whose broadcasts drew huge audiences in the satellite countries of Eastern Europe. The CIA also funded the Congress for Cultural Freedom, the intellectual journal *Encounter*, and a number of newspapers and journals both in Europe (*Der Monad, Preuve*) and in developing countries. That the CIA was financing an array of ostensibly private organizations and media was an open secret in Washington during the 1950s. But those were the days before the press adopted an adversarial attitude toward the institutions of American foreign policy, so no one probed too deeply into the question of just where the institutions that carried out the war of ideas against Communism got their money. But by the late 1960s, media attitudes toward the authority of the federal government had changed. A series of press accounts revealed the pervasive CIA role in providing the funds and, in some cases, setting the political line for organizations that were widely respected both here and abroad. The revelations appeared in a long series of sensationalistic articles that greatly embarrassed the Johnson administration. A presidential panel subsequently recommended an end to CIA funding of private institutions, the only exceptions being Radio Free Europe and Radio Liberty. With the CIA having been removed from the business of democracy promotion, many of the projects that had been sustained with intelligence money went out of business.

The AFL-CIO tried to fill some of the vacuum left by the withdrawal of the CIA. The federation funded non-Communist trade unions and provided some support for dissident exiles and freedom movements both in the Communist bloc and in countries ruled by dictatorships of the right. But the labor movement did not have the resources or the mandate to sustain dissidents, publications, exile organizations, and other instruments of the growing movement for global human rights.

The National Endowment for Democracy thus was formed to support the world's growing ranks of democracy advocates and to do so in an open fashion that was consonant with America's own democratic form of government.

The creation of the NED followed closely on the heels of a 1982 speech that President Reagan delivered before the British Parliament, in which he called for "a global campaign for democracy." Once Reagan gave the NED concept his blessing, events moved rather quickly, and in late 1983, Congress passed legislation calling for the NED's creation. The new agency officially was launched at the end of that year. Kirkland, it is worth noting, invariably dismissed suggestions that Reagan was in any way responsible for the NED's establishment.

The NED was structured along the lines of what in Europe is known as a quasi-governmental organization, or quango. Its policies were set by a board of trustees that was self-perpetuating and not appointed by Congress or the president. Practically all of its funds, however, were to be provided by Congress through the normal appropriations process. The trustees themselves were a blue-chip group of elected officials, former diplomats, educators, labor leaders, and businessmen—men and women who, like Kirkland, could easily have served as diplomats or foreign policy officials in either Republican or Democratic administrations. In theory, the trustees were to act as a firewall against partisan political influence. But as might be expected, NED grants and policies were under constant scrutiny by members of Congress, American ambassadors, the State Department, and other agencies of government involved in international affairs.[10]

Kirkland's stature with both Democratic and Republican congressmen was of critical importance to the NED in its early years, when its long-range prospects were in doubt. The new agency was looked on with suspicion by a number of liberal Democrats, especially those who opposed the Reagan administration's Central America policies and fretted that the NED might be used as a pipeline for material support to the contras. The NED was likewise viewed with skepticism by Republicans of a libertarian or isolationist bent and drew opposition from budget hawks who were convinced that the taxpayers' money was being wasted on a misguided utopian crusade. During the organization's first few years, the bills authorizing its budget were passed by Congress with few votes to spare.[11] In those difficult times, Kirkland's role as an NED advocate helped reassure both hawks and doves that the agency's priorities would conform to its congressionally assigned mandate. Kirkland's importance was amplified by the fact that labor was the only influential institution that put its muscle behind the NED's survival.

From the beginning, the AFL-CIO played a major role in the distribution of NED democracy money abroad. The NED channeled most of its funds through four American institutes: the National Democratic Institute for International Affairs, a project attached to the Democratic Party; the International Republican Institute, a similar entity tied to the GOP; the Center for International Private Enterprise, an affiliate of the United States Chamber of Commerce; and the Free Trade Union Institute, which was attached to the AFL-CIO. The NED did disburse a relatively small part of its grant-giving budget directly to overseas projects. But the bulk of the money was distributed to the institutes, which in turn gave grant money to deserving prodemocracy publications or organizations—human rights monitors, journals of free expression, trade unions, and projects that sought to encourage entrepreneurship and market economics. During the NED's early years, the AFL-CIO was allocated a higher proportion of the annual NED grant budget than were the other institutes, on the theory that labor, with its long history of assisting free institutions in foreign countries, would put the money to its most effective use. Of the amount allotted labor, the Free Trade Union Institute used a portion to support projects in Poland and other East European countries; the rest was distributed through the other AFL-CIO international institutes—the American Institute for Free Labor Development, the Asian-American Free Labor Institute, and the African-American Labor Center.[12]

Initially, it was expected that Allen Weinstein would be appointed as the NED's first president. Weinstein had achieved some notoriety as the author of a book on the Alger Hiss-Whittaker Chambers controversy that concluded that Chambers had told the truth about Hiss's involvement in espionage for the Soviets. Weinstein had drafted the original study that spelled out the structure and mission of the NED and had been functioning as its de facto chief officer. Kirkland, however, preferred another candidate, Carl Gershman, who at the time was serving on the staff of Jeane J. Kirkpatrick, ambassador to the United Nations. Previously, Gershman was executive director of Social Democrats, U.S.A., a position that enabled him to have regular dealings with European social democratic political and labor leaders through the Socialist International. Gershman was a personal friend of Lane and Irena Kirkland; he and Kirkland shared similar political views, including an exasperation with most European social democrats over their willingness to reach political compromise with the Soviets.

"Lane wanted someone who understood and supported labor's objectives," Gershman explained. "He wanted someone who shared labor's view that democracy had to be supported across the board, in Communist dictatorships and in non-Communist, authoritarian dictatorships as well." Another quality sought by Kirkland was the willingness to say "no" to the State Department. "Lane and the others did not want the president to come from the foreign service; they wanted someone with a political background," Gershman noted. "Lane was concerned about whether I would do the right thing if a conflict arose between my judgment and the preferences of the State Department. I told him I would do what I and the board thought was best."[13]

Gershman won the appointment after some intense lobbying by Kirkland. The decision was a tribute to Kirkland's powers of persuasion but also reflected the fact that, outside the government, the AFL-CIO ranked as NED's most important supporter and as something of a model for its operation. The men involved in NED's creation—Frank Fahrenkopf, chairman of the Republican National Committee; Charles Manatt, chairman of the Democratic National Committee; Bill Brock, secretary of labor; Congressman Dante Fascell; Senator Orrin Hatch—often deferred to Kirkland in questions about NED's operation, since Kirkland had strong ideas on democracy building and years of experience in the promotion of independent trade unions in the Third World.[14]

Once the NED money began to flow, Kirkland had a substantial budget for foreign operations at his command, since the AFL-CIO continued to receive generous grants from the United States Agency for International Development. By the mid-1980s, the federation was spending as much for its international programs as it was for all other purposes combined—lobbying, political campaigning, organizing, civil rights, and so on. Kirkland's critics would occasionally raise the issue of the federation's spending on foreign projects as evidence that he was misusing members' money to build a global empire to advance his Cold War objectives. Such charges were a total and, in some cases, deliberate distortion. In fact, practically all the money used for international projects was derived from grants from the Agency for International Development and the NED and did not come from rank-and-file dues.

An early problem revolved around the NED's requirement that its operations be completely transparent—that is, open to inspection by Congress, watchdog agencies like the General Accounting Office, the media, and the public. According to Bill Brock, Kirkland himself was a staunch advocate of openness. "He didn't want NED projects to appear covert or suspect," Brock said. "He argued that if a project were done covertly and information about it became public, it would be all the worse for the recipient."[15] But while Kirkland was strongly in favor of a policy of openness, Irving Brown was less than enthusiastic about the NED's reporting requirements. For decades, Brown had carried out confidential political assignments for the AFL-CIO, including projects to assist democratic-minded trade unionists in societies ruled by Communist dictatorships, European colonialists, and local despots. The people with whom Brown worked often confronted treacherous political conditions in which accusations of collaboration with American interests could lead to dire consequences. Beyond his concerns for the well-being of his friends and contacts, Brown simply didn't like the idea that congressmen, journalists, or GAO auditors should have access to the details of his projects. Brown was a master of bureaucratic obfuscation and used his considerable wiles to prevent the auditors and investigators from learning what Brown believed they didn't need to know. In the end, however, Brown was forced to relent, and the AFL-CIO agreed to adhere to the same rules of transparency that applied to the other NED grantees.[16]

Brown was also a key figure in one of the NED's first mini-scandals. For some years, Brown had maintained close relations with a French organization, the National University Union, or UNI. The UNI was founded by radical 1968ers, veterans of the university uprising of that year; many had been Trotskyites whose opinions had moderated over the years. They were committed to resisting the heavy-handed influence that the French Communist Party exercised over the country's university system.

Brown regarded the UNI as an effective instrument in the ongoing cultural war pitting France's democrats against a Communist movement that, while exhibiting limited electoral potential, commanded impressive influence in the trade union movement, the universities, the press, and intellectual life. He therefore engineered a grant of $575,000 for UNI's activities from the NED, the money to be dispensed over two years. This represented a substantial sum by NED standards; the project was also unusual insofar as NED was not in the habit of sustaining projects whose target country was a democratic ally of the United States.

In 1985, UNI was the subject of a sensationalistic article that appeared in *Libération*, a leftist French newspaper. The article charged that UNI had been created by a shadowy, right-wing paramilitary group called Service d'Action Civique, an organization that had been formed by Charles de Gaulle to assist him in maintaining civic order. *Libération*, in other words, suggested that money from the NED was being used to fund a group of proto-fascists. Gershman immediately dispatched Marc Plattner, a member of the NED staff, and Eugenia Kemble, director of the Free Trade Union Institute, to conduct an investigation. The ensuing report rejected the most sensational charges advanced by *Libération*, especially regarding UNI's relationship with the paramilitary outfit. But it concluded that the grant was not warranted under the NED's guidelines and recommended that the final tranche of $73,000 be withheld. When the issue came before the NED's board of trustees, Kirkland made an impassioned presentation that focused more on the integrity of Irving Brown than on the worthiness of UNI. The trustees thereupon voted to release the final $73,000; there would, however, be no further grants to UNI.[17]

In addition to his service on the NED board, Kirkland was involved in several other institutions that helped to spread democratic ideals. In 1983 the secretary of state, George Shultz, named him to a special advisory panel to review U.S. foreign aid programs.[18] That same year, President Reagan named Kirkland to the Board for International Broadcasting, the governing body for Radio Free Europe and Radio Liberty.[19] Kirkland served on the BIB during the waning years of the Cold War and the first years of post-Communist reconstruction. Among other things, Kirkland helped to dissuade the Clinton administration from shutting the freedom radios down; instead, RFE-RL's headquarters was shifted from Munich to Prague and its broadcasts reoriented toward the encouragement of democratic freedoms in post-Communist trouble spots like Russia, Ukraine, Belarus, and the countries of Central Asia.

As his service on these bipartisan entities suggests, Kirkland was among the members of the Washington elite who believed that politics stops at the water's edge and that political differences need not preclude personal friendship. As a trade union leader, Kirkland almost always supported Democratic candidates and Democratic domestic policies. But he was also convinced that in a successful democracy, there were certain critical issues that required bipartisan cooperation—relations with the Soviets, national defense, Social Security. He thus had no difficulty accepting appointments by Republican presidents to special commissions to study the future of the CIA, Social Security, and American policy toward Central America. In the 1970s, there were many men in Washington who shared Kirkland's notion that the future of America sometimes depended on cooperation between otherwise bitter rivals. By 1995, when he retired, the spirit of bipartisanship was under heavy assault from both right and left.

The Kirklands applied these bipartisan principles in their private lives. They counted among their friends certain members of the trade union inner circle, leading Democratic politicians, prominent members of the Washington press corps, hard-line Cold Warriors, high-ranking diplomats, and freedom fighters from various beleaguered parts of the world. Some of Lane's closer friends were, in fact, conservatives, like William Safire, the *New York Times* columnist, and George Will, a columnist for the *Washington Post*. Lane and Irena were also close friends with David Brinkley, the television anchor, and his wife, Susan. Brinkley and Kirkland were avid fans of the Washington Redskins and often watched games on Lane's large-screen television—both quiet and tense until Washington had rolled up a big enough lead to guarantee victory.

One thing he shared with these men was a love of good writing and speechmaking. Kirkland frequently called George Will to discuss an essay or a speech that he felt was particularly well-crafted. His friends had a high regard for Kirkland's mastery of political writing. Safire wrangled an honorary membership for Kirkland in a club for presidential speechwriters and included one of Lane's speeches in a volume he published.

Kirkland never discussed internal labor matters with his friends outside the movement. But he liked to engage in political debate, and when the discussion turned to President Reagan's domestic agenda or the workings of the global economy, Lane expressed the same views, with the same fervor, that he did in speeches to labor audiences. For these men, however, the core issue facing America was the struggle for freedom, and especially the Cold War struggle against Communism. The attitude of Kirkland's generation of Cold Warriors was summed up by George Will: "If the housing program failed, you could fix it. But if you lost the Cold War, you lost the country."

Kirkland had a strong ego and a sense of the importance of his position. But he never injected his own personality or interests in a political debate. "Lane never sought personal or moral recognition," said Carl Gershman. "Once he was convinced that an injustice was being committed, he fought against it with an unyielding spirit. Those who suffered understood they had a unique friend—a friend with power and influence." In his dealings with his contacts among the Washington political and journalistic elite, Kirkland frequently pressed the case of beleaguered workers at home or repressed freedom advocates abroad. If a conservative columnist or a Republican senator would promote a just cause, it might even be more effective than if a liberal spoke up. But Kirkland had a strict personal rule against using his friends to promote his own interests. He even refrained from discussing his problems with his good friend William Safire when a faction within the labor movement organized to force his retirement in 1995. "I wouldn't have minded if he had tried to use me," Safire recalled, "but he wouldn't."

Kirkland had a powerful sense of solidarity with the Jewish people and a feeling for the Jewish experience. He regarded it as a special mission to support Israel in every venue where he had influence: the AFL-CIO,

American politics, the international labor movement, and the International Labor Organization. Each year the Kirklands hosted their Jewish friends at a special celebration on December 24, and he and Irena often attended a breaking-the-fast meal on Yom Kippur at the home of the Safires. Kirkland also had a special fondness for the Jewish Labor Committee, a once-robust organization that was struggling as Jewish involvement in organized labor declined.

Kirkland shared with Will and Safire a skepticism about claims that a new Soviet leader would institute a wave of reform that would make the system more efficient and less oppressive while retaining the basic structures of Communism. He had witnessed the various Kremlin power shifts and watched in bemusement as one after another general secretary was anointed as the man who would shake things up, modernize the economy, and free the Soviet people from their regimen of totalitarian control.

Kirkland thus was not among those in the West who greeted the changes introduced by Mikhail Gorbachev as evidence that a process of irreversible reform was underway. Adrian Karatnycky, a special assistant for international affairs at the federation, described Kirkland as deeply skeptical about the new Soviet leader's credentials as a democrat. "Lane thought the Gorbachev reforms were a flim-flam, that they were superficial, and that they were introduced not because Gorbachev genuinely believed in democracy, but because he was in a weakened position as the Communist edifice began to crumble."[20]

Other members of the labor leadership were more optimistic about Gorbachev's reformist credentials. Irving Brown, for one, believed that whether by design or otherwise, Gorbachev had set in motion a process that might well lead to a breakup of the system. Even as he was dying of cancer in 1989, Brown focused his energies on events in the Kremlin. "Irving believed that in order to maintain totalitarian control a leader has to be willing to do whatever is necessary, no matter how violent or harsh," said Jim Baker, who worked with Brown in the Paris office. "And Irving thought that Gorbachev would not take those harsh steps when push came to shove."[21]

There was even sentiment to relax the AFL-CIO's long-standing ban on contacts with officials of Communist bloc labor organizations (a sentiment, it should be noted, not shared by Irving Brown). Two executive council members, Jack Sheinkman and William Winpisinger, decided to take the initiative by visiting Moscow—they flew in the Machinists' Union's jet—for private discussions with officials of the All Union Central Committee of Trade Unions and with Gorbachev himself.

Kirkland remained unmoved on the question of contacts with Communist unions. He saw no possible merit in sitting down at a conference table with Communist Party officials who had devoted their lives to the suppression of fundamental worker rights. He also remained dubious about Gorbachev's ability to reform the system. "Gorbachev is finished," Kirkland predicted to Robert S. Strauss, the new American ambassador to Moscow, after Strauss had given him a relatively upbeat briefing on political conditions in the Soviet Union.[22] But Kirkland understood that there was a diversity of opinion within the ranks of labor about the Gorbachev phenomenon. And while Kirkland doubted Gorbachev's sincerity, he entertained the hope that the impulse for change that Gorbachev had unleashed might lead to the collapse of the system and a revolution in the status of the Soviet working population.

Kirkland therefore established a special entity, called the perestroika committee, to provide guidance about the events going on inside the Soviet Union. According to Karatnycky, the creation of the perestroika committee reflected pressure exerted on the federation, both from within its own ranks and by the Bush administration. "Lane felt that even if he doubted that Gorbachev would transform the system, he did recognize that something important was going on. He thus felt there was justifica- tion in reducing the federation's anti-Soviet rhetoric and in assessing the prospects for more reform." Kirkland selected as chairman of the pere- stroika committee a hard-liner whose skepticism about glasnost was every bit as strong as his own—Al Shanker. The committee heard a procession of top Soviet authorities and foreign policy experts, including Brent Scowcroft, Condoleezza Rice, Zbigniew Brzezinski, Richard Pipes, and Steven Sestanovich, and issued a final report that neither endorsed Gorbachev's course nor rejected it as a fraud.[23]

Whatever Kirkland's sentiments about glasnost and perestroika, he was intrigued by the emerging evidence of independent worker move- ments inside the Soviet Union. Kirkland was convinced that the working class represented the most serious threat to Communist stability. He believed that the Poland model could be exported to other Soviet bloc countries. And he was eager to throw the AFL-CIO's resources behind any significant free trade union movement that might exhibit popular support.

Beginning in the late 1980s, labor unrest began to escalate as Gorbachev introduced measures to put the Soviet economy on a more rational basis. The nerve center of worker militancy was the country's vast coal mining regions, located in the Urals, the Donetsk region of Ukraine, parts of Kazakhstan, and Siberia. Miners in these areas abandoned the official party-supervised unions to form independent strike committees that coordinated work stoppages and contributed to the perception that Gorbachev was losing control of events.

In late 1989, Kirkland announced that the federation intended to provide assistance to the new unions, saying he wanted to "test the limits of glasnost." The previous November, Kazimieras Uoka, the president of a new anti-Communist union in Lithuania, had addressed the AFL-CIO's convention, the first time a labor official from the Soviet Union had done so. Then in January 1990, the federation played host to a delegation of Soviet mineworkers who were involved in the wave of strikes during the previous year.[24]

Although the Soviets denied Kirkland a visa to attend a conference of independent trade unionists toward the end of 1989, the Gorbachev government later relented, and in September 1990, Kirkland visited Leningrad and Moscow, traveling with a delegation of Poland's Solidarity officials.[25] On September 4, Soviet workers witnessed the astonishing spectacle of the leader of American labor—a devoted anti-Communist who presided over an organization that had never yielded in its hostility to the Communist idea—addressing a rally of independent trade union activists from the back of a truck not far from the steps of the Winter Palace.

By any reasonable standard this was an event of great symbolic importance, a historic occasion that the press unaccountably failed to note. Lane Kirkland was a principled opponent of the Soviet system. The AFL-CIO was a militant enemy of Communism. Both had been repeatedly demonized by the Soviet press. Yet there stood Kirkland, exhorting Soviet workers—the very class that Communism claimed to represent—to wage the democratic struggle. He spoke at a time of revolutionary change and at a place that had been an icon of Soviet history. He did not camouflage his remarks in the vocabulary of diplomacy; rather, he talked about freedom in phrases that the oppressed of any society could have appreciated.

"Brothers and sisters," Kirkland declared, "I am delighted to bring you warmest fraternal greetings from your 14 million brothers and sisters who belong to the trade unions of the AFL-CIO." Kirkland went on to pledge the support of American labor for the movement for democratic reform that was then sweeping the Communist heartland. "We have great faith that the emergence of free and independent institutions—such as genuine trade unions that truly reflect the will of their members—will ensure that state power withdraws to its proper role in life." Paraphrasing Lenin, he asked, "What then is to be done?" and answered, "Press and test and stretch the limits of liberty, and then press and test again until liberty is finally won." He then concluded:

> Brothers and sisters, keep the faith. Your activism on behalf of social justice and the dignity of every man and woman will soon herald a new era of peace and freedom in your country, and a safer and better world. Then, indeed, we shall build a new world from the ashes of the old.

The following day was Labor Day, and Kirkland delivered his traditional Labor Day address to an audience of reform-minded Soviet trade unionists gathered in Spasso House, the American embassy in Moscow. The workers were involved in forming new independent unions and came from all across the vast Soviet territory, from Belarus and Ukraine in the west to Vorkuta and Sakhalin in Siberia and the Far East. Many had spent days on buses to reach Moscow and meet Kirkland. Although Jack Matlock, the American ambassador, had invited the Western press, the event was largely ignored by the Western media, as most correspondents decided that the Labor Day holiday took precedence over what was, by any reasonable yardstick, a historic occasion.[26]

Kirkland's optimism about the course of Soviet events was dealt a blow in January 1991, when Soviet forces invaded both Lithuania and Estonia in a vain effort to bring the rebellious republics under the authority of the central government. Kirkland wrote to the secretary of state, James A. Baker III, to urge the United States to withdraw from the European Bank for Reconstruction and Development—a mechanism for channeling assistance to post-Communist societies—if it allocated loans or grants to the Soviets.[27]

But by May a measure of calm had been restored, and Kirkland decided to participate in a conference to commemorate the legacy of the great dissident Andrei Sakharov, who had recently died. Kirkland shared the podium with such avowed anti-Communists as Mario Soares, the Portuguese Socialist Party leader who had been instrumental in preventing a Communist takeover of his country; Robert Conquest, the author of definitive histories of the Stalinist terror and the Ukrainian famine; and Mstislav Rostropovich, the cellist and intellectual dissident. Gorbachev also attended the affair. But for Kirkland, the high point was a private session with Boris Yeltsin, who at the time was running for the presidency of the Russian republic and was detested as a renegade by Communist Party loyalists. Yeltsin, who made a point of greeting Irena before shaking hands with Lane, reminded Kirkland of an old-style American politico from the Lyndon Johnson, Tip O'Neill school. He gave Lane and Irena a personal tour of the Kremlin and impressed them both with his warmth and his grasp of the critical issues facing Russia. He described a plan to cut unemployment, praised the AFL-CIO's program to assist independent unions, and blasted Gorbachev for having imposed a ban on strikes. Kirkland left convinced that if Russia achieved democracy, it would be through the leadership of Yeltsin rather than Gorbachev.[28]

Kirkland's belief in trade unions as the key instrument of democratic reform was not limited to the Soviet Union. "Lane believed that the Poland model was exportable," said Adrian Karatnycky. In most of the

East European countries, strike committees had taken root in the waning days of Communist control to challenge the credentials of the official party-dominated unions. Kirkland was hopeful that these dissident committees would supplant the party-affiliated unions as the main institutions of worker power. Furthermore, Kirkland had hopes that East European trade unions would play a crucial role in solidifying the post-Communist socioeconomic order, under which ordinary people would enjoy full democratic rights, as well as the protection of social safety nets and trade unions that would function as the proving ground for future political leaders.[29]

Kirkland decided to help this process along by providing various forms of assistance to the non-Communist union structures. The AFL-CIO established offices throughout Eastern Europe to work with the new unions. It contributed money, office supplies, printing facilities, computers—whatever the unions needed to enable them to compete with the Communist federations. American labor even sent in Rich Bensinger, the director of its organizing institute, to train workers in the basics of organizing at a special conference in Gdansk.[30]

Unfortunately, Kirkland's vision of a democratic trade union movement as the reform vanguard of post-Communist societies was destined to go unfulfilled. In most East European countries, it was the old Communist labor federations that prevailed and not the new insurgent unions. The reasons were complex; a key factor, however, was the disruption in the industrial economies throughout the region that followed on the heels of the collapse of the central command economies, resulting in major unemployment among blue-collar workers.

None of the post-Communist societies moved in the direction preferred by Kirkland. Some opted for shock therapy policies that involved the closure of unprofitable industrial installations that produced unwanted goods on obsolete machines, the privatization of key elements of the economy, policies to entice foreign investment, and a rapid switch to market mechanisms throughout the economy—all of which led to mass unemployment and major impediments to the ability of unions to engage in collective bargaining with employers or to exert influence over the formulation of national economic policy. In other countries, a hybrid system evolved that included some privatization, considerable state involvement in the economy, and pervasive corruption—again with little space for the development of the kind of labor-management relationship that was common in the West. Even in Poland, where the initial non-Communist government was dominated by veterans of Solidarity, the reform movement quickly divided between advocates of free markets, nationalist elements, and those who remained true to Solidarity's trade union roots.[31]

Kirkland found the trend toward what he called an "unfettered" free market deplorable. He had no use for the American consultants who were urging Poland, Russia, and other countries to adopt shock therapy. Kirkland believed that it was possible to move seamlessly from state socialism to social democracy and resented those East European political leaders who, he believed, embraced doctrinaire free market policies at the expense of ordinary people's well-being. So strong were his feelings that he refused to attend an NED conference that included among the speakers Leszek Balcerowicz, who as finance minister was the chief architect of Poland's shock therapy policies. Kirkland was convinced that men like Balcerowicz—especially those who had remained on the sidelines during the struggle against Communism—were betraying the ideals of the democratic revolution that had dispatched Communism to history's dustbin.[32]

Frustrated by the drift of post-Communist events, Kirkland sharpened his anticorporate vocabulary. Recalled Karatnycky, "Lane really resented the role that these advocates of the free market played in Eastern Europe. He would say: 'I don't recall these fat cats at the barricades fighting the Communists. Now they're running in and giving lectures about the necessity of belt tightening and buying off factories and shutting them down and laying off workers.'" Kirkland was particularly upset at suggestions that the Gdansk shipyard be shut down; he found the prospect that such a fate might befall the birthplace of Solidarity outrageous.[33]

Kirkland's mistrust of the corporate world's commitment to freedom predated the fall of Communism. During the 1970s, he frequently criticized business leaders who ignored the totalitarian nature of the Soviet system in their desire for détente and profits. During the 1980s, Kirkland's comments about the role of international business took on a sharper edge. When he referred to business as the "soft underbelly of freedom," he was speaking from conviction. Kirkland genuinely believed that a substantial core of the business community owed allegiance to no flag and no human values. To drive home his point, he liked to repeat the comment of Thomas Theobold, the chief of Citibank, who after the declaration of martial law in Poland was quoted as asserting, "Who knows what political system works best? All we ask is: Can they pay the bills?" Kirkland accused corporate executives like Theobold of practicing a form of "pseudopragmatism," an approach that, he said, "perverts, even as it seems to draw upon, the American tradition."

In June 1992, Kirkland warned the Hungarian government about the dangers of allowing the new democracy's priorities to be dictated by the international business community. Kirkland was visiting Budapest to receive the Freedom Cross of the Order of the Hungarian Republic. After the ceremony, he listened to complaints from the prime minister, József

Antall, about Western businessmen who sought investment opportunities in Hungary and eventually took as partners members of the old Communist Party *nomenklatura*. Kirkland found Antall's lament unsurprising; he told the Hungarian that the behavior he had encountered "was in keeping with the long, opportunistic history of Western capitalism, which maintains that business is business, whether you are doing business with a fraud or a dictator." He added that "the only trustworthy and reliable authors and supporters of human freedom were the working people through their own organizations as the central elements of civil society."[34]

In addition to his support for the use of economic and diplomatic sanctions against countries like Poland and South Africa, Kirkland was an advocate of marshalling America's trade laws in the service of human rights. In 1984, the AFL-CIO successfully fought for the insertion of a provision in the law renewing the General System of Preferences (GSP) that made the granting of GSP conditional on the observance of labor rights standards set by the International Labor Organization. Under the GSP, a list of goods was established that could be imported into the United States without duty. In 1987, the United States, under pressure from the AFL-CIO, dropped Chile from the list of countries that qualified for GSP status because of the Pinochet regime's persecution of a number of the country's leading trade unionists.[35]

The AFL-CIO's role in Chile had generated something of a controversy in the United States. Those who were sympathetic to the government of Salvador Allende had accused the American Institute for Free Labor Development of having supported the 1973 coup that brought Allende down and elevated General Augusto Pinochet to power. While there is little evidence to support the accusation of AIFLD involvement in the coup, it is clear that the AFL-CIO had little use for Allende, an ally of Fidel Castro whose Marxist-leaning government was fast ruining the Chilean economy and pushing the country toward civil war. During the 1980s, however, the AFL-CIO was constantly at odds with Pinochet over his attempts to control the labor movement and the generally repressive nature of the regime. American labor was a crucial source of material and moral support for the forces that were eventually to bring about a restoration of democracy.

Under pressure from both domestic and international sources, Pinochet agreed to hold a plebiscite in October 1988, in which the lone issue to be decided was whether Pinochet should be granted a further presidential term of eight years. A "yes" vote would have postponed a transition to democracy until well into the next decade. The AIFLD lined up strongly behind the campaign for a "no" vote and dispatched some forty-five American trade unionists to serve as election monitors for the plebiscite. On September 15, both Jack Joyce and Bill Doherty were injured during a demonstration to protest the placing of several labor leaders in internal exile. Doherty was the target of a volley from a water cannon and was beaten by security officers. In the event, the "no" vote prevailed by 55 to 45 percent, and Pinochet bowed out of politics, thus paving the way for the restoration of democracy.[36]

Kirkland also mobilized American labor behind the antiapartheid struggle. He never felt quite the same passionate attachment to the majority rule forces in South Africa that he felt toward the Polish workers in Solidarity or the intellectual dissidents in the Soviet Union; he was, nonetheless, strongly opposed to the apartheid system and frequently spoke out in favor of a more vigorous U.S. policy toward the white government in Pretoria. Kirkland was cognizant that members of the South African Communist Party played an important role in the African National Congress, that elements within the freedom movement were drawn to black separatist ideologies, and that the ANC's commitment to democracy was unclear. Kirkland thus concentrated American labor's support on the South African labor unions with which the AFL-CIO had close relations rather than on the ANC or other political movements.

Kirkland, of course, also understood that American liberals regarded South Africa as a litmus-test issue and that the country's fate and, especially, the fate of Nelson Mandela aroused great passions among the black members of the AFL-CIO. In his public statements about apartheid, Kirkland avoided placing the South Africa question within the context of Cold War politics. He consistently defined the issue as one of human rights, democratic rule, racial discrimination, freedom of association, and other universal values.

In 1984, as the pressure of the antiapartheid campaign accelerated, Kirkland met with Secretary of State Shultz to urge a selective boycott in response to the arrest of thirteen black trade unionists.[37] In July 1986, Kirkland was a member of an ICFTU delegation that conducted a study mission on conditions in South Africa. In the course of the visit, the delegation visited Alexandra Township, an impoverished working-class community, without first gaining government permission. Suddenly, the police appeared, complete with hippos, the armored personnel carriers widely used by the South African authorities as riot-control vehicles. A crowd of blacks from the township began gathering as the police interrogated the trade unionists, and the atmosphere grew thick with tension. To calm matters down, Norman Willis, president of the British Trades Union Council, approached the crowd and began leading them in song. He chose the Gilbert and Sullivan favorite whose first line goes, "When constabulary duties are to be done, a policeman's lot is not a happy one." Finally, the officer in charge called someone at headquarters and was apparently told to avoid further confrontation.[38]

Upon his return to the United States, Kirkland issued an impassioned plea to Congress in which he asked that far-reaching sanctions be applied and urged the abandonment of the Reagan administration's policy of "constructive engagement," under which the United States sought change through diplomatic pressure rather than through sanctions. Asked whether he was concerned that his proposal for a withdrawal of American investment might damage the living standards of black workers, Kirkland replied, "They [South African labor leaders] are well aware of the adverse impact such sanctions could have on the black workers of South Africa, but like the workers in Poland and Chile, the victims of oppression in the Soviet Union and the followers of Martin Luther King, they know that freedom is worth any price."[39]

In the end, of course, Mandela was released, apartheid crumbled, and South Africa achieved both black rule and democracy. Kirkland could claim particular satisfaction in the role that trade unions played in the freedom struggle there, a role that further vindicated his belief that free trade unions can alter the course of history.

Kirkland was to meet with less success in his efforts to convince the United States to place human rights at the center of its relations with China. Kirkland regarded China as a society that was every bit as totalitarian as the Soviet Union. He also regarded it as a threat to the living standards of American workers. China, in Kirkland's view, was the nine-hundred-pound gorilla of the global trading system, a repressive society with a huge workforce whose hourly wage rates were well below those of South Korea and Malaysia, not to mention those of the United States. Once China won acceptance as a normal member of the world economic system, Kirkland foresaw a massive hemorrhaging of jobs from America as corporations sought the lowest possible labor costs, a docile workforce, and the absence of genuine trade unions.

There was, however, little that Kirkland could do to influence policies toward China. It seemed to matter little whether the administration in power was Republican or Democratic, whether it gave rhetorical emphasis to human rights or realpolitik, whether it denounced Communism as the focus of evil in the world or sought détente with Moscow—all U.S. presidents from Richard Nixon on through Bill Clinton sought improved diplomatic and economic ties to China and effectively ignored that country's dismal record on political rights and civil liberties. Furthermore, while China did produce a few intellectual dissidents, its democratic advocates were not of the same impressive caliber that one found in the Soviet Union and practically every East European country. There was no Chinese equivalent of Sakharov, Solzhenitsyn, Havel, or Walesa; there were no Helsinki Monitoring Groups or free trade unions of any strength.

As a member of the NED board, Kirkland consistently opposed projects that were carried out inside China. No matter how well-intentioned they might be, Kirkland argued that such undertakings would lend legitimacy to a repressive government and enmesh those involved in potentially unhealthy relations with regime officials. There were, however, a number of human rights projects that focused on abuses inside China that were based in the United States or in Hong Kong that did valuable research into the largely undocumented world of the legal system, the misuse of psychiatry, prison camp labor, and other aspects of Chinese totalitarianism. Kirkland was especially interested in the research conducted by Harry Wu, a Chinese American who made several trips to China to carry out research into the use of political prisoners as slave laborers. In 1995, however, Wu was arrested while carrying out an investigation inside China and was handed a lengthy prison term on charges of stealing state secrets.

Kirkland immediately contacted Henry Kissinger. Just as years earlier, when Kirkland had asked Kissinger, then secretary of state, to intervene on behalf of Soviet dissidents like Vladimir Bukovsky, he now asked Kissinger to intercede with his contacts at the top levels of the Chinese regime on behalf of Harry Wu. Kissinger approached the Chinese leadership and explained that the Wu case "is not a human rights problem, but a problem of Chinese statesmanship" that would lead to endless demonstrations and protests unless it was resolved. Beijing thereupon released Wu from custody and expelled him back to the United States.[40]

Kirkland was often paid tribute by those who regarded him as a brother-in-arms in the freedom struggle. But perhaps the greatest tribute—certainly, the most enduring—was the incorporation of democracy promotion in the foreign policymaking process of the American government. There were others, of course, who made crucial contributions to the modern democracy movement. Kirkland, however, not only argued the case for a policy that formally acknowledged the expansion of human freedom as a core objective, he placed the weight of organized labor behind the struggle as well. By the 1990s, the United States was devoting billions of dollars to assist free media, train human rights workers, strengthen the rule of law, and help independent think tanks in countries where free institutions were fragile or under duress. The model for this ambitious undertaking was the AFL-CIO's long campaign to sustain free trade unions in the world's trouble spots, a project that began in Europe after World War II, was broadened to embrace Latin America and the postcolonial societies of Asia and Africa, and then expanded yet again to include the post-Communist countries of Eastern Europe. If there is any doubt about Kirkland's legacy as a champion of freedom, one need only ask the democratically elected heads of state, the crusading editors, the human rights guardians, and the trade union activists who owe their success, and in some cases their lives, to his commitment to freedom.

10

LABOR UNITY; LABOR PAINS

AT NO TIME IN ITS HISTORY WAS LABOR MORE UNIFIED THAN IN 1989, THE tenth anniversary of Kirkland's leadership. We have already examined Kirkland's success in promoting freedom around the world and in reviving labor's influence in the political arena. Kirkland, however, faced a third challenge: to stem labor's decline at the shop floor, the bargaining table, and the picket line. For organized labor, the 1980s were a time of trouble on several fronts. Kirkland met the challenges with a variety of responses. But his first and most enduring response was to make good on his promise to bring all the "sinners" back into the church.

The unity that Kirkland forged embodied more than the formal expansion of the roster of unions affiliated with the federation. Unity, Kirkland-style, meant a movement that was more inclined to pursue common political goals, to unite around political candidates, and to join together in solidarity in times of duress. It also meant a movement that did not succumb to defeatism, despite the dual challenges of a hostile political climate and an economic environment that triggered membership losses in many of America's largest and most fabled unions and greatly complicated the job of organizing the unorganized.

Kirkland achieved more than labor unity. In another era, his policies would have been hailed as major steps forward for American labor. But the 1980s were difficult times for the union movement. Even as he was rebuilding labor's political apparatus, he was confronted with a series of challenges the likes of which George Meany had never faced. The core of labor's dilemma was to be found not at the polling booth or in the halls of Congress, but rather at assembly lines, mining pits, and construction sites all across America. The decline of labor's strength in private sector employment, a gradual process during the 1960s and 1970s, had worsened during the 1980s, leaving no sector of traditional union strength untouched. It was hastened along by deindustrialization, a phenomenon that spread across the heartland of the old economy like some new and untreatable dread disease. And like AIDS, another scourge of the 1980s, deindustrialization focused its attack on certain vulnerable communities: workers in the Rust Belt factories of South Chicago, Pittsburgh, and Youngstown; employees of textile installations that were susceptible to the impact of foreign trade; and those, like typesetters, whose jobs could be carried out more efficiently by computers or robots.

When asked by reporters about the prospects for a revival of the labor movement, Kirkland could find ample precedent in American history to justify a response that, if not optimistic, was at least less than totally defeatist. But there was no avoiding the harsh facts of labor's predicament. For the first time since the codification of America's basic labor law with the 1935 passage of the Wagner Act, unions were on the defensive, both politically and organizationally. To make matters worse, the decline in labor's fortunes continued even as the economy began to pull itself out of recession. While the 1980s brought prosperity for some, and great riches for a few, this was not a period when the rising tide lifted all the boats. Kirkland responded with anger when corporate boards rewarded CEOs with huge raises in compensation after those very same executives had taken actions that cost thousands of workers their jobs. He remained true to the old New Deal values of sharing the wealth and sharing the sacrifice; during the 1980s, America's elites regarded such notions as hopelessly out of step with the times.

Going a step further, many in the corporate world and among Reagan's economic policymakers believed that the transformation of the American economy required a wholesale weakening of labor strength. Their theory, albeit unspoken, was that there was a direct link between enfeebled unions and the consolidation of an economic order based on free trade; the rapid movement of goods, labor, and capital; and technological change. While Reagan never criticized unions—he continued to speak with sentimental pride of his years as president of the Screen Actors Guild—his appointees were responsible for a dramatic shift in the government's stance toward labor-management relations that was destined to undermine union efforts to organize in the new economy.

From the standpoint of labor's institutional interests, no Reagan appointee was as crucial, or as antagonistic, as Donald R. Dotson. Dotson had been brought into the administration by the labor secretary, Ray Donovan, as assistant secretary for labor-management services—the same post, ironically, that Tom Donahue had occupied during the 1960s. Dotson's credentials for the position were unusual. He had served as chief counsel for the Wheeling-Pittsburgh Corporation, was a friend of Senator Jesse Helms, was an inveterate critic of unions, and had ties to the National Right-to-Work Committee, the organization that was largely responsible for orchestrating the defeat of labor law reform in 1978.

Then, in 1982, Dotson was appointed chairman of the National Labor Relations Board, the agency that functions as referee in unionization elections and in disputes pitting workers and their unions against management. Although he denied an animus toward unions, Dotson made it clear that he believed that the NLRB had been overly attentive to the agenda of the labor leadership. His own writings betrayed a philosophic difference with the very concept of collective bargaining. In a letter to a law journal published during the 1970s, Dotson wrote, "The scheme of organized labor relations in the United States today bears no resemblance to what was intended by the framers of our basic labor law." Dotson went a bit further in a letter published in the *American Bar Association Journal*: "In both the public and private sectors, the strike has come to mean not merely a concerted withholding of labor, but a concerted effort employing violence, intimidation, and political intervention to prevent people who want to work from working. Collective bargaining frequently means labor monopoly, the destruction of individual freedom, and the destruction of the marketplace as the mechanism for determining the value of labor." This last statement represented the classic libertarian critique of trade unions; that the chairman of the NLRB could have written these words was powerful evidence that the old ways of doing things no longer obtained under Ronald Reagan.[1]

With Dotson's confirmation in February 1983, the Reagan administration gained a 4-to-1 majority on the board. Although Republicans had dominated the NLRB at times in the past, their appointees tended to respect the traditional code of labor-management relations, in which unions and collective bargaining were treated as integral and healthy aspects of the American system. This philosophy went unchallenged until the election of Reagan. Within conservatism, there had always been a strain of free market thinking that regarded unions as illegitimate interlopers that distorted markets, impeded productivity, and resisted reform. Donald Dotson and his fellow Reagan appointees wasted little time in demonstrating their sympathy for this philosophy.

Dotson moved rapidly to reorganize and reorient his agency. Among other things, he shifted considerable bureaucratic power to the board's solicitor, a position occupied by Hugh Reilly, an attorney who was hired right out of the National Right-to-Work Committee.[2] That the leading antilabor organization had established a beachhead in the agency that adjudicated differences between labor and management was a development of revolutionary proportions. Soon enough, the board began issuing decisions that reversed earlier pro-union judgments. In case after case, the NLRB gave management more latitude to abrogate union contracts, dismiss workers, and discipline union activists.

When he finally stepped down in December 1987, Dotson left a much different agency from the one he had joined five years earlier. A 1985 AFL-CIO study concluded that under Reaganite leadership, the NLRB found in favor of workers who brought complaints against management 51 percent of the time, a major decrease from the 84 percent figure registered during the Ford and Carter administrations.

The transformation of the NLRB drove home the link between the rise of political conservatism and the deterioration of the trade union as an economic and social institution. For Kirkland, the whole experience was especially frustrating. Kirkland complained to a reporter after Reagan left office that the number of workers fired for their union loyalties had increased "astronomically" under the NLRB, and he accused the president of appointing people "who are beholden to and have served management" to board positions. Kirkland had reached the point where he claimed to favor a return to the "law of the jungle" in industrial relations, whereby unions and bosses could slug it out without the interference of the state. "As between present law and no law, I'd prefer no law," Kirkland declared.[3]

Labor's problems with the NLRB were another reminder of the low spot in the liberal pecking order that trade unions occupied. There were few, if any, protestations by editorialists, commentators, or even members of Congress as the Dotson board handed down one after another unfavorable judgment. By contrast, America's liberal elites issued protests and published statements of outrage over the Reagan administration's tepid affirmative action policies and its appointments of critics of racial preferences to the U.S. Commission on Civil Rights and the Equal Employment Opportunity Commission. Here was yet further evidence that for post-sixties liberalism, race and gender trumped the concerns of the working class and its unions.

Kirkland could console himself that the Department of Labor had been returned to responsible hands. On March 15, 1985, Ray Donovan had resigned after four years of near-constant strife and little achievement. He would have continued in office had he not encountered a new legal challenge: indictment on charges of fraud and larceny. Donovan was the first sitting cabinet secretary to face indictment; his departure was greeted with universal relief by the Reagan inner circle.

As Donovan's successor, the president named Bill Brock, a former senator from Tennessee. On its face, the appointment held little appeal for the AFL-CIO. During his years in the House of Representatives and the Senate, Brock had carved out a reputation that was indistinguishable from that of other new-generation southern Republicans. His voting record was predictably antilabor; Brock received a low COPE rating of fourteen during his six years in the Senate and in 1972 earned a score of zero for the year. After meeting defeat in his 1976 reelection bid, Brock accepted appointment as chairman of the Republican National Committee. He also underwent an ideological shift to the center; at his urging, the party made an attempt to broaden its base among such groups as blacks, Jews, and unions. While his tenure at the RNC was marked by impressive gains in congressional elections, Brock was not considered part of the president's core group of advisers.

Brock began the process of fence-mending with Kirkland immediately upon his appointment. As trade representative, Brock had met regularly with top AFL-CIO officials and had earned their respect as someone who would take their opinions seriously. He was effusive in his praise of Kirkland and hired Stephen Schlossberg, the general counsel to the UAW, as a top aide.[4] Later in the year, Brock drew applause when in the course of a speech to the AFL-CIO convention he attacked outsourcing—the shifting of plants abroad—and the use of union-avoidance tactics by employers. He added, "It would be stupid to try and improve our competitive position by reducing the standard of living of American workers and their families."[5]

Although Kirkland was pleased that Donovan had been replaced by a moderate political professional like Brock, he understood that the shift at the labor department would mean little substantive change in the absence of a commitment by the administration to stem the country's industrial deterioration. He regarded Reagan's treatment of labor as a betrayal of an unwritten code of how politics should be conducted under Cold War conditions. This code dictated that while Republicans and Democrats and business and labor might be divided over matters of domestic policy, they recognized the importance of national unity toward the overriding objective of defeating Communism and winning the Cold War. Eisenhower, Nixon, and Ford had respected the code; the rock-solid Republicans refrained from challenging labor's core interests, supported collective bargaining, and gave labor a hearing when formulating domestic policy. Kirkland believed that during wartime, governments were obliged to embrace policies that unify the citizenry and ensure that if sacrifices are called for, they do not fall disparately on the poorest and most vulnerable.

Among the key elements of Kirkland's strategy to counter Reaganism, deindustrialization, and other threats was an aggressive drive to reunify the labor movement by bringing back to the AFL-CIO those unions—notably, the UAW, the Teamsters, and the Mine Workers—that had disaffiliated or been expelled in past years. The three unions had parted company with the federation for differing reasons. The UMW had withdrawn from the AFL in pre-merger days for reasons that only John L. Lewis, the union's legendary president, completely grasped. Lewis seemed incapable of remaining in any organization where he was less than undisputed leader. His letter of disaffiliation, addressed to William Green, AFL president, was a classic of brevity: "Green: We disaffiliate. Lewis." The Teamsters were expelled from the AFL-CIO at the federation's 1957 convention at George Meany's insistence. Meany believed that the union's record of corruption and the strong-arm methods made notorious by James Hoffa were damaging the entire movement by giving ammunition to those who favored legislation to bring key aspects of labor's internal affairs under federal jurisdiction. After Hoffa was sent to prison on jury tampering charges, Meany forged a working relationship with the new Teamsters chief, Frank Fitzsimmons, but showed no inclination to bring the union back into the federation fold. The UAW withdrew from the AFL-CIO in 1968 due primarily to Walter Reuther's frustration at having consistently been bested by Meany in internal federation disputes.

There were sound reasons—economic, organizational, and political—to pursue labor unity. Each affiliate member paid annual dues, known as the per capita, based on a specified amount for each member in good standing. In 1979, when Kirkland assumed the presidency, the combined strength of the Teamsters and the UAW was over three million, approximately 20 percent of the total AFL-CIO membership. Unity would also enable Kirkland to impose a measure of discipline over the member unions in the establishment of political goals. Kirkland believed that labor should act in concert in supporting a Democratic presidential candidate during the nominating process or should remain strictly neutral until a nominee was elected, thus avoiding a situation whereby different international unions were cutting separate deals with candidates. Moreover, the Teamsters had a consistent record of support for Republican presidential candidates that extended from Richard Nixon to Ronald Reagan. Kirkland hoped that once inside the federation, the Teamsters might agree to throw their muscle behind Democratic nominees. A unified movement would also enhance the prospects for interunion cooperation during organizing campaigns. As an independent, the Teamsters felt no obligation to negotiate with other unions over which had the most compelling claim on a particular class of workers. The Teamsters bragged that they would organize anything that moved; the result was costly competition between the Teamsters and federation-affiliated unions for the allegiance of unorganized workers.

The departure of Meany and Reuther (who died in a 1970 small plane accident) from the scene had removed the main obstacle to reaffiliation by the UAW. Also facilitating unity was the fact that Kirkland and the UAW's president, Douglas Fraser, shared a common liberal perspective on domestic matters. And while differences over international affairs persisted, a major point of dissension, the Vietnam War, had ended.

The principal remaining hurdle was the reluctance of certain members of Reuther's old guard to embrace a return to an institution whose president, Kirkland, remained committed to the Meany tradition. The old guard had beaten back a previous effort at reunification in 1977 because of concern over Kirkland's likely elevation to the federation presidency upon Meany's retirement. Among the issues raised against Kirkland was his prominent role in the Committee for the Present Danger, an organization of foreign policy hawks that lobbied for increased defense spending and for American policies to check the spread of Soviet power. The UAW's outgoing president, Leonard Woodcock (who had been appointed by President Carter as United States representative to Beijing), was a member of a rival organization, the American Committee on U.S.-Soviet Relations, which favored détente with Moscow and advocated, in the words of its mission statement, "a resolute abandonment of the stale slogans and reflexes of the Cold War." The UAW was also unhappy with the AFL-CIO's early critique of President Carter's economic policy.[6]

Once Kirkland ascended to the presidency, negotiations moved along quickly. He had developed a good rapport with Fraser, and other UAW veterans who might have raised objections, like Emil Mazey or Irving Bluestone, had retired or were about to step down. Many in the auto union were appreciative of the assistance Kirkland had extended during the campaign to persuade Congress to approve a financial bailout for the Chrysler Corporation. There was also an unspoken sense that the UAW was no longer dealing from a position of organizational strength in the wake of the recent loss of 300,000 members through layoffs.[7]

The reaffiliation was announced on July 1, 1981, following a vote by the UAW's regional conference that favored the move by a margin of 7,785 to 4,527. There was no ceremony to mark the event, and the official statements by UAW spokesmen were notably low-key, in deference to the substantial portion of the membership that had voted against the proposition. But the only skunk at the party was Victor Reuther, Walter's brother and the former director of international affairs for the UAW. He complained that Kirkland was to the right of Meany, the evidence being his failure to criticize Reagan's military buildup. The UAW, with 1.7 million members, became the federation's largest affiliate. It also became its largest single source of revenue; its per capita contribution would be $2.7 million.[8]

The Teamsters presented Kirkland with a different set of challenges than did the UAW. This was the largest union in the United States, and its leaders had a reputation as labor's most aggressive organizers—a reputation that by the 1980s was of questionable validity. Like other unions whose strength was concentrated in the industries of the old economy, the Teamsters were losing members. The union did not radiate the dynamism that it boasted during Hoffa's time; it had grown sclerotic under mediocre leaders who lacked their predecessor's fierce commitment to the union and were in some cases more corrupt than Hoffa was.

Even before Kirkland assumed the presidency, the AFL-CIO had made overtures to the Teamsters with an eye toward reaffiliation talks. A delegation that included Tom Donahue, Bob Georgine, Jack Lyons, and William Wynn had raised the issue at a Teamsters' executive council meeting, but the Teamsters' leadership showed no interest and the question was dropped. Kirkland might have been able to forge a unity agreement with Frank Fitzsimmons. But Fitzsimmons died in 1981; his successor, Roy Williams, a Teamster leader from Kansas City, was under federal indictment when he assumed office and was soon thereafter convicted and sent to federal prison. Williams in turn was succeeded by Jackie Presser, the powerful chief of the union in Cleveland. Presser himself was under federal investigation even as he took the oath as the international union's president. He was also an FBI informant, a fact that came out after his death.

The Teamsters was a troubled union in the 1980s. A number of its leading figures were serving prison time, facing trial, under indictment, or the focus of investigation by an array of law enforcement agencies. Kirkland was personally intolerant of corruption within the ranks of labor. He was uninterested in the accumulation of riches. He was scrupulously honest in money matters, and he expected others who worked for the AFL-CIO to be the same.

At the same time, Kirkland was a realist. He made the decision to invite the Teamsters to return to the federation without agonizing personal debate. Ken Young had had some troubling encounters with Presser during the 1950s in Cleveland and objected to the reaffiliation. But Kirkland indicated that he preferred the Teamsters inside the fold, where the big union would be more inclined to an attitude of cooperation, than outside, where the Teamsters would be free to cut separate deals with Republican presidents and conduct raiding missions against AFL-CIO affiliated unions. The cooperation of the Teamsters could be critical during organizing drives or strikes, especially in the building trades, the supermarket business, and the hotel and restaurant industry. Kirkland told Young that his one precondition was that the Teamsters adhere to the AFL-CIO constitution.

Kirkland was also disturbed by various proposals to expand the federal government's control over unions suspected of corruption. In 1981, over the objection of several executive council members, Kirkland had endorsed a bill sponsored by Senators Sam Nunn and Warren Rudman that would stiffen the penalties against corrupt labor officials by raising to felony status union-connected crimes involving more than $1,000; removing guilty officials from office after an initial conviction instead of waiting for the appeals process to conclude; and increasing the period during which convicted union officials are barred from union office from five to ten years. "Union office is a calling, not a business," he told a congressional hearing. "The morals of the marketplace will not suffice. Those who enter union office are, and should be, held to a higher standard. If a person holding a union office takes an employer payoff for a substandard contract, misuses the right to strike for his own benefit, or pilfers from the union treasury, that person does not simply tarnish his own honor. He tarnishes the honor of scores of men and women" who serve as honest union officials.[9]

But while Kirkland advocated more rigorous enforcement of existing anticorruption laws, his civil libertarian side was appalled at proposals to extend the reach of the state into the internal affairs of unions. Kirkland described certain ideas that had surfaced during meetings of the President's Commission on Organized Crime as "Orwellian" and a "virtual blueprint for a police state." He was particularly offended by suggestions that federal workers be given regular drug tests and that unions whose officials were found to be corrupt be decertified as bargaining agents.[10]

In objecting to proposals for greater and greater prosecutorial authority, Kirkland was acting within established trade union tradition. He strongly favored the removal of the movement's bad elements. He understood that the corruption of a few reflected badly on the entire movement. He also believed that unions were subject to a double standard, whereby corruption among union officials was judged more harshly than was malfeasance by corporate officers. Opinion polls revealed that Americans' views of labor leaders were strongly influenced by a perception that corruption was pervasive within unions. In fact, corruption was a problem at but a few unions—the President's Commission on Organized Crime identified four problem unions: Teamsters, Laborers, Hotel and Restaurant Workers, and Longshoremen. At a time of trouble, the healthy elements of the movement did not need the additional burden imposed by the corrupt minority. But Kirkland was dismayed at the prospect of handing over to the state the authority to decertify unions, remove union officers, and assume authority over internal union affairs, all of which the Justice Department succeeded in doing to the Teamsters.

Kirkland's opposition to the extension of the federal prosecutorial arm was driven by something more fundamental than labor's institutional interests. Through the years, Kirkland had developed a strong civil libertarian streak, driven in part by his reading of American labor history, with its frequent accounts of state power being deployed to crush strikes and organizing drives. Kirkland was thus alert to government attempts to limit individual rights or violate due process. Kirkland also spoke in opposition to what he considered the misuse of wiretaps, polygraphs, and other forms of electronic snooping. In 1988 Kirkland gave unqualified endorsement to a bill sponsored by Senator Kennedy that would bar the use of lie detectors by private employers. He described lie detectors as "a blatant assault on a worker's right to privacy."[11]

The negotiations that led to the Teamsters' reaffiliation were conducted by a committee of three labor leaders who knew Jackie Presser: Ed Hanley, president of the Hotel and Restaurant Workers Union; William Wynn, president of the United Food and Commercial Workers; and Robert Georgine, president of the AFL-CIO's Building and Construction Trades Department. All three represented workers in industries who relied on Teamster solidarity in their struggles with management.[12]

Hanley, Wynn, and Georgine met with Presser and reported to Kirkland that the Teamsters chief was eager to bring his union back into the federation. There being no serious items for extended negotiation, Kirkland proposed to the executive council that it approve the Teamsters' application. Although the formal council vote was unanimous, the decision was reached only after four hours of intense debate, during which some council members—in particular, Al Shanker—argued against placing the reaffiliation decision on a fast track. Even after the council voted to approve the Teamsters' application, some members continued to harbor misgivings about welcoming Presser into the fold.

The official reaffiliation took place at the federation's 1987 convention, held in Miami Beach. Even as Presser was accepting the applause of the convention delegates, the Justice Department was preparing a civil suit under the Racketeer Influenced and Corrupt Organizations Act (RICO) that would remove the Teamsters' twenty-one-member executive board and hand control of the union to a federal monitor. In comments to the press, Kirkland showed himself sensitive to the notion that the Teamsters were rejoining the federation to exploit its political clout in their struggle to avoid a government takeover. Said Kirkland, "We're giving them no cover, no insulation from their duty to comply with the law." But he also expressed displeasure with the government for "taking shortcuts around this tedious problem of dealing with individuals who are the object of these allegations and imprisoning the entire institution under the control of an appointee of the government." In an address to the convention, Kirkland was even blunter. He blasted "orchestrated leaks and planted press stories" about the Teamsters and added, "A government supervised trade union, like an employer supervised trade union, is a contradiction in terms." The AFL-CIO, he went on, would actively oppose a federal bid for control of the Teamsters.[13]

For many Americans, the most vivid image of Jackie Presser was of his ample frame being carried into a banquet at Caesar's Palace in Las Vegas, clad in a toga and riding in a chariot borne by four men dressed as Roman soldiers, while a loudspeaker boomed, "Hail Caesar." At the AFL-CIO convention, the difference in style between the Teamsters officialdom and the federation leadership was captured by a reporter who wrote of a delegation of men in sharkskin suits (Presser and company) advancing on two men wearing blue blazers and gray slacks (Kirkland and Donahue). Yet another difference was in the generous compensation Presser and his top lieutenants earned as opposed to the far more modest salaries received by Kirkland and other international union presidents. According to one estimate, 117 Teamsters' officials earned over $100,000 annually, a figure that exceeded the salary of the presidents of some well-known international unions. A number of high Teamsters' chieftains earned into the hundreds of thousands by double or triple dipping—that is, receiving salaries from two or three union entities simultaneously. Presser was a triple-dipper: he earned $588,000 from a combination of his job as international president, his home local in Cleveland, and the Ohio Conference of Teamsters. Kirkland, by contrast, earned under $150,000.[14]

Presser's appearance at the convention was relatively brief. The cancer that was soon to kill him was advanced. He had been undergoing chemotherapy, his body had thinned down considerably, and he wore a baseball cap throughout his speech—often incoherent—to conceal his hair loss. Presser was plagued by more than physical illness. He was under indictment for embezzling some $700,000 from a Cleveland local to pay mob figures union salaries for what the government charged were no-show jobs. Presser died before the trial took place, but the government did succeed in placing the Teamsters under the control of a court-appointed monitor. As Kirkland might have predicted, the government, once it gained control of the union, did not surrender it easily; the monitor remained in place not for a brief transition period, but indefinitely.[15]

At the time of reaffiliation, the Teamsters claimed 1.7 million members, well down from the peak of over 2 million. Teamsters dues per capita would amount to 15 percent of the federation budget. Ironically, given its various problems, the AFL-CIO could claim to speak for the largest number of trade unionists, as measured in raw numbers, in its twenty-two-year history: 14.4 million.

Although the United Mine Workers could cite a history that was as noble—and notorious—as either the UAW's or the Teamsters', in the

1980s it was a case study in trade union deterioration. At its height, under the leadership of John L. Lewis, the UMW was America's most powerful union, with a membership of over a half million men and a measure of control over the country's strategic energy supply. By the mid-1980s, however, the union had shriveled to fewer than 100,000 active members, the victim of automation, the replacement of coal by cleaner-burning fuels, and a succession of corrupt and/or ineffective leaders.

In 1982 Richard Trumka, running as an insurgent, defeated the incumbent president, Sam Church, in a bitter and intensely contested election. At thirty-three, Trumka was remarkably young for a union president. He came from a mining family and had himself spent some time working in the pits. But he had made his principal mark as a union lawyer, joining the lengthening list of labor officials who had earned a law degree.

During the Church-Trumka election campaign, officials of several unions affiliated with the AFL-CIO—in particular, William Wynn of the United Food and Commercial Workers—raised campaign funds for Church. The money was raised from individual contributions from union officers and did not come from dues money, and in the end it didn't amount to much. But the pro-Church initiative smacked of the kind of interference in a union's internal affairs that the labor movement had deplored when Ed Sadlowski had solicited campaign money from liberal-left elites in his unsuccessful bid for the Steelworkers presidency. Wynn justified contributions on the grounds that Church had once been a shop steward in a meatcutters' local. But he also accused Trumka of benefiting from outside support, presumably referring to various left-wing activists who were involved in the Trumka campaign.[16] Kirkland himself did not contribute to the Church fund, but he quietly let it be known that he did not disapprove of Wynn's actions.[17]

Trumka seems not to have held a grudge over the pro-Church tilt of Wynn and other labor leaders. Even before his election, the UMW had begun to work in collaboration with the AFL-CIO on various campaigns of mutual concern, a pattern Trumka continued. Trumka himself actively pursued mergers with several unions that represented workers in the energy industry; had the mergers been consummated, the Mine Workers would have joined as a junior partner.

Then in 1989, the UMW found itself locked in a bitter strike against the Pittston Coal Corporation. Pittston had facilities throughout the bituminous region of Kentucky, West Virginia, and Virginia, but the nerve center of the company's operations, and of the strike, was Lebanon, Virginia, a small town in the heart of the state's coal country.

During his long career at the AFL-CIO, Kirkland lent his personal support to innumerable strike campaigns. When traveling to meetings or conferences, he made it a point to join union picket lines in the local community. At one picket line, in Las Vegas, he began arguing with the police after they had arrested the president of the local union but refused to take Kirkland away as well. He directed the federation to develop special strategies to assist unions that were involved in important strikes. He used his influence with presidents, cabinet officials, and key members of Congress to resolve strikes of national significance. He was the personal embodiment of the concept of "labor solidarity."

Kirkland gave total commitment to the Pittston miners. He spoke at rallies; he mobilized broad labor support behind the UMW; he lobbied political leaders. At some point during the strike, Trumka began to discuss the possibility of the UMW's reaffiliating with the federation. He told Young that there was lingering resistance to reaffiliation within his union from those who considered the AFL-CIO insufficiently militant. Trumka inquired whether Kirkland might come to Pittston and court arrest through an act of civil disobedience. Young suggested that rather than Kirkland acting alone, a delegation of labor leaders led by Kirkland visit the strike scene and get themselves arrested. Young then presented the idea to Kirkland—though he did not mention Trumka's suggestion that in exchange for Kirkland's assistance, the UMW would return to the federation. Had Kirkland known there was a quid pro quo, Young believed, he would have refused any involvement whatsoever. And as Young predicted, Kirkland jumped at the opportunity to go to bat for a beleaguered union.[18]

On August 23, Kirkland joined Trumka and a dozen other labor leaders in a sit-down at the county courthouse. This was civil disobedience at its most carefully choreographed; Kirkland and the others were arrested in an almost ceremonial fashion by the sheriff who, in taking Kirkland into custody, declared what an honor it was to meet the number-one man of American labor and then proceeded to introduce Kirkland to his deputies and other hangers-on. Kirkland and the others were soon released after being charged with obstruction of free passage to the courthouse. That night Kirkland addressed a strike rally that drew a crowd of 4,000 despite a steady downpour.[19] Kirkland quoted the early-twentieth-century socialist leader Eugene V. Debs and told the strikers that their commitment was "a tonic" that reinforced his resolve to put his weight behind their cause. At the time, Poland's Solidarity had recently defeated the Communist Party in national elections, and labor unrest was gathering momentum in the Soviet Union. Kirkland thus introduced an international dimension to the Pittston struggle, asserting that it was "time to tell our political leaders that the hard-working trade unionists who exercised their rights in Virginia are just as worthy of their sympathy and support as the workers in Poland and the Soviet Union."

Shortly afterward, Trumka announced that his union had approved a resolution to rejoin the AFL-CIO; reaffiliation was formally consummated at the federation's convention in late 1989.[20] The strike was settled in February 1990, after President Bush's secretary of labor, Elizabeth Dole, rejected the advice of her aides and, at Kirkland's prodding, became personally involved in the conflict. She appointed W. J. Usery, the former labor secretary, as a special mediator, and Usery, whose mediation skills were widely respected, soon brought the two parties to an agreement that gave the miners most of their demands, while giving Pittston the production flexibility it had sought.[21]

Labor's triumph at Pittston did not signal a reversal in its fortunes at the bargaining table. Likewise, the settlement of labor's lengthy struggle with the Coors brewing company did not contain broad implications for future union-organizing efforts. Nonetheless, there was something satisfying for the AFL-CIO in achieving even a partial win over Coors, given the company's antilabor history.

The dispute with Coors had begun in 1977, when the company broke a strike through the use of strikebreakers, some of whom were hired as permanent replacements for members of the Brewery Workers' local at Coors. In response, the AFL-CIO launched a boycott of Coors beer, at the time a popular brand that restricted its distribution to the western part of the United States. Labor pressed the Coors campaign with particular relish because of the Coors family's reputation as partisans of conservative causes and candidates. As it turned out, the timing of the boycott was propitious for labor. Coors was preparing to expand its product base into northeastern states, where unions were strong and boycotts of corporations with records of labor problems were widely honored. Coors met with resistance from consumers when it began selling beer in New York and New Jersey; in Washington, D.C., many hotels declined to carry Coors brands as long as the boycott was in place. At this point Peter Coors, a member of the younger, less political, Coors generation, opened discussions with Tom Donahue, which led to the eventual settlement of the dispute. The boycott campaign—described by Kirkland as a "resounding success"—was called off in August 1987.[22]

The conflict at Eastern Airlines offered a much more formidable challenge than labor had faced at Pittston and Coors. In that encounter, labor faced a series of new adversaries: legislation that transformed labor-management relations in the airline industry, the injection of competition in an industry that had been under strict regulatory control, and a CEO who believed that breaking the power of the airline's unions represented the key to economic recovery. In the end, both sides lost, as Eastern, an airline that millions had flown en route to vacations in Florida and the

Caribbean, went out of existence. But it was the unions and their members who suffered the greatest setback.

Eastern was one of the most financially distressed operations to emerge from deregulation. In the mid-1980s it was purchased by Texas Air, a small nonunion carrier run by Frank Lorenzo. Earlier in the decade, Texas Air had purchased Continental Airlines, another troubled carrier. From the outset, Lorenzo made a target of Continental's union contracts, first demanding major concessions and then abrogating union agreements after taking the airline into bankruptcy. When Lorenzo insisted on major concessions from Eastern's machinists and baggage handlers, a strike was called.

Although ostensibly pitting Eastern's management against its unions, the strike in reality also involved Frank Lorenzo against the American labor movement. Kirkland had little respect for Lorenzo, whom he regarded as emblematic of a new type of buccaneer capitalist, an "adventurer" who acquires, scavenges, and liquidates an enterprise with little concern for the well-being of its workers or their families. Kirkland made a strong effort to resolve the strike through political intervention. But on this occasion, Elizabeth Dole declined to place her authority on the line, while President Bush vowed to veto legislation that would establish an emergency board to help settle the conflict.[23] Although Lorenzo scored a victory over the unions, he was unable to keep the airline aloft; Eastern was liquidated in 1991, resulting in the loss of tens of thousands of jobs.

The impact of the economic transformation on an established, heavily unionized industry was also on display in the failed strike at the Hormel meatpacking facility in Austin, Minnesota, which began in 1985. The United Food and Commercial Workers had attempted to stem job losses in the industry by offering Hormel and other companies a four-year wage freeze. But conditions failed to improve, and after the companies made demands for further concessions, the UFCW agreed to a master pay rate that was below the prevailing level of $10.69 per hour.

Not all the union's meatpacking locals were content with the agreement. Some locals, whose members were fearful of plant closings, were willing to agree to even deeper concessions. At the other extreme, the union's P-9 local, which represented workers at Hormel's Austin facility, was determined to accept no givebacks whatsoever.

The ensuing strike resulted in a highly public setback for labor. To plan a strike strategy, the local hired Ray Rogers, a veteran organizer who had made an important contribution to the success of the Amalgamated Clothing and Textile Workers' campaign to organize the workers of the J. P. Stevens textile firm. Rogers was an advocate of the corporate campaign, in which strikes are transformed into social cause movements and efforts are made to embarrass members of the corporation's board and financial institutions that have ties to the company. This strategy had worked well at J. P. Stevens, and Rogers was confident that it could work at Hormel.

But conditions at Hormel were in no way comparable to the situation in the textile industry. Stevens had resisted unionization efforts for years and had a record of multiple violations of federal labor law. Hormel, by contrast, had a lengthy history of reasonably amicable relations with unions and had made no overt effort to break the UFCW at its installations. Furthermore, public support for a strike against concessions was limited; most Americans were aware that workers in many industries had been forced to agree to givebacks, often as a last-ditch measure to keep a company from falling into bankruptcy.[24]

The strike was broken the next January when Hormel reopened the plant with the assistance of the National Guard. Hormel used a combination of nonstriking workers and striker replacements to keep operations going. A number of workers lost their jobs entirely.

In addition to its strike against Hormel, Local P-9 found itself in bitter dispute with UFCW's national leadership. The union's president, William Wynn, had disavowed the strike, which he saw as an exercise in futility and which violated the settlement reached by the UFCW with the major meatpackers for a reduction in the master rate. Local P-9 had dispatched roving pickets to march in front of plant gates at other Hormel installations in the Midwest; the UFCW ordered its members to ignore the pickets and report to work. Eventually, the UFCW leadership took over negotiations from the local and reached an accommodation with Hormel, after which it placed P-9 in trusteeship.[25]

Most experienced labor leaders blamed Ray Rogers for what they regarded as a tragedy that need not have occurred. Both Kirkland and Donahue saw Rogers as irresponsible and publicity-mad. They were sympathetic to the workers' fury over an agreement that effectively reduced their standard of living. But concessions were an unfortunate element in collective bargaining during the 1980s. Rogers was an experienced organizer who, in their view, should have been aware of the pitfalls of ultra-militancy in the prevailing economic climate.

Things came to a head, and nearly to blows, at the February 1987 executive council meeting in Bal Harbour. Rogers showed up, with James Guyette, P-9's president, in tow. Rogers was a constant presence, taunting Wynn and other trade union leaders and providing the press with a stream of quotes, invective, and charges, all directed at the UFCW leadership.[26] Kirkland met with Wynn and Guyette in an effort to mediate the dispute, but the local president refused to be placated, and nothing was resolved. At this point Kirkland publicly sided with Wynn, asserting that the UFCW had given "wise and sound advice" on the strike. Kirkland was irritated by press accounts that interpreted Hormel as another sign of labor's rapid organizational decline. He said that the "high-flown highfalutin rhetoric" of some journalists had conveyed the impression that the "decline and fall of the labor movement hinges on [the Hormel outcome]—I think that's malarkey."[27]

In both Hormel and Eastern, a principal weapon of management was the hiring of strikebreakers on a permanent basis. The use of striker replacements was a relatively new phenomenon, made popular in the Reagan years. Striker replacements were not illegal, but they had been considered a breach of labor-management etiquette until the 1980s. The main example was, of course, the air controllers. This was followed by the use of replacement workers to defeat strikes at Continental, Greyhound, Phelps Dodge, and the Danly Machine Corporation. In each case, management went out and rounded up enough of what Kirkland called "an army of long-term unemployed" to keep the company going during the strike.[28]

It was rare for labor to score a victory once permanent replacements entered the picture. But in 1991, the Steelworkers won something of a triumph after a long and angry strike at the Ravenswood Aluminum Company in West Virginia.

Ravenswood's management had hired replacement workers from out of town to take the jobs of some 1,400 of the 1,700 workers at the installation after a strike was called in 1989. That act in itself stirred up resentment in the tightly knit Ravenswood community. The union then launched a multipronged campaign against the company, beginning with a series of complaints filed with the NLRB and a boycott of Ravenswood's aluminum products, that paid dividends when corporate giants like Coca-Cola and Stroh's brewery agreed not to use the company's cans.

But the key ingredient at Ravenswood was a highly public campaign directed against the man who labor claimed held the controlling interest in the company—Marc Rich. Rich was living in Zug, Switzerland, an exile in flight from prosecution by the Justice Department on tax charges. Rich acknowledged that he had an investment interest in Ravenswood but insisted that his company did not have a controlling stake. Yet despite his fabulous wealth and global influence, Rich proved to be the most vulnerable link in the company structure. Rich was desperate to return to the United States. First, however, he wanted the pending criminal charges dropped (Rich was finally granted a pardon in one of Bill Clinton's last, and most controversial, acts as president). Rich's campaign depended on the support of influential Americans; under these circumstances, he could not afford accusations of union busting.

The strategy devised by labor called for a corporate campaign with a personal twist. The federation dispatched a team to Rich's Swiss retreat at Zug, where they picketed his office and engaged in puppet theater, in which Rich was portrayed as the villain. Labor also targeted Rich with "wanted" posters that were distributed throughout Europe. In addition, trade unionists in Romania, Czechoslovakia, and Russia worked to disrupt Rich's efforts to expand his financial empire to those countries. In effect, an international picket line was erected around Rich's ventures in Europe.

At this point Rich decided that action had to be taken to resolve the dispute. At the request of the Steelworkers, Kirkland met privately with Rich at his retreat in Zug. An outline of an agreement was reached. Afterward, Kirkland met with a Rich associate, Willy Strathotte, who had engineered the purchase of a majority interest in Ravenswood and then dismissed the company CEO, R. Emmett Boyle, who was principally responsible for the hard-line stance against the unions. Leonard Garment, a Washington attorney who represented Rich during his exile, arranged for a meeting involving the Steelworkers leadership, Kirkland, and Strathotte. The meeting was held on Strathotte's boat, anchored off Ft. Lauderdale. The principals reached an agreement involving some improvement in salary and the rehiring of the locked-out workers, and the strike was settled.[29]

The chief participant for the Steelworkers was George Becker, a high union official who would soon succeed Lynn Williams as president. Several years later, Becker would be among those who engineered the coup that forced Kirkland into premature retirement.

Despite the mounting troubles facing the union movement, Kirkland maintained his quick wit and sense of irony. He often used aphorisms in summing up debates during executive council sessions. At some point, Lenore Miller, president of the Retail, Wholesale, and Department Store Workers and a Kirkland admirer, began writing down some of Lane's favorite maxims. "Another victory for hope over experience," was a favorite, as was, "If we don't have a solution, we don't have a problem." One of Miller's favorites, and one she took to heart, was, "If you're on the right side, everything else comes easy." Miller felt that Lane tried to live by his own maxim: "Even though he was a political realist, he wanted to be on the right side." Kirkland also liked to borrow quotes from the movie *Casablanca* to drive home a point. Among his favorites: "Round up the usual suspects," and, "I am shocked, shocked!"

Huey Long provided Lane with fodder for some of his favorite stories, particularly the two yarns that ended with the punch line "Well, son, you're just going to have to go out there and tell them the governor lied." And, "those of you who endorse me now get the goodies, those of you who endorse me after Labor Day get what's left and the rest of you get good guv'mint."

Clearly, Kirkland had an ironic wit, usually aimed at a political subject. Whenever his dachshund, Stanley, rolled on his back in a pose of abject surrender, Kirkland would describe the dog as having assumed "the full State Department position."

Once, during a meeting of union officials, the idea was put forward that the AFL-CIO should create its own think tank. "We don't need a think tank," Tom Donahue replied. "We have Lane Kirkland."

Kirkland's powers of strategic thinking were severely tested by the challenges labor faced during the 1980s. He recognized that American society was undergoing a far-reaching transformation that carried unsettling implications for labor's future. Kirkland made frequent visits to the American heartland, where he met with local labor officials, toured plants, and listened to the frustrations and complaints of the rank and file. Along with United Steelworkers president Lynn Williams, Kirkland toured the Monongahela Valley, where rusting and inactive steel mills dotted the landscape, a sad emblem of the demise of the old steel economy. On another occasion, accompanied by Mario Cuomo, then New York governor, he walked through a brand-new steel facility, where a handful of workers produced steel by keystrokes on a computer—the new steel economy, a robotized and computerized world where few human beings, and therefore few potential union members, earned a living.

Kirkland saw clearly that the old ways of doing things were no longer sufficient. He continued to believe that a turnaround in labor's fortunes would require a shift in the political environment. But he also recognized that labor would continue to lose members, and influence, unless the union movement focused greater attention on organizing the unorganized. To be sure, most unions claimed that they devoted a substantial portion of their overall budget to organizing efforts. But these figures could be misleading, since unions tended to lump in spending for the servicing of local unions with that of organizing new members. Many unions, in fact, allocated few resources to organizing campaigns and were psychologically ill-equipped to cope with the workforce complexities of the new economy.

Kirkland was quietly encouraging union presidents to reassess their organizational mission in light of the emergence of an economy that stressed technology and information. He was particularly interested in the Communications Workers of America (CWA), a union whose membership had historically been concentrated in the Bell Telephone system. In 1985 Kirkland asked the CWA president, Morton Bahr, to take in the

International Typographers' Union (ITU), a once powerful union whose membership had been decimated by the introduction of computers in the newsroom. The Teamsters, then still outside the federation fold, had initiated merger talks with the ITU, a development that Kirkland was determined to thwart. Bahr was skeptical. The CWA, he told Kirkland, was a telephone workers' union; it had never organized in the newspaper world. Kirkland responded that Bahr should begin to think of the CWA as evolving into a different type of union, one in which the membership was not focused on a single industry but instead regarded itself as a union for workers of the communications industry, writ large. He urged Bahr to expand the CWA's horizons to embrace everything from the telecommunications industry to the news media to the entertainment industry. Bahr took Kirkland's advice to heart: the CWA subsequently incorporated the typographers, the Newspaper Guild, a number of film and theater associations, and the International Union of Electrical Workers. By the 1990s it enjoyed a reputation as the leading voice of labor in the new economy.[30]

Kirkland also established a special body in 1984 called the Evolution of Work Committee, to study the changing nature of the workplace and the role of the labor union in the postindustrial economy. Donahue served as chairman, and the committee engaged a number of academics and opinion pollsters to draft a series of studies and reports that was designed to provide a framework for a labor strategy that took into account shifting attitudes of workers toward their jobs and unions, the legal and political environment, technology change, trade—in short, to examine every aspect of the movement's condition and propose a road map for revival.

An unstated purpose of the committee was to force a labor leadership that was not inclined toward self-examination to confront its own shortcomings. Dick Wilson, who served as director of the AFL-CIO's organizing department during the 1980s, put it this way: "Most union leaders wanted to believe that our problems with membership were the result of union busters or Reagan or foreign trade. They didn't want to hear the message that something fundamental had changed in the American economy."[31] Although labor would continue to place primary blame for its reversals on the attitudes of corporate management, the political climate, and the nature of the country's labor laws, the committee's findings drove home the message, as Donahue put it, "that workers had different attitudes towards jobs and bosses than they did in the 'thirties."

Not to mention different attitudes to unions. For some time, opinion pollsters had been reporting that American workers held ambivalent attitudes toward unions, praising their contribution to higher wages and benefits, while expressing coolness toward labor's political involvement and the ethical standards of its leaders. Donahue came to realize the extent of the problem when he observed a focus group on workplace issues conducted by the pollster Peter Hart. The experience was painful. On the one hand, the workers clearly desired some form of workplace mechanism to resolve disputes and represent their interests. As elaborated by the focus group participants, the mechanism closely resembled a labor union. But when the word *union* was introduced to the discussion, the participants immediately exhibited discontent. Recalled Donahue, "You could see by their body language that the word bothered them; they actually pulled away from the table. They seemed to be frightened or repelled by the word *union*. I was startled by this response. These workers wanted something that could bring them together but found the notion of a union frightening."[32]

The committee's most important findings were issued in February 1985. Entitled "The Changing Situation of Workers and Their Unions," the report was blunt in its tone of self-criticism. Its observations were not new, by and large, but the fact that the source was the AFL-CIO, not some critic from a university or an academic journal, was important. The report spoke of a workplace environment that was not hospitable to unionization, lagging membership, and growth concentrated in nonunion industries and in regions of the country where unions were weak. It noted the growing instability of employment, where workers might spend a few years at a job instead of several decades, as another hurdle to union growth. And it noted the increased percentage of the labor force that was defined as managers, supervisors, or contract workers—employees who were either ineligible for union representation or who were subject to reprisal for pro-union sympathies.

Among the most disturbing findings was the marked change in employer attitudes toward unions. According to the report, 95 percent of employers opposed unions, and a full 75 percent used consultants or advisers to assist in maintaining a union-free workplace. This wave of antiunion sentiment contributed to a major increase in the sacking of workers for union activity, from 872 NLRB cases in 1957 to some 10,000 in 1980. The impact of employer hostility, the report concluded, was considerable. During the same period that unionism in the private sector had declined, union strength among public workers had exhibited steady—and, in some sectors, spectacular—gains. Although municipal and state governments might not welcome the unionization of their employees, they seldom engaged in the aggressive antilabor tactics that had become common practice in the private sector. The report urged the expansion of the kind of corporate campaigns that had proved so successful in the J. P. Stevens boycott. It also encouraged the formation of organizing committees, separate from the structure of specific unions, to plan and coordinate unionization drives against difficult targets.

A controversial proposal called for unions to establish a new form of membership—associate memberships—for workers in facilities where the union did not enjoy bargaining rights. The proposal was advanced as a means of maintaining ties with workers who had voted for union representation in an election where the antiunion sentiment had prevailed. The report suggested that unions might solidify the loyalty of associate members by offering them certain benefits: low-cost health, auto, and home insurance; credit cards; and possibly an IRA.

One consequence of the report was the creation of a new entity, the Organizing Institute. The institute was to function as a training facility for young organizers from international unions and as an instrument for the study of new organizing techniques and strategies. The AFL-CIO hired Richard Bensinger as director; he joined the federation with an impressive record as an organizer in the western states for the Amalgamated Clothing and Textile Workers Union. Bensinger was enthusiastic, tireless, and abrasive—a fanatic who didn't mind ruffling the feathers of influential labor leaders. Bensinger's unique abilities as a trainer of organizers were recognized throughout the labor movement, and the graduates of the Organizing Institute went on to high positions in various international unions. Bensinger himself was appointed director of the AFL-CIO's Department of Organization after John J. Sweeney's election as president in 1995, only to be summarily fired by Sweeney, apparently at the behest of labor officials who found Bensinger's combative style irritating.

The report also inspired the establishment of the Strategic Approaches Committee, whose goal was to develop strategies and provide aid for beleaguered unions locked in important strike campaigns. Such assistance was provided to the Steelworkers in a strike against the USX corporation (formerly known as U.S. Steel), to a National Football League players' strike, and to the unions striking against Eastern—in the latter case, to the tune of some $2 million.

Kirkland had established a new entity, the Labor Institute for Public Affairs, to strengthen the movement's ability to get its message across to the press and to its own members. But while he appreciated the importance of effective public relations, he did not see it as a panacea for labor's problems. He had mixed feelings about the corporate campaign. Although Kirkland was impressed by the role played by corporate campaigns in the triumphs of J. P. Stevens and a few other cases, and while he recognized that in the prevailing climate creative tactics were needed to augment the traditional strike weapon, he regarded some of the corporate campaign's most fervent advocates as irresponsible hustlers.

Kirkland was also a realist about labor's prospects, which is why he stressed the adverse impact of the country's labor laws, the impact of the antilabor political climate, and the importance of organizing workers in the new high-tech economy. Polls showed that even as most nonunion workers were dubious about the relevance of union membership to their workplace life, a substantial minority declared that they would have joined a union if it were possible. Had unions organized even half of this pro-union minority, the media would have proclaimed that labor was undergoing a renewal, instead of incessantly pointing to its decline. Did these workers remain outside the union fold because labor organizers lacked aggressiveness and creativity? Or was the principal roadblock corporate threats to fire union partisans, liquidate the plant, or export jobs to a foreign country? Lynn Williams, who as a Canadian had worked his way up the ranks of the Steelworkers in a society with a much more union-friendly legal environment, was of the view that Kirkland and other American union leaders were doing everything possible to cope with the organizing crisis, given the political handicaps they faced.[33] Kirkland was familiar with the power and the respect that unions enjoyed in Canada and Western Europe; he found it a great source of frustration that unions in America should be compelled to devise extraordinary measures like corporate campaigns to organize a single corporation or even a single workplace. In other civilized democracies, workers determined whether their workplace would be unionized through the simple procedure of voting on the issue, up or down.

Had Kirkland been free to pursue his long-range vision for trade union revival, he would have moved to refashion American labor relations to more effectively meet the needs of a changing workforce and an evolving, international economy. Although Kirkland had no model in mind, he admired certain characteristics of labor relations in Europe but understood that European templates could not be grafted onto the much different cultural environment of the United States. Kirkland may have hoped that the Evolution of Work Committee would play a crucial role in changing the mindset of American trade unionists, who were still committed to the traditional system of us-against-them collective bargaining and were resistant to any but the most modest reforms. But even if a united labor movement under the leadership of a farsighted chief like Kirkland had put forward a scheme for a different sort of relation between unions and the corporation, the men who held the reins of business power would have rejected the proposition without a second thought. Kirkland therefore placed his hopes on a reversal in political conditions. Eventually, he reasoned, the Democrats would return to power. At that point, the trade union movement would be in position to present its case to an administration that owed its election to labor's work in the political trenches and thus could not ignore its needs.

Meanwhile, the decade of the 1980s that had been so thoroughly unkind to the trade union movement ended on a high note. The administration of the kinder, gentler George Bush was more willing to give labor's case a hearing than was Reagan's. In Congress, the AFL-CIO had mounted a full legislative agenda, including trade and safety laws, a parental leave bill, a bill to require corporations to provide prior notification before shutting down major installations, an increase in the minimum wage, and a measure restricting the private sector's ability to use lie detector tests. Most would eventually win passage.

Indeed, the federation's 1989 convention—an event that marked the tenth anniversary of Kirkland's presidency—was a celebration of achievements on the home front and internationally. One reason for the sense of optimism was the unprecedented degree of labor unity that Kirkland had forged. A highlight was the introduction of the representatives from the unions that had returned to the church, not just the UAW, the Mine Workers, and the Teamsters, but smaller unions, such as the Brotherhood of Locomotive Engineers, the International Longshoremen's and Warehousemen's Union (the West Coast longshoremen had been pushed out of the CIO years earlier because of the Communist sympathies of its leader, Harry Bridges), and the Writers Guild of America, East. There were also delegations from unions involved in strikes at Pittston, Eastern, and Nynex, where the CWA and the International Brotherhood of Electrical Workers were involved in a struggle with management.

Another highlight at that convention was an appearance by Lech Walesa. The convention itself was designed around the theme "Solidarity at Home and Throughout the World." Kirkland was inspired; he hoped that the example of Solidarity could infuse the global working class with a spirit of unity. As he put it in his keynote speech:

> If we are to advance in this hostile climate, there is only one way for trade unionism to turn, and that is to each other. . . . A new spirit of solidarity among the workers of the world has placed trade unionism at the head of the movement for democracy and human rights. . . . Today, more than ever, the solidarity of labor is the instrument of history and the lever that moves the world.

He vowed to capitalize on the momentum generated by developments in Poland to organize new members and influence the passage of social legislation. "No matter what or where the front, we remain engaged," said Kirkland.

Walesa made his entrance on November 14. As he and other Solidarity leaders wound their way through the hall en route to the podium, the delegates stood and cheered raucously for a full fifteen minutes. Garment workers jumped on chairs to snap Walesa's picture; steelworkers gave the victory sign; a paperworker held aloft a sign in Polish that denounced Frank Lorenzo, labor's number-one hate object. "Lech, Lech, Lech," the delegates chanted.[34] Walesa was overwhelmed by the response, as were the members of his entourage. "I never knew it was like this," Bronislaw Geremek whispered to Adrian Karatnycky as they walked through the hall. Geremek and other Solidarity activists understood that Solidarity had the support of Kirkland and a few other top leaders; the surprise was the emotional depth of support throughout the ranks of the American union movement.[35]

"Today, I am here as a trade unionist," Walesa shouted. He ended the speech with "Solidarity forever" in Polish and then brought down the house with, "Union, Yes!" in English, the theme of an AFL-CIO public relations drive then featured on American television. "One easily finds friends when one is successful," Walesa said, "but when you are in trouble there is suddenly hardly anybody to be seen. But at least you can know for sure that those that stayed with you are the ones you can rely on. And this is the kind of friendship you can value the most, even when you are surrounded by new allies and sympathizers attracted by your new success."[36]

In later years, after Kirkland retired under pressure from a segment of the labor leadership, he would be criticized as being complacent in the face of crisis. But the record of his first decade in office is that of a leader who was engaged in a series of skirmishes on a wide variety of battlefields. He bolstered labor's political machine even as the movement suffered a series of setbacks in relations with the corporate world. He walked numerous picket lines, addressed dozens of strike rallies, and took steps to deepen the involvement of the rank and file in union affairs. He encouraged the more farsighted union leaders to develop new strategies for organizing workers and new ways of relating to the great mass of unorganized workers. On another level, Kirkland made shrewd use of his influence as a Washington insider to resolve strikes, win passage of legislation, and generally advance the cause of organized labor during difficult political times.

At the same time, Kirkland continued to believe that the solution to labor's declining numbers woes lay in Washington, through legislation that would even out the playing field during organizing campaigns. And, increasingly, he began to draw the connection between labor's organizational difficulties and a global trade environment that was rendering the very notion of a prosperous working class obsolete. He would soon emerge as a leading figure in a movement to change the rules of the international economic system to ensure that workers, as well as investors, would benefit from globalization.

11

CIVIL RIGHTS
Keeping the Faith

ALTHOUGH HE HAD BEEN RAISED UNDER CONDITIONS OF RACIAL separation in one of America's most segregated states, Lane Kirkland believed in racial equality from an early age. He derived his racial liberalism in part from his home environment. His father would not tolerate expressions of bigotry, and Kirkland himself enjoyed easy friendships with black people in both Camden and Newberry. Other white southerners from small-town backgrounds had similar relationships with black children, and yet as adults joined the resistance to civil rights. Kirkland was different. During his years on the AFL-CIO staff, he gained a reputation as a civil rights partisan and was prominently involved in the development of labor's positions on desegregation legislation and the formulation of plans to accelerate the integration of the trade union movement itself. But while he condemned segregation as immoral, Kirkland never treated racial injustice as a problem exclusive to the South. Experience had taught him that prejudice could be as virulent in New York as in South Carolina.

Kirkland was convinced that economic inequality lay at the core of America's racial problems. He was therefore not surprised at the escalation of racial turmoil that occurred after the enactment of the 1964 Civil Rights Act, the bill that prohibited most forms of legal discrimination. Kirkland never sketched out a specific road map for racial change and was scornful of those who advanced one or another nostrum aimed at the transformation of the racial landscape. Kirkland regarded all such propositions—whether separatist schemes advanced by black nationalists, minority capitalist strategies proposed by conservatives, or community control demands put forward by race chauvinists—as different variants of ideological snake oil. Kirkland instead believed in the traditional labor-liberal strategy of helping blacks to advance to the middle class through stimulus policies that would encourage job creation, public works projects that would provide employment to unskilled workers, reindustrialization programs to salvage the kind of "old economy" jobs that had been the traditional instruments of middle-class advancement for minorities, and affirmative action programs to compensate for the impact of discrimination. Thus while Kirkland recognized racial discrimination as a stain on American democracy, he saw no reason why blacks couldn't participate in the American dream through the passage of enlightened laws, their strict enforcement, and special measures to elevate blacks into the economic mainstream. Moreover, he was convinced that social class was more central to inequality than was race, and he favored government initiatives that crossed class lines over strategies narrowly tailored for a particular minority constituency.

Kirkland did not share the liberal's guilt over the legacy of slavery and segregation. He had known black people his entire life as friends, colleagues, and political allies. He never doubted that blacks were endowed with the same potential as everyone else. But at the same time, he never believed that blacks had superior wisdom or a higher sense of morality than other Americans. Nor did he sentimentalize race relations. Unlike many white southern liberals, Kirkland did not dwell obsessively on racial matters or return again and again to the theme of race as the country's original sin.

Kirkland almost always endorsed the goals of the NAACP and other mainstream civil rights organizations, including policies, like busing for school integration, that were unpopular with white union members. But he much preferred to address the problems of ordinary Americans and the poor without regard to gender or racial classifications.

Kirkland's closest ally in the civil rights community was Bayard Rustin. Like his mentor, A. Philip Randolph, Rustin had been a political radical, having flirted with Communism before gravitating to a movement of socialist pacifists led by A. J. Muste. Rustin developed a close association with Randolph during the 1940s; he served as a deputy during Randolph's successful campaign to persuade President Roosevelt to establish a Fair Employment Practices Commission during World War II that would open up jobs for blacks in the defense industry. Rustin subsequently served as an organizer for several integration projects initiated by Randolph during the late 1950s, while simultaneously serving as a tactician for Dr. Martin Luther King Jr. during his campaigns to end segregation in the South.

Rustin was an electric presence. Tall, with an athlete's build, finely chiseled features, and a shock of salt-and-pepper hair, he often became the central figure at demonstrations and rallies. When the mood struck, he could deliver a powerful oration to an impressive variety of audiences: black church people, building trades unionists, Jewish organizations. He was also a brilliant political movement strategist. A student of Gandhian methods of nonviolent civil disobedience, Rustin played an important role in the development of the protest tactics that the civil rights movement employed so effectively in the South. Rustin also counseled King against expanding the protest campaign to the North and strongly urged that King not move to align civil rights protest with the movement against the Vietnam War. Rustin's advice was sound on both counts, but King chose to proceed anyway, with disastrous consequences for the black cause.

In 1963, Randolph named Rustin as the organizer of the March on Washington. The appointment created some controversy within the civil rights movement and among the civil rights movement's enemies. Indeed, Strom Thurmond, the segregationist senator from South Carolina, denounced Rustin as a radical and a homosexual. Randolph, however, refused to heed the advice of those who argued that Rustin's prominent presence might hurt the march's credibility. Rustin remained as organizer, and in the aftermath of the march's success, his role within the civil rights and labor movements was never again seriously questioned.

Were it not for his homosexuality, Rustin might have risen to a more visible leadership position within the civil rights arena. Ironically, the labor movement, whose leading figures included men who spoke with open contempt of gays, treated Rustin with respect and sought his counsel on a range of civil rights matters. Labor also provided him with a base of operations for his work to solidify the tattered relations between unions and the mainstream civil rights community. That base was the A. Philip Randolph Institute, an organization established in the mid-1960s with Rustin as president and Norman Hill, a young veteran of civil rights and labor struggles, as his deputy.

Rustin believed that the strategy of advancing the interests of black workers by fighting trade union discrimination—an approach adopted by Randolph in a forerunner organization, the Negro-American Labor Council—would lead to endless confrontation and few tangible results. Instead, Rustin believed that the most effective course was the development of a black leadership within the various unions. Rustin also believed that blacks would continue their march into the economic mainstream only to the degree that labor was able to win political support for its legislative program; he therefore opposed strategies that might weaken the AFL-CIO's influence in Washington.

As AFL-CIO president, Kirkland was spared the controversies that had plagued Meany: clashes over building trades segregation, black radicalism on the shop floor, and protests by black nationalists and their white radical allies against "racist" and "fascist" hard-hats. There was, to be sure, the ongoing issue of the lack of diversity on the AFL-CIO executive council. Kirkland had demonstrated a willingness to break with tradition in order to increase the percentage of women and minorities on the council by reaching out below the level of international union president for new members. But it soon became evident that there was a limit to the transformation of the council from one dominated by white men to one that, to borrow a phrase from Bill Clinton, looked like America, or at least more closely resembled the membership of the AFL-CIO. Executive council membership was automatic for the presidents of the largest and most influential unions. It was also important to have representation from the various occupation categories: basic industry, construction, public employees, transportation, the railroad brotherhoods. Unions cherished council membership; small unions lobbied as earnestly as did larger ones for positions on the body. When blacks or women rose to the position of union president, it was usually in a small, politically weak union; to enhance diversity, then, Kirkland decided to reach down below the position of union president and name a lower-level official or staff member. Despite the pressure from some black union officials, Kirkland remained unwilling to take the more ambitious step of expanding the council from its traditional thirty-five members to some larger figure.

Kirkland made a priority of solidifying the relationship between the AFL-CIO and the mainstream civil rights community, especially the NAACP. Kirkland insisted on scheduling several black leaders as speakers at rallies and conventions—Bayard Rustin; Ben Hooks, director of the NAACP; Vernon Jordan, director of the National Urban League; and Coretta Scott King, the widow of Martin Luther King, all made frequent appearances, as did Jesse Jackson and members of the Congressional Black Caucus, such as William Clay and John Lewis. In turn, Kirkland frequently addressed the conventions and protests organized by civil rights groups. Both labor and the civil rights leadership believed that a strengthened alliance was essential in the face of a hostile political environment. On almost every front—from economic policy to appointments to regulatory agencies, to Supreme Court nominations, to the trimming of social spending programs—labor and blacks felt under a constant state of siege during the Reagan years. Under these conditions, the civil rights and labor leaderships decided that differences on subsidiary issues should be set aside for the sake of a revived liberal alliance.

Although Kirkland invited Jesse Jackson to address rallies and never criticized him in public, he did not have a high opinion of Jackson. Kirkland thought Jackson's entry into the 1984 presidential campaign was an exercise in ego gratification that had weakened Walter Mondale's presidential chances. He believed that Jackson's foreign policy positions—his embrace of Fidel Castro and the Sandinistas, his pro-PLO stance, his demands for huge and unilateral cutbacks in defense spending, and his blithe dismissal of concerns about Soviet objectives—represented the kind of radical posturing that had contributed to a loss of Democratic Party credibility on national security issues. And he also resented Jackson's lectures to the labor movement about its alleged deficiencies, as well as his attitude that he, Jackson, was more qualified to speak for working Americans than were the leaders of the labor movement.

While there was some lingering discontent over the low level of minority and female representation on the executive council, there were no complaints from these groups over the civil rights policies adopted by labor under Kirkland's leadership. Whether the issue was affirmative action, comparable worth, or the conflicts over Supreme Court nominations, Kirkland invariably supported the stance of the mainstream civil rights and feminist organizations. And here there was a subtle difference between the Kirkland and Meany approaches. While both were reliable civil rights liberals, Meany made clear his dislike for affirmative action plans that involved the use of quotas or preferential treatment. And on two of the most volatile social issues—gay rights and abortion—Meany flatly ruled out internal debate within the ranks of labor, much less the adoption of a formal position. Kirkland, by contrast, barely paid lip service to concerns over quotas in his public utterances about affirmative action, offered no objection to the federation's taking a position that effectively endorsed equal rights for gays, and moved the federation in the direction of support for the legalization of abortion.

There is no evidence that the federation's alignment with the civil rights agenda weakened its credibility with its white membership. On only one hot button social issue, abortion, did the trade union leadership receive intense grassroots lobbying, and there is reason to believe that the source for the avalanche of postcards that reached the federation leadership was the antiabortion lobby rather than rank-and-file union members. But union members did have strong opinions on a number of social issues, particularly affirmative action. Some union locals, especially in police, firefighter, and civil services unions, experienced bitter upheaval over affirmative action plans that gave preference to minority or women candidates. In his speeches and press conferences, Kirkland seldom took sides regarding individual cases of affirmative action at the workplace. He and the federation did, however, support the position of a firefighters' local in Memphis that opposed an affirmative action plan that called for whites with higher seniority rights to be laid off while blacks with less seniority retained their jobs during a period of municipal budget crisis. The firefighters' union prevailed when the case reached the Supreme Court.

Kirkland identified the roll back of affirmative action that took place during the 1980s as one element in a broad-gauged conservative strategy to emasculate the social achievements of previous Democratic administrations stretching back to FDR. In 1989, he characterized a series of Supreme Court decisions that had narrowed the scope of workplace affirmative action as "the legal lynching of black America's hope . . . to become partners in the American dream."[1]

In addition to his support for affirmative action, Kirkland placed the federation firmly behind another controversial measure designed, its advocates claimed, to level the economic playing field. In this case the advocates were women's organizations, and the issue was known as *comparable worth*. Comparable worth emerged as a serious issue in the 1980s. According to civil rights law, American workers regardless of race or sex were to be given equal pay for equal work, whether as receptionist, cab driver, or electrician. But according to some feminist theorists, the doctrine of equal pay for equal work was insufficient. They asserted that jobs traditionally held by women were devalued precisely because they were women's occupations. To rectify this state of affairs, they urged a new doctrine; instead of equal pay for equal work, the reigning principle should be equal pay for jobs of comparable worth.

Comparable worth or, as it is sometimes referred to, pay equity, sought to rearrange wage scales not simply for workers doing jobs that were relatively similar, say, a subway motorman and a long-haul trucker, but also jobs that were highly dissimilar—a truck driver and a registered nurse, for example. Pay equity called for sweeping job evaluations to determine whether certain positions were undervalued because they were predominantly filled by women and whether some jobs were overvalued because they were predominantly held by men.

Although adopted without serious public controversy when it first came before an AFL-CIO convention in 1979, a resolution endorsing the concept privately drew opposition from federation staff and a number of international union presidents. Kirkland, however, intervened to prevent a floor fight, and the resolution was passed. Labor support for pay equity was solidified as the recruitment of women into the ranks of unions became a priority and as polls indicated a high degree of enthusiasm for comparable worth among women workers. In practice, however, comparable worth's impact was largely restricted to public employees.

Although in private a supporter of the legalization of abortion, Kirkland remained studiously uncommitted in his public comments on this most controversial of hot-button issues. Kirkland regarded abortion as a peripheral concern that labor could justifiably evade given the divisions within its ranks, although his pragmatism may have been tempered by his civil libertarian's conviction that the state should not meddle in matters of private conscience.

But the issue would not go away. As the Supreme Court, exhibiting

the growing dominance of Reagan appointees, moved in a steadily conservative direction, feminist organizations escalated their demands that
politicians and politically influential organizations take a clear stand in
favor of abortion rights. Within the AFL-CIO, the Coalition of Labor
Union Women, as well as some male leaders, pressed Kirkland to move
away from the traditional stance of no position.

The issue came to a boil at the federation's 1989 convention. Pro-
abortion forces were unsettled by a recent Supreme Court decision that
gave states the right to restrict abortions in public hospitals and to compel abortion clinics to perform abortion procedures under hospital-like
conditions and by President Bush's veto of legislation that would have
permitted federal funding of some abortions. At the labor convention, six
separate resolutions were put forward that would have placed the federation in favor of abortion rights. Although the resolutions were withdrawn,
observers sensed that a majority of the labor delegates were in favor of the
federation adopting a pro-choice position. In the end, the resolutions'
sponsors agreed to put the issue aside after Kirkland agreed to establish a
special committee to study the matter and make recommendations for
further federation action.[2]

Kirkland planned to establish the committee, formally known as the
Ad Hoc Committee on Reproductive Issues, at the February 1990 executive council meeting. By the time the labor leadership assembled in Bal
Harbour, both the pro-choice and pro-life forces had launched what was
to become an unprecedented lobbying effort on a matter of internal AFL-
CIO policy. On one side, feminist organizations, along with activist trade
union women, were pressing for a shift from neutrality to one favoring
abortion rights. Patricia Ireland, the president of the National
Organization for Women, was candid in expressing the hope that a pro-
choice position might enable the labor federation to add its lobbying
muscle to upcoming campaigns to prevent the adoption of restrictive legislation at the state level. At the same time, women trade unionists were
attempting to counter the argument that labor should steer clear of the
issue because it did not affect the core workplace concerns of trade
unions. Thus Joyce Miller noted that trade unionism's ability to grow
depended on the recruitment of women, pointing out that the previous
year labor had suffered a net loss of male members while winning a net
gain of 200,000 women.

The modest campaign to persuade the federation to adopt a pro-
choice position paled in comparison to the pressure exercised by the
antiabortion movement. Even before the committee was appointed, the
National Right to Life Committee and elements within the Catholic
Church were threatening a campaign to urge members to withhold a

portion of their dues if a pro-abortion stance was embraced. The right-to-life organization first sent out an action alert to its membership urging those who were members of unions to try to stop Kirkland from even appointing the committee, on the grounds that once installed, the committee would be likely to recommend a pro-choice stance. And just as NOW had expressed the hope that labor would put its influence behind the campaign for abortion rights, so the antiabortion forces expressed the fear that the impact of a pro-choice resolution would be to "unleash the AFL-CIO's massive organizational resources in support of the pro-abortion cause." The right-to-life committee demonstrated its seriousness when it followed up the alert by asking union members to post in their workplaces a flier warning that "Radical pro-abortion feminists want your union and the entire AFL-CIO on record in support of abortion. Do you want your union dues used to oppose pro-life pro-labor candidates in 1990 and beyond?"[3]

Kirkland initially appointed fourteen members to the committee, nine of whom, including the chairman, William Wynn, were regarded as having pro-choice views. The committee also included the three women members of the executive council. Subsequently, four other executive council members were added at their own request. That Kirkland would not have minded a recommendation in favor of abortion rights is suggested by the committee's composition and the fact that a pro-life recommendation was not among the stated options for the committee. But Kirkland also made it clear that he wanted a position that could be supported by a consensus of the labor leadership; he did not want a rancorous internal conflict over abortion when labor was facing a hostile political environment.[4]

Sensing labor's vulnerability, the antiabortion movement raised the specter of a grassroots rebellion in the event of a pro-choice outcome. Cardinal John O'Connor, the archbishop of New York and a clergyman with a strong record of support for labor's objectives, issued a statement that said that union members should be allowed to direct part of their union dues to a pro-life organization should the federation embrace the pro-choice option. O'Connor's concerns were echoed by Msgr. George Higgins, a professor of theology at Catholic University and a lifelong labor partisan. Higgins warned that a pro-abortion stand would risk alienating a large segment of the union membership "just when labor is on the defensive and desperately needs to put a high premium on unity and solidarity."[5]

At a press conference in Bal Harbour, Kirkland said the committee would not be swayed by the massive letter-writing campaign undertaken by right-to-life advocacy groups. "I've been around awhile, and I think I can tell the difference between grass roots and Astroturf," he commented, suggesting that the letters were not coming from union members. The committee, he added, "will not be moved by threats of reprisals."[6] But at least one member of the committee, Morton Bahr, president of the Communications Workers of America, found the experience unsettling. After the *Washington Post* published the names of the committee members, Bahr received thousands of letters and postcards from antiabortion partisans, most of whom came from outside the union. Some letters included disturbing photos of aborted fetuses. Bahr also received numerous phone calls from abortion opponents, the overwhelming majority of which came from men. His membership on the committee made abortion an issue of controversy within the CWA and left Bahr regretting that he had agreed to serve on the panel.[7]

The committee met several times over the next five months, heard witnesses on both sides of the issue, and agonized over its recommendation. But in the end, the committee urged a continuation, with slight modification, of the traditional position of neutrality, and the executive council accepted the recommendation, with three dissenting votes from pro-choice members. Kirkland explained to the press that the council majority felt "that this was an issue of deep, personal conviction, conscience, and religion, and that one's individual moral views are not likely to be influenced by any stand the trade union movement at large would take." The pro-choice forces within labor could take some solace, however, for the resolution included language that suggested that in choosing neutrality, labor was opting for a neutrality in favor of abortion rights. In a key passage, the resolution declared that labor "has staunchly and fervently defended the rights of all persons to privacy, to personal belief, and to self-determination in matters of religion, thought, conscience, and family. We resent and resist government intrusion into matters that are essentially private."[8]

Abortion and affirmative action were at the core of the controversy over President Reagan's selection of Robert Bork, a federal district court judge in Washington, to the Supreme Court. The Bork nomination presented Kirkland with something of a dilemma. Although his judicial record was clearly conservative, Bork had not issued decisions that could be characterized as consistently antilabor, and his capabilities as a jurist were beyond dispute. Kirkland's initial response was thus to postpone a decision on a labor endorsement, pending a review of Bork's record by the federation's lawyers. The previous year, the federation had gone on record in opposition to the appointment of Justice William Rehnquist as chief justice and ultimately decided to add labor's name to the long list of liberal cause organizations that had made the defeat of Bork a litmus-test issue. Bork's chances to win a position of labor neutrality were not helped by his failure to visit federation headquarters and, as a courtesy, discuss his judicial perspective. In the end, however, the executive council decided to oppose the nomination because of Bork's judicial record.[9]

In contrast to the complexities of the Bork nomination, the selection for the Supreme Court of Clarence Thomas was for Kirkland a clear-cut case of an unqualified ideologue who did not merit Senate confirmation. Shortly after President Bush announced Thomas's appointment in July 1991, the executive council, then meeting in Chicago, issued a sharp statement that opposed Thomas and condemned what it called Bush's "apparent resolve to make the court the preserve of the right wing." Kirkland also blasted Thomas for believing that "unfettered markets and private property are sacrosanct" and expressed doubt that Thomas could "rise above his ideological biases and render the impartial justice expected of the nation's court."[10]

Throughout the long, ugly debate over Thomas's fitness for the high court and the allegations of his sexual harassment of Anita Hill, who had worked for Thomas when he was director of the Equal Employment Opportunity Commission, Kirkland restricted his remarks to two issues: Thomas's opposition to affirmative action and his tendency to integrate his conservative economic views into his judicial decision-making. Kirkland was also withering in his criticism of the strategy adopted by the nominee's handlers of refusing to discuss issues of judicial philosophy during the confirmation hearings. In testimony before the Senate Judiciary Committee, Kirkland denounced the "transparent effort to create an image of moderation and open-mindedness" adopted by Thomas while refusing to take clear positions on issues of substance. Kirkland charged that Bush had selected Thomas because of his willingness to serve as a "gladiator in the ideological arena." "The pamphleteer's ability to reduce complex issues to caricature and to belittle those who have a different social vision made him a hero of the right and a candidate for Justice [Thurgood] Marshall's seat."

To drive home the seriousness of labor's opposition to the confirmation, Kirkland criticized a Thomas opinion that actually sided with a New York building trades union in a job discrimination case. Kirkland reminded the committee that labor was in large measure responsible for the inclusion of job discrimination in the 1964 Civil Rights Act. He then went on to attack the proposition that in deciding cases of employment bias, courts should restrict their decisions to the impact on the individual victim, instead of issuing judgments affecting entire classes or broad groups of workers.

Asked by Senator Arlen Specter, a Pennsylvania Republican, whether he thought it was important to have a black justice on the court, Kirkland responded:

> I think it is rather outrageous that over so many years there has been no representative of the black community on the Supreme Court, and then only one. And then that he should be replaced by a person whose views are so diametrically opposed, I believe, to the measures that have been designed in this country to address the problems of the afflicted and the underprivileged, and who has chosen to ally himself with the forces of privilege and of power in this country, and I believe that consideration overrides the question of ethnic representation.

Whether because of racial sensitivities or because the Republicans were better prepared for a protracted struggle after the Bork experience, Thomas won confirmation, though by the slimmest of margins. But while they had failed to deny confirmation to a second conservative nominee, the members of the broad coalition of liberal interest groups had established themselves as a permanent lobbying presence on federal judicial appointments.

Kirkland never wavered in his conviction that government had the responsibility to level the playing field for those who had been the victims of discrimination. The man who had argued with President Kennedy over the inclusion of a job discrimination provision in the 1964 Civil Rights Act was still prodding presidents to stand firm in the 1990s, when affirmative action and racial preferences were the main subject of debate. In one of his last acts as president of the AFL-CIO, Kirkland issued a statement that praised President Clinton for a speech in which he reaffirmed support for affirmative action, then under withering attack from various quarters:

> Our society has not yet achieved the ideal of being color-blind and gender neutral. The hard fact is that a long history of discrimination cannot be made to disappear in a few short years. And the equally hard reality is that for the foreseeable future, affirmative action programs are necessary and essential to correcting the failures of the past and improving the prospects for the future.

12

TWO CHEERS FOR CLINTON

IT WAS ELECTION DAY 1992, AND BY MIDAFTERNOON KIRKLAND HAD already received some of the best news of his career. His chief political aides had seen the results of the early exit polls, and it was clear that Bill Clinton would be the next president of the United States. Kirkland was delighted; he took pride in labor's role in Clinton's triumph, as the early indications pointed to a heavy Clinton vote by trade union families. (The final exit poll findings showed Clinton with a two-to-one margin over the incumbent Republican, George H. W. Bush.)

Kirkland was already looking forward to leading labor in a close alliance with Clinton. He had had some initial ambivalence about the Democratic nominee but had grown increasingly enthusiastic about Clinton's candidacy as the campaign progressed. He was impressed by Clinton's toughness under fire and was heartened by the liberal domestic agenda Clinton had spelled out during the campaign. Champagne bottles were popped open, and the staff at the federation headquarters had its first real victory party since 1976, when Jimmy Carter was declared the winner in the post-midnight hours. The era of the Reagan Democrat had finally been put to rest, Kirkland told associates.[1]

For labor, the path to victory in 1992 had begun in 1984, when Kirkland mobilized the united union effort behind Fritz Mondale. The AFL-CIO emerged from the Mondale campaign with its reputation reinforced as one of America's preeminent political machines. By securing the nomination for Mondale and by turning back the challenge mounted by Gary Hart, labor had signaled that despite a membership slippage, it had lost none of its ability to influence the course of political events. Labor had money, manpower, leadership, and convictions; a candidate who enjoyed the united support of the trade union movement in the Democratic primaries would immediately qualify as a front-runner. But the party feared the power of the special-interest label. Republicans continued to pound away at the Democrats as a party that sought not to represent the broad interests of the great American middle class but that preferred to appease the insatiable appetites of a long and ever-expanding list of self-pleaders. Labor was, in fact, the one part of the Democratic coalition whose program cut across racial, cultural, and gender lines. But Democrats were more willing to distance themselves from labor's agenda than to oppose the laundry list of demands advanced by Jesse Jackson or the National Organization for Women. In the wake of the Mondale defeat, a group of centrist Democrats formed a new organization, the Democratic Leadership Council, as a response to the growing influence of the interest groups. Among other things, the DLC believed that the party's losing streak was due to the part labor had played in shaping a domestic agenda that continued to favor generous spending for social needs; it also saw labor as an unrepentant opponent of economic deregulation.

Kirkland was no fan of the DLC, which he saw as another sign that the Democrats were evolving from a party of working people to one that catered to the interests of suburbia. He would have mobilized the AFL-CIO behind a Democratic presidential candidate in the 1988 primaries if there had been one around whom a consensus could be forged. With Reagan leaving office and George Bush regarded as beatable, many Democrats were lining up for the contest, including a number of whom labor thought highly. But there were no Kennedys, Humphreys, or Mondales to rally the trade union leadership; the one candidate who might have drawn widespread union support, Senator Joseph Biden, withdrew before the campaign officially got underway, after it was revealed that he had plagiarized speech excerpts from British Labour Party leader Neil Kinnock.

The AFL-CIO had little trouble supporting the eventual nominee, Governor Michael Dukakis of Massachusetts. Dukakis was reasonably well-liked by trade unions in Massachusetts and had carved an image that placed him somewhere between the old labor-liberal Democrats and the New Politics wing of the party that appealed to the suburban constituencies that had flocked to Gary Hart four years earlier. But while Dukakis's poll ratings were impressive during the summer, by autumn he had fallen well behind: he had failed to demonstrate a grasp of national security issues and, on the domestic front, he had chosen to stress his competence as a public official instead of setting forth a vision for America's future that differed substantially from the Reagan agenda. Bush, who stressed a "kinder, gentler" version of Reaganism, won easily.

Labor found Bush's policies preferable to Reagan's only at the margins. Kirkland was pleased with the appointment of Elizabeth Dole as secretary of labor and considered the new administration's appointees to the National Labor Relations Board (NLRB) less objectionable than those named by Reagan. But Bush's economic course differed little from that of his predecessor. And Bush operated under the further constraint of a huge federal deficit, rendering any significant spending initiatives an impossibility. Bush, like most Republicans, had a high degree of respect for Kirkland, stemming from Kirkland's contribution to America's Cold War objectives. Nevertheless, when Kirkland made inquiries about the possibility of reinstating the air controllers, Bush, who could easily have decided that eight years of punishment was enough, turned down the request.

Although Bush did agree to a compromise measure that increased the minimum wage, he rejected practically all other labor-backed bills. And as his term neared its end, Bush took several steps that Kirkland regarded as gratuitous slaps at labor—steps whose only rationale was as a gesture of pacification to the Republican Party's right wing.

Kirkland took special offense at Bush's efforts to hinder labor from using dues money for political purposes. Under federal law, workers in a union shop who chose not to join the union could still be compelled to pay dues for the services provided by the union. In 1988, the Supreme Court, in *Communications Workers of America v. Beck*, ruled that workers could not be required to pay that portion of the dues that was used for lobbying and political campaigns.

The Bush administration had done little to enforce the *Beck* ruling—that is, until April 1992, when Bush came under fire from the leader of his party's isolationist-populist wing, Pat Buchanan. At that point, the president issued an executive order directing federal contractors to post notices advising employees of their right to object to the use of their dues money for political purposes. The impact of *Beck* was not significant, since there were few workers in the category of nonmembers who were employed in union shops and fewer still who would take the trouble to demand a partial dues refund. But labor was concerned that *Beck* would inspire the right to seek further restrictions on union political activism. Labor often complained about the scrutiny devoted to its political spending: Why, union leaders asked, wasn't the same intense attention directed to the contributions given to Republican candidates by major corporations? But labor was vulnerable; an estimated 30 to 40 percent of union members regularly voted against Democratic candidates, while the unions gave over 90 percent of their campaign contributions to Democrats.[2]

Bush certainly was not inclined to support a bill popularly known as striker replacement legislation. The measure was introduced in 1991 at labor's behest, in an effort to curb the growing practice of hiring permanent new workers to replace employees who had gone out on strike. Under the National Labor Relations Act, the permanent replacement of strikers was legal. But until the PATCO sackings, corporations—or, for that matter, government agencies—had seldom invoked this right; a company might hire scab labor to keep a plant in operation during a strike, but after the strike was settled, the strikers were welcomed back to their old jobs. The rules changed after Reagan dismissed the air traffic controllers; subsequently, a number of blue-chip corporations resorted to the hiring of permanent replacements to defeat unions during strikes.

While *Beck* was a marginal issue, striker replacement went directly to the heart of labor's organizational troubles. The willingness of corporations, including some with histories of friendly relations with unions, to in effect fire any worker engaged in a strike was exerting a chilling effect on organizing and collective bargaining. Even though only a relatively small number of companies had taken the extreme step of striker replacement, the very threat that other businesses might follow suit discouraged workers from making use of the strike. The impact of the corporate world's post-PATCO tactics can be seen by Bureau of Labor Statistics figures, which indicated that among companies with over 1,000 workers, the average annual number of strikes during the 1980s was 80 (only 45 in 1990). By contrast, in the previous three decades, the low was 181 in 1963; the high, 437, came in 1953.[3]

Like the earlier labor law reform, striker replacement had wide enough support to secure majorities in both the House and the Senate. But like previous labor law measures, it was destined for failure, given the certainty of a presidential veto or a Republican filibuster. On this go-round, it was the Bush administration that killed off labor reform.

In the wake of America's triumph over Iraq in Operation Desert Storm, Bush looked invincible, with poll ratings reaching positive levels never attained by Reagan. But as the economy continued to decline, so did Bush's poll numbers. Then, in November 1991, a relatively unknown Democrat, Harris Wofford, defeated Dick Thornburgh, the former U.S. attorney general, in a special senatorial election in Pennsylvania. Kirkland had been alert to signs of rising voter discontent over the declining state of the economy and had gotten labor solidly behind the Wofford effort. The victory in Pennsylvania convinced Kirkland to begin making plans for a massive labor election drive on behalf of the Democratic presidential nominee.

To carry the fight against Bush, labor preferred New York's then governor, Mario Cuomo. But Cuomo declined to run, leaving the field open to a number of new faces: Paul Tsongas, former Massachusetts governor; Tom Harkin, senator from Iowa; Bob Kerrey, senator from Nebraska; Paul Simon, senator from Illinois; Bill Clinton, governor of Arkansas; and one old face, Jerry Brown, former governor of California. There being no obvious front-runner, Kirkland invited the entire group of Democratic contenders to the federation's biannual convention in Detroit in late 1991. Kirkland had no strong preferences at this point. But he did make clear the kind of Democrat he hoped would carry the party's banner: "I, for one, would like to see a meat-and-potatoes Democrat, a campaign in which the traditional Democratic message is finally tested." Harkin was one candidate who met Kirkland's definition of a "meat and potatoes" fundamentalist, a labor-liberal of the old school who, before trade union audiences, would roar that when he became president "every double-breasted, scab-hiring, union-hurting employer in the United States will know that the working people of America have a friend in the White House."[4] But Harkin carried the aura of a loser. Lane thus kept his counsel; more than anything, he wanted a candidate whose views were broadly compatible with labor's, who could unite the party's discordant factions, and who could prevail at the polls. Harkin did not measure up, and the executive council decided to remain neutral during the primaries.

While Kirkland preferred a nominee in the Humphrey-Johnson mold, he also wanted a candidate who could achieve victory by expanding his base to draw the support of moderate Democrats and independents. The remainder of the Democratic field consisted of clear losers—Simon and Brown—and candidates who embraced, in varying degrees, the New Democrat label: unfettered by ties to special interests, prudent in taxing and spending matters, willing to attack Big Government. Of these, the most intriguing was Clinton. Unlike Tsongas, who had made a fetish of his break with mainstream liberal ideals, Clinton had strong ties to just about every wing of the Democratic Party and had succeeded in maintaining his liberal credentials while winning election after election in Arkansas.

Kirkland was increasingly attracted to Clinton. To be sure, there were differences to be surmounted. A meeting between Clinton and Kirkland had been arranged by Seymour Martin Lipset, the respected sociologist who was affiliated with the Progressive Policy Institute, the research arm of the Democratic Leadership Council. The very fact that Clinton was involved with the DLC was enough to make Kirkland wary, and the meeting had its rough spots. While Clinton and Kirkland agreed on a broad list of domestic issues, they disagreed on trade. Kirkland pressed Clinton on the North America Free Trade Agreement (NAFTA), which was then being pushed in Congress by the Bush administration. According to Jim Baker, who had recently succeeded Ken Young as Kirkland's executive assistant, Clinton argued that with the emergence of the European Union as a single economic entity and with Japan forging cooperative relationships with other Asian economic powers, a North American economic union was essential to America's ability to maintain its competitive edge.

But while Clinton was straightforward in his endorsement of the NAFTA concept, he was vague when the discussion turned to labor's demand that strict regulations to protect worker rights be written into the treaty.[5]

Kirkland, however, became more enthusiastic about Clinton as the campaign progressed. The core of Clinton's domestic agenda lay within the labor-liberal tradition of using the government to facilitate the mobility of the lower classes and protect the gains of the working class. Kirkland was also impressed by Clinton's resilience under fire. He had seen other politicians wilt when attacked by their adversaries and the press. Clinton, by contrast, had toughed it out when accused of sexual affairs with Gennifer Flowers and other women, private issues that, Lane believed, should never have been injected into the campaign. Clinton had the aura of a winner, and labor responded by mobilizing its forces for an all-out effort on behalf of the Democratic ticket. Even the Teamsters, now under the leadership of a new reform-minded president, Ron Carey, broke with recent tradition and supported the Democrat.[6]

The more Kirkland learned about Clinton, the greater his enthusiasm for the campaign. Although Clinton eschewed the liberal label, his platform, anchored on proposals for universal medical insurance and social investment, focused on the kind of broad-based liberal objectives that Kirkland had been advocating for years. Clinton was not a labor-liberal in the tradition of Fritz Mondale, but he displayed a toughness of character during the campaign that, Lane believed, suggested a firmness of leadership as president.

Throughout his long career, Kirkland had occasionally been mentioned as an ideal candidate for a foreign policy position—secretary of state or CIA director, for example—by his admirers in the press. Early on in his administration, Clinton approached Kirkland and offered him the ambassadorship to Poland. Kirkland politely turned the offer down with hardly a second thought.[7] Kirkland regarded himself first and last as a trade unionist; he had no special hankering to serve in the diplomatic corps. In fact, Lane believed that he could achieve more good for the new democracies of Eastern Europe by remaining right where he was and continuing to use the influence of organized labor to pressure the American government toward policies of generous assistance. Furthermore, having spent practically his entire stint as AFL-CIO president under Republican administrations, Kirkland looked forward to a period of accomplishment for the members of America's trade unions and for working people generally. He especially relished the prospect of the upcoming campaign to enact a system of national health insurance—item number one on Clinton's domestic agenda, and an issue that the AFL-CIO had been advocating for decades. Kirkland anticipated the adoption of some form of health-care reform, a popular issue with Americans and an issue that, more than any other, had propelled Clinton to the presidency. Kirkland thus looked forward to presiding over a massive mobilization of trade union forces behind health-care reform, in much the same way that Meany had mobilized labor's troops for the successful campaign for Medicare.

Unfortunately, the administration chose as its first legislative priority not medical insurance but, instead, the passage of NAFTA.

This would be the second time NAFTA had come before Congress. During the waning days of the Bush administration, both houses had voted to give the president what is known as fast-track authority—that is, the authority to negotiate the details of the agreement with the two other countries involved, Mexico and Canada. Under fast-track, the agreement that was hammered out could be voted up or down by Congress but was not subject to congressional amendment. If labor was dissatisfied with the treaty, its only recourse was to press for NAFTA's defeat.

As an economic document, NAFTA was similar to the economic provisions of the agreement that created the European Union, in that it lowered most tariff and other trade barriers among the three signatory countries. Unlike the EU accords—and this is a point that Kirkland emphasized and reemphasized throughout the debate—NAFTA contained no social dimension of any consequence. Where the EU covenant called for the member countries to maintain similar levels of worker rights and environmental standards, NAFTA left these concerns to the discretion of the member states. Where Spain and Portugal had to meet certain social and political criteria before being allowed to join the rest of Europe, Mexico was being asked to make no such commitments.

Kirkland was a realist. He privately expressed doubts that NAFTA could be defeated, considering the widespread support it enjoyed among political and economic elites. And he was fully aware that American corporations would continue to shift manufacturing jobs to Mexico, whether or not the treaty passed. If labor and its allies were somehow to defeat NAFTA, Kirkland hoped that the United States would reorient its trade strategy to countries that shared America's standard of living and a commitment to worker rights and other social guarantees. And if, as he fully anticipated, NAFTA was adopted, he sought at a minimum to establish the principle that every new trade agreement negotiated by Washington should include worker rights clauses with strong enforcement mechanisms. Kirkland would have much preferred that Clinton either abandon NAFTA or renegotiate the agreement to incorporate worker rights provisions in the main treaty text. If the administration had followed this course, Mexico would almost certainly have withdrawn from NAFTA, which would have been fine with Kirkland, who believed it was utter folly for countries with such widely differing levels of economic and political development to be creating free trade zones.

During the presidential campaign, Clinton and his economic advisers had made repeated pledges to negotiate tough worker rights and environmental protection side agreements once in office. That position was reinforced shortly after the election by Mickey Kantor, soon to be appointed as the administration's chief trade official. According to Kirkland, Kantor told him and Tom Donahue that "he would not accept a side agreement that did not have enforcement provisions just as strong and effective as the enforcement provisions . . . governing intellectual property rights."[8] But astute observers remained unimpressed by these promises. Mexico's economic strong suit was its low-wage workforce; the average pay of Mexico's manufacturing workers was well below the minimum wage in the United States. It made no sense for Mexico to agree to an accord that included the worker rights provisions that the AFL-CIO was urging. It might just as well continue to lure American-owned installations without a treaty.

Even as he was gearing up for a battle over trade, Kirkland was determined that differences over NAFTA would not seriously damage the relationship between labor and the new administration. He admired the boldness of Clinton's domestic program, was impressed by the president's command of both the policies and the politics of an issue, and hoped to forge a partnership with the administration toward the fulfillment of medical insurance and other social reforms. Shortly after the election, Kirkland was invited to dine with Clinton at the home of the president-elect's friend and adviser Vernon Jordan. Jordan and Warren Christopher, a key member of the transition team, paid several visits to Kirkland to discuss a range of issues, including NAFTA, health care, and the conflict in Bosnia.[9] Kirkland was also invited to Little Rock to meet with the president-elect for a discussion of policies and appointments.

Kirkland's public utterances about the new president ranged from positive to outright glowing. In an April 6 speech to the International Union of Operating Engineers, Kirkland spoke of a "new day in Washington," described Clinton as a president "who is living up to his promises to bring change to this country," and asserted that Clinton "has set the stage for sweeping change from the old order."

The early months of the Clinton presidency were notable for a series of blunders and missteps, ranging from the controversy over the role of gays in the military, to rancor over Clinton's appointments policies, to questions about the "co-presidency" role of First Lady Hillary Clinton. These problems were compounded by a decision by congressional Republicans to adopt a stance of hard-edged opposition and to deny

Clinton the honeymoon grace period usually accorded a new administration in its early months. By April, administration officials were adding NAFTA to the lengthening list of trouble zones. Budget director Leon Panetta was reporting that NAFTA was doomed in the House unless Clinton took steps to revive it, with almost all of the freshman Democratic contingent leaning toward a "no" vote. Given an early warning, the White House began putting together a congressional pro-NAFTA coalition that included leading Republicans, as well as Democrats. At the same time, the business community announced the formation of a blue-chip group called USA/NAFTA to put some lobbying muscle behind the pro-treaty forces. Meanwhile, the government of Carlos Salinas, the Mexican president, swung into action; it made threatening noises about pulling out of the treaty if the United States insisted on the kind of labor rights provisions being demanded by the AFL-CIO, deeming such measures a threat to the country's sovereignty.

Despite its tough rhetoric, labor remained willing to adopt a position of neutrality if the administration could reach a reasonable compromise on the side agreements. Mark Anderson, a trade specialist for the AFL-CIO who played a central role in the NAFTA fight, was in regular contact with the administration's trade negotiating team:

> After twelve years in the wilderness and with a government that was more friendly to labor's goals, we wanted to work with the administration to see if an agreement on the side agreements could be reached that met our goals. That's why we adopted the slogan, "Not This NAFTA," meaning that we were open to an agreement that was consistent with our interests. We were genuinely open to working with the administration for a NAFTA that was better, from labor's perspective.[10]

For months, Clinton's trade representatives maintained that they were remaining resolute in talks over the side agreements. Then, in August, they informed Anderson that labor's goals would not be met. "The Clinton people told us, 'We tried our hardest, but the Mexicans just wouldn't go along.' But we believed that it was the American business community that was the main obstacle." Instead of side agreements with enforcement mechanisms, the treaty called for each country to set up commissions to monitor compliance with environmental and labor standards. But the accord established no new supranational standards or enforcement instruments. Instead, the new commissions were asked to monitor each country's compliance with its own established environmental and labor standards and did not mandate new standards that would have affected Mexico.[11]

Kirkland called the side agreements a "bad joke . . . a Rube Goldberg structure of committees leading nowhere." Kirkland declined to blame Clinton for the treaty's shortcomings, calling the accord "a poison pill left over from the previous administration." But he vowed an all-out fight against the treaty, calling it "a way to bring peonage to America."[12] Kirkland also escalated his attacks on Mexico's political system, telling Daniel Schorr in the course of a radio interview that Mexico "brings to this agreement one basic thing—cheap and plentiful labor kept in place by a one-party system."[13]

While Kirkland and other labor leaders remained highly supportive of Clinton, they were less forbearing toward his secretary of labor, Robert Reich. Labor officials stewed over Reich's musing that "the jury is still out on whether the traditional union is necessary for the new workplace." Reich raised hackles a bit further when he accused unions of engaging in Luddite-like "policies of preservation grounded in fear." Nor were unions impressed by his advocacy of retraining as the answer to unemployment caused by trade or technological obsolescence. Union officials were familiar with the failure of past job-retraining schemes.[14]

Kirkland approached the NAFTA fight with resolve. He wrote a series of op-ed articles, gave numerous news conferences, and went out on the hustings to deliver stump speeches to labor audiences. At a forum in Minneapolis, where he shared the platform with Paul Wellstone, the Senate's most liberal member, Kirkland pounded away at the constellation of organizations and institutions that was providing NAFTA with its intellectual credibility. On think-tank intellectuals, he declared, "There are plenty of academic call girls who will to do anything for a modest honorarium and a round-trip first-class ticket." On pro-NAFTA editorialists, "The free press belongs to those who own it." On the support for NAFTA voiced by four past presidents (Carter, Reagan, Bush, and Ford), "It symbolizes reality. It's the elite versus the people." Kirkland then took up the claim that workplace cooperation would render unions irrelevant. His voice nearly a whisper, he declared, "Adversarial is supposed to be outmoded. . . . We get lectured about how we don't understand the new global economy—that we must adapt our ways, our thinking." Then, a little louder, "Our members aren't in the think tanks or in the halls of academe. But we didn't just fall out of the back of the watermelon truck, either." Then, thundering and pounding the lectern, "This is about jobs, jobs, jobs, going south, south, south. It's about workers being paid a buck an hour, or less. People living in cardboard shacks. It's about streams polluted by those high-minded American industrialists who talk about trust and cooperation."[15]

Kirkland also offered for consideration his own version of NAFTA, a

North Atlantic Free Trade Agreement that would link the United States and Canada with the established capitalist democracies of Western Europe and would exclude Mexico. Kirkland recognized that at this late juncture, the proposal was not likely to be given serious consideration as a substitute for NAFTA. His purpose was to place on the table issues that were being brushed aside by the champions of NAFTA-style agreements. The United States and Canada, he said, would benefit from an accord with Europe through links to countries with "high wages, strong consumer purchasing power, and high standards of living." American workers would profit from the incorporation of clauses that would compel the signatory countries to meet European standards for vocational training, comparable worth, and an expansive interpretation of the right of union organization. The proposed agreement would also reinforce transatlantic ties and political stability. As Kirkland argued, "The New NAFTA would anchor the U.S. in Europe in the post–Cold War era, acting as a compelling antidote for isolationist voices that have been a persistent and dangerous undercurrent in American political life." To a devoted Atlanticist like Kirkland, a North Atlantic economic alliance was the logical follow-on to NATO, the Helsinki Accords, and the other treaties and agreements that forged ever-closer ties between Europe and the United States. That his concept had not been embraced, he felt, was due to "financial elites" bent on the exploitation of Mexican workers.[16]

In girding for battle over NAFTA, labor found itself facing determined adversaries on many fronts. Indeed, it was labor's ill fortune that the administration, whose first months had been marked by political ineptitude, responded to the NAFTA challenge with an exhibition of deal-making and political infighting that would have made the modern Democratic Party's two great wheeler-dealers, FDR and LBJ, marvel. As for the business lobby, this imposing juggernaut had been largely ineffective until it was prodded into action by Clinton's people rather late in the game. The Mexican government was another factor, spending lavishly to ensure the enactment of the right kind of agreement, one in which labor and environmental standards remained under the sole control of each signatory country's laws. Finally, labor found itself again arrayed against the power of American elite opinion, which, from the moderate left to the free market right, treated NAFTA as a touchstone issue; to break ranks meant to risk being labeled an enemy of progress, an isolationist, a racist, a Luddite, or a flat earther.

Labor did have an asset in its own near-unanimous support for the war against NAFTA. The degree of unity was impressive, especially given the fact that for many unions, trade had little direct effect on their membership. Indeed, only a minority of unions, notably those representing the shrinking percentage of workers in manufacturing jobs, had an obvious stake in the NAFTA outcome. A few other unions were tangentially affected by the shifting winds of trade policy; many other unions, including some of the largest in the service and public employee sectors, represented workers whose jobs were seemingly unaffected by trade. In similar past situations, administrations had been successful in breaking labor solidarity by winning over or neutralizing unions that did not have a direct interest in the issue at hand. But labor solidarity held firm throughout the NAFTA struggle, in part because Kirkland and Tom Donahue were able to convince the trade union leadership that adoption of the treaty would further weaken the ability of all unions to organize workers and represent them in collective bargaining. Labor was convinced that as long as corporations could quash union-organizing efforts by threatening to pull up stakes and move facilities to Mexico, all organizing efforts, even those in which the export of jobs was not possible, were in jeopardy. Kirkland and Donahue also drove home the point that industrial jobs lost through trade had a reverberating impact throughout a community that affected property taxes, government services, schools, retail sales—indeed, just about every aspect of economic life.

The lobbying offensive put forward by the AFL-CIO ranked as one of the most impressive legislative campaigns in labor's history. Tom Donahue, who had been in charge of past trade projects, formed a special NAFTA task force and mobilized what amounted to the lobbying version of total war. In addition to the usual Capitol Hill arm-twisting, labor dispatched organizers to mobilize opposition at the state and local levels and assigned its writers and researchers to churn out position papers and commercials. Mark Anderson presided over a war room that spewed out material to be fed to local labor officials in the districts of 143 members of Congress who were regarded as undecided. If the congressman said something that signaled a possible shift in position, this information was relayed immediately to his district, along with the AFL-CIO's most updated position.[17]

In the House, labor could count on the support of key members of the Democratic leadership, like Dick Gephardt and David Bonior, along with its traditional allies from blue-collar districts. The American people also seemed to be leaning against the treaty. In opinion polls, Americans expressed concern about the export of jobs and wariness of closer economic ties with Mexico; an August Gallup Poll showed Americans coming down against NAFTA by over two-to-one when the issue was framed as pitting job losses against increased exports.[18]

On October 7, Clinton traveled to San Francisco to address the AFL-CIO convention. Clinton could boast of having taken several measures favored by labor. He had announced his intention to sign a revision of Hatch Act rules to end restrictions on the political involvement of public workers, had revoked both the Bush administration's directive on *Beck* and a Bush decree that seemed to favor nonunion contractors, and had indicated his intention to end the prohibition on the rehiring of the PATCO members. He had also appointed William Gould IV, a pro-union academic from Stanford, as chairman of the NLRB. And, of course, he was planning to introduce a comprehensive medical health insurance plan in 1994. Although some delegates wore "No NAFTA" buttons, the convention gave the president an enthusiastic welcome.[19]

During his presidential campaign, Clinton had shown consummate skill in distancing himself from core Democratic constituent groups without rupturing relations with the party base. Now, in the heat of the NAFTA struggle, Clinton directed some calculated fire at organized labor. Appearing on *Meet the Press* on November 6, Clinton singled out labor for criticism, making reference to the "roughshod, muscle-bound" tactics of unions that were threatening to withdraw political support from pro-NAFTA Democrats. Clinton went on to exhort business leaders to speak out and, in effect, twist congressional arms on behalf of the agreement. Clinton spoke eleven days before the House vote, just as a CNN poll was released that showed Americans opposing the treaty by 48 to 36 percent.[20]

Clinton's strategy depended less on attacking labor than on persuading wavering members of Congress, a process that involved incorporating in the agreement provisions to exclude certain items, especially agricultural products, from its reach. In an effort to expand the base of Republican support, Clinton forged an alliance with the House minority leader, Newt Gingrich—an interesting move, given Gingrich's reputation as a hard-edged anti-Clinton ideologue. Then, a few days before the scheduled vote, Clinton made the astonishing announcement that he would defend Republican congressmen in the next election who came under criticism for voting for NAFTA. This brought forth an angry Kirkland accusation that "the president has clearly abdicated his role as leader of the Democratic Party." "I'm afraid the bitterness will linger and will be difficult to overcome," he said on the eve of the vote.[21] When asked about the broad support for NAFTA from former presidents, Kirkland declared:

> There is not a drop of blood of presidents or IMF economists in the streets of Gdansk, because they weren't there when the issue of worker rights was brought out. . . . That's what rests on this vote: some indication of whether or not that's still a value. Or whether governments are reared among men in the service of flagless corporations who have no

country and who have demonstrated that they'll abandon communities and leave them hollowed out and vacant of jobs.[22]

In the end, the Clinton strategy paid dividends. NAFTA passed by the surprisingly large margin of 234 to 200. The Democrats opposed the agreement, but the margin, 156 to 102, was not enough to overcome a huge Republican majority for the pact. Kirkland was stoic in defeat. He said he was proud of labor's effort. "Working people . . . were the only ones whose interests were not taken into account," he said. "Amid all the planes, trains, and bridges—and all the protections for citrus, peanuts, sugar, and wheat—there was not one word about the rights of workers on both sides of the border to obtain decent wages or safe working conditions or to defend themselves from gross exploitation." Some union leaders muttered about retribution against Democrats who were expected to oppose NAFTA but who, at the last minute and under intense White House pressure, had supported it. "We'll make sure we get even at the polls," remarked Bill Bywater, president of the International Union of Electrical Workers. Kirkland himself showed his frustration as his voice broke during a press conference when he spoke of the workers whose jobs would be lost due to NAFTA.[23] At the same time, union leaders spoke of the campaign against the treaty as one of labor's finest moments and predicted that the grassroots lobbying effort would serve as a model for future campaigns against trade accords not to labor's liking. John J. Sweeney declared that "out of this momentous struggle, the political power of organized workers has been resoundingly reaffirmed."

Kirkland quickly put NAFTA aside and moved on to the issues around which labor and the administration could make common cause. Clinton invited him to the White House for meetings about health care, and Kirkland announced that labor would spend "whatever it takes" to secure passage of a reform plan. He made plans to place labor's weight behind the Clinton health insurance plan in much the same way that, in earlier times, the unions had supported Medicare, civil rights legislation, and jobs programs. To demonstrate to the political world that, the Clinton-labor partnership had been revived, Kirkland was seated to Hillary Clinton's immediate left for the State of the Union address; on her right was Jack Smith, chief executive officer of General Motors.[24]

A further step toward healing the differences was made at the February 1994 executive council meeting in Bal Harbour. The Democratic leadership was on hand in full force: Vice President Gore; George Mitchell, Senate majority leader; House Speaker Tom Foley; and Gephardt. Gore engaged in a "candid" discussion about NAFTA, but Kirkland preferred to accentuate the federation's commitment to health care.[25]

The rest of 1994 proved difficult for Clinton and labor, as the newly emboldened congressional Republicans worked tenaciously, and with considerable effectiveness, to bury the administration's domestic program. In July, striker replacement failed once again, this time falling seven votes short of the number needed to survive a Republican filibuster.

Then, on November 6, came the most devastating development of all: a massive, across-the-board Republican midterm election landslide. Under the leadership of Newt Gingrich, Clinton's NAFTA ally, the GOP replaced the Democrats as the majority in both the House and the Senate and won a majority of governorships as well. The GOP had not held sway in the House for forty years, and its margin, 230 to 204, shocked even Republican optimists. The casualties included Speaker Foley and a number of labor's close allies; in their place would be a class of Republicans that had a goodly share of young, hard-edged conservatives from right-to-work states. Once the new Congress was installed, Gingrich would become the Speaker. He was already touting a conservative legislative agenda, enshrined in the so-called Contract with America, that included a series of legislative proposals, every one of which was abhorrent to labor.

For labor, the election results were a source of gloom. Clinton, whose election had elicited such high hopes, and his administration had failed on the issues about which unions cared most passionately; its most signal success, ironically, was on the one issue, NAFTA, to which unions were most determinedly opposed. Labor, of course, was not directly responsible for the electoral calamity. Indeed, the principal culprit was the Clinton administration, which had chosen to fight a divisive issue, NAFTA, before it launched its effort to win the enactment of what should have been a unifying and popular issue, health-care reform. But there is no question that in the aftermath of NAFTA, labor found it difficult to summon up intensity and zeal for the election, especially for Democrats who had opted to support the trade treaty.

The decision to go to war over NAFTA had always been a calculated gamble. There are certain issues around which America's political and business elites, conservative and liberal alike, can be expected to rally. The list of such issues is not long, but free trade certainly ranks near the top. Although it would be wrong to claim that opposing NAFTA was an exercise in futility—after all, most Americans opposed the treaty at the time of the House vote—the pro-NAFTA forces gained an unstoppable momentum once the administration and the business community put their combined weight behind the accords. As Tom Donahue now says, "I still don't know why our case didn't prevail. But I would agree that NAFTA and other similar trade bills are inevitable. It would have passed even if we could have proved that all the negative consequences we predicted would come to pass actually did come to pass. The free traders would simply respond that we don't understand the hidden benefits."[26]

In fact, the NAFTA campaign waged by the AFL-CIO did have an enduring impact. Some future trade agreements did include worker rights provisions, and pressure has continued to mount for the incorporation of labor standards in the various regional and bilateral trade accords proposed by the United States in the wake of NAFTA. At the same time, Kirkland's skepticism about NAFTA's ability to fulfill its advocates' expectations was seemingly vindicated by the accord's unimpressive record over its first ten years. NAFTA was sold to American voters as an agreement that would enhance the living standards of Mexican workers and stem the flow of illegal immigrants across the Rio Grande. It accomplished neither. In fact, Mexican workers found it increasingly difficult to find stable manufacturing employment, in light of the growing trend of multinational corporations to move jobs from Mexico to China. At the same time, NAFTA contributed to the impoverishment of rural Mexico, which in turn spurred an even greater migration of undocumented workers to the United States. In 2004, on the tenth anniversary of the agreement, the critics of the treaty included, incredibly enough, Senator Hillary Rodham Clinton and Mickey Kantor, President Clinton's special trade representative.

On August 8, Kirkland was presented with the Presidential Medal of Freedom, the highest honor bestowed on civilians in the United States. Lane took quiet pride in being selected as a Medal of Freedom winner. He had a strong sense of patriotism and a genuine appreciation for America's achievements at home and abroad during his lifetime. Because of his leadership, organized labor had made a major contribution to the expansion of freedom in postwar America.

Kirkland was among an eminent group of Americans who received the Medal of Freedom from President Clinton. There was Dorothy Height, the long-time president of the National Council of Negro Women, and Barbara Jordan, America's first black congresswoman and one of the country's most impressive public officials. Another labor figure, Cesar Chavez, the founder of the United Farm Workers of America, was honored posthumously.

President Clinton was at his eloquent best in his presentation to Kirkland. Kirkland, he said, "is a hero of the modern labor movement— a man who has spent his life forging solidarity among the men and women whose sweat and toil have built our world." Clinton added:

Ever resolute in his quest to enhance opportunities for working people, he has tirelessly worked to strengthen democracy and to further the cause of human rights. During the Cold War, his vital assistance to the Solidarity movement in Poland spurred the forces of freedom towards victory in Eastern Europe, just as his guidance here at home helped to renew and fortify the American economy. As a people, we are indebted to Lane Kirkland for his talented leadership efforts as an advocate for unity and social justice.

This was a fitting tribute as Kirkland neared the end of his long and distinguished service to American labor. Lane had already begun discussing the prospect of retirement with Irena. He had yet to set the date. The most likely occasion, however, was the next federation convention, scheduled for October 1995. Yet as he was pondering his future plans, Lane was unaware that 1995 would prove the most difficult and painful year of his long life in labor.

13

THE COUP

JIM BAKER WAS AT HOME, READING THE *WASHINGTON POST*, WHEN LANE Kirkland called. Although it was a Saturday morning, Baker was not surprised to hear from his boss, given the startling item on the newspaper's front page: an article that reported, in the words of its headline, that "Key Union Leaders Want Kirkland to Leave."

According to the article, which appeared on January 28, 1995, a number of presidents of large and influential unions believed that it was time for Kirkland to retire. How many union leaders shared this alleged desire for new leadership was unclear. The author, labor reporter Frank Swoboda, named no names; the quotes were in every case anonymous. Some of the complaints aired by the reporter's sources were rehashes of issues that had been raised in the past, such as the charge that Kirkland devoted too much of his time and energy to international affairs. Gerald McEntee, president of the American Federation of State, County, and Municipal Employees, had frequently struck a "Come home, Lane," theme at labor gatherings, and there was immediate suspicion that he was the one responsible for the material in the *Post* piece. Clearly, however, much of the labor leadership's discontent was motivated by the Republican landslide in the November elections and the emergence of triumphalist, hard-right, antiunion Republican leadership in the House under Speaker Newt Gingrich.

Kirkland was incensed by the airing of differences in the press; he was angry that those who had spoken to Swoboda had never expressed their differences to him personally or in executive council meetings, and he was infuriated that his accusers hid behind the anonymity of the confidential source. "Lane didn't have the same kind of ego as elected officials," said Baker. "He expected that people would take him on when they disagreed with him. But he was really bothered by the anonymity. And he was upset that the criticisms that were aired in the press had never been brought before the executive council or other federation bodies."[1]

This was not the first time that discontent with the AFL-CIO leadership had been expressed, anonymously, in the press. From the time of George Meany's presidency onward, there was a tradition of retirement rumors or mutterings of disgruntlement, sometimes placed by aspirants to the top position or by their supporters. But there was something more ominous in the tone of the *Post* article. One of Swoboda's sources declared that if Kirkland sought reelection at the federation's convention the next October, he would face open opposition.

Kirkland, in fact, had already told Irena and a few close friends that he intended to retire in the near future. He had not as yet made this decision widely known. Nor had he set a date—although his friends assumed that he would make the decision public before the convention. But it was one thing to choose the time and venue for a farewell speech to the movement he had served and loved for nearly a half-century and another to be pushed out by a group of malcontents. Kirkland felt a sense of betrayal. He had treated his labor colleagues with respect and collegiality; he had been responsive in times of crisis; he had joined picket lines to demonstrate solidarity; and he had used his influence within Washington elite circles to help unions in times of duress or to secure important legislation. He had also taken the lead in developing a strategy to deal with the impact of the global economy on American jobs. Kirkland had always adhered to a code of behavior that dictated that differences be settled face-to-face, not in the press or through intrigue. He believed that the ethical standards that held sway within the labor movement were superior to those of business or the political world. Kirkland felt that his antagonists, by secretly organizing a coup against him, had embraced the morals of partisan politics, with its deal-making and shifting allegiances. When presidents of international unions challenged his opinions during meetings of the executive council or in private sessions, he always treated the critics with respect and never sought to punish or isolate those who clashed with him. He expected that his colleagues would extend him the same type of consideration.

Who was involved in the movement against Kirkland? Aside from McEntee, speculation centered on Rich Trumka. Jim Baker recalls hearing several months prior to the *Post* article that Trumka was "up to something," although the precise nature of the "something" was unclear. David St. John, Kirkland's speechwriter, had also heard rumors of growing dissent. But the rumors remained rumors—inchoate, unspecific, with no hint that a movement against Kirkland was being quietly organized.

It was around this time that John J. Sweeney, president of the Service Employees International Union, emerged as an important representative of the group that had mobilized to oppose Kirkland. According to Baker, Sweeney paid Kirkland a visit a few days before the *Post* article appeared.

Kirkland had heard a few rumors of discontent among executive council members and wanted to ascertain whether there was anything serious afoot. A member of the executive council since 1980, Sweeney had supported Kirkland on every major struggle—the air traffic controllers, the Mondale campaign, NAFTA. His own union had undergone impressive membership growth over the previous fifteen years, shooting up from 650,000 to over 1.1 million, an expansion that was divided between mergers with smaller unions and the acquisition of new members, mostly in the service and health-care fields. Kirkland told Baker afterward that Sweeney had indicated that some executive council members favored a change in leadership. Kirkland added that when he pressed Sweeney on his own position, Sweeney had replied, "I'm with you, Lane." Lane told associates that Sweeney had added that he did not intend to seek the presidency, that he wanted Lane to run.

A second Sweeney-Kirkland meeting took place the week after the Swoboda article had been published. Sweeney's purpose in seeking the meeting was to inform Kirkland that the gist of the *Post* article was accurate, that a number of union leaders favored a change in leadership. According to Sweeney, he told Kirkland that a group of important international union presidents felt it was "time for a change." Sweeney mentioned the Clinton administration's offer of the ambassadorship to Poland; Kirkland responded that he had turned it down and was not interested in the diplomatic life. The conversation, obviously strained, went on for a while. Eventually, Sweeney acknowledged that he was among those who believed that a leadership change was in everybody's best interest.[2]

Meanwhile, several of Kirkland's strongest allies began to speak up in his defense. Swoboda's article had listed Jack Joyce as among those mentioned as potential successors as federation president. Joyce thereupon circulated a letter that expressed total support for Kirkland and denied any interest in the presidency. Among other things, the letter declared that "one of our most important assets is that the two top leaders are also the most powerful intellects in the movement." Joyce made a point of praising Kirkland's international activities; Kirkland, he said, was fighting for the interests of American workers when he engaged in the struggle against NAFTA and other trade measures that cost American jobs. Joyce's sentiments were echoed by another major union president, John J. Barry of the International Brotherhood of Electrical Workers. Barry said the sniping at Kirkland "can only provide aid and comfort to those in the political and business circles who would like nothing better than to see the whole work force unorganized." Barry said that Kirkland's "formidable intellect and commitment to the causes of working people" stood out "in an era of cheapened politics and glib arguments."[3]

The federation's annual executive council retreat in Bal Harbour was coming up in late February; Kirkland decided that the council session would provide a suitable opportunity for all involved to air their grievances, man-to-man and without the media present. At the council session on February 21, Kirkland said that he had been reading "a lot of crap" in the press, in which anonymous sources had critical things to say about his performance and the direction of the AFL-CIO. He therefore proposed that the council meet in executive session, which only the thirty-five trade union leaders would attend, with staff excluded.

The executive session lasted a full five hours. Participants recall the atmosphere as "tense," "electric." Kirkland went into the meeting already irritated by a quote in another Frank Swoboda article, in which an unnamed executive council member said he "didn't even think [Kirkland] knew my name."[4] Kirkland took pride in knowing the biography of every international union president and the condition of his union—its strengths, weaknesses, whether it was involved in merger discussions, the organizing campaigns it was involved in, its effectiveness in lobbying and political campaigning. He began the meeting by going around the room to remind his critics that he was familiar with the details of their careers and the state of their unions and from there went on to recall his role in the strikes, lobbying campaigns, organizing drives, and other projects where his personal involvement had made a difference. He reminded George Kourpias, president of the Machinists, of how he had worked to win a measure of justice for his members when the union was battling Frank Lorenzo at Eastern Airlines. He inquired whether George Becker recalled his assistance in resolving the Ravenswood strike. He reminded Rich Trumka, whose name was popping up in press accounts as a potential candidate for the presidency, of the many actions he had taken to win a settlement for the Pittston miners.

Kirkland was tough, articulate, combative. John Barry emerged from the meeting to tell Kirkland's staff members that he had "scored a knockout."[5] But even as Kirkland was engaged in a defense of his stewardship, he was made aware that his critics were not likely to back down. Kirkland still commanded great authority with the elected leaders of organized labor and enjoyed the support of a majority on the executive council. But the executive session revealed that a substantial minority of the council, concentrated among leaders of large and powerful unions, were adamant in their desire for Kirkland to retire. Most of the critics tried to soften the blow by emphasizing their respect for Kirkland and their appreciation for his achievements. Trumka reportedly told Kirkland, "I love you like a brother." Another compared Kirkland to a coach of a losing football team; no matter how brilliant the coach might be, he sometimes had to quit after a losing season. Others, such as McEntee, dispensed with the niceties and launched a direct attack, charging Kirkland with devoting too much time to Eastern Europe, showing insufficient interest in organizing the unorganized, and failing to be more aggressive in mounting a public relations initiative on behalf of labor's positions and ideas.[6]

The executive session left Kirkland disturbed. "I sensed disbelief on Lane's part that this could be happening," said Lenore Miller, a Kirkland supporter. "He felt it was unjust and outside the trade union tradition." Tom Donahue had a similar reaction: "I think Lane was set back by what happened in that meeting. The Saturday after the session, Lane called me to his hotel room. We had a drink; he said that maybe we should both retire and let these bastards find a new leadership. That was his mood then."[7]

For perhaps the only time in his career, Kirkland was unsure of his course of action. A few months earlier, when there had been rumblings of frustration after the midterm elections, Jim Baker had urged Kirkland to announce that he intended to seek reelection and begin mobilizing support within the ranks of labor. Had Kirkland made his intentions clear at an early date, Baker believes that he might have squelched the opposition before it gathered momentum. At this point, Lane had decided to retire at the October convention. But he did not want to make a premature announcement out of concern that it might trigger a period of instability within the federation, with factions mobilizing to support opposing candidates for leadership positions. Likewise, a firm public retirement decision would have enabled the federation leadership to come together around the choice of a successor, who almost certainly would have been Tom Donahue. Now, however, Kirkland, though leaning toward retirement, was undecided. "Lane wasn't sure what he wanted to do," Baker said. "I urged him to announce anyway. But he didn't want to say he planned to do something when in fact he didn't know if he really wanted to do it."[8]

At the time of the executive council, the leaders of ten unions had joined the opposition to Kirkland. All except Trumka represented unions with substantial membership: besides McEntee, Trumka, Becker, Kourpias, and Sweeney, the oppositionists were Owen Bieber, UAW; Arthur Coia, Laborers; Sigurd Lucassen, Carpenters; Frank Hanley, Operating Engineers; and Ron Carey, Teamsters. The ten unions represented some 6 million of the federation's 13.5 million members. Although not a majority, the opposition faction was sufficiently strong to warrant confidence that it could force Kirkland to give way or could defeat him if matters came to a head at the convention. Conditions could change, of course, if members of the faction wavered or switched sides. To avoid such an outcome, the members of the original coup faction swore what one member called a blood oath to remain united throughout the struggle ahead. An added irony was the involvement in the opposition of the leadership of the unions that Kirkland had brought into the federation as part of his unity campaign: UAW, Teamsters, Mine Workers. The role of the UAW and the Teamsters was crucial; without their votes, the opposition might never have gotten off the ground.

Shortly after returning to Washington from Bal Harbour, Kirkland asked George Kourpias to come to his office. Of all the members of what had blossomed into an organized opposition, Kourpias enjoyed Kirkland's greatest respect. Kourpias had joined the opposition in large measure because he believed that a trade union leader should retire at a certain age; his union, the Machinists, had a 65-and-out rule, and he believed that a similar policy made good sense for the federation as well. In the course of their meeting, Kirkland asked whether Kourpias would be interested in seeking the federation presidency. Kourpias declined and suggested Tom Donahue instead. Kirkland replied that Donahue either—accounts here vary—was not interested in the position or was ambivalent. (Donahue, in fact, was refusing to say anything that could be interpreted as indicating an interest in succeeding Kirkland.) Kourpias then mentioned John Sweeney as a possibility. Kirkland responded with a flat "no." Although he did not elaborate in his discussion with Kourpias, Kirkland no longer trusted Sweeney, whom he believed had misled him during their earlier conversations.[9] Kirkland subsequently had talks with Douglas Dority, president of the United Food and Commercial Workers Union, about the federation presidency. Dority, who had only recently assumed his union's top position, declined interest.

Ironically, even as the opposition began to organize itself as a formal faction, signs of a labor recovery began to emerge. On the political front, President Clinton began to deliver on promises he had made to Kirkland. He announced his intention to veto a series of measures opposed by labor that were working their way through the Republican-controlled Congress, effectively killing their chances of adoption. He also signed an executive order prohibiting employers who used permanent striker replacements from bidding on federal contracts. And he announced the lifting of the prohibition on the hiring of the air traffic controllers fired by Reagan fourteen years earlier. There was also a bit of good news from the Bureau of Labor Statistics. For the second consecutive year, organized labor had gained membership, to the tune of 150,000 in 1994.[10] Finally, there were signs of renewed interest in Kirkland's idea for a free trade area of the North Atlantic. Jean Chretien, the prime minister of Canada, had endorsed the concept, as had Alain Juppe, the French foreign minister, and Jacques Santer, president of the European Union.[11]

In the midst of his difficulties, Kirkland got welcome relief at an event where he was honored in the name of the president he most revered: Franklin D. Roosevelt. At a ceremony in Warm Springs, Georgia, to mark the fiftieth anniversary of FDR's death, Kirkland was one of several notable liberals honored by the Roosevelt Institute's Four Freedoms awards; the others were the civil rights leader Andrew Young; Elliott Richardson, the former attorney general; the columnist Mary McGrory; and former President Jimmy Carter. But it was Kirkland, who received the Freedom From Want award, who brought the assembled Roosevelt admirers to their feet when he declared, "When they ask me whether I'm a 'liberal' or 'conservative' or 'misanthrope,' I can only respond that I'm a New Dealer, pure, simple, and unreconstructed."[12] He continued:

> The more fiercely the current debate rages about the appropriate role of the federal government, the more clearly I remember a lot of things about our country before there was such a role.
>
> There were county poorhouses out on the edge of town. That's where the people went when they were too old or too sick to work. Then Social Security came and tore those poorhouses down.
>
> The rivers of my state ran brick red from the erosion of farms, and the topsoil of the Great Plains literally blew away—turning thousands upon thousands of farm families into homeless nomads.
>
> Then came the tree-planting of the CCC and the farm programs of the New Deal. Today those rivers are black and clear. Free enterprise such as the paper, forest products, and agribusiness industries shared abundantly in those government initiatives.
>
> I am proud to acknowledge that I am a child of Franklin Roosevelt's New Deal. But then, every person alive today, regardless of age or previous condition, is an heir of that great period in our nation's life.

The turmoil within the federation placed Tom Donahue in a difficult and even painful position. He had served with Kirkland for sixteen years as secretary-treasurer. He admired Kirkland, supported his policies, shared his philosophy of the federation's role, and thought of himself as part of a leadership team. He was also John Sweeney's long-standing friend. In a sense, Donahue was responsible for Sweeney's position within the labor leadership, as it was he who had gotten Sweeney his first job on the Service Employees' staff.

Now the press began quoting members of the opposition caucus to the effect that Donahue would make an ideal successor to Lane Kirkland. Donahue made it clear in public and in private that he would never collaborate with those seeking to push Kirkland out. Just to drive the point across, he had praised Kirkland during the executive session in Bal Harbour and had emphasized that he had been a part of all the policies during Kirkland's tenure, stood by those policies, and credited Kirkland with a record of achievement during his presidency.

At the same time, Donahue had aspirations to the federation presidency should Kirkland retire. He had several conversations with Kirkland about the future during the time when Kirkland was oscillating between retirement and making the race for another term. The discussions were somewhat uncomfortable; Kirkland sometimes urged Donahue to join him in retirement. Donahue, for his part, said that each man should make up his own mind about his future in the labor leadership. He also told Kirkland that he was not likely to run for another term as secretary-treasurer but would be interested in seeking the presidency should Kirkland retire.[13]

In early May Kirkland announced his intention to stand for reelection. In this, he was influenced by speeches made by McEntee and Trumka at a conference sponsored by the AFL-CIO's Industrial Union Department, in which the theme was struck that a new labor leadership was emerging and that the current leadership should "follow or get out of the way." The speeches infuriated Kirkland. He told Donahue, "You know, I was only thinking about when I would retire, at which council meeting I would make the announcement. But I'm not going to be pushed out like this."[14]

Despite his troubles, Kirkland retained his rapier wit. At an executive council meeting in the spring, he proposed that the federation become more aggressive in embracing the new information technology, especially the Internet. This proposition aroused the attention of Gerald McEntee. McEntee urged the movement to move cautiously in making use of the Internet and said something to the effect that dissident members of AFSCME were "saying the most outrageous things about me."

"And how does it feel, Gerry?" Kirkland shot back, without missing a beat.[15]

Somewhat later, shortly before Lane's retirement, Rex Hardesty found his boss in a glum mood. "What does it matter?" Lane told Hardesty. "These are not our people and this is not our trade union movement." Even at this point, Kirkland's biting sense of humor did not desert him. In a variation on the devastating put-down of Dan Quayle by Lloyd Bentsen in their 1988 vice presidential debate, Kirkland joked, "I knew Jerry Wurf; Jerry Wurf was a friend of mine. McEntee, you're no Jerry Wurf!" Wurf was McEntee's predecessor as president of AFSCME and the man credited with transforming a weak union into one of the largest and most influential trade union organizations.

On May 9 Donahue announced publicly his decision not to seek reelection to his post as secretary-treasurer. Some interpreted this as signaling his desire not to serve another term with Kirkland. This was not true; Donahue was simply not prepared to serve two more years under conditions that would be dominated by bickering, complaint, and intrigue. In his letter of retirement, Donahue said, "I have been injected into a debate in which I have made it clear that I will not participate. I have been part of [Lane Kirkland's] administration for sixteen years and have been privy to, and supportive of, every policy followed in those years."

Kirkland had the support of a number of important union leaders, including Dority, Joyce, Barry, Al Shanker, Morton Bahr, Bob Georgine, and Lenore Miller. But on May 17, seven smaller unions joined the opposition faction. Gerald McEntee, who was serving as the opposition's spokesman, claimed that his group now had sufficient votes to defeat Kirkland at the October convention, for while Kirkland commanded the support of more unions than did the opposition, the selection of the federation president was determined by a system that allocated each union a number of votes that coincided with the number of dues-paying members, as reflected in the per capita tax paid by each affiliate to the federation. At the same time, the opposition group announced that it was holding a series of meetings to piece together a ticket to oppose the leadership slate. An abrasive and polarizing figure, McEntee declared that he did not intend to seek the presidency. Much of the speculation thus focused on John Sweeney. By this time there was no ambiguity about where Sweeney stood in the leadership struggle. Along with McEntee and Trumka, Sweeney was emerging as Kirkland's sharpest critic. He signed a memo to the unions affiliated with the AFL-CIO that urged them to join the opposition and asserted that "the decline of the labor movement must be stopped by any means possible." And in a widely quoted statement that particularly angered Kirkland, Sweeney declared that unions "are irrelevant to the vast majority of unorganized workers" and were in danger of being regarded as similarly irrelevant by unionized workers as well.[16]

In fact, Kirkland's critics seldom leveled specific charges of leadership failure against the administration, at least not for attribution. There were, to be sure, anonymous complaints that were echoed in the press. Most were unwarranted or simply wrong. Kirkland's involvement in international affairs had not detracted from his other responsibilities, as his leadership in the NAFTA struggle and the health-care debate demonstrated. To blame Kirkland for the NAFTA setback was to miss the point entirely. Organized labor had never succeeded in defeating a piece of trade legislation sought by the country's economic elites; the real story was how close labor had come to defeating the combined forces of the business community, the Republican Party, the Clinton administration, and the editorial pages. Likewise with striker replacement. In the postwar period, labor had never prevailed when pitted against corporate America on crucial labor-management issues like labor law reform. Labor had failed to prevent the enactment of Taft-Hartley and Landrum-Griffin at a time when unions represented over one-third of the workforce. Likewise, it had been unable to repeal section 14(b) or enact labor law reform, even with Democratic majorities in both houses of Congress and a Democratic president in the White House.

There were, of course, issues on which legitimate differences existed between Kirkland and the opposition. One key question was the federation's role in organizing campaigns. The opposition was demanding that 30 percent of the federation budget be allocated to organizing drives. Kirkland was willing to spend more resources to strengthen labor's organizing capability. He was convinced, however, that the success or failure of organizing depended on the international unions, not on the federation. The federation did have a proper role in organizing; it could train organizers and coordinate drives in which a number of different unions were engaged in campaigns to organize an entire industry or many employers in a region. Kirkland had demonstrated his commitment to organizing by establishing the Organizing Institute. But the federation's resources were not unlimited, and Kirkland believed that they were put to more effective use if devoted to lobbying and electing candidates who would support labor's agenda in Washington. Lane also believed that the policies his administration had introduced were beginning to pay off, as was suggested by the rise in labor membership during the preceding year.

Then there was the question of media relations. McEntee asserted that the president of the AFL-CIO should be on television interview programs at least once a month, presenting labor's case directly to the American people. Despite his mixed feelings about the press, Kirkland had given frequent interviews to reporters from the leading newspapers and magazines. And while he had a reputation for involved, complex sentences, Kirkland gave the press its share of sound bites, ranging from "Where's the beef?" to "I know the difference between Astroturf and grass roots." But he had no intention of appearing on the new generation of television interview programs, such as CNN's *Crossfire*, which featured rapid-fire questioning and placed a premium on loudness and the ability to elbow other speakers aside to get your point across. Kirkland described such programs as "gong shows" and said it would be demeaning for the president of American labor to participate in such spectacles. "Public relations at large is not a panacea," he told a reporter. "I'd like someone to point out the time when the trade union movement was accepted by the . . . news media."[17]

On June 9, Kirkland followed his initial instinct and made the irrevocable decision to retire. Retirement had been his preference from the beginning of the struggle with the opposition. He had remained in the race because of pride, a fierce competitiveness, and the conviction that the opposition was wrong in its assessment of his policies and mistaken in its prescribed course for labor's future. But Kirkland was a realist in political affairs. He had met with three of his closest friends in the movement—Al Shanker, Bob Georgine, and Morton Bahr. They told him they would support him to the bitter end, but they reported that the momentum was moving in the opposition's direction.[18] Kirkland was also influenced by his experiences in a series of regional AFL-CIO meetings during the spring. At each session, members from the opposition unions—led by McEntee and staff members from AFSCME—had harassed and hectored Kirkland and had made it nearly impossible for him to present an effective defense of his policies. Finally, after a particularly rough regional session in Boston, Kirkland informed Tom Donahue, while they were waiting at Logan Airport to board their flight home, that he planned to step aside.[19]

The decision was made public on June 12. Kirkland said the decision "stems from my own personal preferences as well as my duty to do my best to see that the future course of the AFL-CIO will be in the hands of one who places the solidarity and best interests of labor as a whole above other considerations." He added, "Service in the cause of free men and democratic trade unionism is a privilege, and I am secure in the conviction that I have been faithful to it. A life spent in that service is a happy one and I regret nothing." The retirement was to take effect at an executive council meeting scheduled for August 1.

The announcement of Kirkland's retirement brought Donahue back into the race for president. In his retirement statement, Kirkland gave Donahue his endorsement, praising him for his support for a policy of "constructive change" and calling him the best man to preserve the "integrity of the federation."

But conditions had changed in the months since members of the opposition had indicated support for Donahue as Kirkland's successor. Although Sweeney had yet to formally announce his candidacy, the opposition had reached a firm decision to put forward its own slate. The opposition was no longer inclined to coalesce around Donahue; according to Sweeney, he and others in the opposition faction did not believe that Donahue would push through the sweeping changes that they believed were essential to labor's revival.[20] Some Kirkland supporters are convinced that from the very outset, the opposition faction intended to nominate Sweeney or another Kirkland critic and to institute a thoroughgoing overhaul of the federation, not simply promote incremental changes.

In a last-ditch effort to forestall a full-scale leadership brawl, Donahue and Sweeney had a long dinner meeting that ended inconclusively. As the two prepared to leave, Donahue said that, given their years of friendship and collaboration, it would be a tragedy for the two to oppose each other for the presidency. Sweeney, Donahue recalled, agreed, leaving Donahue with the impression that he might not make the race. Sweeney suggested that Donahue take the matter up with McEntee. The next morning, then, McEntee paid a visit to Donahue's office, accompanied by two other members of the faction, George Kourpias and Frank Hanley. Donahue began by saying that he was interested in the presidency and hoped to reach an accommodation that would spare labor an internal brawl. McEntee then proceeded to wave his finger in Donahue's face and shout, "You gotta get out of this race." Voices got louder and louder, and obscenities flew back and forth, to the point where the secretaries in Donahue's outer office feared that things might end in violence.

To defeat Sweeney, Donahue needed to detach several of the larger unions from the opposition coalition. He got some help when Sigurd Lucassen was replaced as president of the Carpenters by Douglas McCarron, a move that shifted the union from the Sweeney to the Donahue camp. But Donahue got something of a jolt when he sought to persuade Frank Hanley to bring the Operating Engineers behind him. Donahue had known Hanley for many years, and his brother had worked with Hanley in the building trades back in New York. But Hanley couldn't be moved. "You don't understand, Tom," Donahue recalls him as saying. "These guys have big plans; big plans! They're going to do a whole lotta things; it's not just Lane."[21]

On August 1, Lane made his final appearance as president of the AFL-CIO. For the last time, he addressed the executive council, which was meeting in Chicago. "My life in the trade union movement has been an entirely happy one," he told his fellow labor leaders. "There has not been a day when I have not felt singularly fortunate to be engaged in a central way in the most important undertaking of which human beings are capable. I have given it my best shot and I have no regrets whatsoever."

Lane did not offer a point-by-point defense of his leadership. He did stress that the federation's political action was "far, far superior in design, staffing, and direction" to the efforts of previous eras. And he went out of his way to praise the federation staff, a target of criticism by the insurgents.

At the same meeting both Donahue and Sweeney were nominated as president of the AFL-CIO to serve until the October convention, at which the convention delegates would choose between them. While Donahue won the executive council vote by a margin of 22 to 11—and got the votes of the women and the minorities on the council—Sweeney maintained control of the largest unions. By this time, both men had announced their running mates. Donahue selected Barbara Easterling, an official of the Communications Workers of America and the daughter of a coal miner, to run as a candidate for secretary-treasurer. In order to get a woman on his slate, Sweeney proposed the creation of a new office, that of executive vice president, and selected Linda Chavez-Thompson, a Hispanic woman from Texas and a vice president of AFSCME, to run along with Rich Trumka, his nominee for secretary-treasurer.

The rest of the campaign was anticlimactic. Sweeney and Donahue were alike in many respects: two New York Irishmen of roughly the same age (Sweeney was sixty-two; Donahue, sixty-six) who had begun their careers in the same union and had been in agreement on most issues of importance to the movement through the years. The two engaged in several debates during the campaign, as well as an unprecedented debate at the convention. But the major difference seemed to be Sweeney's willingness to trump Donahue's proposal on whatever issue was under discussion. Donahue agreed that the executive council could be expanded to enhance racial and gender diversity; Sweeney proposed a whopping increase in its membership, from thirty-five members to fifty-four. Both agreed that more resources should be devoted to organizing, but Sweeney proposed a massive infusion of funds, while Donahue proposed a less expensive program. During the convention debate, Sweeney promised a militant administration that would "block bridges" if that was what was required to gain justice for workers, a reference to the Service Employees' having literally blocked bridges in Washington, D.C., during a campaign to organize janitors in that city. Donahue, by contrast, derided Sweeney's words as counterproductive to labor's long-term goals; he asserted that labor needed to "build bridges" to the political and business communities. Neither the debate nor last-minute behind-the-scenes maneuvering resulted in changes in commitments to the two candidates. In the end, the opposition caucus held firm; the Sweeney slate led by a margin of 7.3 million delegates to 5.7 million, when Donahue conceded and allowed Sweeney to be elected by acclamation.

Once in office, Sweeney moved swiftly to institute sweeping changes in just about every aspect of the federation's structure and work. Almost immediately, Sweeney began an overhaul of the staff at federation headquarters. In department after department, Lane's people were replaced. Although few were fired outright, they were made to understand that there was no place for them in the new administration. Many left after receiving buyout settlements, at a cost to the federation that was to contribute to financial problems in future years. Where Kirkland and Donahue had tended to draw staff from within the labor movement,

Sweeney often filled vacancies by going outside labor's ranks and hiring veterans of social cause movements. Sweeney also made a top-to-bottom change in the federation's public relations operation, toward the goals of more aggressively pushing labor's case to the press and a "repositioning" of the federation's image as a militant and radical institution. As part of this effort, Sweeney and his associates sought to reignite an alliance with left-wing academics. Sweeney addressed campus audiences and implemented a new project, dubbed "union summer," in which thousands of student volunteers were dispatched to assist in union-organizing drives around the country. Sweeney also joined Democratic Socialists of America, an organization founded by the socialist author Michael Harrington.

In the realm of politics, the new administration moved to forge a more organic relationship with the Democratic Party, essentially abandoning the tradition of Gompersian nonpartisanship that had guided labor under Meany and Kirkland. Where Kirkland had refused to address official party functions, Sweeney addressed the Democratic National Convention in 2000. Sweeney also moved the federation into a central role in the antiglobalization movement, which emerged in the late-1990s as the major focus of activity for the forces of the political left. This represented another departure from the Kirkland tradition. For while Kirkland had been a biting critic of the global economy's impact on American workers— Kirkland, in fact, had been attacking the workings of the international economy before the term *globalism* became part of the political lexicon— he eschewed alliances with the kinds of hard-left and, in some cases, violent forces that engaged in demonstrations against the World Trade Organization (WTO) and other international finance institutions.

The initial response to Sweeney and his New Voice leadership was largely positive. Journalists, especially those of a leftish orientation, wrote of a new energy and a sense of mission in labor's ranks. The emphasis on organizing workers on the lower rungs of the economy—one of the first campaigns launched under Sweeney was a drive to unionize immigrant strawberry pickers in California—appealed to those who believed that organized labor should reinvent itself as an engine of social activism, instead of regarding itself as an institution of the American mainstream. The new leadership was also greeted with enthusiasm on the university campus. Students flocked to sign up for summer jobs as organizers, while their professors spoke expectantly of their hopes that the "new" labor movement would play the leading role in the revival of the political left.

Soon enough, however, bumps appeared along the road. The first serious setback was a scandal over illegal fund-raising methods in Ron Carey's campaign for reelection as president of the Teamsters. Pitted against Carey was James P. Hoffa, the son of Jimmy Hoffa. The election was expected to be close; to boost Carey's chances, a scheme to siphon money into his campaign was devised that involved several international unions, the Democratic National Committee, a left-wing organization called Citizen Action, and, some charged, the AFL-CIO. The initial election, won by Carey, was annulled after details about the fund-raising scheme became public. Carey was subsequently expelled from the union, and Hoffa emerged victorious in a second election. Among the casualties was Rich Trumka, whose name surfaced during a federal investigation and who invoked his Fifth Amendment right against self-incrimination during congressional hearings. While no charges were brought against him, his credibility as a spokesman for labor was damaged. Labor itself suffered, insofar as the scandal reinforced the impression that, under Sweeney, labor had turned away from its tradition of independent nonpartisanship and evolved into a left-wing appendage of the Democratic Party.

Sweeney did fulfill his promise to add more diversity to the AFL-CIO executive council. The new council accommodated fifty-four members, and whereas 17 percent of the old council had consisted of women or minorities, 27 percent of the new expanded council fell into those categories. But while the new council was more diverse, it was less involved in determining federation policy than under Kirkland. Increasingly, the role of the traditional decision-making instruments—the executive council and the convention—was de-emphasized, as authority gravitated to Sweeney and a small group of aides. Policies to enhance diversity seemed meaningless under circumstances in which the newly diverse bodies were effectively without power. In early 2003, the federation shifted yet again by establishing a new entity, an executive committee that was to meet monthly with Sweeney. The committee was to have seventeen members, one-half the number of the old, Kirkland-era executive council, the very instrument that had been criticized as an obstacle to diversity.

The biggest disappointment, however, was the failure to reverse the steady decline in trade unionism's membership strength. Indeed, the accumulated problems afflicting the Sweeney administration would have been largely forgotten if union membership had grown by significant numbers under the new leadership. Although the New Voice leadership devoted millions of dollars and a great deal of creative thinking to the challenge of recruiting new members to the ranks of labor, membership has actually declined since 1995, both in raw terms and as a proportion of the national workforce. Within the total workforce, the percentage of union workers has dipped to 13.8 percent. Particularly disturbing is the fact that the percentage of workers in the private sector represented by unions has dropped to 8.2 percent, according to Bureau of Labor

Statistics figures for 2003. Today well over half of organized labor's membership is concentrated in the public sector. Even as the economy achieved near full employment during the boom years of Bill Clinton's second term, labor's ranks continued to decline. In response, Sweeney and other federation officials began to point the finger of blame at the international unions for a lack of effort in organizing new members, in effect agreeing with Kirkland's contention that the unions, and not the federation, were ultimately responsible for organizing.

The inability of the new leadership to achieve tangible membership results contributed to a setback on the public relations front. After a honeymoon period in which the press concentrated its coverage on the innovations introduced by the Sweeney team, press coverage reverted to form and focused on scandals and membership decline. While the press remained sympathetic toward Sweeney, Sweeney himself was not particularly effective in articulating labor's case to the broader public, in large measure due to his discomfort when speaking without a prepared text. As his term progressed, quotes from Sweeney on the issue of the day seldom appeared in the press, and he was not often asked to appear on the major news talk programs.

Even in the realm of electoral politics, where the new leadership scored some early gains, things seemed to unravel as the years passed. Organized labor's performance in the Democratic primaries of 2004 seemed especially disorganized and inept. Labor divided between Dick Gephardt, a long-time friend, who was backed by the core industrial unions, and Howard Dean, who was supported by the Service Employees and AFSCME. Both Gephardt and Dean fared poorly in the Iowa caucuses, a particular embarrassment for labor, given that the caucus system is tailor-made for unions that have strong membership-mobilization capabilities. Compounding the appearance of disarray, the unions that had backed Dean immediately distanced themselves from his candidacy; Gerald McEntee went as far as to withdraw AFSCME's endorsement while Dean was still a candidate. The upshot was to paint labor as lacking both political muscle and loyalty. Kirkland, by contrast, had forged a unified labor movement behind Fritz Mondale in 1984. Labor had played a major role in Mondale's crucial triumph in Iowa, and labor had stuck with Mondale even as his candidacy faltered over the "special interests" issue.

Finally, organized labor no longer figures as an important force in the broad debates over national policy. Perhaps a decline in influence was inevitable, in view of the movement's membership shrinkage. Yet even in the later years of Kirkland's presidency, the AFL-CIO's views on war and peace, social reform, global trade, cabinet appointments, and other critical matters were given a respectful audience by policymakers. Under the new leadership, organized labor had little to say about the broad issues that shaped foreign and domestic policy, unless it was an issue that directly affected the labor constituency. Labor's voice was notably absent after September 11, 2001. Despite the heroic efforts of thousands of unionized police, firefighters, paramedics, and construction workers in the rescue and cleanup operations in New York, labor had little to say about the war on terror and was deeply divided on the war in Iraq. Republicans, by contrast, never missed an opportunity to appear in the company of New York's Finest or Bravest.

As many of its supporters liked to say, the new labor movement was not the labor movement of Kirkland or Meany. But what exactly was this new entity? What did it stand for? What were its values? What was its role in American society? To these important questions, no answer emerged from the new leadership.

Sweeney never uttered a critical word about Kirkland once in office. But he seldom mentioned his predecessor's contributions, except in speeches at formal gatherings where Kirkland's role in labor or American society was honored. And it seemed to Kirkland's associates that the federation's public relations repositioning involved a reinterpretation of American labor history so as to eliminate Kirkland from the story. Like a Communist official who had grown into disfavor, Kirkland was treated as a nonperson whose contributions were ignored or minimized.

Lane Kirkland never offered a public comment about his successor. In the few interviews he gave in retirement, he made it clear that he had no second thoughts about his administration's policies. Whatever doubts he maintained about the course taken by Sweeney he kept private. He did, however, write in the fragmentary memoirs he left that the new administration was driven by a "public relations über alles" mindset.

When he assumed the presidency in 1979, Kirkland told Ken Young that organized labor was not the sole interest in his life and that he intended to retire at the proper moment to pursue the projects that engaged his intellect or simply gave him enjoyment. Mentally, he had been prepared for life after the AFL-CIO—that is, until the opposition had made his tenure a factional issue. Kirkland would never entirely forgive those who had turned against him. But there were still things he wanted to do, places he wanted to visit, and friends to break bread with. The next phase in his life was about to start, and Kirkland intended to make the most of it.

14

FREEDOM'S FIVE-STAR GENERAL

IN RETIREMENT, LANE HAD AMPLE TIME TO DEVOTE TO HIS MANY AND eclectic interests. Lane was a man of many dimensions with a wide-ranging curiosity. He loved archaeology and modern art, classical ballet, and gardening. He read extensively in history, with particular interest in the Civil War and the history of organized labor. He was an ardent fan of the Redskins who also appreciated the splendors of the Swiss Alps during hill-walking expeditions. Lane could now devote himself to these pursuits and tackle projects that he had put off while president of the AFL-CIO.

Lane had use of an office at the George Meany Center for Labor Education, which he visited to work on several writing projects and meet old friends, such as Ken Young, Tom Donahue, Rex Hardesty, and Bob Georgine. He greatly enjoyed talking to students and trade unionists who were attending seminars at the center. They often introduced themselves in the cafeteria. Some simply wanted to shake his hand and express their appreciation for his service to the movement; others asked his opinion on some question of labor history—one of Lane's favorite topics. He made plans to write a book that would be a combination of memoir and history of American labor. The fragments he left include a number of amusing or illuminating anecdotes from his life in South Carolina and the earlier years of his service in labor. But Lane found it difficult to expound on his achievements. His writings convey a deep love for Irena and a profound respect for his father and for George Meany. But when Lane was forced to confront his own role in labor, he wrote more as an observer than as a participant and omitted references to his acts of leadership.

He declined to comment publicly on the policies of the new AFL-CIO administration. But he remained interested in labor's developments and was known to have made acerbic comments to close friends about "the gang that couldn't shoot straight," after the scandal over Ron Carey's fund-raising scheme made the headlines.

Lane maintained an involvement in international affairs by serving on a blue-ribbon committee that sought to promote the expansion of NATO through the incorporation of those former Communist states that had achieved a degree of democratic stability. Lane was a strong advocate of NATO enlargement, which he saw as an important step in the integration of Central Europe into the Western democratic orbit. While still at the AFL-CIO, Lane had urged President Clinton to place the United States fully behind expansion at a time when the foreign policy community was divided on the issue. He also continued to serve on the boards of organizations like Freedom House and the International Rescue Committee, institutions that had upheld the best ideals of Cold War liberalism and had remained strong advocates of freedom and American engagement in the post–Cold War era.

His love of art reflected the unpredictable side of his personality. For many years he had been intensely interested in archaeology. As was always the case with his avocations, Lane felt compelled to gain a mastery of the subject. He read widely on antiquities, gained a rudimentary knowledge of hieroglyphics, and assembled a small collection of Etruscan, Greek, and Egyptian objects that he purchased at various places in the United States and Europe. He especially liked to visit a small shop that dealt in antiquities, situated on a side street near Claridge's in London. Lane and the proprietor enjoyed discussing archaeology and ancient art, the proprietor no doubt appreciating a customer who could speak intelligently about their shared interest. Lane was later astonished to discover that the proprietor was the former chief of MI 6, the British equivalent of the CIA.

Along with ancient art, Lane was fascinated by a new and thoroughly modern tendency called the Art and Technology movement. Art and Technology developed during the 1960s as an attempt to use the latest technology—the machines people worked with—to create art of all kinds, from murals and sculptures to music and modern dance. Robert Rauschenberg was a notable figure among the movement's founders. The composer John Cage and the choreographer Merce Cunningham were also involved. The movement attracted an eclectic group of supporters who were fascinated by the proposition that the tools and machines of everyday work could be used to create superb works of art. Lane was drawn to Art and Technology, as was Theodore Kheel, a New York attorney who had gained prominence as a labor negotiator. Lane developed a friendship with Rauschenberg, and he commissioned a mural by the artist that was hung in the AFL-CIO headquarters.

Lane was now well into his seventies. Although he had led an active life, he never enjoyed formal exercise. And he stubbornly refused to abandon the nicotine habit that dated back to his teenage years in Newberry, when he and Rannie had started smoking rabbit tobacco in pipes. Lane continued to smoke, even as many of his friends quit the habit and even though Irena begged him to stop.

In September 1998, Lane fell ill after returning from a European trip. The illness lingered, but it was not until the following spring that doctors from the Johns Hopkins Hospital found a malignancy on his lung. Lane had had two previous bouts with cancer: a melanoma on his back during the 1960s and kidney cancer in the late 1980s. Because of the condition of his kidneys, chemotherapy was not an option. Lane grew steadily weaker over the next six months. He was unable to be present at a ceremony where he and his old friend from Solidarity, Lech Walesa, were honored for their contribution to freedom by the National Endowment for Democracy. The tribute declared that Lane "manages to illuminate more principles in absentia than most mortals do in person."

During his final months, Lane was visited by a number of friends of long standing. Walesa skipped a meeting at the White House to be with Lane. Several days before Lane's death, Henry Kissinger stopped by after attending a ceremony for the presentation of the Presidential Medal of Freedom. Lane was particularly happy to hear that among those honored was Evelyn Dubrow, the long-time lobbyist for the International Ladies' Garment Workers Union and one of labor's most beloved personalities. About the same time, Daniel Schorr, the political commentator, and his wife visited the Kirklands. The Kirklands and the Schorrs had dinner together; it would be the last time Lane was with friends.

To the end, Lane remained emotionally strong and stoic. With Henry Kissinger and the Schorrs, Lane talked about the sorts of things that had always interested him; he did not dwell on his condition. Henry Kissinger actually thought Lane might be on the way to recovery; their last words were an expression of hope that they would see each other at Thanksgiving. In fact, the apparent improvement in Lane's condition was a reflection of his iron will; he had summoned up all his reserves of energy for Kissinger, as he did for his other visitors during the last days. On August 14, 1999, Lane Kirkland died at the age of seventy-seven, at his home in Washington, with his beloved Irena at his side.

Lane was buried at Arlington National Cemetery. On September 23, a memorial service was held at Georgetown University. The venue was fitting; not only was Georgetown Lane's alma mater, it was where William Green had inspired him to pursue a career in organized labor.

The memorial service was both a tribute to Lane and a reflection of his career and the many causes he took on. In attendance at the service were high officials of both parties, including President Clinton. There were the intellectual giants of the foreign policy community, led by Henry Kissinger. There were the leaders of the labor movement, friends like Tom Donahue and Bob Georgine, as well as John Sweeney, the man who had succeeded him. Kirkland's daughters and grandchildren were present. Also on hand were his friends from the world of journalism and a representation of older men who had devoted themselves to winning the Cold War and who had come to pay tribute to one of their own. The audience included foreign diplomats who came to honor the man whose commitment to their countries' freedom never wavered. The music was, appropriately, recorded spirituals sung by Bayard Rustin.

In his remarks, Tom Donahue reminded people of Lane's many sides, describing him as "thinker and activist, idealist and practical leader, philosopher and tactician." Lane, he said, was a man of "absolute honor and integrity, morally correct, honest, and tough." Donahue mentioned another trait, his intelligence. "He won the presidency of the AFL-CIO because he was, by a wide margin, the smartest among us." Bob Georgine struck a similar theme. "Lane saw things we couldn't see; he anticipated problems we hadn't even thought of."

Lane was honored by the two countries, other than America, to which he had the most intense attachment and to which he had made the greatest contribution: Israel and Poland. It was announced that the government of Israel and the Histadrut, the Israeli labor federation, had jointly donated a grove of trees in his honor. And the Polish ambassador presented Irena with the Order of the White Eagle, the country's highest honor, which was given to Lane posthumously for his service to Polish freedom.

President Clinton, who had been the beneficiary of Kirkland's support but also the occasional target of his criticism, described him as "a true five-star general in the global fight for human liberty" and a man who was "almost irrationally passionate about the things he knew to be right."

Lech Walesa was there, having come from Poland to pay final tribute to his friend. "One gets to know true friends under great hardship. And Lane proved to be a very tested friend." He added, "I knew I could always count on him. I didn't have to tell him what to do. He always knew instinctively what we needed." Perhaps thinking about himself as well, Walesa said that Lane "belonged to that generation of trade union leaders who are now perishing, men of charisma and strong leadership."

Henry Kissinger stressed Lane's modesty and patriotism. "He did his duty as he saw it, not for accolades. Freedom was his mission; social justice, his cause; opposition to totalitarianism, his vocation." Lane, Kissinger said, "was never ambivalent about his country's worth or about its indispensable role in resisting totalitarianism. He emphatically rejected, indeed, he could not understand, the tendency to use America's imperfections as an alibi for America's withdrawal from the world."

Carl Gershman spoke of Lane's iron commitment to democracy and to the rights of workers. Gershman had done work for the commission chaired by Henry Kissinger on Central America policy. He recalled how Lane, a commission member, went through each page of the commission's final report, editing it to ensure that it reflected his principles on democracy and worker rights. Lane even caught Kissinger up when he tried to skip a page, just to see if Kirkland was paying attention. He was certainly paying attention.

More honors flowed in after the memorial. A special project, the Lane Kirkland Scholarship Program, was established in Poland. It brings together Poles and students from neighboring countries—Ukraine, Russia, Belarus, Slovakia, Lithuania—to study Poland's experience at making the transition to democracy. The goal of the program is very much in the Kirkland tradition: to promote and strengthen democratic practices and economic reforms, with an eye toward enhancing the relationship between what later came to be called New Europe and Old Europe and to further relations between a newly united Europe and the United States.

In 2002 it was announced that a new conference facility at the Meany labor education center would be named for Lane. This was an appropriate tribute for a labor leader with a deep knowledge and respect for the history of the American trade union movement.

On April 6, 2000, Irena attended a ceremony where Lane was honored for his service to Israel. Lane's friends gathered on American Independence Hill above Jerusalem, where a grove of trees was dedicated in his name. The event was organized by three of Lane's oldest Israeli friends: Simcha Dinitz, the former ambassador to the United States; Nachik Navoth, who served with Dinitz at the embassy; and Teddy Kollek, the former mayor of Jerusalem. Kirkland was remembered as a stalwart friend of the Jewish state and as an influential man who had used his power to advance Israel's cause with successive presidential administrations.

Kirkland was a member of the World War II generation—the greatest generation, it is often called. He was as close to the perfect embodiment of that generation's best ideals as could be found. Having played his part in a war for world freedom, he never lost the conviction that the fight for free institutions and free minds was worth the sacrifice. Nor did he ever reject the proposition that American leadership is essential if freedom is to make headway. Lane came to manhood at a time when the first signs of racial ferment were stirring. Although his roots were in a state that counted itself as among the most resistant to the equality of black people, Lane became a strong supporter of the civil rights program. On the other hand, his South Carolina roots inspired his conviction that government was obliged to assist those who existed at society's margins. He had seen grinding rural poverty, and he had witnessed the changes wrought by the New Deal. He could never accept the idea that America should step away from its responsibility to the less fortunate.

Lane had an opportunity given to few men of translating his strongly held beliefs into government policy. His fingerprints can be found on practically all the important social legislation, including the landmark civil rights laws, enacted during the last half of the twentieth century.

Perhaps his greatest and most enduring achievement is the modern democracy movement. When Kirkland and a few others initially proposed that the promotion of democracy should be recognized as a priority of American foreign policy, the idea was regarded as radical, utopian, or naive. Lane was undaunted, and he used his considerable pull to bring about the creation of the National Endowment for Democracy. In pressing this campaign for democracy promotion, he could cite the example of organized labor, which under his guidance became the single most powerful American force for the advancement of freedom outside the U.S. government. It is in part due to Kirkland that today concepts such as democracy promotion, support for civil society, and humanitarian intervention have become normal and accepted aspects of American policy.

But not all of Kirkland's aspirations were fulfilled. His hopes for a broad-based labor movement whose voice is heard in every policy debate and whose actions are anchored by mainstream liberal principles have been derailed as the new generation of labor leaders moved in an increasingly partisan and left-wing direction. His view that patriotic Americans should suppress their political differences when America is under threat has also been rejected, as American foreign policy has become more polarized, partisan, and angry. The time when Lane and George Meany met with Richard Nixon and Henry Kissinger to offer their critiques of American policy seems like a distant era today.

Lane's death brought to a close a once-respectable tradition of first-rate trade union speechmaking. Unless someone emerges from the younger generation of union leadership, Kirkland may have been the last labor leader to deliver speeches that combined an oratorical flair with an intelligent and organized development of ideas. Many of the younger union presidents tend to repeat liberal verities or to speak in an outmoded vocabulary of class warfare, directing their attack at the lords of globalism, rather than at the captains of industry. One of Kirkland's finest addresses was delivered at the 1985 graduation ceremony at South Carolina University. Lane was the commencement speaker.

Lane's theme in that speech was the growing irrelevance of the two great ideological labels of American politics: liberal and conservative. As the speech occurred during the Reagan years, Lane touched ironically on the Reaganite contention that government is the enemy and not the friend of the common man. "I would suggest that the citizens of a modern republic should not go too far in support of those who would dismantle or ruin the benign capacity of their government, for they may need it badly some day. When it happens to you, you'll know it's true." He then turned his attention to the isolationism that had infected liberalism in the wake of the Vietnam War. "If, as has been said, a modern 'liberal' is someone who believes that his country's adversaries are probably right, I strongly reject that label."

For others of Kirkland's generation, and for greater numbers of younger Americans, the dilemma of politics in the late twentieth century was brilliantly summed up in the phrases Kirkland delivered to the graduating students of his native state. This was especially true for liberals, who were engaged in a seemingly interminable debate over the proper role of government in economic and social life and the proper use of American power throughout the world.

Lane Kirkland had no doubts about where he stood. His actions as the leader of American trade unionism were rooted in iron conviction. Yet he was one of the best in Washington at the art of politics. The greatness of his achievements derived from his unusual combination of commitment and practicality. He knew when to negotiate and when to hold firm. During the years of crisis in Poland, he held firm when fainter hearts were prepared to surrender the fight, and history was changed because of his steadfast example.

Kirkland also set an example of a kind of informed patriotism that seems to be dying off as American politics grows ever more rancorous. He was not a flag waver, but he had a deep appreciation for the richness and complexities of American society. He understood that America's mistakes were overshadowed by its achievements. And he recognized that America—its government, its institutions, and its people—was an indispensable force behind the wave of freedom that swept the world during the years that he presided over the AFL-CIO.

When Lane died, one of the EMS medics who responded to the call took Irena aside. He told her he was the shop steward in his unit and went on to say how grateful he and his fellow workers were for everything Lane had done for them. He was not alone in his sentiment. Others—workers in the United States; freedom advocates in Poland, Russia, Israel, and elsewhere—remembered Lane Kirkland as a hero of democracy and a friend to ordinary workers. For Lane, there could be no greater tribute than to be remembered as someone who fought for the freedoms of working men and women around the world.

NOTES

1. Southern Roots

1. Randolph W. Kirkland, unpublished family genealogy, housed at Randolph W. Kirkland's home.
2. Ibid.
3. "1860 Census Abstracts: Kirkland, Withers, Nichols: Colleton and Kershaw Districts."
4. Mary Withers, unpublished fragmentary memoirs.
5. Randolph W. Kirkland, unpublished genealogy; author interview with Randolph W. Kirkland.
6. "Thomas J. Kirkland," unpublished memoir; author interview with Randolph W. Kirkland.
7. Ibid.
8. Author interview with Randolph W. Kirkland.
9. "Recollections of William Lennox Kirkland," unpublished memoir.
10. Alan Richardson, "Biography of Charles Richardson," unpublished manuscript.
11. Alan Richardson, "Sketch of the Lives of Joseph Lane Richardson and Mary Jacobs Jones Richardson," unpublished memoir.
12. Ibid.
13. Ibid.; author interview with Randolph W. Kirkland.
14. "The Descendants of Thomas J. Kirkland and J. L. Richardson," genealogy prepared by Randolph W. Kirkland.
15. Unpublished memoirs of Lane Kirkland. Unless otherwise noted, subsequent mentions of "Lane Kirkland memoirs" refer to the fragmentary memoirs written by Kirkland after his retirement from the AFL-CIO. Author interview with Randolph W. Kirkland.
16. Lane Kirkland memoirs.
17. Ibid.
18. Author interview with Randolph W. Kirkland.
19. Lane Kirkland memoirs.
20. Lane Kirkland, "My Journey from Camden to Warsaw" (address to the South Carolina Historical Society, Columbia, S.C., February 24, 1996).
21. Author interview with Thomas J. Kirkland.
22. Lane Kirkland, "My Journey."
23. Lane Kirkland memoirs.
24. Author interviews with Randolph W. Kirkland, Thomas J. Kirkland, and Katharine Kirkland Crockett.
25. William Lennox Kirkland, "Recollections."

26. Author interview with Randolph W. Kirkland.
27. Author interviews with Randolph W. Kirkland and Katharine Kirkland Crockett.
28. Author interview with Randolph W. Kirkland.
29. Author interviews with Thomas J. Kirkland and Katharine Kirkland Crockett.
30. Author interviews with Randolph W. Kirkland, Thomas J. Kirkland, and Katharine Kirkland Crockett.
31. Author interview with Katharine Kirkland Crockett.
32. Ibid.
33. Lane Kirkland memoirs.
34. Ibid.
35. Ibid.
36. Ibid.
37. Ibid.
38. Author interview with Thomas J. Kirkland.
39. Lane Kirkland memoirs.
40. "AFL-CIO Pres. Kirkland Recalls War Service as Seaman," *Seafarers' Log* (June 1993).
41. Lane Kirkland memoirs.
42. Author interviews with Katharine Kirkland Crockett and Thomas J. Kirkland.
43. Lane Kirkland memoirs.
44. Ibid.
45. Randolph W. Kirkland, "The Descendants of Thomas J. Kirkland and J. L. Richardson," genealogy.

2. Education of a Trade Unionist

Unless otherwise noted, the source for this chapter is the fragmentary memoirs written by Kirkland after his retirement from the AFL-CIO.

1. Author interviews with Edith Hollyday, Rikki Condon, and Lucy Schoenfeld.
2. Theodore H. White, *The Making of the President 1968* (New York: Atheneum, 1969), pp. 364–365.
3. Ibid., p. 365.
4. Richard Gid Powers, *Not without Honor: The History of American Anticommunism* (New York: Free Press, 1995), pp. 324–325.
5. Joseph Goulden, *Meany: The Unchallenged Strong Man of American Labor* (New York: Atheneum, 1972), pp. 371–402 passim.

3. Expanding Horizons

1. Kirkland was elected by the executive council in May 1969. "Meany Is Reported Picking Successor," *New York Times*, May 7, 1969.
2. "AFL-CIO Picks 9 Vice Presidents; 3 Are New Yorkers," Associated Press, May 8, 1969.
3. Author interview with George Shultz.
4. Ibid.
5. Meany's attitude to Nixon related to author by Tom Kahn, an aide to both Meany and Kirkland.
6. "Nixon Names 14 to Panel on Financial Structure," *New York Times*, June 16, 1970.
7. "10 Members Are Added to Productivity Panel," *New York Times*, October 8, 1971.

8. "Rockefeller Names First Panels of Critical Choices Commission," *New York Times*, February 5, 1974.

9. Clifton Daniel, "The Rockefeller Panel and Its CIA Mission," *New York Times*, January 20, 1975.

10. "Members of Panel in Study on CIA," *New York Times*, June 10, 1975.

11. Seymour M. Hersh, "CIA Told to Curb Activities Abroad," *New York Times*, January 7, 1975.

12. Author interview with William Safire.

13. Henry A. Kissinger, *Years of Renewal* (New York: Simon and Schuster, 1999), p. 327.

14. Lane Kirkland memoir; author interview with Irena Kirkland.

15. Peter Kihss, "100,000 Rally at the UN against Palestinian Voice," *New York Times*, November 5, 1974.

16. "No End but Dishonor," *Free Trade Union News*, December 1974.

17. "U.S. Labor Asks Ban on All Imports of Arab Oil," *New York Times*, November 3, 1974; Anthony Ripley, "Labor Chiefs Urge a Curb on Arab Oil; Support Rationing," *New York Times*, January 24, 1975.

18. Reginald Stuart, "Zumwalt Heads Energy Group," *New York Times*, July 11, 1975.

19. Author interviews with Vladimir Bukovsky and Henry A. Kissinger.

20. Author interview with Vladimir Bukovsky.

21. Bernard Gwertzman, "U.S. Bows to Policy of Unions and Bars 3 Soviet Labor Aides," *New York Times*, April 17, 1977.

22. "Senate Votes to Restrict Visas for Puppet 'Labor Leaders,' PLO," *Free Trade Union News*, June 1979.

23. Theodore H. White, *The Making of the President—1972* (New York: Atheneum, 1973), p. 38.

24. Ibid., p. 212.

25. Ibid., pp. 212–213.

26. Ibid., pp. 229–230.

27. Ibid., p. 347.

28. Author interview with Penn Kemble.

29. Ibid.

30. Jack W. Germond and Jules Witcover, *Wake Us When It's Over: Presidential Politics of 1984* (New York: Macmillan, 1986), p. 266; author interview with Rachelle Horowitz.

31. A. H. Raskin, "Labor: Leaders Giving Priority to Reviving Economy and Jobs," *New York Times*, September 5, 1976.

32. Edward Cowan, "Labor Leader Says Economy Needs Permanent Tax Cut of $25 Billion," *New York Times*, December 14, 1976.

33. Lee Dembart, "Modern Labor Defended by AFL-CIO Official," *New York Times*, September 1, 1977.

34. James W. Singer, "Already Crying the Blues," *National Journal*, February 19, 1977.

35. Author interview with Landon Butler.

36. Lane Kirkland memoirs.

37. Author interview with Thomas R. Donahue.

38. Author interview with Walter Mondale.

39. Philip Shabecoff, "Labor Official Denounces Carter," *New York Times*, April 6, 1977.

40. Hobart Rowen, "AFL-CIO Mounts Bitter Attack on Carter's Policies," *Washington Post*, April 6, 1977.

41. James W. Singer, "Already Crying the Blues," *National Journal*, February 19, 1977.

42. Anthony Lewis, "The Cold Warriors," *New York Times*, December 16, 1976; David Binder, "AFL-CIO Reported to Oppose Sorensen," *New York Times*, January 5, 1977.

43. Author interview with Bruce Miller.

44. Helen Dewar, "Labor Plight in '78; Ambitious Program Is Proving Elusive," *Washington Post*, September 4, 1978.

45. Author interviews with Rachelle Horowitz and Ken Young.

46. David Pauly, "Slings and Arrows," *Newsweek*, April 18, 1977.

47. "House Passes Labor Law Reform Bill," *Facts on File World News Digest*, October 22, 1977.

48. Robert A. Dobkin, Associated Press, July 20, 1977.

49. Ward Sinclair, "Computer Mail Spews a Blizzard of Influence on Congress," *Washington Post*, January 29, 1978.

50. "Kirkland Foresees Defeat of Labor Bill Leading to Friction," *New York Times*, May 26, 1978.

51. Philip Shabecoff, "Business Interests Unite for Fight Over Labor Laws," *New York Times*, June 24, 1977.

52. Philip Shabecoff, "Breach Grows as Top Labor Official Quits U.S. Posts," *New York Times*, December 20, 1978.

53. David S. Broder, "Union Chief Decries Meany's Attacks on Carter's Policies," *Washington Post*, December 12, 1978.

4. Captain of the Ship

1. Helen Dewar, "Old George Meany Just Keeps Rolling as Brothers Sigh," *Washington Post*, February 26, 1979.

2. Helen Dewar, "Labor Suggests Nationalization of U.S. Oil Industry," *Washington Post*, August 9, 1979; David Moberg, "Nationalize Oil, Says Union Council," *In These Times*, August 15–21, 1979.

3. Helen Dewar, "AFL-CIO Gives Its Qualified Support to SALT II Treaty," *Washington Post*, August 8, 1979; author interview with Landon Butler.

4. William Serrin, "AFL-CIO Sees Danger in Exporting Critical Technology to Soviet Union," *New York Times*, August 9, 1979.

5. David Moberg, "Nationalize Oil, Says Union Council," *In These Times*, August 15–21, 1979.

6. Helen Dewar, "Meany to Step Down as AFL-CIO President," *Washington Post*, September 29, 1979.

7. Author interviews with Irena Kirkland and Christopher Gersten.

8. Philip Shabecoff, "Two Seek Kirkland's Post at AFL-CIO," *New York Times*, October 23, 1979.

9. Walter Shapiro, "Labor's New Chief Punches In," *Washington Post*, November 18, 1979.

10. Text of Kirkland speech, keynote address to AFL-CIO Convention, November 18, 1979, New York.

11. Author interview with Rex Hardesty.

12. Author interviews with John Perkins and Adrian Karatnycky.

13. Author interview with Ken Young.

14. Ibid.

15. Helen Dewar, "Time Intrudes on AFL-CIO," *Washington Post*, November 15, 1979.

16. Warren Brown, "AFL-CIO Shifts on Makeup of Executive Unit," *Washington Post*, November 21, 1979.

17. Author interviews with Thomas R. Donahue and Ken Young.

18. Damon Statson, "Kennedy Criticizes Reagan in Speech at Labor Meeting," *New York Times*, November 19, 1981; author interview with Ken Young.

19. Material on Kirkland's leadership style from author interviews with Ken Young, Thomas R. Donahue, Jack Joyce, Rex Hardesty, and Lynn Williams.

20. Author interviews with Rex Hardesty and Ken Young.

21. On Kirkland's relations with Carter, author interviews with Landon Butler, Ken Young, and Thomas R. Donahue were particularly helpful.

22. Lane Kirkland memoirs.

23. James W. Singer, "Carter in 1980—Not Ideal, but May Be Labor's Best Hope," *National Journal*, July 28, 1979; James W. Singer, "Courting the Labor Vote," *National Journal*, October 27, 1979.

24. Lane Kirkland memoirs.

25. Walter Shapiro, "Labor's New Chief Punches In," *Washington Post*, November 18, 1979.

26. Art Pine, "Dunlop's Late Mandate," *Washington Post*, October 7, 1979; Lane Kirkland memoirs.

27. Walter Shapiro, "Labor's New Chief Punches In," *Washington Post*, November 18, 1979; author interview with Landon Butler; Lane Kirkland memoirs.

28. Art Pine, "Dunlop's Late Mandate," *Washington Post*, October 7, 1979; Lane Kirkland memoirs.

29. Martin Schram, "Managing to Upstage Kennedy," *Washington Post*, September 30, 1979.

30. Edward Cowan, "Pay Panel's Debate on Guideline Is Inconclusive," *New York Times*, October 30, 1979.

31. Hobart Rowan, "AFL-CIO Supports Carter 'With Some Enthusiasm,'" *Washington Post*, July 20, 1980.

32. Ibid.

33. James W. Singer, "Closing Ranks behind Carter," *National Journal*, July 8, 1980.

34. Martin Schram and T. R. Reid, "Deft Politics in a Dance for Unity," *Washington Post*, August 15, 1980; author interview with Ken Young.

35. William Serrin, "AFL-CIO Executive Council Pledges to Campaign for Carter," *New York Times*, August 21, 1980; Owen Ullman, "AFL-CIO Leaders Divided on Endorsement Strategy," Associated Press, August 20, 1980.

36. Philip Shabecoff, "Fear of Reagan Is the Major Impetus for a Major Labor Effort for Carter," *New York Times*, October 29, 1980.

37. Philip Shabecoff, "Voter Shifts and Conservatives' Gain Worry Labor," *New York Times*, November 9, 1980.

38. Philip Shabecoff, "AFL-CIO Weighing New Campaign," *New York Times*, December 7, 1980.

39. Ibid.

5. Labor Versus Reagan

1. Walter Shapiro, "Skirmishing for Labor," *Washington Post*, December 2, 1980.

2. Warren Brown, "Donovan Selection Prompts a 'Who Is He?' Chorus by Labor Leaders," *Washington Post*, December 17, 1980.

3. Author interview with Donald Devine.

4. Warren Brown, "Donovan to Reorganize the Department of Labor," *Washington Post*, July 10, 1981.

5. Philip Shabecoff, "Labor and the White House Trading Blame on Silence," *New York Times*, May 11, 1981; author interviews with Thomas R. Donahue and Ken Young.

6. Philip Shabecoff, "Labor and the White House Trading Blame on Silence," *New York Times*, May 11, 1981; author interviews with Thomas R. Donahue and Ken Young.

7. Author interview with Ken Young.

8. Philip Shabecoff, "Economic Plan Rejected by Labor Chiefs as Unfair," *New York Times*, February 20, 1981.

9. Martin Tolchin, "Kirkland Declares Budget Inequitable," *New York Times*, March 5, 1981.

10. Howell Raines, "Reagan Reversing Many U.S. Policies," *New York Times*, July 3, 1981.

11. "Kirkland Vows Labor Will Oppose Lower Minimum Wage for Youths," *New York Times*, March 20, 1981.

12. Kathy Sawyer, "Rights, Labor Groups Protest Affirmative Action Proposals," *Washington Post*, June 7, 1981.

13. Richard Corrigan, "Miners Rally to Block Black Lung Cuts," *National Journal*, March 28, 1981.

14. Warren Brown, "Kirkland Hits Trade Policy as 'Fairy Tale' Approach," *Washington Post*, July 14, 1981; Clyde H. Farnsworth, "Kirkland Asks Curbs on Imports," *New York Times*, July 14, 1981.

15. Author interview with Douglas Fraser.

16. Kirkland telegram to Reagan, June 10, 1981, Ronald Reagan Presidential Library (RR Library).

17. Author interview with Thomas R. Donahue.

18. Stuart Taylor, "Strikers and the Law," *New York Times*, August 5, 1981.

19. William J. Lanouette, "Sing Labor a Message," *National Journal*, August 22, 1981.

20. Reagan note to PATCO convention, May 18, 1981, RR Library.

21. David Moberg, "As PATCO Goes, So Go the Unions," *In These Times*, August 26–September 1, 1981.

22. Tom Morgenthau, "Who Controls the Air," *Newsweek*, August 17, 1981.

23. Warren Brown and Laura A. Kiernan, "Reagan Threatens to Fire Striking Controllers," *Washington Post*, August 4, 1981.

24. William Serrin, "Kirkland Defends Strike Decision," *New York Times*, August 4, 1981.

25. Author interview with Douglas Fraser.

26. A. H. Raskin, "The Air Strike Is Ominous for Labor," *New York Times*, August 16, 1981; William Serrin, "AFL-CIO Defers Action to Back Up Air Controllers," *New York Times*, August 7, 1981.

27. Warren Brown, "U.S. Rules Out Rehiring Striking Air Controllers," *Washington Post*, August 7, 1981.

28. Author interview with Donald Devine.

29. Author interview with Richard V. Allen.

30. William Serrin, "AFL-CIO Defers Action to Back Up Air Controllers, *New York Times*, August 7, 1981."

31. Fred W. Fielding memorandum, August 14, 1981, RR Library.

32. Author interviews with Howard Baker, Ken Young, and Rex Hardesty.

33. Howell Raines, "Labor and Reagan Remain Far Apart," *New York Times*, September 6, 1981.
34. "CBS Cancels Kirkland Speech as Attack on Administration," *New York Times*, September 5, 1981.
35. Author interviews with Ken Young, Rex Hardesty, and Thomas R. Donahue.
36. Michael Oreskes, "100,000 March Up Fifth Avenue to Celebrate Centennial of Labor," *New York Times*, September 8, 1981.
37. Author interview with John Perkins.
38. William Serrin, "After Solidarity Day, Organizers Must Set Agenda," *New York Times*, September 21, 1981.
39. Author interview with John Perkins.
40. David Broder, "AFL-CIO Leader Riding a Big Bet," *Washington Post*, September 20, 1981.
41. William Safire, "Kirkland Comes to Call," *New York Times*, November 29, 1981.
42. Author interview with Douglas Fraser.
43. Steven R. Weisman, "Reagan, at Meeting with Union Chiefs, Urges Mutual Consultation," *New York Times*, December 3, 1981; Leonard Silk, "Reagan Policy: Protests Grow," *New York Times*, December 4, 1981; Michael Wright and Carolyn Rand Herron, "Tradesmen Use Front Entrance," *New York Times*, December 6, 1981.
44. William Serrin, "Solidarity Day's Enigmatic Organizer," *New York Times*, September 19, 1981.
45. Seth S. King, "AFL-CIO Challenges Reagan on Budget," *New York Times*, February 16, 1982; William Serrin, "Big Labor's New View: Military Now in Critical Focus," *New York Times*, February 18, 1982.
46. David Broder and Kathy Sawyer, "Liberal, Labor Groups Frustrated by Vote of Senators They Back," *Washington Post*, August 5, 1982.
47. Kathy Sawyer, "List Labor as One of the Midterm Winners," *Washington Post*, November 9, 1982.
48. Seth S. King, "U.S. Jobless Rate Climbs to 10.8%, a Postwar Record," *New York Times*, December 4, 1982.

6. All Out for Fritz

1. Kathy Sawyer, "Organization Man Leads Labor into Unusually Gutsy Gamble," *Washington Post*, October 2, 1983.
2. Peter Goldman, "A Last Round-Up of the Old Coalition," *Newsweek*, Election Special, November–December 1984.
3. Author interview with John Perkins.
4. David S. Broder, "Why Mondale?" *Washington Post*, August 14, 1983; David S. Broder and Kathy Sawyer, "Mondale Is AFL-CIO Front Runner," *Washington Post*, February 17, 1983.
5. Kathy Sawyer, "AFL-CIO to Endorse in October; Decision Is Regarded as Large Boost for Mondale," *Washington Post*, August 10, 1983.
6. Kathy Sawyer, "Exuberant AFL-CIO Delegates Wrap Up Endorsement of Mondale," *Washington Post*, October 6, 1983; Howell Raines, "Confident Mondale Accepts Labor's Endorsement," *New York Times*, October 6, 1983; AFL-CIO press release, October 5, 1983.
7. Kathy Sawyer, "Special Interest Denied; Kirkland Hits Back at Label," *Washington Post*, October 4, 1983.

8. Bernard Weinraub, "Mondale Woos His Party's Conservative Wing," *New York Times*, November 15, 1983.

9. Howell Raines, "Moving to Regain Labor's Lost Power," *New York Times*, January 17, 1983; author interview with Dick Wilson.

10. AFL-CIO press release, October 5, 1983.

11. Robert Pear, "Record Shows Hart Focuses on Arms, Energy, and Deficit," *New York Times*, March 18, 1984; George Lardner Jr., "'New Ideas' Democrat Has Long Had His Eye on the Presidency," *Washington Post*, January 17, 1984; author interview with Chris Gersten.

12. Author interview with Ken Young.

13. Howell Raines, "At the AFL-CIO, Blue Notebooks for Mondale," *New York Times*, November 8, 1983.

14. Kathy Sawyer, "Union Support of Costly Phone Banks Jangles Mondale's Democratic Rivals," *Washington Post*, February 10, 1984; Kathy Sawyer, "Iowa Caucuses Prove the Worth of Labor Backing," *Washington Post*, February 23, 1984.

15. Howell Raines, "Mondale to Bolster Lead as Others Adjust to New Lineup," *New York Times*, February 22, 1984; George F. Will, "The Democrats Get Serious," *Washington Post*, February 22, 1984.

16. David S. Broder, "Other Hopefuls Attack Mondale in Iowa Debate," *Washington Post*, February 12, 1984.

17. Author interviews with Walter Mondale, Rachelle Horowitz, and Ken Young.

18. Kathy Sawyer, "Organized Labor Tries to Assess Damage to Mondale, Itself," *Washington Post*, March 1, 1984; David S. Broder, "Hart Defeats Mondale in Maine Caucuses," *Washington Post*, March 5, 1984.

19. Bill Keller, "The Uneasiness between Blacks and Union Leaders," *New York Times*, May 13, 1984.

20. Author interview with Ken Young.

21. Kathy Sawyer, "Labor's Voice Crackles with Political Tension," *Washington Post*, April 3, 1984; Margot Hornblower, "Mondale Returns Hart's Fire on Foreign Policy Positions," *Washington Post*, March 28, 1984; Margot Hornblower, "AFL-CIO President Denounces Hart; Kirkland Compares Senator with Reagan," *Washington Post*, March 25, 1984.

22. "Labor Head Bids Hart Return '80 Donations," United Press International, *New York Times*, April 29, 1984.

23. "AFL-CIO Leader Criticizes Hart," Associated Press, March 12, 1984.

24. Germond and Witcover, *Wake Us When It's Over*, p. 266.

25. Kathy Sawyer, "Kirkland Says Union Unity for Mondale Vindicated," *Washington Post*, May 8, 1984; Bill Peterson, "Hart, in Nebraska, Criticizes Mondale on 'Protectionism,'" *Washington Post*, May 11, 1984.

26. Kathy Sawyer, "Kirkland Wants an Olive Branch; Hart Can Still Kindle Labor's Lost Love," *Washington Post*, June 8, 1984.

27. "AFL-CIO Political Aide Predicts Party Unity behind Mondale," *Washington Post*, July 6, 1984.

28. "Thousands of Unionists Parade for Democrats," *New York Times*, July 16, 1984.

29. Howell Raines, "Mondale Changes at the Last Minute," *New York Times*, July 16, 1984; Germond and Witcover, *Wake Us When It's Over*, pp. 304–305; author interviews with John Perkins and Ken Young.

30. Author interview with Dick Wilson.

31. Germond and Witcover, *Wake Us When It's Over*, pp. 408–411.

32. Bill Keller, "Labor Chiefs Motivated by Fear of Reagan Second Term," *New York Times*, August 19, 1984.
33. Author interview with Ken Young.
34. Bill Keller, "Unionists Reassess Mondale Support," *New York Times*, November 9, 1984.

7. Solidarity Forever

1. Author interview with Lech Walesa; James F. Shea and Don R. Kienzle, "An Interview with Lane Kirkland," conducted for the Labor Diplomacy Oral History Project, 1996.
2. "Press Questions Kirkland on AFL-CIO Support for Polish Workers," *Free Trade Union News*, September 1980.
3. William Serrin, "AFL-CIO Names a Woman to Its Executive Board," *New York Times*, August 22, 1980.
4. Fred Barbash, "Unions in West Helped Poles, UAW President Says," *Washington Post*, September 1, 1980; "Union Sent Money to Striking Polish Workers," Associated Press, September 1, 1980.
5. George Gedda, "AFL-CIO Aids Polish Workers," Associated Press, September 4, 1980; author interview with Eric Chenoweth.
6. Flora Lewis, "Let the Poles Do It," *New York Times*, September 5, 1980.
7. George Gedda, "Carter's Stand on Poland Swayed by Politics, Sources Say," Associated Press, September 5, 1980.
8. John Darnton, "Polish Officials Tell U.S. Embassy Money Aid May Hurt New Unions," *New York Times*, September 10, 1980.
9. Bradley Graham, "Poles Criticize AFL-CIO for Aiding New Unions," *Washington Post*, September 11, 1980.
10. Thomas Kent, "Kremlin Promises More Food, Manufactured Goods to Poland," Associated Press, September 12, 1980.
11. "Muskie Informed Soviets of Unions' Plan to Help Poles," *New York Times*, September 12, 1980; note to Secretary of State Muskie from U.S. embassy, Moscow, September 1980.
12. "Polish Strike Leader Thanks U.S. Labor," Associated Press, September 12, 1980.
13. Author interview with Lech Walesa.
14. "There's a Good Fighting Chance They Can Make It Work," *U.S. News and World Report*, September 15, 1980.
15. Robert M. Gates, *From the Shadows* (New York: Simon and Schuster, 1996), p. 144.
16. Daniel Southerland, "AFL-CIO Sending Aid to Polish Unionists," *Christian Science Monitor*, December 8, 1980; author interviews with Adrian Karatnycky and Lech Walesa.
17. Zbigniew Brzezinski, *Power and Principle* (New York: Farrar, Straus, and Giroux, 1982), p. 467.
18. Charles J. Hanley, "U.S., Other Unions Pour Aid into Poland," Associated Press, January 14, 1981.
19. Bayard Rustin, "Report on Poland," unpublished manuscript, personal collection of Dick Wilson.
20. David L. Anderson, "AFL-CIO Denied Visas," Associated Press, September 25, 1981.
21. Author interview with Wiktor Kulerski.

22. Shea and Kienzle, "An Interview with Lane Kirkland."

23. AFL-CIO press release, December 15, 1981; United Press International, December 14, 1981.

24. Paul Bremer memo to James Nance, December 17, 1981.

25. Shea and Kienzle, "An Interview with Lane Kirkland."

26. Author interview with Alexander Haig.

27. Haig memo to Reagan, December 26, 1981.

28. AFL-CIO press release, January 30, 1981.

29. Leslie H. Gelb, "Reprieve on Polish Debt," *New York Times*, February 3, 1982.

30. Hedrick Smith, "Reagan's Sanctions," *New York Times*, December 25, 1981; Ed Towns, "AFL-CIO to Reagan: Get Tough on Polish Situation," *Christian Science Monitor*, December 30, 1981.

31. Juan J. Walte, "AFL-CIO Calls for Stern Action Over Poland," United Press International, December 28, 1981.

32. United Press International, February 5, 1982; Seth S. King, "Labor Council Urges More Drastic Action on Poland Situation," *New York Times*, February 19, 1982; Warren Brown, "Haig Calls Halt on Grain to Soviets Self-Defeating," *Washington Post*, February 20, 1982.

33. Paul Moses, "AFL-CIO President Calls Reagan Soft on Poland," Associated Press, April 13, 1982; "AFL-CIO Leader Brands Warsaw Government 'Fascist Junta,'" Associated Press, May 18, 1982.

34. United Press International, September 1, 2002.

35. George Lardner Jr., "Kirkland Says U.S. Should Force Poland into Bankruptcy," *Washington Post*, October 11, 1982.

36. Gregory Domber, "Interview with Thomas Simons," unpublished, undated paper.

37. Jonathan Kwitney, *Man of the Century* (New York: Holt, 1997), p. 472.

38. "AFL-CIO Calls Lifting of Martial Law 'Sham,'" Associated Press, July 22, 1983.

39. Merrill Hartson, Associated Press, October 5, 1983.

40. Bernard Gwertzman, "U.S. Intends to Ease Polish Curbs; AFL-CIO Vows Opposition," *New York Times*, November 1, 1983.

41. Author interview with Janusz Onyszkiewicz.

42. Domber, "Interview with Thomas Simons."

43. Author interview with Bronislaw Geremek.

44. Author interview with Zbigniew Romaszewski.

45. Domber, "Interview with Thomas Simons"; author interview with James Baker.

46. Maralee Schwartz and Frank Swoboda, "AFL-CIO Leader Tosses Early Jabs at Bush, Quayle," *Washington Post*, August 23, 1988.

47. Author interview with Joanna Pilarska.

48. Author interview with Bronislaw Geremek.

49. Richard Wilson, "In Solidarity: The AFL-CIO and Solidarnosc, 1980–1990," unpublished manuscript.

50. Author interview with Joanna Pilarska.

51. Author interview with Janusz Onyszkiewicz.

52. Author interview with Wiktor Kulerski.

53. Author interview with Irena Lasota.

54. Author interview with Czeslaw Bielecki.

55. Bogdan Turek, United Press International, January 18, 1985.

56. Author interview with Bogdan Borusewicz.

57. Gates, *From the Shadows,* p. 237.

58. Shea and Kienzle, "An Interview with Lane Kirkland."

59. Author interview with Bronislaw Geremek.

60. Author interview with Janusz Onyszkiewicz.

61. Author interview with Czeslaw Bielecki.

62. Author interview with Andrzej Celinski.

63. Lane Kirkland memoirs.

8. Central America: Fighting the Good Fight at Home and Abroad

1. Author interview with Gordon Ellison.

2. Author interview with William C. Doherty Jr.

3. Ibid.

4. Richard Oulahan, unpublished, undated memoir; author interview with William C. Doherty Jr.

5. Ambassador Robert White memo to Secretary of State, March 1980, National Security Archives.

6. Author interview with Gordon Ellison.

7. Ibid.

8. Ibid.

9. United States Embassy, El Salvador, memo to State Department, October 1983, National Security Archives.

10. Author interview with William C. Doherty Jr.

11. Lane Kirkland memo to State Federation Presidents, March 23, 1983.

12. Author interviews with George F. Will and Adrian Karatnycky.

13. Author interviews with Henry A. Kissinger and John Silber.

14. Author interview with Henry A. Kissinger.

15. Ibid.

16. "Report of the National Bipartisan Commission on Central America," United States government report, 1984, pp. 126–127.

17. Charles Kernaghan, undated memo.

18. Lane Kirkland memo to State Federation Presidents, August 29, 1985.

19. "AFGE President Slams Contra Aid," Labor Report on Central America, July–August 1986.

20. Alvin Guthrie letter to Lane Kirkland, May 28, 1985.

21. Ibid.

22. Michael Hammer Jr. letter to Arthur Osborne, September 30, 1985.

23. Lane Kirkland letter to Ronald Fortune, October 1985.

24. Author interview with David Jessup.

25. Ibid.

26. Transcript of proceedings, AFL-CIO convention, October 1985, George Meany Memorial Archives.

27. Ibid.

28. Author interview with David Jessup.

29. Federal News Service Information, January 18, 1989; "Idea of Expelling AFL-CIO Mission Resurrected," *Latino*, April 26, 1988.

30. Lane Kirkland letter to Jose Napoleon Duarte, November 18, 1987; Lane Kirkland letter to George Shultz, January 7, 1988.

31. Jack T. Joyce, John J. Sweeney, and Gene Upshaw letter to Daniel Ortega, October 17, 1986; Don Slaiman memo to John Henning, September 8, 1986.

32. Lane Kirkland memo to State Federations, March 23, 1987.

33. Jack T. Joyce memo to local affiliates, International Union of Bricklayers and Allied Craftsmen, April 1, 1987.

34. David Jessup letter to John J. Sweeney, March 30, 1987; author interviews with David Jessup and Joel Freedman.

35. "The Shrinking of Democracy," *AIFLD Briefs*, September 28, 1989.

36. Author interview with Bernard Aronson.

37. "Democracy Wins in Nicaragua," *AIFLD Briefs*, March 9, 1990.

38. *The Guardian*, September 14, 1988.

39. Author Interview with John Silber.

9. Mr. Democracy

1. Author interviews with James Baker and Adrian Karatnycky.

2. Author interview with Adrian Karatnycky.

3. Anthony Carew, Michel Dreyfus, and Marcel Van Der Linden, *The International Confederation of Free Trade Unions*, The ICFTU (London: Peter Lang Publishing, 2000), pp. 323–331.

4. Lane Kirkland, "The Future of the ILO," *Free Trade Union News*, October 1975; Lane Kirkland, "Mixed Results from 1976 ILO Meetings," *Free Trade Union News*, July 1976.

5. Eugenia Kemble, "The USA Returns to the ILO," *Free Trade Union News*, July 1980.

6. Lane Kirkland, "Labor, Foreign Policy, and Defense," *Free Trade Union News*, January 1983.

7. Lane Kirkland, "On the Future of NATO," *London Times*, May 29, 1984.

8. Lane Kirkland, "Free Trade Unions: Force for Democracy," *Free Trade Union News*, excerpts from a speech before the Chicago Council on Foreign Relations, June 1978.

9. Ibid.

10. Author interview with Carl Gershman.

11. David Lowe, "Idea to Reality: A Brief History of the National Endowment for Democracy," paper published by the National Endowment for Democracy, 1999.

12. Author interviews with Eugenia Kemble, Bill Brock, Orrin Hatch, Carl Gershman, and Adrian Karatnycky.

13. Author interview with Carl Gershman.

14. Author interviews with Eugenia Kemble, Bill Brock, and Carl Gershman.

15. Author interview with Bill Brock.

16. Author interview with James Baker.

17. Author interviews with Eugenia Kemble and Carl Gershman; David K. Shipler, "Missionaries for Democracy: U.S. Aid for Global Pluralism," *New York Times*, June 1, 1986.

18. "Panel to Advise on Foreign Aid," *New York Times*, February 23, 1983.

19. "3 Named to Broadcast Board," Associated Press, May 17, 1983.

20. Author interview with Adrian Karatnycky.

21. Author interview with James Baker.

22. Author interview with Dick Wilson.

23. Author interviews with Adrian Karatnycky and Joel Freedman.

24. Frank Swoboda, "AFL-CIO to Aid Labor Groups in Soviet Union," *Washington Post*, December 20, 1989.

25. "Soviets Deny AFL-CIO Request for Visa," *New York Times*, November 30, 1989.

26. "Labor Day in Moscow," *Free Trade Union News*, September 1990.

27. "The Soviet Union: Hope and Despair," *Free Trade Union News*, January 1991; Clyde H. Farnsworth, "U.S. Role in Aid Bank Draws Fire," *New York Times*, April 12, 1990.

28. "The Sakharov Memorial Congress," *Free Trade Union News*, May 1991; author interviews with Irena Kirkland, James Baker, and Adrian Karatnycky.

29. Author interviews with Adrian Karatnycky, James Baker, and Dick Wilson.

30. Author interview with Dick Wilson.

31. Author interviews with Adrian Karatnycky and Dick Wilson.

32. Author interviews with Adrian Karatnycky and Carl Gershman.

33. Author interview with Adrian Karatnycky.

34. "Kirkland Comments on Western Businessmen," *Free Trade Union News*, July 1992.

35. "Workers' Rights: Using Trade Pressures," *Free Trade Union News*, January 1988; author interview with Mark Anderson.

36. "Chile: The Tide Turns," *Free Trade Union News*, October 1988; author interview with William C. Doherty Jr.

37. "A Movement Reborn?" *Newsweek*, December 10, 1984; Shea and Kienzle, "An Interview with Lane Kirkland."

38. Robert O. Boorstin, "Tear Gas Used on Churchgoers in South Africa," *New York Times*, July 21, 1986.

39. "South African Blacks Support Sanctions, AFL-CIO Chief Says," *Washington Post*, July 25, 1986.

40. Author interview with Henry A. Kissinger.

10. Labor Unity; Labor Pains

1. Seth King, "New Tone and Tilt on Labor Board," *New York Times*, February 2, 1984.

2. Roger Fillott, Associated Press, May 5, 1983.

3. Martin Tolchin, "AFL-CIO Chief Laments State of Labor Laws," *New York Times*, August 30, 1989.

4. David S. Broder, "Nominee Attracts Wide-Ranging Praise," *Washington Post*, March 21, 1985.

5. Peter Perl, "Brock Urges Union-Industry Accord," *Washington Post*, October 31, 1985.

6. "UAW Delays Federation Return," *New York Times*, January 12, 1977.

7. David Moberg, "The UAW Repents Its Independence," *In These Times*, May 20–26, 1981.

8. Iver Peterson, "After 13 Years, Auto Union Joins AFL-CIO Again," *New York Times*, April 29, 1981; Philip Shabecoff, "Move to Rejoin Labor Alliance Gains in UAW," *New York Times*, April 29, 1981.

9. Warren Brown, "Kirkland Supports Stiffer Penalties in Bill," *Washington Post*, November 4, 1981; "Kirkland for Corruption Curb," *New York Times*, November 4, 1981.

10. "A Divided Commission," *National Journal*, August 2, 1986.

11. Helen Dewar, "Senate Votes to Limit Private Job Polygraphs," *Washington Post*, March 4, 1988; author interviews with William Safire and Thomas R. Donahue.

12. Author interview with Ken Young.

13. Kenneth B. Noble, "Teamsters Gain Readmittance to AFL-CIO," *New York Times*, October 25, 1987; Kenneth B. Noble, "Kirkland Pledges to Help Teamsters Fight Any Government Takeover," *New York Times*, October 27, 1987.

14. Kenneth B. Noble, "AFL-CIO and a New Obsession with Presser," *New York Times*, October 28, 1987.

15. Frank Swoboda, "Top Teamster Comes Home to AFL-CIO," *Washington Post*, October 30, 1987.

16. Ben A. Franklin, "Miners' Chief Gets Uncommon Campaign Aid," *New York Times*, April 4, 1982.

17. Author interviews with Ken Young and Thomas R. Donahue.

18. Ibid.

19. Dana Priest, "Labor Leaders Arrested in Va.," *Washington Post*, August 24, 1989.

20. Frank Swoboda, "Mine Workers Decide to Affiliate with AFL-CIO," *Washington Post*, October 5, 1989.

21. Dana Priest, "Contract Approved by Miners," *Washington Post*, February 21, 1990.

22. Lynda Richardson and Mary Jordan, "AFL-CIO Agrees to End Its Boycott of Coors Beer," *Washington Post*, August 30, 1987; author interview with Dick Wilson.

23. Martha M. Hamilton and Frank Swoboda, "Union Tactics Shift as Strike Drags On," *Washington Post*, August 20, 1989.

24. Ronald Brownstein, "Labor Wants Respect," *National Journal*, November 2, 1985.

25. David Moberg, "Hormel Settlement Leaves Unionists Bitterly Divided," *In These Times*, September 24–30, 1986.

26. William Serrin, "Images of Labor," *New York Times*, February 21, 1986.

27. Kenneth B. Noble, "Kirkland Joins in Parent Union's Criticism of Hormel Strikers," *New York Times*, February 18, 1987.

28. John Hoerr, "A Host of Strikebreakers Is Tipping the Balance against Labor," *Business Week*, July 15, 1985.

29. Author interview with Leonard Garment; Barbara Presley Noble, "Different Tactics in Labor's Battles," *New York Times*, September 6, 1991; Maria Mallory and Michael Schroeder, "How the USW Hit Marc Rich Where It Hurt," *Business Week*, May 11, 1992.

30. Author interview with Morton Bahr.

31. Author interview with Dick Wilson.

32. Author interview with Thomas R. Donahue.

33. Author interview with Lynn Williams.

34. Mike Feinsilber, "A Bearhug for the Union Movement," Associated Press, November 14, 1989.

35. Author interview with Adrian Karatnycky.

36. "Walesa the Latest Star in 'Union Yes' Campaign," Associated Press, November 16, 1989.

11. Civil Rights: Keeping the Faith

1. Les Byard, "Nostalgic March Criticizes 'Legal Lynching' of Civil Rights," Associated Press, August 26, 1989.

2. John King, "Abortion Debate Undermines Labor's Week of Solidarity," Associated Press, November 16, 1989.

3. Frank Swoboda, "Abortion Political Debate Beckons Organized Labor," *Washington Post*, February 19, 1990.

4. Frank Swoboda, "AFL-CIO Names Panel to Weigh Abortion Issue," *Washington Post*, February 20, 1990.

5. Harry Bernstein, "AFL-CIO Leadership Is Still Divided on Abortion," *Los Angeles Times*, February 20, 1990.
6. Karen Ball, "Labor Leaders Doubt Major Policy Change from Reagan Era," Associated Press, February 20, 1990.
7. Author interview with Morton Bahr.
8. "AFL-CIO Takes No Stand on Abortion," United Press International, July 30, 1990; Philip Dine, "Keeping Clear: Labor Leaders Avoid Taking Abortion Stance," *St. Louis Post-Dispatch*, August 1, 1990.
9. Henry Weinstein and Ronald Ostrow, "AFL-CIO Expected to Oppose Bork," *Los Angeles Times*, August 15, 1987; author interview with Irena Kirkland.
10. *PR Newswire*, July 31, 1991.

12. Two Cheers for Clinton

1. Author interview with Adrian Karatnycky.
2. Robert Pear, "Bush Attacks the Way Unions Are Using Nonmembers' Fees," *New York Times*, April 12, 1992.
3. Peter T. Kilborn, "Ban on Replacing Strikers Faces Veto Threat," *New York Times*, March 7, 1991.
4. George F. Will, "Smothering the Private Sector," *Washington Post*, November 24, 1991.
5. Author interview with James Baker.
6. Author interview with John Perkins.
7. Author interview with Irena Kirkland.
8. NAFTA Roundtable, November 15, 1993, text released by AFL-CIO.
9. Philip Dine, "Great Expectations: Labor Approaches Clinton with Pent-Up Demands," *St. Louis Post-Dispatch*, November 22, 1992.
10. Author interview with Mark Anderson.
11. "Industry Backs NAFTA with Qualified Support," *Chemical Marketing Reporter*, August 23, 1993.
12. Frank Swoboda, "Kirkland: No Compromise on NAFTA," *Washington Post*, September 1, 1993.
13. National Public Radio interview, September 18, 1993.
14. Peter T. Kilborn, "Hailing Health Plan but Denouncing Trade Pact, Big Labor Is Heard Again," *New York Times*, September 16, 1993.
15. Doug Grow, "Labor's Stand Is Nowhere Near Clinton's Bully Pulpit," *Minneapolis Star-Tribune*, September 21, 1993.
16. Lane Kirkland, "A Trade Marriage Made in Heaven," *Washington Post*, May 19, 1993.
17. Frank Swoboda, "President Woos Labor on NAFTA," *Washington Post*, October 5, 1993; author interview with Mark Anderson.
18. William Schneider, "NAFTA Has the White House Spooked," Federal News Service, August 19, 1993.
19. Stephen Franklin, "Unions Overlook Clinton's Position on NAFTA for Marriage's Sake," *Chicago Tribune*, October 1, 1993.
20. *The McNeil-Lehrer NewsHour*, November 8, 1993.
21. Robert Naylor Jr., "Union Leader Warns of Damaged Relations Over NAFTA," Associated Press, November 16, 1993.
22. Terence Hunt, "Clinton Presses to Pick Up Needed NAFTA Votes," Associated Press, November 15, 1993.

23. Michael Putzel, "Enraged Union Leaders Say They Won't Forget," *Boston Globe*, November 19, 1993.

24. "Clinton Delivers State of the Union Address," *Facts on File*, January 27, 1994.

25. Frank Swoboda, "Gore Seeks Peace at Labor Gathering," *Washington Post*, February 22, 1994; Robert Naylor Jr., "Labor Makes Passage of Clinton Health Plan Top Priority," Associated Press, February 22, 1994; Robert Naylor Jr., "Union Chiefs Say Clinton Lax on Striker Replacement," Associated Press, November 24, 1994.

26. Author interview with Thomas R. Donahue.

13. The Coup

1. Author interview with James Baker.

2. Author interviews with Thomas R. Donahue, James Baker, and John J. Sweeney.

3. Philip Dine, "U.S. Labor Movement Is Detecting Discontent Over AFL-CIO President," *St. Louis Post-Dispatch*, February 10, 1995.

4. Frank Swoboda, "Lane Kirkland Signals He'll Fight to Keep His Job," *Washington Post*, February 20, 1995; author interview with Rex Hardesty.

5. Author interview with Rex Hardesty.

6. Author interviews with Thomas R. Donahue, Rex Hardesty, James Baker, and David St. John.

7. Author interview with Thomas R. Donahue.

8. Author interview with James Baker.

9. Author interviews with George Kourpias and Thomas R. Donahue.

10. "Unions Show Membership Gain," *Industry Week*, March 20, 1995.

11. Nathaniel C. Nash, "Is a Trans-Atlantic Pact Coming Down the Pike?" *New York Times*, April 15, 1995.

12. John F. Harris, "Among New Deal Believers, Clinton Has Skeptics," *Washington Post*, April 13, 1995.

13. Author interview with Thomas R. Donahue.

14. Ibid.

15. Author interviews with David St. John and Thomas R. Donahue.

16. Leslie Kaufman, "Union Solidarity Forever? Not This Year," *Newsweek*, May 22, 1995.

17. Stephen Franklin, "AFL-CIO's Kirkland Not Stepping Aside," *Chicago Tribune*, June 9, 1995.

18. Author interview with Morton Bahr.

19. Author interview with Thomas R. Donahue.

20. Author interview with John J. Sweeney.

21. Author interview with Thomas R. Donahue.

INDEX

Page numbers in *italic* type refer to photos.